PREFACE

Henry Clarke Warren's *Buddhism in Translations* was first published in 1896. It appeared as Volume Three of the Harvard Oriental Series, a series of books founded by the generosity of Warren and at that time edited by his teacher and friend Charles R. Lanman. The book long remained the most popular volume of the Series and was reprinted time and again. In the course of these reprintings several pages were successively added. Among the additions were a prefatory note by Lanman, a memorial of Henry Warren's life, and a descriptive list of other volumes of the Series. In the present student's edition all this supplementary matter has been excluded. Since the cost of publishing has trebled since the time of the first edition, other changes have been made in format and binding. But not a word of Warren's text has been omitted or changed.

Warren's book remains an admirable introduction to the basic teachings of Buddhism. Buddhist studies, it is true, have advanced since Warren's time; many more texts have been edited and translated. Particularly is this true with regard to Mahayana or Northern Buddhism, with which Warren did not deal. But no one has organized this new material with the skill which Warren showed in dealing with the material available in his day. The picture of Theravada or Southern Buddhism given by Warren's selections is singularly well balanced. And his renderings have the special merit of being readable as well as scholarly.

Warren's attitude toward Buddhism was one neither of acceptance nor of disapproval. He disapproved of only one thing: the forming of opinions about Buddhism or India or Asia at second and third hand. It was to help Westerners form an opinion of Buddhism at close acquaintance that he wrote this book. And it is for the same purpose that his book is now reissued.

DANIEL H. H. INGALLS

Editor, Harvard Oriental Series

Cambridge, Massachusetts, 1953

CONTENTS

CHAPTER III.

KARMA AND REBIRTH.

CHAPTER IV.

MEDITATION AND NIRVANA.

CHAPTER V.

THE ORDER.

APPENDIX.

ABBREVIATIONS.

A. . . . . . Aṅguttara-Nikāya. Edited by Rev. Richard Morris. Pāli
          Text Society, London, 1885–8.
CV. . . . . Culla-Vagga. Edited by Hermann Oldenberg. Vinaya-Piṭaka,
          vol. ii., London, 1880.
D. . . . . . Dīgha-Nikāya, vol. i. Edited by T. W. R. Davids and J. E.
          Carpenter. P. T. S., 1890.
Dhp. . . . Dhammapada. Edited by V. Fausböll. Copenhagen. 1855.
Grimblot. Sept Suttas Pālis. Edited by P. Grimblot. Paris, 1876.
J. . . . . . Jātaka, together with its Commentary, 5 vols. Edited by V.
          Fausböll, 1877–91.
JPTS. . . Journal of the Pāli Text Society.
JRAS. . . Journal of the Royal Asiatic Society, London.
M. . . . . . Majjhima-Nikāya. Edited by V. Trenckner. P. T. S., 1888.
Mil. . . . . Milindapañha. Edited by V. Trenckner. London, 1880.
MPS. . . . Mahā-Parinibbāna-Sutta. Edited by R. C. Childers, London,
          1878. JRAS., new series, vii.; also separately.
MSS. . . Mahā-Satipaṭṭhāna-Sutta. Colombo, 1883.
MV. . . . . Mahā-Vagga. Edited by Hermann Oldenberg. Vinaya-Piṭaka,
          vol. i., London, 1879.
P's Aut. . Mrs. Piozzi's Autobiography. Edited by Hayward. Boston,
          1861.
S. . . . . . Saṁyutta-Nikāya. Edited by Léon Feer. P. T. S., 1884–94.
Sum Vil. . Sumaṅgala-Vilāsinī. Edited by T. W. R. Davids and J. E.
          Carpenter. P. T. S., 1886.
Ud. . . . . Udāna. Edited by Paul Steinthal. P. T. S., 1885.
Vis. . . . . Visuddhi-Magga, in manuscript.

The abbreviations and numbers at the upper inside corners of the
pages of this book refer, as precisely as may be, to the chapter and
other subdivisions or to the volume and page and line of the original
work from which the *beginning* of the page concerned is translated.

NOTE ON THE PRONUNCIATION OF PALI NAMES

Short *a*, as in *organ*, or like the *u* in *but*. The other vowels, as in the
key-words, *far, pin, pīque, pull, rūle,* (and roughly) *they, so*. Pronounce
c like *ch* in *church*, and *j* as in *judge*. The "aspirates" are true aspirates: thus, *th, dh, ph*, as in *hothouse, madhouse, uphill*. They are not
spirants as in *thin, graphic*. The underdotted *ṭ, ḍ, ṇ,* etc. are pronounced
(by the Hindus, at least) with the tip of the tongue turned up and
drawn back. Dotted *ṁ* indicates nasalization of the preceding vowel.

THE THREE CHARACTERISTICS.

Translated from the Aṅguttara-Nikāya (iii. 134[1]).

Whether Buddhas arise, O priests, or whether Buddhas do not arise, it remains a fact and the fixed and necessary constitution of being, that all its constituents are transitory. This fact a Buddha discovers and masters, and when he has discovered and mastered it, he announces, teaches, publishes, proclaims, discloses, minutely explains, and makes it clear, that all the constituents of being are transitory.

Whether Buddhas arise, O priests, or whether Buddhas do not arise, it remains a fact and the fixed and necessary constitution of being, that all its constituents are misery. This fact a Buddha discovers and masters, and when he has discovered and mastered it, he announces, teaches, publishes, proclaims, discloses, minutely explains, and makes it clear, that all the constituents of being are misery.

Whether Buddhas arise, O priests, or whether Buddhas do not arise, it remains a fact and the fixed and necessary constitution of being, that all its elements are lacking in an Ego. This fact a Buddha discovers and masters, and when he has discovered and mastered it, he announces, teaches, publishes, proclaims, discloses, minutely explains, and makes it clear, that all the elements of being are lacking in an Ego.

GENERAL INTRODUCTION.

The materials for this book are drawn ultimately from the Pāli writings of Ceylon and Burma, — that is to say, they are to be found in palm-leaf manuscripts of those countries, written in the Singhalese or Burmese alphabet, as the case may be, but always in the same Pāli language, a tongue very nearly akin to the Sanskrit. These Pāli writings furnish the most authoritative account of The Buddha and his Doctrine that we have; and it is therefore to be regretted that, inasmuch as so little has been known in the Occident until recently of either Pāli or Pāli literature, the information of the public concerning Buddhism has been so largely drawn from books based on other, non-Pāli, sources, on works written in the Singhalese, Chinese, and Tibetan languages, and in the Buddhist-Sanskrit of Nepaul. But a large number of Pāli manuscripts have now been edited and printed in the publications of the Pāli Text Society of London, and in scattered works both in England and in other European countries, and several volumes of translations into English have appeared, so that all excuse for not deriving our knowledge of Buddhism from the most authentic sources is fast disappearing.

As the work on this book has been done wholly in America, my main reliance has naturally been on printed texts. Still, I have had the use of a number of Pāli manuscripts. In Brown University at Providence, Rhode

Island, there are many manuscripts, in the Burmese character, of works belonging to the Buddhist Scriptures. These were presented by the Rev. Dr. J. N. Cushing, Baptist missionary to Burma, and an alumnus of the University. But the manuscripts which, as being both important and unedited, have proved of most value to me, are four copies of the extensive and systematic treatise on Buddhist Doctrine composed by the famous Buddhaghosa, who flourished in the fourth century A. D. It is called the "Way of Purity" (in Pāli, Visuddhi-Magga). These four manuscripts have come to me from England: one is from the private collection of Prof. T. W. Rhys Davids, Secretary of the Royal Asiatic Society; the second belonged to the late Rev. Dr. Richard Morris of Harold Wood, Essex; the third to Henry Rigg, Esq., consulting engineer to the Government of India, for railways; while for the loan of the fourth, a Burmese manuscript, my thanks are due to the India Office Library.

The Pāli literature chiefly consists of the Buddhist Scriptures and their commentaries. These form an extensive body of works, many of which are individually very large. The Singhalese canon proper — that is to say, the texts without the commentaries — has been estimated by Prof. Rhys Davids to contain about twice as much matter as the Christian Bible. From this estimate Professor Davids excludes the repetitions, which, as he well says, are " some of them very frequent, and others very long." The Christian Bible is divided into two Testaments, whereas the Buddhist canon, or Bible, has three main divisions called " Baskets " (in Pāli, Piṭaka), and the Buddhist Bible, consequently, is called " The Three Baskets " (Ti-Piṭaka).

The first Testament, Basket, or Piṭaka has been edited and published by Oldenberg, and a translation of a large part of it has appeared in the "Sacred Books of the East." This Piṭaka gives the various rules and ordinances to be observed by the Buddhist Order, and is therefore called the "Discipline-Basket" (in Pāli, Vinaya-Piṭaka). A large part of this Piṭaka is dry and technical reading; but by no means all of it is of this nature, for there is interspersed much narrative of events in the life of The Buddha. The Buddha himself is supposed to have laid down all these rules as occasion suggested their necessity, and the object of these stories is to explain the circumstances under which he did so. The works of this Piṭaka are five, as follows: —

Bhikkhu-Vibhaṅga;	Culla-Vagga;
Bhikkhunī-Vibhaṅga;	Parivāra-Pāṭha.
Mahā-Vagga;	

The second of the three Testaments, or Baskets, is called the Sutta-Piṭaka, which may be translated the "Sermon-Basket." It consists of a great number of sermons and discourses in prose and verse, delivered by The Buddha or some one of his disciples, and is extremely interesting to any one studying the philosophy and folk-lore of Buddhism. The list of the works which, according to the Singhalese canon, belong to this Piṭaka is as follows: —

Dīgha-Nikāya;
Majjhima-Nikāya;
Saṁyutta-Nikāya;
Aṅguttara-Nikāya;
Khuddaka-Nikāya, consisting of

Khuddaka-Pāṭha;	Therī-Gāthā;
Dhammapada;	Jātaka;
Udāna;	Niddesa;
Itivuttaka;	Paṭisambhidā-Magga;
Sutta-Nipāta;	Apadāna;
Vimāna-Vatthu;	Buddha-Vaṁsa;
Peta-Vatthu;	Cariyā-Piṭaka.
Thera-Gāthā;	

The works composing the third and last Piṭaka are, of all the Buddhist Scriptures, the dreariest and most forbidding reading, and this is saying a great deal. However, like the desert of Sahara, they are to be respected for their immensity; and when they are all printed, no doubt something can be made of them. The title of this Piṭaka is the " Metaphysical Basket " (in Pāli, Abhidhamma-Piṭaka). It is composed of the following works : —

Dhamma-Saṅgaṇi ;　　　Dhātu-Kathā ;
Vibhaṅga ;　　　　　　　Yamaka ;
Kathā-Vatthu ;　　　　　Paṭṭhāna.
Puggala-Paññatti ;

This completes the list of the works composing the Tipiṭaka or Buddhist Scriptures. A number of them have not been printed in their entirety, and still others not at all.[1]

The non-canonical works consist of numerous commentaries on the Tipiṭaka, and of several other writings of more or less importance. The Buddhaghosa above mentioned was a most prolific commentator, and his Sumaṅgala-Vilāsinī, or commentary on the Dīgha-

---

[1] Since the above was written, the King of Siam, who has long been a patron of Pāli studies, has presented Harvard College and a number of other institutions of learning with an edition of Tipiṭaka works. This gift was made on the occasion of the twenty-fifth anniversary of his accession to the throne, and consists of thirty-nine volumes printed in the Siamese character. The first and third Piṭakas are complete, as well as the first four Nikāyas of the second Piṭaka ; but of the Khuddaka-Nikāya I find only the Khuddaka-Pāṭha, Dhammapada, Udāna, Itivuttaka, Sutta-Nipāta, Niddesa, and Paṭisambhidā-Magga. Most of the other works of this Nikāya have been or are being edited in Europe, so that the only Tipiṭaka work which has not appeared, at least partially, in type is the Apadāna. This splendid present made by the King of Siam was, I am sorry to say, received too late to be drawn upon for selections for this volume.

Nikāya, is in the Providence collection, and has also partially appeared in type. Of others of his commentaries I have seen only fragments; but, as above stated, I have his general work entitled the Visuddhi-Magga.

Of works which are not commentaries, there is a dictionary of synonyms written in verse, and called the Abhidhāna-ppadīpikā. Then there is the Milindapañha (Questions of Milinda). Milinda (Greek Menander) was a Greek king who carried on the Greek dominion in Bactria founded by Alexander the Great. He probably lived in the second century B. C., and the Milindapañha was probably composed about the beginning of our era. The Milindapañha is, strictly speaking, a North Buddhist work, but it is considered so orthodox by the South Buddhists, i. e. by the Buddhists of Ceylon, Burma, and Siam, that I have felt bold to draw upon it freely in this book. Then there are the Abhidhammattha-Sangaha, the Sārasangaha, the Anāgata-Vaṁsa, and some other works on grammar, history, and so forth, the names of which I spare the reader, as no translation from them occurs in this book.

After long bothering my head over Sanskrit, I found much more satisfaction when I took up the study of Pāli. For Sanskrit literature is a chaos; Pāli, a cosmos. In Sanskrit every fresh work or author seemed a new problem; and as trustworthy Hindu chronology and recorded history are almost nil, and as there are many systems of philosophy, orthodox as well as unorthodox, the necessary data for the solution of the problem were usually lacking. Such data, I mean, as who the author was, when he lived and wrote, what were the current beliefs and conceptions of his day, and what his own position was in respect of them; such data, in short, as are necessary in order to know what to think of an author, and fully to understand what he says. Now the subject-matter of Pāli literature is nearly always the same, namely, the definite system of religion propounded by The Buddha. Indeed, in a large part of the writings, The Buddha appears as a dramatis persona. We have volumes and volumes of sermons, discourses, and moral tales credited to him, and hundreds of incidents related, apropos of which he pronounced some dictum. And the place of such utterance is usually given. Consequently, although there is a large field for text criticism — a field on which I have not felt it desirable to enter in this book — there is, in a general way and in respect of subject-matter, considerable unity in Pāli literature.

The aim of the present work is to take different ideas and conceptions found in Pāli writings, and present them to the reader in English. Translation has been the means employed as being the most effectual, and the order pursued is in the main that of the Buddhist "Three Jewels" (in Pāli, Ti-Ratana), to wit, The Buddha, the Doctrine, and the Order. The selections of the first chapter are on The Buddha; next follow those which deal chiefly with the Doctrine; while others concerning the Order and secular life constitute the closing chapter of the book.

CHAPTER I.

THE BUDDHA.

Introductory Discourse.

In reading the Pāli Scriptures one is impressed with the strong personal influence exercised by The Buddha over the hearts of his followers. He was regarded, not as a mere formulator of dry metaphysical propositions, but as a very wise and compassionate friend of his fellow-men. He was full of tact, and all his ways were ways of peace. To allay discord he would tell a little story or fable with a moral, and his epithet for one of whom he disapproved was merely "vain man." Anger, in fact, had no place in his character, and the reader of this book will find that it had equally none in his religio-philosophic system.

The term "Buddha" means "Enlightened One," and signifies that the person to whom it is applied has solved the riddle of existence, and discovered the doctrine for the cessation of misery. It was by his attainment of this supreme "Enlightenment" or Wisdom that Gotama became a Buddha. During the thirty-five years of his life previous to that event, and during all previous existences from the time he set out towards the Buddhaship, he was a Bodhisatta, — a term which I have freely translated "Future Buddha," but which is more literally rendered "He whose essence is Wisdom."

The Buddha's given name would appear to have been Siddhattha; but as the word means "Successful in his Objects," it looks as though it might be a simple epithet. The

Buddha belonged to the Sakya clan. The word "Sakya"
means "Powerful;" and the families that bore the name had
a reputation for pride and haughtiness. They were of the
warrior caste, but cultivated the peaceful arts of agriculture.
By his contemporaries The Buddha is usually called Gotama,
or, as the word is sometimes Anglicized, the Gotamid. It is
not quite clear why he and others of his clan should bear the
name of Gotama in addition to that of Sakya. It may be
they claimed descent from the ancient sage Gautama (Sanskrit "Gautama" becomes "Gotama" in Pāli), to whom are
attributed some of the hymns of the Rig-Veda; or it may
be, as Burnouf has suggested, "because Gautama was the
sacerdotal family name of the military race of Sakyas, who,
being of the warrior caste, had no ancestor or tutelar saint
like the Brahmans, but might, as the Hindu law permits,
have taken the name of the sage to whose family belonged
their spiritual guide."

The Buddha was a Hindu, born not far from the Ganges,
and during his long ministry wandered about from place to
place in the section of country about Benares, very much as
did Christ in Samaria and Judea. And just as Christ once
left his native country and went to Egypt, so The Buddha is
said by native authorities to have paid a couple of visits to
Ceylon; but the statement is, I fear, somewhat mythical.

The date of Gotama Buddha is considered to be the sixth
century before Christ. It would appear that he lived to his
eightieth year, and the time of his death is given by scholars
as about 480 B. C.

The first eight sections of the present chapter are from
the general introduction to the Jātaka ("Book of Birth-
Stories"). These Birth-Stories, five hundred and fifty in
number, are so called because they are tales of the anterior
existences of Gotama Buddha, while he was as yet but a

Future Buddha. The Jātaka is an extensive work; five volumes have already been edited by Professor V. Fausböll, of Copenhagen, and more is yet to come. It consists of the Birth-Stories themselves, with a commentary and a long introduction. Examples of these Birth-Stories will be given further on; here we have only to do with the Introduction, the author of which and of the commentary is unknown.

After a few preliminary remarks concerning the inception and plan of his work, the author begins by quoting entire the Story of Sumedha as contained in the metrical work called the Buddha-Vaṁsa ("History of the Buddhas"). He does not quote it all consecutively, but a few stanzas at a time as authority for his prose statements. In this prose is also some matter of a commentary nature, apparently later glosses and not a part of the original text. In my first translation I give the Story of Sumedha as quoted in this Introduction to the Jātaka, but I give it consecutively and omit the prose, except that of some of the more interesting and explanatory passages, of the glosses especially, I have made foot-notes.

After the Story of Sumedha our author gives formal descriptions of each of the twenty-four Buddhas that preceded Gotama. These descriptions, however, are tedious, and are not here translated. They mainly concern themselves with such details as the height of each Buddha, his length of life, how many conversions he made, the names of his father, mother, chief disciples, etc. But from the point where my second section begins to the end of the eighth I follow the native text without making any omissions. I have divided one continuous text into seven parts, and then given these divisions titles of my own devising.

The reader is thus brought up to the ministry of The Buddha. This ministry lasted some forty-five years, and an account of part of it is given by the author of the Introduc-

tion. It is, however, only a part that he gives, just enough
to conduct his reader up to the time when The Buddha was
presented with Jetavana monastery, the importance of which
event to our author will be readily perceived when it is
remembered that this was the monastery in which The
Buddha is represented as having related the greater part of
the Birth-Stories. As our author fails to give us a complete
life of The Buddha, and as I know of none in Pāli literature,
none is attempted in this book. But in order that the reader
may have at an early stage an idea of what the matters were
wherein The Buddha considered himself "enlightened," two
passages are translated from the Mahā-Vagga. Then follows
a description of the daily routine of The Buddha's ministry,
and the last section of this chapter gives the Pāli account
of how The Buddha died. It is not because the philosophical
ideas expressed and the references to meditation and trance
made in these four sections are supposed to be self-explana-
tory, that I make no comment on them in this chapter; but
because the next three chapters, as I have already stated
in my General Introduction, are devoted to the Doctrine,
and constitute the philosophical and systematic part of this
work. It appeared desirable to give the reader a general
idea of what the Buddhists consider to be the salient features
of their system of religion before beginning its detailed
discussion.

§ 1.   THE STORY OF SUMEDHA.[1]

Translated from the Introduction to the Jātaka (i.3¹).

12.   A hundred thousand cycles vast
      And four immensities ago,
      There was a town named Amara,
      A place of beauty and delights.
      It had the noises ten complete [2]
      And food and drink abundantly.

13.   The noise of elephant and horse,
      Of conch-shell, drum, and chariot,
      And invitations to partake —
      " Eat ye, and drink ! " — resounded loud.

14.   A town complete in all its parts,
      Where every industry was found,
      And eke the seven precious gems,[3]
      And foreigners from many lands.
      A prosperous city of the gods,
      Full·of good works and holy men.

15.   Within this town of Amara
      Sumedha lived, of Brahman caste,
      Who many tens of millions had,
      And grain and treasure in full store.

16.   A student he, and wise in spells,
      A master of the Vedas three.
      He fortunes told, tradition knew,
      And every duty of his caste.

---

[1] This entire story is related by The Buddha to his disciples, and describes how, in his long-ago existence as the Brahman Sumedha, he first resolved to strive for the Buddhaship. In stanzas 12–16 he speaks of himself, that is, of Sumedha, in the third person, but elsewhere in the first.

[2] Only six of the ten noises indicative of a flourishing town are here mentioned.   For the complete list, see p. 101.

[3] Probably gold, silver, pearls, gems (such as sapphire and ruby), cat's-eye, diamond, and coral; or perhaps as given on p. 101, note.

17. In secret then I sat me down,
   And thus to ponder I began:
   "What misery to be born again!
   And have the flesh dissolve at death!

18. "Subject to birth, old age, disease,
   Extinction will I seek to find,
   Where no decay is ever known,
   Nor death, but all security.

19. "What if I now should rid me of
   This body foul, this charnel-house,
   And go my way without a care,
   Or least regret for things behind!

20. "There is, there must be, an escape!
   Impossible there should not be!
   I'll make the search and find the way,
   Which from existence shall release!

21. "Even as, although there misery is,
   Yet happiness is also found;
   So, though indeed existence is,
   A non-existence should be sought.

22. "Even as, although there may be heat,
   Yet grateful cold is also found;
   So, though the threefold fire[1] exists,
   Likewise Nirvana should be sought.

23. "Even as, although there evil is,
   That which is good is also found;
   So, though 't is true that birth exists,
   That which is not birth should be sought.

24. "Even as a man befouled with dung,
   Seeing a brimming lake at hand,
   And nathless bathing not therein,
   Were senseless should he chide the lake;

---

[1] Lust, hatred, and infatuation. Compare page 59, and also the "Fire-sermon," page 351.

25.   " So, when Nirvana's lake exists
      To wash away corruption's stain,
      Should I not seek to bathe therein,
      I might not then Nirvana chide.

26.   " Even as a man hemmed in by foes,
      Seeing a certain safe escape,
      And nathless seeking not to flee,
      Might not the blameless pathway chide;

27.   " So, when my passions hem me in,
      And yet a way to bliss exists,
      Should I not seek to follow it,
      That way of bliss I might not chide.

28.   " Even as a man who, sore diseased,
      When a physician may be had,
      Should fail to send to have him come,
      Might the physician then not chide;

29.   " So, when diseased with passion, sore
      Oppressed, I seek the master not
      Whose ghostly counsel me might cure,
      The blame should not on him be laid.

30.   " Even as a man might rid him of
      A horrid corpse bound to his neck,
      And then upon his way proceed,
      Joyous, and free, and unconstrained;

31.   " So must I likewise rid me of
      This body foul, this charnel-house,
      And go my way without a care,
      Or least regret for things behind.

32.   " As men and women rid them of
      Their dung upon the refuse heap,
      And go their ways without a care,
      Or least regret for what they leave;

33.   " So will I likewise rid me of
        This body foul, this charnel-house,
        And go my way as if I had
        Cast out my filth into the draught.

34.   " Even as the owners leave and quit
        A worn-out, shattered, leaky ship,
        And go their ways without a care,
        Or least regret for what they leave ;

35.   " So will I likewise rid me of
        This nine-holed,[1] ever-trickling frame,
        And go my way, as owners do,
        Who ship disrupted leave behind.

36.   " Even as a man who treasure bears,
        And finds him in a robber-gang,
        Will quickly flee and rid him of
        The robbers, lest they steal his gold ;

37.   " So, to a mighty robber might
        Be likened well this body's frame.
        I 'll cast it off and go my way,
        Lest of my welfare I be robbed."

38.   Thus thinking, I on rich and poor
        All that I had in alms bestowed ;
        Hundreds of millions spent I then,
        And made to Himavant [2] my way.

39.   Not far away from Himavant,
        There was a hill named Dhammaka,
        And here I made and patterned well
        A hermitage and hut of leaves.

---

[1] The two eyes, ears, and so forth, as enumerated at page 298.

[2] The Himalaya mountains. *Himālaya* and *Himavant* are Sanskrit words of almost identical signification. The former means " snow-abode," and is a compound of *hima*, " snow," and *ālaya*, " settling-down place," or " abode." *Hima-vant* means " snow-y."

40. A walking-place I then laid out,
     Exempted from the five defects, [1]
     And having all the virtues eight; [2]
     And there I gained the Six High Powers.

41. Then ceased I cloaks of cloth to wear,
     For cloaks possess the nine defects, [3]

---

[1] Native gloss: Jātaka, vol. i., p. 7, l. 14: *Exempted from the five defects:* The following are the five defects in a walking-place: hardness and unevenness; trees in the midst; dense underbrush; excessive narrowness; excessive width. For if the walking-place be on hard and uneven ground, then any one who uses it hurts and blisters his feet, so that he fails of concentration of mind, and his meditation is broken up; while he who walks at ease on a soft and even surface succeeds in meditation. Therefore hardness and unevenness of surface are to be reckoned as one defect. If a walking-place have trees in it, whether in the middle or at the end, then any one who uses it is liable, if not careful, to strike his forehead or his head against them. Therefore trees in the midst are a second defect. If a walking-place be overgrown with a dense underbrush of grass, vines, and so forth, any one who uses it in the dark is liable to tread upon snakes and other creatures and kill them, or they may bite and injure him. Thus a dense underbrush is a third defect. If a walking-place be excessively narrow, say only a cubit or half a cubit wide, then any one who uses it is liable to stumble at the borders and stub his toes and break his toe-nails. Therefore excessive narrowness is a fourth defect. If a walking-place be excessively wide, then any one who uses it is liable to have his mind wander and fail of concentration. Thus excessive width is a fifth defect. A walking-place should be a path a cubit and a half in breadth, with a margin of a cubit on either side, and it should be sixty cubits in length, and it should have a surface soft and evenly sprinkled with sand.

[2] Ibidem, l. 30. *And having all the virtues eight:* Having the eight advantages for a monk. The following are the eight advantages for a monk: it admits of no storing-up of treasure or grain; it favors only a blameless alms-seeking; there one can eat his alms in peace and quiet; there no annoyance is experienced from the reigning families when they oppress the kingdom with their levies of the precious metals or of leaden money; no passionate desire arises for furniture and implements; there is no fear of being plundered by robbers; no intimacies are formed with kings and courtiers; and one is not shut in in any of the four directions.

[3] Native gloss: Jātaka, vol. i., p. 8, l. 27: *For cloaks possess the nine defects: . . .* For one who retires from the world and takes up the life of an anchorite, there are nine defects inherent in garments of cloth. The great cost is one defect; the fact that it is got by dependence on others is another; the fact that it is easily soiled by use is another, for

> And girded on a barken dress,
> Which is with virtues twelve endued.¹

42.   My hut of leaves I then forsook,
      So crowded with the eight defects,²
      And at the foot of trees I lived,
      For such abodes have virtues ten.³

when it has been soiled it must be washed and dyed ; the fact that when it is much worn it must needs be patched and mended is another; the difficulty of obtaining a new one when needed is another ; its unsuitableness for an anchorite who has retired from the world is another; its acceptableness to one's enemies is another, for it must needs be guarded lest the enemy take it; the danger that it may be worn for ornament is another ; the temptation it affords to load one's self down with it in travelling is another.

¹ The bast, or inner bark of certain trees, was much used in India as cloth, to which indeed it bears a striking resemblance. — Native gloss : Jātaka, vol. i., p. 9, l. 2 : *Which is with virtues twelve endued :* Possessing twelve advantages. For there are twelve advantages in a dress of bark. It is cheap, good, and suitable ; this is one advantage. You can make it yourself ; this is a second. It gets dirty but slowly by use, and hence time is not wasted in washing it; this is a third. It never needs sewing, even when much used and worn ; this is a fourth. But when a new one is needed, it can be made with ease; this is a fifth. Its suitableness for an anchorite who has retired from the world is a sixth. That it is of no use to one's enemies is a seventh. That it cannot be worn for ornament is an eighth. Its lightness is a ninth. Its conducing to moderation in dress is a tenth. The irreproachableness and blamelessness of searching for bark is an eleventh. And the unimportance of its loss is a twelfth.

² Native gloss : Jātaka, vol. i., p. 9, l. 11 : *My hut of leaves I then forsook, So crowded with the eight defects : . . .* (L. 36) For there are eight evils connected with the use of a leaf-hut. The great labor involved in searching for materials and in the putting of them together is one evil. The constant care necessary to replace the grass, leaves, and bits of clay that fall down is a second. Houses may do for old men, but no concentration of mind is possible when one's meditation is liable to be interrupted ; thus the liability to interruption is a third. The protection afforded against heat and cold renders the body delicate, and this is a fourth. In a house all sorts of evil deeds are possible ; thus the cover it affords for disgraceful practices is a fifth. The taking possession, saying, "This is mine," is a sixth. To have a house is like having a companion ; this is a seventh. And the sharing of it with many others, as for instance with lice, bugs, and house-lizards, is an eighth.

³ Ibidem, p. 10, l. 9 : *And at the foot of trees I lived, For such abodes have virtues ten : . . .* The following are the ten virtues. The smallness of

43. No sown and cultivated grain
     Allowed I then to be my food;
     But all the many benefits
     Of wild-fruit fare I made my own.

44. And strenuous effort made I there,
     The while I sat, or stood, or walked;
     And ere seven days had passed away,
     I had attained the Powers High.

45. When I had thus success attained,
     And made me master of the Law,
     A Conqueror, Lord of All the World,
     Was born, by name Dīpaṁkara.

46. What time he was conceived, was born,
     What time he Buddhaship attained,
     When first he preached, — the Signs[1] appeared.
     I saw them not, deep sunk in trance.

47. Then, in the distant border-land,
     Invited they this Being Great,
     And every one, with joyful heart,
     The pathway for his coming cleared.

---

the undertaking is one virtue, for all that is necessary is simply to go to the tree. The small amount of care it requires is a second; for, whether swept or unswept, it is suitable for use. The freedom from interruption is a third. It affords no cover for disgraceful practices; wickedness there would be too public; thus the fact that it affords no cover for disgraceful practices is a fourth. It is like living under the open sky, for there is no feeling that the body is confined; thus the non-confinement of the body is a fifth. There is no taking possession; this is a sixth. The abandonment of all longings for household life is a seventh. When a house is shared with others, some one is liable to say, "I will look after this house myself. Begone!" Thus the freedom from eviction is an eighth. The happy contentment experienced by the occupant is a ninth. The little concern one need feel about lodgings, seeing that a man can find a tree no matter where he may be stopping, — this is a tenth.

[1] Translated from the prose of the Jātaka, vol. i., p. 10, last line but one: At his [Dīpaṁkara's] conception, birth, attainment of Buddhaship, and when he caused the Wheel of Doctrine to roll, the entire system of ten thousand worlds trembled, quivered, and shook, and roared with a mighty roar; also the Thirty-Two Prognostics appeared. [For the Thirty-Two Prognostics, see page 44.]

48.   Now so it happened at this time,
        That I my hermitage had left,
        And, barken garments rustling loud,
        Was passing o'er them through the air.

49.   Then saw I every one alert,
        Well-pleased, delighted, overjoyed;
        And, coming downward from the sky,
        The multitude I straightway asked:

50.   " Well-pleased, delighted, overjoyed,
        And all alert is every one;
        For whom is being cleared the way,
        The path, the track to travel on?"

51.   When thus I asked, response was made:
        " A mighty Buddha has appeared,
        A Conqueror, Lord of All the World,
        Whose name is called Dīpaṁkara.
        For him is being cleared the way,
        The path, the track to travel on."

52.   This word, " The Buddha," when I heard,
        Joy sprang up straightway in my heart;
        " A Buddha! Buddha!" cried I then,
        And publishèd my heart's content.

53.   And standing there I pondered deep,
        By joyous agitation seized:
        " Here will I now some good seed sow,
        Nor let this fitting season slip."

54.   " For a Buddha do ye clear the road?
        Then, pray, grant also me a place!
        I, too, will help to clear the way,
        The path, the track to travel on."

55.   And so they granted also me
        A portion of the path to clear,
        And I gan clear, while still my heart
        Said " Buddha! Buddha!" o'er and o'er.

56. But ere my part was yet complete,
     Dīpaṁkara, the Mighty Sage,
     The Conqueror, came that way along,
     Thronged by four hundred thousand saints,
     Without depravity or spot,
     And having each the Six High Powers.

57. The people then their greetings gave,
     And many kettle-drums were beat,
     And men and gods, in joyous mood,
     Loud shouted their applauding cries.

58. Then men and gods together met,
     And saw each other face to face;
     And all with joinèd hands upraised
     Followed The Buddha and his train.

59. The gods, with instruments divine,
     The men, with those of human make,
     Triumphant music played, the while
     They followed in The Buddha's train.

60. Celestial beings from on high
     Threw broadcast over all the earth
     The Erythrina flowers of heaven,
     The lotus and the coral-flower.

61. And men abiding on the ground
     On every side flung up in air
     Champakas, salaḷas, nīpas,
     Nāgas, punnāgas, ketakas.

62. Then loosened I my matted hair,
     And, spreading out upon the mud
     My dress of bark and cloak of skin,
     I laid me down upon my face.

63. " Let now on me The Buddha tread,
     With the disciples of his train;
     Can I but keep him from the mire,
     To me great merit shall accrue."

64.   While thus I lay upon the ground,[1]
       Arose within me many thoughts:
       "To-day, if such were my desire,
       I my corruptions might consume.

65.   "But why thus in an unknown guise
       Should I the Doctrine's fruit secure?
       Omniscience first will I achieve,
       And be a Buddha in the world.

66.   "Or why should I, a valorous man,
       The ocean seek to cross alone?
       Omniscience first will I achieve,
       And men and gods convey across.

67.   "Since now I make this earnest wish,
       In presence of this Best of Men,
       Omniscience sometime I'll achieve,
       And multitudes convey across.

68.   "I'll rebirth's circling stream arrest,
       Destroy existence's three modes;
       I'll climb the sides of Doctrine's ship,
       And men and gods convey across.

69.   "A human being,[2] male of sex,
       Who saintship gains, a Teacher meets,
       As hermit lives, and virtue loves,
       Nor lacks resolve, nor fiery zeal,
       Can by these eight conditions joined,
       Make his most earnest wish succeed."

---

[1] Native gloss: Jātaka, vol. i., p. 13, l. 31: As he lay in the mud, he opened his eyes again, and gazing upon the Buddha-glory of Dipaṁkara, The Possessor of the Ten Forces, he reflected as follows: "If I so wished, I might burn up all my corruptions, and as novice follow with the congregation when they enter the city of Ramma; but I do not want to burn up my corruptions and enter Nirvana unknown to any one. What now if I, like Dipaṁkara, were to acquire the supreme wisdom, were to cause multitudes to go on board the ship of Doctrine and cross the ocean of the round of rebirth, and were afterwards to pass into Nirvana! That would be something worthy of me!"

[2] Native gloss: Jātaka, vol. i., p. 14, l. 20: For it is only a human being that can successfully wish to be a Buddha; a serpent, or a bird,

70. Dīpaṁkara, Who Knew All Worlds,
     Recipient of Offerings,
     Came to a halt my pillow near,
     And thus addressed the multitudes:

71. "Behold ye now this monk austere,
     His matted locks, his penance fierce!
     Lo! he, unnumbered cycles hence,
     A Buddha in the world shall be.

---

or a deity cannot successfully make the wish. Of human beings it is only one of the male sex that can make the wish: it would not be successful on the part of a woman, or of a eunuch, or of a neuter, or of a hermaphrodite. Of men it is he, and only he, who is in a fit condition by the attainment of saintship in that same existence, that can successfully make the wish. Of those in a fit condition it is only he who makes the wish in the presence of a living Buddha that succeeds in his wish; after the death of a Buddha a wish made at a relic-shrine, or at the foot of a Bo-tree, will not be successful. Of those who make the wish in the presence of a Buddha it is he, and only he, who has retired from the world that can successfully make the wish, and not one who is a layman. Of those who have retired from the world it is only he who is possessed of the Five High Powers and is master of the Eight Attainments that can successfully make the wish, and no one can do so who is lacking in these excellences. Of those, even, who possess these excellences it is he, and only he, who has such firm resolve that he is ready to sacrifice his life for The Buddhas that can successfully make the wish, but no other. Of those who possess this resolve it is he, and only he, who has great zeal, determination, strenuousness, and endeavor in striving for the qualities that make a Buddha that is successful. The following comparisons will show the intensity of the zeal. If he is such a one as to think: "The man who, if all within the rim of the world were to become water, would be ready to swim across it with his own arms and get to the further shore, — he is the one to attain the Buddhaship; or, in case all within the rim of the world were to become a jungle of bamboo, would be ready to elbow and trample his way through it and get to the further side, — he is the one to attain the Buddhaship; or, in case all within the rim of the world were to become a *terra firma* of thick-set javelins, would be ready to tread on them and go afoot to the further side, — he is the one to attain the Buddhaship; or, in case all within the rim of the world were to become live coals, would be ready to tread on them and so get to the further side, — he is the one to attain the Buddhaship," — if he deems not even one of these feats too hard for himself, but has such great zeal, determination, strenuousness, and power of endeavor that he would perform these feats in order to attain the Buddhaship, then, but not otherwise, will his wish succeed.

72. " From the fair town called Kapila
     His Great Retirement shall be made.
     Then, when his Struggle fierce is o'er,
     His stern austerities performed, —

73. " He shall in quiet sit him down
     Beneath the Ajapāla-tree;
     There pottage made of rice receive,
     And seek the stream Nerañjarā.

74. " This pottage shall The Conqueror eat,
     Beside the stream Nerañjarā,
     And thence by road triumphal go
     To where the Tree of Wisdom stands.

75. " Then shall the Peerless, Glorious One
     Walk to the right, round Wisdom's Throne,
     And there The Buddhaship achieve,
     While sitting at the fig-tree's root.

76. " The mother that shall bring him forth,
     Shall Māyā callèd be by name;
     Suddhodana his father's name;
     His own name shall be Gotama.

77. " Kolita, Upatissa[1] too, —
     These shall his Chief Disciples be;
     Both undepraved, both passion-free,
     And tranquil and serene of mind.

78. " Ānanda shall be servitor
     And on The Conqueror attend;
     Khemā and Uppalavaṇṇā
     Shall female Chief Disciples be,

79. " Both undepraved, both passion-free,
     And tranquil and serene of mind.
     The Bo-tree of this Blessed One
     Shall be the tree Assattha[1] called."

---

[1] Better known as Moggallāna and Sāriputta, respectively.
[2] Ficus religiosa.

80. Thus spake Th' Unequalled, Mighty Sage;
     And all, when they had heard his speech,
     Both men and gods rejoiced, and said:
     " Behold a Buddha-scion here! "

81. Now shouts were heard on every side,
     The people clapped their arms and laughed.
     Ten thousand worlds of men and gods
     Paid me their homage then and said:

82. " If of our Lord Dīpaṁkara
     The Doctrine now we fail to grasp,
     We yet shall stand in time to come
     Before this other face to face.

83. " Even as, when men a river cross,
     And miss th' opposing landing-place,
     A lower landing-place they find,
     And there the river-bank ascend;

84. " Even so, we all, if we let slip
     The present Conqueror that we have,
     Yet still shall stand in time to come
     Before this other, face to face."

85. Dīpaṁkara, Who All Worlds Knew,
     Recipient of Offerings,
     My future having prophesied,
     His right foot raised and went his way.

86. And all who were this Conqueror's sons,
     Walked to the right around me then;
     And serpents, men, and demigods,
     Saluting me, departed thence.

87. Now when The Leader of the World
     Had passed from sight with all his train,
     My mind with rapturous transport filled,
     I raised me up from where I lay.

88. Then overjoyed with joy was I,
   Delighted with a keen delight;
   And thus with pleasure saturate
   I sat me down with legs across.

89. And while cross-leggèd there I sat,
   I thus reflected to myself:
   "Behold! in trance am I adept,
   And all the Powers High are mine.

90. "Nowhere throughout a thousand worlds
   Are any seers to equal me;
   Unequalled in the magic gifts
   Have I this height of bliss attained."

91. Now while I sat with legs across,
   The dwellers of ten thousand worlds
   Rolled forth a glad and mighty shout:[1]
   "Surely a Buddha thou shalt be!

92. "The presages that erst were seen,
   When Future Buddhas sat cross-legged,
   These presages are seen to-day —
   Surely a Buddha thou shalt be!

93. "All cold is everywhere dispelled,
   And mitigated is the heat;
   These presages are seen to-day —
   Surely a Buddha thou shalt be!

94. "The system of ten thousand worlds
   Is hushed to quiet and to peace;
   These presages are seen to-day —
   Surely a Buddha thou shalt be!

---

[1] There have been many beings who, like Sumedha here, were to become Buddhas, and who were therefore called Bodhi-sattas or "Future Buddhas." The certainty of their ultimate "Illumination," or Buddhaship, was always foretokened by certain presages. The "dwellers of ten thousand worlds" describe in the following stanzas what these presages were, declare that they are reappearing now, and announce to Sumedha their prophetic inference that he will attain Buddhaship.

95. "The mighty winds then cease to blow,
      Nor do the rivers onward glide;
      These presages are seen to-day —
      Surely a Buddha thou shalt be!

96. "All plants, be they of land or stream,
      Do straightway put their blossoms forth;
      Even so to-day they all have bloomed —
      Surely a Buddha thou shalt be!

97. "And every tree, and every vine,
      Is straightway laden down with fruit;
      Even so to-day they're laden down —
      Surely a Buddha thou shalt be!

98. "In sky and earth doth straightway then
      Full many a radiant gem appear;
      Even so to-day they shine afar —
      Surely a Buddha thou shalt be!

99. "Then straightway music's heard to play
      'Mongst men on earth and gods in heaven;
      So all to-day in music join —
      Surely a Buddha thou shalt be!

100. "There falleth straightway down from heaven
      A rain of many-colored flowers;
      Even so to-day these flowers are seen —
      Surely a Buddha thou shalt be!

101. "The mighty ocean heaves and roars,
      And all the worlds ten thousand quake;
      Even so is now this tumult heard —
      Surely a Buddha thou shalt be!

102. "Straightway throughout the whole of hell
      The fires ten thousand all die out;
      Even so to-day have all expired —
      Surely a Buddha thou shalt be!

103.   " Unclouded then the sun shines forth,
       And all the stars appear to view;
       Even so to-day do they appear —
       Surely a Buddha thou shalt be !

104.   " Straightway, although no rain hath fallen,
       Burst springs of water from the earth;
       Even so to-day they gush in streams —
       Surely a Buddha thou shalt be !

105   " And bright then shine the starry hosts
       And constellations in the sky;
       The moon in Libra now doth stand —
       Surely a Buddha thou shalt be !

106.   " All beasts that lurk in holes and clefts,
       Then get them forth from out their lairs;
       Even so to-day they 've left their dens —
       Surely a Buddha thou shalt be !

107.   " Straightway content is all the world,
       And no unhappiness is known;
       Even so to-day are all content —
       Surely a Buddha thou shalt be !

108.   " Then every sickness vanishes,
       And hunger likewise disappears;
       These presages are seen to-day —
       Surely a Buddha thou shalt be !

109.   " Then lust doth dwindle and grow weak,
       And hate, infatuation too;
       Even so to-day they disappear —
       Surely a Buddha thou shalt be !

110.   " Then fear and danger are unknown;
       All we are freed from them to-day;
       And by this token we perceive —
       ' Surely a Buddha thou shalt be !'

111.   " No dust upwhirleth towards the sky;
       Even so to-day this thing is seen;
       And by this token we perceive —
       ' Surely a Buddha thou shalt be ! '

112.   " All noisome odors drift away,
       And heavenly fragrance fills the air;
       Even so the winds now sweetness waft —
       Surely a Buddha thou shalt be !

113.   " Then all the gods appear to view,
       Save those that hold the formless realm;
       Even so to-day these all are seen —
       Surely a Buddha thou shalt be !

114.   " Then clearly seen are all the hells,
       However many be their tale;
       Even so to-day may all be seen —
       Surely a Buddha thou shalt be !

115.   " Through walls, and doors, and mountain-rocks,
       One finds an easy passage then;
       Even so to-day they yield like air —
       Surely a Buddha thou shalt be !

116.   " Existence then forbears its round
       Of death and rebirth for a time;
       Even so to-day this thing is seen —
       Surely a Buddha thou shalt be !

117.   " Do thou a strenuous effort make !
       Do not turn back !. Go on !   Advance !
       Most certainly we know this thing:
       ' Surely a Buddha thou shalt be ! ' "

118.   When I had heard The Buddha's speech,
       And what the worlds ten thousand said,
       Well-pleased, delighted, overjoyed,
       I thus reflected to myself:

119. " The Buddhas never liars are ;
     A Conqueror's word ne'er yet was vain ;
     Nothing but truth The Buddhas speak —
     Surely a Buddha I shall be !

120. " As clods thrown upward in the air
     Fall surely back upon the earth,
     So what the glorious Buddhas speak
     Is sure and steadfast to the end.
     Nothing but truth The Buddhas speak [1] —
     Surely a Buddha I shall be ! [1]

121. " As also for each living thing
     The approach of death is ever sure,
     So what the glorious Buddhas speak
     Is sure and steadfast to the end.
     Nothing but truth The Buddhas speak [1] —
     Surely a Buddha I shall be ! [1]

122. " As at the waning of the night
     The rising of the sun is sure,
     So what the glorious Buddhas speak
     Is sure and steadfast to the end.
     Nothing but truth, *etc.* [1]

123. " As, when he issues from his den,
     The roaring of the lion 's sure,
     So what the glorious Buddhas speak
     Is sure and steadfast to the end.
     Nothing but truth, *etc.* [1] .

124. " As when a female has conceived,
     Her bringing forth of young is sure,
     So what the glorious Buddhas speak
     Is sure and steadfast to the end.
     Nothing but truth The Buddhas speak [1] —
     Surely a Buddha I shall be ! [1]

---

[1] This refrain is added to these stanzas in the Buddha-Vaṁsa. In the Jātaka it is omitted.

125.   '' Come now! I'll search that I may find
       Conditions which a Buddha make —
       Above, below, to all ten [1] points,
       Where'er conditions hold their sway.''

126.   And then I searched, and saw the First
       Perfection, which consists in Alms,
       That highroad great whereon of old
       The former seers had ever walked.

127.   '' Come now!   This one as first adopt,
       And practise it determinedly;
       Acquire perfection in thine Alms,
       If thou to Wisdom wouldst attain.

128.   '' As when a jar is brimming full,
       And some one overturneth it,
       The jar its water all gives forth,
       And nothing for itself keeps back;

129.   '' So, when a suppliant thou dost see,
       Of mean, or high, or middling rank,
       Give all in Alms, in nothing stint,
       E'en as the overturnèd jar.

130.   '' But now there must be more than these
       Conditions which a Buddha make:
       Still others will I seek to find
       That shall in Buddhaship mature.''

131.   Perfection Second then I sought,
       And lo! the Precepts came to view,
       Which mighty seers of former times
       Had practised and had follow'd.

132.   '' Come now! as second this adopt,
       And practise it determinedly;
       The Precepts to perfection keep,
       If thou to Wisdom wouldst attain.

---

[1] The four cardinal points of the compass, the four intermediate points, the zenith and nadir.

133.   " As when a Yak cow's flowing tail
        Is firmly caught by bush or thorn,
        She thereupon awaits her death,
        But will not tear and mar her tail; [1]

134.   " So likewise thou in stages four,
        Observe and keep the Precepts whole,
        On all occasions guard them well,
        As ever Yak cow does her tail.

135.   " But now there must be more than these
        Conditions which a Buddha make;
        Still others will I seek to find
        That shall in Buddhaship mature."

136.   And then Perfection Third I sought,
        Which is Renunciation called,
        Which mighty seers of former times
        Had practised and had follow'd.

137.   " Come now! this one as third adopt,
        And practise it determinedly;
        Renounce, and in perfection grow,
        If thou to Wisdom wouldst attain.

138.   " Even as a man who long has dwelt
        In prison, suffering miserably,
        No liking for the place conceives,
        But only longeth for release;

139.   " So likewise thou must every mode
        Of being as a prison view —
        Renunciation be thy aim;
        Thus from existence free thyself.

140.   " But now there must be more than these
        Conditions which a Buddha make;
        Still others will I seek to find
        That shall in Buddhaship mature."

___

[1] As Fausböll observes, a very similar statement is made by Aelian,
περὶ ζώων, xvi. 11.   See also Visuddhi-Magga, chapter i.

141.   And then I sought and found the Fourth
       Perfection, which is Wisdom called,
       Which mighty seers of former times
       Had practised and had follow'd.

142.   " Come now! this one as fourth adopt,
       And practise it determinedly;
       Wisdom to its perfection bring,
       If thou to Wisdom wouldst attain.

143.   " Just as a priest, when on his rounds,
       Nor low, nor high, nor middling folk
       Doth shun, but begs of every one,
       And so his daily food receives;

144.   " So to the learned ay resort,
       And seek thy Wisdom to increase;
       And when this Fourth Perfection's gained,
       A Buddha's Wisdom shall be thine.

145.   " But now there must be more than these
       Conditions which a Buddha make;
       Still others will I seek to find
       That shall in Buddhaship mature."

146.   And then I sought and found the Fifth
       Perfection, which is Courage called,
       Which mighty seers of former times
       Had practised and had follow'd.

147.   " Come now! this one as fifth adopt,
       And practise it determinedly;
       In Courage perfect strive to be,
       If thou to Wisdom wouldst attain.

148.   "Just as the lion, king of beasts,
       In crouching, walking, standing still,
       With courage ever is instinct,
       And watchful always, and alert;

149.   " So thou in each repeated birth,
        Courageous energy display;
        And when this Fifth Perfection's gained,
        A Buddha's Wisdom shall be thine.

150.   " But now there must be more than these
        Conditions which a Buddha make;
        Still others will I seek to find
        That shall in Buddhaship mature."

151.   And then I sought and found the Sixth
        Perfection, which is Patience called,
        Which mighty seers of former times
        Had practised and had follow'd.

152.   " Come now! this one as sixth adopt,
        And practise it determinedly;
        And if thou keep an even mood,
        A Buddha's Wisdom shall be thine.

153.   " Just as the earth, whate'er is thrown
        Upon her, whether sweet or foul,
        All things endures, and never shows
        Repugnance, nor complacency;

154.   " E'en so, or honor thou, or scorn,
        Of men, with patient mood must bear;
        And when this Sixth Perfection's gained,
        A Buddha's Wisdom shall be thine.

155.   " But now there must be more than these
        Conditions which a Buddha make;
        Still others will I seek to find
        That shall in Buddhaship mature."

156.   And then I sought and found the Seventh
        Perfection, which is that of Truth,
        Which mighty seers of former times
        Had practised and had follow'd.

157. " Come now! this one as seventh adopt,
       And practise it determinedly;
       If thou art ne'er of double speech,
       A Buddha's Wisdom shall be thine.

158. " Just as the morning star on high
       Its balanced course doth ever keep,
       And through all seasons, times, and years,
       Doth never from its pathway swerve;

159. " So likewise thou in all thy speech
       Swerve never from the path of truth;
       And when this Seventh Perfection's gained,
       A Buddha's Wisdom shall be thine.

160. " But now there must be more than these
       Conditions which a Buddha make;
       Still others will I seek to find
       That shall in Buddhaship mature."

161. And then I sought and found the Eighth
       Perfection, Resolution called,
       Which mighty seers of former times
       Had practised and had follow'd.

162. " Come now! this one as eighth adopt,
       And practise it determinedly;
       And when thou art immovable,
       A Buddha's Wisdom shall be thine.

163. " Just as a rocky mountain-peak,
       Unmovèd stands, firm-stablishèd,
       Unshaken by the boisterous gales,
       And always in its place abides;

164. " So likewise thou must ever be
       In Resolution firm intrenched;
       And when this Eighth Perfection's gained,
       A Buddha's Wisdom shall be thine.

165.   " But now there must be more than these
       Conditions which a Buddha make ;
       Still others will I seek to find
       That shall in Buddhaship mature."

166.   And then I sought and found the Ninth
       Perfection, which is called Good-will ;
       Which mighty seers of former times
       Had practised and had follow'd.

167.   " Come now ! this one as ninth adopt,
       And practise it determinedly ;
       Unequalled be in thy Good-will,
       If thou to Wisdom wouldst attain.

168.   " As water cleanseth all alike,
       The righteous and the wicked, too,
       From dust and dirt of every kind,
       And with refreshing coolness fills ;

169.   " So likewise thou both friend and foe,
       Alike with thy Good-will refresh,
       And when this Ninth Perfection 's gained,
       A Buddha's Wisdom shall be thine.

170.   " But now there must be more than these
       Conditions which a Buddha make ;
       Still others will I seek to find
       That shall in Buddhaship mature."

171.   And then I sought and found the Tenth
       Perfection, called Indifference ;
       Which mighty seers of former times
       Had practised and had follow'd.

172.   " Come now ! this one as tenth adopt,
       And practise it determinedly ;
       And when thou art of equal poise,
       A Buddha's Wisdom shall be thine.

173.   " Just as the earth, whate'er is thrown
         Upon her, whether sweet or foul,
         Indifferent is to all alike,
         Nor hatred shows, nor amity;

174.   " So likewise thou in good or ill,
         Must even-balanced ever be;
         And when this Tenth Perfection's gained,
         A Buddha's Wisdom shall be thine.

175.   " But earth no more conditions hath
         That in The Buddhaship mature;
         Beyond these are there none to seek;
         So practise these determinedly."

176.   Now pondering these conditions ten,
         Their nature, essence, character, —
         Such fiery vigor had they all,
         That all the worlds ten thousand quaked.

177.   Then shook and creaked the wide, wide earth,
         As doth the sugar-mill at work;
         Then quaked the ground, as doth the wheel
         Of oil-mills when they're made to turn.

178.   Th' entire assemblage that was there,
         And followed in The Buddha's train,
         Trembled and shook in great alarm,
         And fell astonied to the ground.

179.   And many thousand waterpots,
         And many hundred earthen jars,
         Were one upon another dashed,
         And crushed and pounded into dust.

180.   Excited, trembling, terrified,
         Confused, and sore oppressed in mind,
         The multitudes together came,
         And to Dīpaṁkara approached.

181.   " Oh, tell us what these signs portend.
         Will good or ill betide the world?
         Lo! terror seizes hold on all.
         Dispel our fears, All-Seeing One!"

182.   The Great Sage, then, Dīpaṁkara,
         Allayed and pacified their fears: —
         " Be comforted; and fear ye not
         For that the world doth quake and shake.

183.   " Of whom to-day I made proclaim —
         ' A glorious Buddha shall he be,' —
         He now conditions pondereth,
         Which former Conquerors fulfilled.

184.   " 'T is while on these he is intent,
         As basis for The Buddhaship,
         The ground in worlds ten thousand shakes,
         In all the realms of gods and men."

185.   When thus they'd heard The Buddha speak,
         Their anxious minds received relief;
         And all then drawing near to me,
         Again they did me reverence.

186.   Thus on the road to Buddhaship,
         And firm determined in my mind,
         I raised me up from off my seat,
         And reverenced Dīpaṁkara.

187.   Then as I raised me from my seat,
         Both gods and men in unison
         Sweet flowers of heaven and flowers of earth
         Profusely sprinkled on my head.

188.   And gods and men in unison
         Their great delight proclaimed aloud: —
         " A mighty prayer thou now hast made;
         Succeed according to thy wish!

189.   " From all misfortunes be thou free,
         Let every sickness disappear!

Mayst thou no hindrance ever know,
And highest Wisdom soon achieve!

190.   " As, when the time of spring has come,
The trees put forth their buds and flowers,
Likewise dost thou, O Hero Great,
With knowledge of a Buddha bloom.

191.   " As all they who have Buddhas been,
The Ten Perfections have fulfilled,
Likewise do thou, O Hero Great,
The Ten Perfections strive to gain.

192.   " As all they who have Buddhas been,
On Wisdom's Throne their insight gained,
Likewise do thou, O Hero Great,
On Conqueror's Throne thy insight gain.

193.   " As all they who have Buddhas been,
Have made the Doctrine's Wheel to roll,
Likewise do thou, O Hero Great,
Make Doctrine's Wheel to roll once more.

194.   " As on the mid-day of the month
The moon in full perfection shines,
Likewise do thou, with perfect mind,
Shine brightly in ten thousand worlds.

195.   " As when the sun, by Rāhu freed,
Shines forth exceeding bright and clear,
So thou, when freed from ties of earth,
Shine forth in bright magnificence.

196.   " Just as the rivers of all lands
Into the ocean find their way,
May gods and men from every world
Approach and find their way to thee."

197.   Thus praised they me with glad acclaim;
And I, beginning to fulfil
The ten conditions of my quest,
Re-entered then into the wood.

END OF THE STORY OF SUMEDHA.

§ 2. A LIST OF FORMER BUDDHAS.

Translated from the Introduction to the Jātaka (i.43²⁸).

Now in the same world-cycle that saw Dīpaṃkara, The
One Possessing the Ten Forces, there were also three other
Buddhas; but as none of them prophesied concerning the
Future Buddha, I have not mentioned them. In the Com-
mentary, however, all the Buddhas are mentioned from the
beginning of that world-cycle on, as follows : —

247. " Taṇhaṃkara, Medhaṃkara,
       And also Saraṇaṃkara,
       Dīpaṃkara, the Buddha great,
       Koṇḍañña, of all men the chief,

248. " Maṅgala, and Sumana too,
       Revata, Sobhita, the sage,
       Anomadassi, Paduma,
       Nārada, Padumuttara,

249. " Sumedha, and Sujāta too,
       Piyadassi, the glorious one,
       Atthadassi, Dhammadassi,
       Siddhattha, guide of every man,

250. " Tissa, Phussa, the Buddha great,
       Vipassi, Sikkhi, Vessabhū,
       Kakusandha, Koṇāgamana,
       Kassapa also, guide for men, —

251. " All these aforetime Buddhas were,
       Tranquil, from every passion free.
       And like the sun, the many-rayed,
       They chased away the darkness dense,
       And having flamed like tongues of fire,
       Became extinct with all their train."

Our Future Buddha, in his passage through four immensities and a hundred thousand world-cycles to the present time,

has made his wish under twenty-four of these Buddhas,
beginning with Dīpaṁkara. But since Kassapa, The
Blessed One, there has been no Supreme Buddha excepting
our present one. Accordingly, our Future Buddha has received recognition at the hands of twenty-four Buddhas,
beginning with Dīpaṁkara.

---

§ 3. THE CHARACTERISTICS OF A FUTURE BUDDHA.

Translated from the Introduction to the Jātaka (i.44[20]).

> " A human being, male of sex,
> Who saintship gains, a Teacher meets,
> As hermit lives, and virtue loves,
> Nor lacks resolve, nor fiery zeal,
> Can by these eight conditions joined,
> Make his most earnest wish succeed."

These eight conditions were all united in him when he made
his earnest wish at the feet of Dīpaṁkara, saying, —

> " Come now! I 'll search that I may find
> Conditions which a Buddha make."

Thereupon, putting forth a strenuous effort, — as it is said, —

> " And then I searched, and found the First
> Perfection, which consists in alms," —

he discovered, not only the perfection which is called alms,
but also all the others that go to make a Buddha. And
in fulfilling them he reached his Vessantara existence.[1] In
so doing, all the blessings celebrated in the following stanzas
as belonging to Future Buddhas who make the earnest wish
were attained by him : —

---

[1] The Vessantara Birth-Story is the last of the five hundred and fifty,
and is not yet published.

252.   " Such men in every virtue trained,
        And destined for the Buddhaship,
        In all their weary rounds of birth,
        Though cycle-millions come and go,

253.   " Are never born inside of hell,
        Nor in the intermundane voids.
        They never share the Manes' thirst,[1]
        Their hunger or ferocity,[1]
        And though sometimes of low estate,
        Are never of the insect class.

254.   " When they appear among mankind,
        'T is not as blind from birth they come,
        Deafness they never have to bear,
        Nor dumbness have they to endure.

255.   " They 're never of the female sex,
        Nor as hermaphrodites appear,
        As eunuchs are they never classed,
        Those destined for the Buddhaship.

256.   " From all the five great crimes exempt,
        And pure in all their walks in life,
        They follow not vain heresy,
        For well they know how karma works.

257.   " Though in the heavens they may be born,
        Yet ne'er 'mongst those perception-reft ;
        Nor are they destined to rebirth
        ' Mongst dwellers in the Pure Abodes.[2]

258.   " These pleasure-abnegating men
        Live unattached in every birth,
        And ever toil to help the world,
        While all perfections they fulfil."

---

[1] I despair of giving in metre more than the general drift of these two lines. See Hardy, " Manual of Budhism," chap. ii. § 11.

[2] See page 289.

Now in accomplishing these Ten Perfections there was no limit to the number of existences in which he fulfilled the perfection of almsgiving; as when he was born as the Brahman Akitti, the Brahman Saṁkha, king Dhanañjaya, Mahā-Sudassana, Mahā-Govinda, king Nimi, prince Canda, Visayha the treasurer, king Sivi, and king Vessantara. But the acme was reached when as the Wise Hare [1] he said, —

> 259.   "There came a beggar, asked for food;
> Myself I gave that he might eat.
> In alms there's none can equal me;
> In alms have I perfection reached."

Thus, in this offering up of his own life, he acquired the perfection of almsgiving in its highest degree.

Likewise there was no limit to the number of existences in which he fulfilled the precepts; as when he was born as the elephant-king Sīlava, the snake-king Campeyya, the snake-king Bhūridatta, the elephant-king Chaddanta, and prince Alīnasattu, son of king Jayaddisa. But the acme was reached when, as related in the Saṁkhapāla Birth-Story, he said, —

> 260.   "They pierced me through with pointed stakes,
> They hacked me with their hunting-knives;
> Yet gainst these Bhojans raged I not,
> But kept the precepts perfectly."

Thus, in giving up his own life, he acquired perfection in the keeping of the precepts.

Likewise there was no limit to the number of existences in which he fulfilled the perfection of abnegation by aban-

---

[1] The story of the Future Buddha's existence as the Wise Hare is given further on under the caption, "The Hare-Mark in the Moon." It is the only one of the numerous Birth-Stories above-mentioned that is to be found in this book. The stanza quoted, however, is not taken from that account, but from another work called the Cariyā-Piṭaka, which is wholly in poetry. The Cariyā-Piṭaka consists of Birth-Stories, and, besides the Wise Hare, gives several others of those here mentioned. Some are also briefly alluded to in the ninth chapter of the Visuddhi-Magga; but of course the great treasure-house for Birth-Stories is the Jātaka itself.

doning his throne; as when he was born as prince Somanassa, prince Hatthipāla, and the pandit Ayoghara. But the acme was reached when, as related in the Lesser Sutasoma Birth-Story, he said, —

> 261. " A kingdom dropped into my hands;
> Like spittle vile I let it fall,
> Nor for it felt the smallest wish,
> And thus renunciation gained."

Thus, free from attachment, he renounced a kingdom and retired from the world, and by so doing acquired the perfection of abnegation in its highest degree.

Likewise there was no limit to the number of existences in which he fulfilled the perfection of knowledge; as when he was born as the pandit Vidhūra, the pandit Mahā-Govinda, the pandit Kuddāla, the pandit Araka, the wandering ascetic Bodhi, and the pandit Mahosadha. But the acme was reached when, as the pandit Senaka of the Sattubhatta Birth-Story, he said, —

> 262. " With wisdom sifted I the case,
> And freed the Brahman from his woe;
> In wisdom none can equal me:
> In wisdom I've perfection reached,"

and displayed to all present the serpent which lay concealed in the bag, and in so doing acquired the perfection of wisdom in its highest degree.

Likewise there was no limit to the number of existences in which he fulfilled the perfection of courage. But the acme was reached when, as related in the Greater Janaka Birth-Story, he said, —

> 263. " Far out of sight of land were we,
> The crew were all as dead of fright;
> Yet still unruffled was my mind:
> In courage I've perfection reached."

Thus it was in crossing the ocean he acquired the perfection of courage in its highest degree.

Likewise in the Khantivāda Birth-Story, where he said, —

264.   " Like one insensible I lay,
        While with his hatchet keen he hacked,
        Nor raged I gainst Benares' king:
        In patience I 've perfection reached,"

in enduring great suffering, while appearing to be uncon-
scious, he acquired the perfection of patience in its highest
degree.

Likewise in the Greater Sutasoma Birth-Story, where he
said, —

265.   " I kept the promise I had made,
        And gave my life in sacrifice,
        A hundred warriors set I free:
        In truth have I perfection reached,"

in keeping his word at the sacrifice of his life, he acquired
the perfection of truth in its highest degree.

Likewise in the Mūgapakkha Birth-Story, where he said, —

266.   " 'T is not that I my parents hate,
        'T is not that glory I detest,
        But since omniscience I held dear,
        Therefore I kept my firm resolve,"

in resolving on a course of conduct that cost him his life, he
acquired the perfection of resolution in its highest degree.

Likewise in the Ekarāja Birth-Story, where he said, —

267.   " No fear has any one of me,
        Nor have I fear of any one,
        In my good-will to all I trust,
        And love to dwell in lonely woods,"

in the exercise of feelings of good-will, and in taking no
thought for his life, he acquired the perfection of good-will
in its highest degree.

Likewise in the Lomahaṁsa Birth-Story, where he said,—

268.   " I laid me down among the dead,
        A pillow of their bones I made;
        While from the villages around,
        Some came to mock, and some to praise,"

while village children flocked about him, and some spat and others showered fragrant garlands upon him, he was indifferent alike to pleasure and pain, and acquired the perfection of indifference in its highest degree.

The above is an abridgment, but the full account is given in the Cariyā-Pitaka.

Having thus fulfilled all the perfections, he said, in his existence as Vessantara, —

> 269. "This earth, unconscious though she be,
>   And ignorant of joy or grief,
>   E'en she then felt alms' mighty power,
>   And shook and quaked full seven times."

And having thus caused the earth to quake by his mighty deeds of merit, at the end of that existence he died, and was reborn in the Tusita heaven.

Accordingly the period from the time when he fell at the feet of Dīpaṁkara to his birth in the city of the Tusita gods constitutes the Distant Epoch.

§ 4. THE BIRTH OF THE BUDDHA.

Translated from the Introduction to the Jātaka (i.47²¹).

Now while the Future Buddha was still dwelling in the city of the Tusita gods, the "Buddha-Uproar," as it is called, took place. For there are three uproars which take place in the world, — the Cyclic-Uproar, the Buddha-Uproar, and the Universal-Monarch-Uproar. They occur as follows: —

When it is known that after the lapse of a hundred thousand years the cycle is to be renewed, the gods called Loka-byūhas, inhabitants of a heaven of sensual pleasure, wander about through the world, with hair let down and flying in the wind, weeping and wiping away their tears with their hands, and with their clothes red and in great disorder. And thus they make announcement: —

"Sirs, after the lapse of a hundred thousand years, the cycle is to be renewed; this world will be destroyed; also the mighty ocean will dry up; and this broad earth, and Sineru, the monarch of the mountains, will be burnt up and destroyed, — up to the Brahma heavens will the destruction of the world extend. Therefore, sirs, cultivate friendliness; cultivate compassion, joy, and indifference; wait on your mothers; wait on your fathers; and honor your elders among your kinsfolk."

This is called the Cyclic-Uproar.

Again, when it is known that after a lapse of a thousand years an omniscient Buddha is to arise in the world, the guardian angels of the world wander about, proclaiming:

"Sirs, after the lapse of a thousand years a Buddha will arise in the world."

This is called the Buddha-Uproar.

And lastly, when they realize that after the lapse of a hundred years a Universal Monarch is to arise, the terrestrial deities wander about, proclaiming: —

"Sirs, after the lapse of a hundred years a Universal Monarch is to arise in the world."

This is called the Universal-Monarch-Uproar. And these three are mighty uproars.

When of these three Uproars they hear the sound of the Buddha-Uproar, the gods of all ten thousand worlds come together into one place, and having ascertained what particular being is to be The Buddha, they approach him, and beseech him to become one. But it is not till after omens have appeared that they beseech him.

At that time, therefore, having all come together in one world, with the Cātum-Mahārājas, and with the Sakka, the Suyāma, the Santusita, the Paranimmita-Vasavatti, and the Mahā-Brahma of each several world, they approached the Future Buddha in the Tusita heaven, and besought him, saying, —

"Sir, it was not to acquire the glory of a Sakka, or of a Māra, or of a Brahma, or of a Universal Monarch, that you fulfilled the Ten Perfections; but it was to gain omniscience

in order to save the world, that you fulfilled them.   Sir, the
time and fit season for your Buddhaship has now arrived."

But the Great Being, before assenting to their wish,
made what is called the five great observations.   He observed, namely, the time, the continent, the country, the
family, and the mother and her span of life.

In the first of these observations he asked himself whether
it was the right time or no.   Now it is not the right time
when the length of men's lives is more than a hundred
thousand years.   And why is it not the right time?   Because
mortals then forget about birth, old age, and death.   And if
The Buddhas, who always include in their teachings the Three
Characteristics, were to attempt at such a time to discourse
concerning transitoriness, misery, and the lack of substantive
reality, men would not think it worth while listening to them,
nor would they give them credence.   Thus there would be no
conversions made; and if there were no conversions, the dispensation would not conduce to salvation.   This, therefore,
is not the right time.

Also it is not the right time when men's lives are less
than a hundred years.   And why is it not the right time?
Because mortals are then exceedingly corrupt; and an exhortation given to the exceedingly corrupt makes no impression,
but, like a mark drawn with a stick on the surface of the
water, it immediately disappears.   This, therefore, also is not
the right time.

But when the length of men's lives is between a hundred
years and a hundred thousand years, then is it the right time.
Now at that time men's lives were a hundred years; accordingly the Great Being observed that it was the right time
for his birth.

Next he made the observation concerning the continent.
Looking over the four continents with their attendant isles,
he reflected: "In three of the continents the Buddhas are
never born; only in the continent of India are they born."
Thus he decided on the continent.

Next he made the observation concerning the place.
"The continent of India is large," thought he, "being ten

thousand leagues around. In which of its countries are The Buddhas born?" Thus he decided on the Middle Country.

The Middle Country is the country defined in the Vinaya as follows:—

"It lies in the middle, on this side of the town Kajaṅgala on the east, beyond which is Mahā-Sāla, and beyond that the border districts. It lies in the middle, on this side of the river Salalavatī on the southeast, beyond which are the border districts. It lies in the middle, on this side of the town Setakaṇṇika on the south, beyond which are the border districts. It lies in the middle, on this side of the Brahmanical town Thūṇa on the west, beyond which are the border districts. It lies in the middle, on this side of the hill Usīraddhaja on the north, beyond which are the border districts."

It is three hundred leagues in length, two hundred and fifty in breadth, and nine hundred in circumference. In this country are born The Buddhas, the Private Buddhas,[1] the Chief Disciples, the Eighty Great Disciples, the Universal Monarch, and other eminent ones, magnates of the warrior caste, of the Brahman caste, and the wealthy householders. "And in it is this city called Kapilavatthu," thought he, and concluded that there he ought to be born.

Then he made the observation concerning the family. "The Buddhas," thought he, "are never born into a family of the peasant caste, or of the servile caste; but into one of the warrior caste, or of the Brahman caste, whichever at the time is the higher in public estimation. The warrior caste is now the higher in public estimation. I will be born into a warrior family, and king Suddhodana shall be my father." Thus he decided on the family.

Then he made the observation concerning the mother. "The mother of a Buddha," thought he, "is never a wanton, nor a drunkard, but is one who has fulfilled the perfections through a hundred thousand cycles, and has kept the five precepts unbroken from the day of her birth. Now this queen Mahā-Māyā is such a one; and she shall be my mother."—

---

[1] See index, s. v.

" But what shall be her span of life ? " [1] continued he.   And
he perceived that it was to be ten months and seven days.

Having thus made the five great observations, he kindly
made the gods the required promise, saying, —

" Sirs, you are right.   The time has come for my Buddhaship."

Then, surrounded by the gods of the Tusita heaven, and
dismissing all the other gods, he entered the Nandana Grove
of the Tusita capital, — for in each of the heavens there is a
Nandana Grove.   And here the gods said, " Attain in your
next existence your high destiny," and kept reminding him
that he had already paved the way to it by his accumulated
merit.   Now it was while he was thus dwelling, surrounded
by these deities, and continually reminded of his accumulated
merit, that he died, and was conceived in the womb of queen
Mahā-Māyā.   And in order that this matter may be fully
understood, I will give the whole account in due order.

It is related that at that time the Midsummer Festival
had been proclaimed in the city of Kapilavatthu, and the
multitude were enjoying the feast.   And queen Mahā-Māyā,
abstaining from strong drink, and brilliant with garlands and
perfumes, took part in the festivities for the six days previous
to the day of full moon.   And when it came to be the day of
full moon, she rose early, bathed in perfumed water, and dis-
pensed four hundred thousand pieces of money in great lar-
gess.   And decked in full gala attire, she ate of the choicest
food ; after which she took the eight vows, and entered her
elegantly furnished chamber of state.   And lying down on
the royal couch, she fell asleep and dreamed the following
dream : —

The four guardian angels came and lifted her up, together
with her couch, and took her away to the Himalaya Mountains.   There, in the Manosilā table-land, which is sixty
leagues in extent, they laid her under a prodigious sal-tree,

---

[1] That is, " How long is she to live after conceiving me ? "   And the
answer is, " Ten lunar [that is, the nine calendar] months of my mother's
pregnancy, and seven days after my birth."

seven leagues in height, and took up their positions respectfully at one side.   Then came the wives of these guardian
angels, and conducted her to Anotatta Lake, and bathed her,
to remove every human stain.   And after clothing her with
divine garments, they anointed her with perfumes and decked
her with divine flowers.   Not far off was Silver Hill, and in
it a golden mansion.   There they spread a divine couch with
its head towards the east, and laid her down upon it.   Now
the Future Buddha had become a superb white elephant,
and was wandering about at no great distance, on Gold
Hill.   Descending thence, he ascended Silver Hill, and approaching from the north, he plucked a white lotus with his
silvery trunk, and trumpeting loudly, went into the golden
mansion.   And three times he walked round his mother's
couch, with his right side towards it, and striking her on her
right side, he seemed to enter her womb.   Thus the conception took place in the Midsummer Festival.

On the next day the queen awoke, and told the dream to
the king.   And the king caused sixty-four eminent Brahmans
to be summoned, and spread costly seats for them on ground
festively prepared with green leaves, Dalbergia flowers, and
so forth.   The Brahmans being seated, he filled gold and
silver dishes with the best of milk-porridge compounded with
ghee, honey, and treacle; and covering these dishes with others,
made likewise of gold and silver, he gave the Brahmans to
eat.   And not only with food, but with other gifts, such as
new garments, tawny cows, and so forth, he satisfied them
completely.   And when their every desire had been satisfied,
he told them the dream and asked them what would come
of it.

" Be not anxious, great king ! " said the Brahmans; " a
child has planted itself in the womb of your queen, and it is
a male child and not a female.   You will have a son.   And
he, if he continue to live the household life, will become a
Universal Monarch; but if he leave the household life and
retire from the world, he will become a Buddha, and roll
back the clouds of sin and folly of this world."

Now the instant the Future Buddha was conceived in the

womb of his mother, all the ten thousand worlds suddenly quaked, quivered, and shook. And the Thirty-two Prognostics appeared, as follows: an immeasurable light spread through ten thousand worlds; the blind recovered their sight, as if from desire to see this his glory; the deaf received their hearing; the dumb talked; the hunchbacked became straight of body; the lame recovered the power to walk; all those in bonds were freed from their bonds and chains; the fires went out in all the hells; the hunger and thirst of the Manes was stilled; wild animals lost their timidity; diseases ceased among men; all mortals became mild-spoken; horses neighed and elephants trumpeted in a manner sweet to the ear; all musical instruments gave forth their notes without being played upon; bracelets and other ornaments jingled; in all quarters of the heavens the weather became fair; a mild, cool breeze began to blow, very refreshing to men; rain fell out of season; water burst forth from the earth and flowed in streams; the birds ceased flying through the air; the rivers checked their flowing; in the mighty ocean the water became sweet; the ground became everywhere covered with lotuses of the five different colors; all flowers bloomed, both those on land and those that grow in the water; trunk-lotuses bloomed on the trunks of trees, branch-lotuses on the branches, and vine-lotuses on the vines; on the ground, stalk-lotuses, as they are called, burst through the overlying rocks and came up by sevens; in the sky were produced others, called hanging-lotuses; a shower of flowers fell all about; celestial music was heard to play in the sky; and the whole ten thousand worlds became one mass of garlands of the utmost possible magnificence, with waving chowries, and saturated with the incense-like fragrance of flowers, and resembled a bouquet of flowers sent whirling through the air, or a closely woven wreath, or a superbly decorated altar of flowers.

From the time the Future Buddha was thus conceived, four angels with swords in their hands kept guard, to ward off all harm from both the Future Buddha and the Future Buddha's mother. No lustful thought sprang up in the mind of the Future Buddha's mother; having reached the pinnacle of good fortune and of glory, she felt comfortable and well, and experienced no exhaustion of body. And within her womb she could distinguish the Future Buddha, like a white thread passed through a transparent jewel. And whereas a womb that has been occupied by a Future Buddha is like the shrine of a temple, and can never be occupied or used again, therefore it was that the mother of the Future Buddha died when he was seven days old, and was reborn in the Tusita heaven.

Now other women sometimes fall short of and sometimes run over the term of ten lunar months, and then bring forth either sitting or lying down; but not so the mother of a Future Buddha. She carries the Future Buddha in her womb for just ten months, and then brings forth while standing up. This is a characteristic of the mother of a Future Buddha. So also queen Mahā-Māyā carried the Future Buddha in her womb, as it were oil in a vessel, for ten months; and being then far gone with child, she grew desirous of going home to her relatives, and said to king Suddhodana, —

"Sire, I should like to visit my kinsfolk in their city Devadaha."

"So be it," said the king; and from Kapilavatthu to the city of Devadaha he had the road made even, and garnished it with plantain-trees set in pots, and with banners, and streamers; and, seating the queen in a golden palanquin borne by a thousand of his courtiers, he sent her away in great pomp.

Now between the two cities, and belonging to the inhabitants of both, there was a pleasure-grove of sal-trees, called Lumbini Grove. And at this particular time this grove was one mass of flowers from the ground to the topmost branches, while amongst the branches and flowers hummed swarms of bees of the five different colors, and flocks of various kinds of birds flew about warbling sweetly. Throughout the whole of Lumbini Grove the scene resembled the Cittalatā Grove in Indra's paradise, or the magnificently decorated banqueting pavilion of some potent king.

When the queen beheld it she became desirous of disport-

ing herself therein, and the courtiers therefore took her into
it. And going to the foot of the monarch sal-tree of the
grove, she wished to take hold of one of its branches. And
the sal-tree branch, like the tip of a well-steamed reed, bent
itself down within reach of the queen's hand. Then she
reached out her hand, and seized hold of the branch, and
immediately her pains came upon her. Thereupon the people hung a curtain about her, and retired. So her delivery
took place while she was standing up, and keeping fast hold
of the sal-tree branch.

At that very moment came four pure-minded Mahā-
Brahma angels bearing a golden net; and, receiving the
Future Buddha on this golden net, they placed him before
his mother and said, —

"Rejoice, O queen! A mighty son has been born to
you."

Now other mortals on issuing from the maternal womb
are smeared with disagreeable, impure matter; but not so
the Future Buddha. He issued from his mother's womb like
a preacher descending from his preaching-seat, or a man coming down a stair, stretching out both hands and both feet,
unsmeared by any impurity from his mother's womb, and
flashing pure and spotless, like a jewel thrown upon a vesture
of Benares cloth. Notwithstanding this, for the sake of hon-
oring the Future Buddha and his mother, there came two
streams of water from the sky, and refreshed the Future
Buddha and his mother.

Then the Brahma angels, after receiving him on their
golden net, delivered him to the four guardian angels, who
received him from their hands on a rug which was made of
the skins of black antelopes, and was soft to the touch, being
such as is used on state occasions; and the guardian angels
delivered him to men who received him on a coil of fine
cloth; and the men let him out of their hands on the ground,
where he stood and faced the east. There, before him, lay
many thousands of worlds, like a great open court; and in
them, gods and men, making offerings to him of perfumes,
garlands, and so on, were saying, —

" Great Being ! There is none your equal, much less your superior."

When he had in this manner surveyed the four cardinal points, and the four intermediate ones, and the zenith, and the nadir, in short, all the ten directions in order, and had nowhere discovered his equal, he exclaimed, " This is the best direction," and strode forward seven paces, followed by Mahā-Brahma holding over him the white umbrella, Suyāma bearing the fan, and other divinities having the other symbols of royalty in their hands. Then, at the seventh stride, he halted, and with a noble voice, he shouted the shout of victory, beginning, —

" The chief am I in all the world."

Now in three of his existences did the Future Buddha utter words immediately on issuing from his mother's womb: namely, in his existence as Mahosadha ; in his existence as Vessantara ; and in this existence.

As respects his existence as Mahosadha, it is related that just as he was issuing from his mother's womb, Sakka, the king of the gods, came and placed in his hand some choice sandal-wood, and departed. And he closed his fist upon it, and issued forth.

" My child," said his mother, " what is it you bring with you in your hand ? "

" Medicine, mother," said he.

Accordingly, as he was born with medicine in his hand, they gave him the name of Osadha-Dāraka [Medicine-Child]. Then they took the medicine, and placed it in an earthenware jar; and it was a sovereign remedy to heal all the blind, the deaf, and other afflicted persons who came to it. So the saying sprang up, " This is a great medicine, this is a great medicine ! " And thus he received the name of Mahosadha [Great Medicine-Man].

Again, in the Vessantara existence, as he was issuing from his mother's womb, he stretched out his right hand, and said, —

" Pray, mother, is there anything in the house ? I want to give alms."

Then, after he had completely issued forth, his mother said, —

"It's a wealthy family, my son, into which you are born;" and putting his hand in her own, she had them place in his a purse containing a thousand pieces of money.

Lastly, in this birth he shouted the shout of victory above-mentioned.

Thus in three of his existences did the Future Buddha utter words immediately on issuing from his mother's womb. And just as at the moment of his conception, so also at the moment of his birth appeared the Thirty-two Prognostics.

Now at the very time that our Future Buddha was born in Lumbini Grove there also came into existence the mother of Rāhula, and Channa the courtier, Kāḷudāyi the courtier, Kanthaka the king of horses, the Great Bo-tree, and the four urns full of treasure. Of these last, one was a quarter of a league in extent, another a half-league, the third three quarters of a league, and the fourth a league. These seven[1] are called the Connate Ones.

Then the inhabitants of both cities took the Future Buddha, and carried him to Kapilavatthu.

---

§ 5. THE YOUNG GOTAMID PRINCE.

Translated from the Introduction to the Jātaka (i.54¹¹).

On this same day the happy and delighted hosts of the Heaven of the Thirty-three held a celebration, waving their cloaks and giving other signs of joy, because to king Suddhodana in Kapilavatthu had been born a son who should sit at the foot of the Bo-tree, and become a Buddha.

Now it came to pass at that time that an ascetic named Kāladevala, who was an intimate friend of king Suddhodana, and practised in the eight stages of meditation, went, after

---

[1] In making up this number the Future Buddha is to be counted as number 1, and the four urns of treasure together as number 7.

his daily meal, to the Heaven of the Thirty-three to take
his noon-day rest. And as he was sitting there resting, he
noticed these gods, and said, —

"Why do you frolic so joyously? Let me too know the
reason."

"Sir," replied the gods, "it is because a son has been born
to king Suddhodana, who shall sit at the foot of the Bo-tree,
and become a Buddha, and cause the Wheel of the Doctrine
to roll; in him we shall be permitted to behold the infinite and masterful ease of a Buddha, and shall hear the
Doctrine."

On hearing this, the ascetic descended from the world of
the gods in haste, and entered the dwelling of the king; and
having seated himself on the seat assigned to him, he said, —

"Great king, I hear that a son has been born to you. I
would see him."

Then the king had the prince magnificently dressed, and
brought in, and carried up to do reverence to the ascetic.
But the feet of the Future Buddha turned and planted themselves in the matted locks of the ascetic. For in that birth
there was no one worthy of the Future Buddha's reverence;
and if these ignorant people had succeeded in causing the
Future Buddha to bow, the head of the ascetic would have
split in seven pieces.

"It is not meet that I compass my own death," thought
the ascetic, and rose from his seat, and with joined hands did
reverence to the Future Buddha. And when the king had
seen this wonder, he also did reverence to his son.

Now the ascetic could look backward into the past for
forty world-cycles, and forward into the future for forty
world-cycles, — in all, eighty world-cycles. And, noting on
the person of the Future Buddha all the lucky marks and
characteristics, he began to reflect and consider whether or
not they prophesied his Buddhaship. And perceiving that
undoubtedly he would become a Buddha, he thought to himself, "What a marvellous personage he is!" and smiled.

Next he considered in his mind whether he would live to
see him attain the Buddhaship; and he perceived that he was

not to have that opportunity. For he would die before that time, and be reborn in the formless mode of existence, where it would be out of the power of even a hundred or a thousand Buddhas to come and enlighten him. And he thought, "It will not be mine to behold this so marvellous a personage when he has become a Buddha. My loss, alas, will be great," and wept.

The people noticed his behavior, and said to him, —

"Our good father smiled but a moment ago, and now has begun to weep. Reverend sir, is any misfortune to happen to our young master?"

"No misfortune is to happen to him. He will become a Buddha without any manner of doubt."

"Then why did you weep?"

"I wept at the thought of my own great loss; for, alas, I am not to have an opportunity of seeing this marvellous person after he has become a Buddha."

Next he considered in his mind whether or not any of his relatives were to have the opportunity; and he saw that his sister's child Nālaka was to have it. And he went to his sister's house, and inquired, —

"Where is your son Nālaka?"

"Good father, he is in the house."

"Call him hither."

"My child," said he to the lad when he had come, "a son has been born in the family of Suddhodana the king, who is the coming Buddha. Thirty-five years from now he will become a Buddha, and you will have an opportunity of seeing him. Retire from the world this very day."

And the child did so, although he belonged to a family possessing eight hundred and seventy millions of treasure; for he thought, "My uncle would not lay such a command upon me for any trifling reason." Sending to the bazaar, he procured some yellow garments, and an earthenware bowl, and cut off his hair and his beard, and put on the yellow garments. And stretching out his joined hands in the direction of the Future Buddha, he said, "I retire from the world to follow earth's greatest being." Then he prostrated him-

self, so that he touched the ground with the fivefold contact.
Having thus done reverence, he placed the bowl in his scrip,
slung the latter over his shoulder, and going to the Himalaya
Mountains, he there performed the duties of a monk.

And after the Great Being had achieved the absolute and
supreme wisdom, Nālaka came to him, and had him prescribe
the Nālaka course of conduct.[1]   Then, returning to the
Himalaya Mountains, he attained to saintship, and adopted
that excellent course.   And keeping alive for seven months
more, and being at the time near a certain Gold Hill, he
passed out of existence by that final extinction in which
none of the elements of being remain.

Now on the fifth day they bathed the Future Buddha's
head, saying, " We will perform the rite of choosing a name
for him."   And they prepared the royal palace by anointing
it with four kinds of perfumes, and by scattering Dalbergia
blossoms and other flowers, five sorts in all.   And making
some porridge of whole rice-grains boiled in milk, they
invited one hundred and eight Brahmans, men who had
mastered the three Vedas.   And having seated these Brahmans in the royal palace, and fed them with delicate food,
and showed them every attention, they asked them to observe
the marks and characteristics of the Future Buddha's person,
and to prophesy his fortune.

Among the hundred and eight, —

270.   " Rāma, Dhaja, Lakkhaṇa, also Manti,
        Kondañña, Bhoja, Suyāma, Sudatta,
        These Brahmans eight were there with senses six subdued;
        They from the magic books disclosed his fortune."

These eight Brahmans were the fortune-tellers, being the
same [2] who had interpreted the dream of the night of the

---

[1] The Nālaka course of conduct is given in the Nālaka Sutta of the
Sutta-Nipāta, and consists of a number of precepts for leading the holy
life.

[2] See p. 43.   They presumably were the spokesmen for the sixty-
four, as here for the one hundred and eight.

conception. Seven of these raised two fingers each, and
gave a double interpretation, saying, "If a man possessing
such marks and characteristics continue in the household
life, he becomes a Universal Monarch; if he retire from the
world, he becomes a Buddha." And then they set forth all
the glory of a Universal Monarch.

But the youngest of them all, a youth whose clan-name
was Koṇḍañña, after examining the splendid set of marks
and characteristics on the person of the Future Buddha,
raised only one finger, and gave but a single interpretation,
saying, "There is here naught to make him stay in the household life. He will most undoubtedly become a Buddha, and
remove the veil of ignorance and folly from the world." For
this Koṇḍañña was one who had made an earnest wish under
former Buddhas, and was now in his last existence. Therefore it was that he outstripped the other seven in knowledge,
and saw but one future; inasmuch as a person possessed of
such marks and characteristics would never stay in the household life, but would undoubtedly become a Buddha. So he
raised only one finger, and gave that interpretation.

Then the seven Brahmans went home and said to their
sons, "Children, we are old, but whether we ourselves are
alive or not when the son of Suddhodana the king shall
attain omniscience, you, at least, should then retire from the
world under his dispensation."

And after these seven persons had lived out their term
of life they passed away according to their deeds; but
Koṇḍañña, being younger, was still alive and hale. And
when the Great Being, after making the great retirement in
pursuit of wisdom, had arrived at Uruvelā in his progress
from place to place, he thought: "How pleasant indeed
is this spot! How suitable for the struggles of a young
man desirous of struggling!" and took up his abode there.
Koṇḍañña heard the news that the Great Being had retired
from the world, and drawing near to the sons of those seven
Brahmans, he spoke to them as follows: —

"I hear that prince Siddhattha has retired from the world.
Now he will unquestionably become a Buddha, and if your

fathers were alive they would follow after him this very day.
If you also would like to retire from the world, come with
me. I mean to follow after that man in his retirement from
the world."

But they could not all agree; and three of them did not
retire from the world. But the remaining four did so, and
made the Brahman Koṇḍañña their chief. And these five
persons became known as the "Band of Five Elders."

Then said the king, "What shall my son see to make him
retire from the world?"

" The four signs."

" What four?"

" A decrepit old man, a diseased man, a dead man, and a
monk."

" From this time forth," said the king, "let no such persons be allowed to come near my son. It will never do for
my son to become a Buddha. What I would wish to see is
my son exercising sovereign rule and authority over the four
great continents and the two thousand attendant isles, and
walking through the heavens surrounded by a retinue thirty-
six leagues in circumference." And when he had so spoken
he placed guards for a distance of a quarter of a league in
each of the four directions, in order that none of these four
kinds of men might come within sight of his son.

On this same day, also, eighty thousand clansmen assembled together in the festival-hall, and each dedicated a son,
saying, —

" Whether the young prince become a Buddha or a king,
we will each one give a son : so that if he become a Buddha,
he shall be followed and surrounded by monks of the warrior
caste ; and if he become a king, by nobles of the warrior
caste."

And the king procured nurses for the Future Buddha, —
women of fine figure, and free from all blemish. And so the
Future Buddha began to grow, surrounded by an immense
retinue, and in great splendor.

Now on a certain day the king celebrated the Sowing

Festival, as it was called.   On that day they used to decorate
the whole city, so that it looked like a palace of the gods;
and all the slaves and other servants would put on new
tunics; and, perfumed and garlanded, they would assemble
together at the king's palace, where a thousand plows were
yoked for the royal plowing.

On this occasion there were one hundred and eight
plows, all save one ornamented with silver, as were also the
reins for the oxen and the cross-bars of the plows.   But the
plow that was held by the king was ornamented with red
gold, as also the horns, the reins, and the goads for the
oxen.   And the king issued forth with a large retinue,
taking his son along with him.   And in the field where
the plowing was to be done was a solitary rose-apple tree of
thick foliage and dense shade.   Underneath this tree the
king had a couch placed for the young prince, and spread
over his head a canopy that was studded with gold stars; and
he surrounded him with a screen, and appointed those that
should watch by him; and then, decked with all his ornaments and surrounded by his courtiers, he proceeded to the
place where they were to plow.   On arriving there, the king
took the gold plow, and the courtiers took the silver plows,—
one hundred and eight save one, and the farmers the other
plows; and then all plowed forward and back.   The king
went from the hither side to the farther side, and from the
farther side back again; and the pomp and magnificence of
the festival was at its climax.

Now the nurses who were sitting about the Future
Buddha came out from behind the screen to behold the
royal magnificence.   And the Future Buddha, looking hither
and thither and seeing no one, arose in haste and sat him
down cross-legged, and mastering his inspirations and his
expirations, entered on the first trance.   The nurses delayed a little, being detained by the abundance of good
things to eat.   And the shadows of the other trees passed
over to the east, but the shadow of the rose-apple tree
remained steadily circular.   Suddenly the nurses remembered that they had left their young master alone; and

raising the screen, they entered and saw the Future Buddha sitting cross-legged on the couch, and also noticed the miracle of the shadow. Then they went and announced to the king, —

"Sire, thus and so is the prince sitting; and the shadows of the other trees have passed over to the east, but the shadow of the rose-apple tree remains steadily circular."

And the king came in haste, and seeing the miracle, he did obeisance to his son, saying, "This, dear child, is my second obeisance."

And thus, in due course, the Future Buddha attained to the age of sixteen years. And the king built three palaces for the Future Buddha, suited to the three seasons, — one of nine stories, another of seven stories, and another of five stories. And he provided him with forty thousand dancing girls. And the Future Buddha, with his gayly dressed dancers, was like a god surrounded by hosts of houris; and attended by musical instruments that sounded of themselves, and in the enjoyment of great magnificence, he lived, as the seasons changed, in each of these three palaces. And the mother of Rāhula was his principal queen.

Now while he was thus enjoying great splendor, one day there arose the following discussion among his relatives : —

"Siddhattha is wholly given over to pleasure, and is not training himself in any manly art. What could he do if war were to occur?"

The king sent for the Future Buddha, and said, —

"My child, your relatives are saying that you are not training yourself, but are wholly given over to pleasure. Now what do you think we had best do?"

"Sire, I do not need to train myself. Let the crier go about the city beating the drum, to announce that I will show my proficiency. On the seventh day from now I will show my proficiency to my relatives."

The king did so. And the Future Buddha assembled together bowmen that could shoot like lightning and at a hair's-breadth ; and in the midst of the populace, and before his kinsfolk, he exhibited a twelvefold skill, such as none of the other bowmen could equal. All of which is to be understood after the manner related in the Sarabhañga Birth-Story. So the assembly of his kinsfolk doubted him no longer.

---

§ 6. THE GREAT RETIREMENT.

Translated from the Introduction to the Jātaka (i.58⁸¹).

Now on a certain day the Future Buddha wished to go to the park, and told his charioteer to make ready the chariot. Accordingly the man brought out a sumptuous and elegant chariot, and adorning it richly, he harnessed to it four state-horses of the Sindhava breed, as white as the petals of the white lotus, and announced to the Future Buddha that everything was ready. And the Future Buddha mounted the chariot, which was like to a palace of the gods, and proceeded towards the park.

"The time for the enlightenment of prince Siddhattha draweth nigh," thought the gods; "we must show him a sign:" and they changed one of their number into a decrepit old man, broken-toothed, gray-haired, crooked and bent of body, leaning on a staff, and trembling, and showed him to the Future Buddha, but so that only he and the charioteer saw him.

Then said the Future Buddha to the charioteer, in the manner related in the Mahāpadāna, —

"Friend, pray, who is this man? Even his hair is not like that of other men." And when he heard the answer, he said, "Shame on birth, since to every one that is born old age must come." And agitated in heart, he thereupon returned and ascended his palace.

"Why has my son returned so quickly?" asked the king.

"Sire, he has seen an old man," was the reply; "and

because he has seen an old man, he is about to retire from
the world."

" Do you want to kill me, that you say such things?
Quickly get ready some plays to be performed before my
son. If we can but get him to enjoying pleasure, he will
cease to think of retiring from the world." Then the king
extended the guard to half a league in each direction.

Again, on a certain day, as the Future Buddha was going
to the park, he saw a diseased man whom the gods had fashioned; and having again made inquiry, he returned, agitated
in heart, and ascended his palace.

And the king made the same inquiry and gave the same
orders as before; and again extending the guard, placed them
for three quarters of a league around.

And again on a certain day, as the Future Buddha was
going to the park, he saw a dead man whom the gods had
fashioned; and having again made inquiry, he returned, agitated in heart, and ascended his palace.

And the king made the same inquiry and gave the same
orders as before; and again extending the guard, placed
them for a league around.

And again on a certain day, as the Future Buddha was
going to the park, he saw a monk, carefully and decently
clad, whom the gods had fashioned; and he asked his charioteer, " Pray, who is this man? "

Now although there was no Buddha in the world, and
the charioteer had no knowledge of either monks or their
good qualities, yet by the power of the gods he was inspired
to say, " Sire, this is one who has retired from the world;"
and he thereupon proceeded to sound the praises of retirement from the world. The thought of retiring from the
world was a pleasing one to the Future Buddha, and this
day he went on until he came to the park. The repeaters of
the Dīgha,[1] however, say that he went to the park after
having seen all the Four Signs on one and the same day.

When he had disported himself there throughout the day,

---

[1] Dīgha-Nikāya : see General Introduction.

and had bathed in the royal pleasure-tank, he went at sunset and sat down on the royal resting-stone with the intention of adorning himself. Then gathered around him his attendants with diverse-colored cloths, many kinds and styles of ornaments, and with garlands, perfumes, and ointments. At that instant the throne on which Sakka was sitting grew hot. And Sakka, considering who it could be that was desirous of dislodging him, perceived that it was the time of the adornment of a Future Buddha. And addressing Vissakamma, he said, —

"My good Vissakamma, to-night, in the middle watch, prince Siddhattha will go forth on the Great Retirement, and this is his last adorning of himself. Go to the park, and adorn that eminent man with celestial ornaments."

"Very well," said Vissakamma, in assent; and came on the instant, by his superhuman power, into the presence of the Future Buddha. And assuming the guise of a barber, he took from the real barber the turban-cloth, and began to wind it round the Future Buddha's head; but as soon as the Future Buddha felt the touch of his hand, he knew that it was no man, but a god.

Now once round his head took up a thousand cloths, and the fold was like to a circlet of precious stones; the second time round took another thousand cloths, and so on, until ten times round had taken up ten thousand cloths. Now let no one think, "How was it possible to use so many cloths on one small head?" for the very largest of them all had only the size of a sāma-creeper blossom, and the others that of kutumbaka flowers. Thus the Future Buddha's head resembled a kuyyaka blossom twisted about with lotus filaments.

And having adorned himself with great richness, — while adepts in different kinds of tabors and tom-toms were showing their skill, and Brahmans with cries of victory and joy, and bards and poets with propitious words and shouts of praise saluted him, — he mounted his superbly decorated chariot.

At this juncture, Suddhodana the king, having heard that

the mother of Rāhula had brought forth a son, sent a messenger, saying, " Announce the glad news to my son." ,

On hearing the message, the Future Buddha said, " An
impediment [rāhula] has been born; a fetter has been
born."

" What did my son say?" questioned the king; and
when he had heard the answer, he said, " My grandson's
name shall be prince Rāhula from this very day."

But the Future Buddha in his splendid chariot entered
the city with a pomp and magnificence of glory that enrap-
tured all minds.   At the same moment Kisā Gotamī, a vir-
gin of the warrior caste, ascended to the roof of her palace,
and beheld the beauty and majesty of the Future Buddha, as
he circumambulated the city; and in her pleasure and satisfaction at the sight, she burst forth into this song of joy:—

> 271.   " Full happy now that mother is,
>   Full happy now that father is,
>   Full happy now that woman is,
>   Who owns this lord so glorious!"

On hearing this, the Future Buddha thought, " In beholding a handsome figure the heart of a mother attains
Nirvana, the heart of a father attains Nirvana, the heart of
a wife attains Nirvana.   This is what she says.   But wherein
does Nirvana consist?"   And to him, whose mind was already averse to passion, the answer came: " When the fire
of lust is extinct, that is Nirvana; when the fires of hatred
and infatuation are extinct, that is Nirvana; when pride,
false belief, and all other passions and torments are extinct,
that is Nirvana.   She has taught me a good lesson.   Certainly,
Nirvana is what I am looking for.   It behooves me this very
day to quit the household life, and to retire from the world in
quest of Nirvana.[1]   I will send this lady a teacher's fee."   And

---

[1] The Future Buddha puns upon the word " happy " in Kisā Gotamī's
verses.   The word in Pāli is *nibbuta*, and is in form a past passive participle of a verb which perhaps does not occur in Pāli in any finite form, but
which appears in Sanskrit as *nirvṛ*.   Now there is a Pāli verb of which
the third person singular present indicative is *nibbāyati*, and from this

loosening from his neck a pearl necklace worth a hundred
thousand pieces of money, he sent it to Kisā Gotamī. And
great was her satisfaction at this, for she thought, "Prince
Siddhattha has fallen in love with me, and has sent me a
present."

And the Future Buddha entered his palace in great splendor, and lay on his couch of state. And straightway richly
dressed women, skilled in all manner of dance and song, and
beautiful as celestial nymphs, gathered about him with all
kinds of musical instruments, and with dance, song, and
music they endeavored to please him. But the Future
Buddha's aversion to passion did not allow him to take pleasure in the spectacle, and he fell into a brief slumber. And
the women, exclaiming, "He for whose sake we should perform has fallen asleep. Of what use is it to weary ourselves
any longer?" threw their various instruments on the ground,
and lay down. And the lamps fed with sweet-smelling oil
continued to burn. And the Future Buddha awoke, and
seating himself cross-legged on his couch, perceived these
women lying asleep, with their musical instruments scattered
about them on the floor, — some with their bodies wet with
trickling phlegm and spittle; some grinding their teeth, and
muttering and talking in their sleep; some with their mouths
open; and some with their dress fallen apart so as plainly to

---

verb is formed the verbal noun *nibbāna* (Sanskrit, *Nirvāṇa*). *Nibbuta*
is constantly made to do duty as past passive participle to this verb, so
that what would be the true form (*nibbāta*) is never found. The Future
Buddha therefore puns when he pretends that Kisā Gotamī was using
nibbuta as the participle of *nibbāyati*, and was urging him to Nirvana.

The verb *nibbāyati* means "to be extinguished," as the flame of a
candle; and, when used as a metaphysical term, refers to the fires of
lust, desire, etc. And as when fire is extinguished coolness results (a
consummation devoutly to be wished in a hot climate like India), the
verb acquires the further meaning of "be assuaged," "become happy."
And in like manner the verbal noun Nirvana (in Pāli *nibbāna*), meaning
both literally and metaphorically "becoming extinguished," comes to
stand for the *summum bonum.*

I add a retranslation of the passage, to show the punning meanings given by the Future Buddha to the words, *nibbuta, nibbāyati,* and
Nirvana: —

disclose their loathsome nakedness. This great alteration in their appearance still further increased his aversion for sensual pleasures. To him that magnificent apartment, as splendid as the palace of Sakka, began to seem like a cemetery filled with dead bodies impaled and left to rot; and the three modes of existence appeared like houses all ablaze. And breathing forth the solemn utterance, "How oppressive and stifling is it all!" his mind turned ardently to retiring from the world. "It behooves me to go forth on the Great Retirement this very day," said he; and he arose from his couch, and coming near the door, called out, —

"Who's there?"

"Master, it is I, Channa," replied the courtier who had been sleeping with his head on the threshold.[1]

"I wish to go forth on the Great Retirement to-day. Saddle a horse for me."

"Yes, sire." And taking saddle and bridle with him, the courtier started for the stable. There, by the light of lamps fed with sweet-smelling oils, he perceived the mighty steed Kanthaka in his pleasant quarters, under a canopy of cloth beautified with a pattern of jasmine flowers. "This is the

> "Nirvana hath that mother gained,
> Nirvana hath that father gained,
> Nirvana hath that woman gained,
> Who owns this lord so glorious!"

On hearing this, the Future Buddha thought, "In beholding a handsome form the heart of a mother is made happy (*nibbāyati*), the heart of a father is made happy, the heart of a wife is made happy. This is what she says. But wherein does happiness (*nibbuta*) consist?" And to him whose mind was already averse to passion, the answer came: "When the fire of lust is assuaged (*nibbuta*), that is happiness (*nibbuta*); when the fires of hatred and infatuation are assuaged, that is happiness; when pride, false belief, and all other passions and torments are assuaged, that is happiness. She has taught me a good lesson. Certainly, happiness (Nirvana) is what I am looking for. It behooves me this very day to quit the household life and to retire from the world in quest of happiness. I will send this lady a teacher's fee."

[1] In India it is customary to hang doors at the height of about two feet from the ground for the sake of coolness and ventilation. The threshold is thus exposed even when the door is shut.

one for me to saddle to-day," thought he; and he saddled Kanthaka.

" He is drawing the girth very tight," thought Kanthaka, whilst he was being saddled; " it is not at all as on other days, when I am saddled for rides in the park and the like. It must be that to-day my master wishes to issue forth on the Great Retirement." And in his delight he neighed a loud neigh. And that neigh would have spread through the whole town, had not the gods stopped the sound, and suffered no one to hear it.

Now the Future Buddha, after he had sent Channa on his errand, thought to himself, " I will take just one look at my son; " and, rising from the couch on which he was sitting, he went to the suite of apartments occupied by the mother of Rāhula, and opened the door of her chamber. Within the chamber was burning a lamp fed with sweet-smelling oil, and the mother of Rāhula lay sleeping on a couch strewn deep with jasmine and other flowers, her hand resting on the head of her son. When the Future Buddha reached the threshold, he paused, and gazed at the two from where he stood.

" If I were to raise my wife's hand from off the child's head, and take him up, she would awake, and thus prevent my departure. I will first become a Buddha, and then come back and see my son." So saying, he descended from the palace.

Now that which is said in the Jātaka Commentary, " At that time Rāhula was seven days old," is not found in the other commentaries. Therefore the account above given is to be accepted.

When the Future Buddha had thus descended from the palace, he came near to his horse, and said, —

" My dear Kanthaka, save me now this one night; and then, when thanks to you I have become a Buddha, I will save the world of gods and men." And thereupon he vaulted upon Kanthaka's back.

Now Kanthaka was eighteen cubits long from his neck to his tail, and of corresponding height; he was strong and swift, and white all over like a polished conch-shell. If he neighed or stamped, the sound was so loud as to spread

through the whole city; therefore the gods exerted their
power, and muffled the sound of his neighing, so that no one
heard it; and at every step he took they placed the palms of
their hands under his feet.

The Future Buddha rode on the mighty back of the
mighty steed, made Channa hold on by the tail, and so
arrived at midnight at the great gate of the city.

Now the king, in order that the Future Buddha should
not at any time go out of the city without his knowledge,
had caused each of the two leaves of the gate to be made so
heavy as to need a thousand men to move it. But the Future
Buddha had a vigor and a strength that was equal, when
reckoned in elephant-power, to the strength of ten thousand
million elephants, and, reckoned in man-power, to the strength
of a hundred thousand million men.

" If," thought he, " the gate does not open, I will straightway grip tight hold of Kanthaka with my thighs, and, seated
as I am on Kanthaka's back, and with Channa holding on
by the tail, I will leap up and carry them both with me over
the wall, although its height be eighteen cubits."

" If," thought Channa, " the gate is not opened, I will
place my master on my shoulder, and tucking Kanthaka
under my arm by passing my right hand round him and
under his belly, I will leap up and carry them both with me
over the wall."

" If," thought Kanthaka, " the gate is not opened, with
my master seated as he is on my back, and with Channa
holding on by my tail, I will leap up and carry them both
with me over the wall."

Now if the gate had not opened, verily one or another of
these three persons would have accomplished that whereof he
thought; but the divinity that inhabited the gate opened it
for them.

At this moment came Māra,[1] with the intention of per-

---

[1] The Buddhists recognize no real devil. Māra, the ruler of the
sixth and highest heaven of sensual pleasure, approaches the nearest
to our Satan. He stands for the pleasures of sense, and hence is The
Buddha's natural enemy.

suading the Future Buddha to turn back; and standing in
the air, he said, —

"Sir, go not forth! For on the seventh day from now
the wheel of empire will appear to you, and you shall rule
over the four great continents and their two thousand attendant isles. Sir, turn back!"

"Who are you?"

"I am Vasavatti."

"Māra, I knew that the wheel of empire was on the
point of appearing to me; but I do not wish for sovereignty.
I am about to cause the ten thousand worlds to thunder with
my becoming a Buddha."

"I shall catch you," thought Māra, "the very first time
you have a lustful, malicious, or unkind thought." And,
like an ever-present shadow, he followed after, ever on the
watch for some slip.

Thus the Future Buddha, casting away with indifference
a universal sovereignty already in his grasp, — spewing it out
as if it were but phlegm, — departed from the city in great
splendor on the full-moon day of the month Āsālhī,[1] when
the moon was in Libra. And when he had gone out from
the city, he became desirous of looking back at it; but no
sooner had the thought arisen in his mind, than the broad
earth, seeming to fear lest the Great Being might neglect to
perform the act of looking back, split and turned round like
a potter's wheel.[2] When the Future Buddha had stood a
while facing the city and gazing upon it, and had indicated
in that place the spot for the "Shrine of the Turning Back of
Kanthaka," he turned Kanthaka in the direction in which he
meant to go, and proceeded on his way in great honor and
exceeding glory.

For they say the deities bore sixty thousand torches in
front of him, and sixty thousand behind him, and sixty

---

[1] About the first of July.

[2] I think the conception here is that a round portion of the earth,
on which the Future Buddha stood, turned around like a modern rail-
road turn-table, thus detaching itself from the rest and turning the
Future Buddha with it.

thousand on the right hand, and sixty thousand on the left
hand.   Other deities, standing on the rim of the world, bore
torches past all numbering; and still other deities, as well as
serpents and birds, accompanied him, and did him homage
with heavenly perfumes, garlands, sandal-wood powder, and
incense.   And the sky was as full of coral flowers as it is of
pouring water at the height of the rainy season.   Celestial
choruses were heard; and on every side bands of music
played, some of eight instruments, and some of sixty, —
sixty-eight hundred thousand instruments in all.   It was
as when the storm-clouds thunder on the sea, or when the
ocean roars against the Yugandhara rocks.

Advancing in this glory, the Future Buddha in one night
passed through three kingdoms, and at the end of thirty
leagues he came to the river named Anomā.

But was this as far as the horse could go? Certainly not.
For he was able to travel round the world from end to end,
as it were round the rim of a wheel lying on its hub, and yet
get back before breakfast and eat the food prepared for him.
But on this occasion the fragrant garlands and other offerings which the gods and the serpents and the birds threw
down upon him from the sky buried him up to his haunches;
and as he was obliged to drag his body and cut his way
through the tangled mass, he was greatly delayed.   Hence
it was that he went only thirty leagues.

And the Future Buddha, stopping on the river-bank, said
to Channa, —

" What is the name of this river? "

" Sire, its name is Anomā [Illustrious]."

" And my retirement from the world shall also be called
Anomā," replied the Future Buddha.   Saying this, he gave
the signal to his horse with his heel; and the horse sprang
over the river, which had a breadth of eight usabhas,[1] and
landed on the opposite bank.   And the Future Buddha, dis-
mounting and standing on the sandy beach that stretched
away like a sheet of silver, said to Channa, —

---

[1] An usabha is 140 cubits.

"My good Channa, take these ornaments and Kanthaka and go home. I am about to retire from the world."

"Sire, I also will retire from the world."

Three times the Future Buddha refused him, saying, "It is not for you to retire from the world. Go now!" and made him take the ornaments and Kanthaka.

Next he thought, "These locks of mine are not suited to a monk; but there is no one fit to cut the hair of a Future Buddha. Therefore I will cut them off myself with my sword." And grasping a simitar with his right hand, he seized his top-knot with his left hand, and cut it off, together with the diadem. His hair thus became two finger-breadths in length, and curling to the right, lay close to his head. As long as he lived it remained of that length, and the beard was proportionate. And never again did he have to cut either hair or beard.

Then the Future Buddha seized hold of his top-knot and diadem, and threw them into the air, saying, —

"If I am to become a Buddha, let them stay in the sky; but if not, let them fall to the ground."

The top-knot and jewelled turban mounted for a distance of a league into the air, and there came to a stop. And Sakka, the king of the gods, perceiving them with his divine eye, received them in an appropriate jewelled casket, and established it in the Heaven of the Thirty-three as the "Shrine of the Diadem."

272.   "His hair he cut, so sweet with many pleasant scents,
     This Chief of Men, and high impelled it towards the sky;
     And there god Vāsava, the god with thousand eyes,
     In golden casket caught it, bowing low his head."

Again the Future Buddha thought, "These garments of mine, made of Benares cloth, are not suited to a monk."

Now the Mahā-Brahma god, Ghatīkāra, who had been a friend of his in the time of the Buddha Kassapa, and whose affection for him had not grown old in the long interval since that Buddha, thought to himself, —

"To-day my friend has gone forth on the Great Retirement. I will bring him the requisites of a monk."

273.   " Robes, three in all, the bowl for alms,
        The razor, needle, and the belt,
        And water-strainer, — just these eight
        Are needed by th' ecstatic monk."

Taking the above eight requisites of a monk, he gave them to him.

When the Future Buddha had put on this most excellent vesture, the symbol of saintship and of retirement from the world, he dismissed Channa, saying, —

"Channa, go tell my father and my mother from me that I am well."

And Channa did obeisance to the Future Buddha; and keeping his right side towards him, he departed.

But Kanthaka, who had stood listening to the Future Buddha while he was conferring with Channa, was unable to bear his grief at the thought, " I shall never see my master any more." And as he passed out of sight, his heart burst, and he died, and was reborn in the Heaven of the Thirty-three as the god Kanthaka.

At first the grief of Channa had been but single; but now he was oppressed with a second sorrow in the death of Kanthaka, and came weeping and wailing to the city.

---

§ 7. THE GREAT STRUGGLE.

Translated from the Introduction to the Jātaka (i.65²⁹).

Now the Future Buddha, having thus retired from the world, — in that place there was a mango-grove named Anupiya, and here he first spent a week in the joy of having retired from the world, — in one day went on foot to Rājagaha, a distance of thirty leagues, and entering the city, he begged for food from house to house without passing any by. By the beauty of the Future Buddha, the whole city was thrown into a commotion, like that into which Rājagaha was thrown by the entrance of Dhanapālaka, or like that into which the

heavenly city was thrown by the entrance of the chief of the
Titans.

Then ran the king's men to the palace, and made announcement, —

"Sire, there is a being of such and such appearance going
about the city begging for food. Whether he be a god, or a
man, or a serpent, or a bird, we do not know."

Then the king, standing on the roof of his palace, and
thence beholding the Great Being, became amazed and
astonished, and commanded his men, —

"Look ye now! Go and investigate this! If this person be not a man, he will vanish from sight as soon as he
leaves the city; if, namely, he be a god, he will depart by way
of the air; if a serpent, he will sink into the ground. But if
he be a human being, he will eat the food he has obtained in
alms."

Now the Great Being, after collecting a number of scraps,
sufficient, as he judged, for his sustenance, left the city by
the same gate he had entered, and sitting down with his face
to the east, in the shade of Paṇḍava rock, he attempted to
eat his meal. But his stomach turned, and he felt as if his
inwards were on the point of coming out by his mouth.
Thereupon, in the midst of his distress at that repulsive food,
— for in that existence he had never before so much as seen
such fare, — he began to admonish himself, saying, "Siddhattha, although you were born into a family having plenty to
eat and drink, into a station in life where you lived on fragrant third season's rice [1] with various sauces of the finest
flavors, yet when you saw a monk clad in garments taken
from the rubbish heap, you exclaimed, 'Oh, when shall I be
like him, and eat food which I have begged? Will that time
ever come?' And then you retired from the world. And

---

[1] A garment new, a new-built house,
A new umbrella, and a bride, —
The new is good; but long-kept rice
And long-kept servants men do praise.

From the Sanskrit of the *Nītipradīpa*, 15, as given by Böhtlingk,
Indische Sprüche, 3410.

now that you have your wish, and have renounced all, what, pray, is this you are doing?" When he had thus admonished himself, his disgust subsided, and he ate his meal.

Then the king's men went and announced to the king what they had seen. And the king, on hearing the report of the messengers, issued hastily from the city, and approaching the Future Buddha, and being pleased with his deportment, he tendered him all his kingly glory.

"Great king," replied the Future Buddha, "I do not seek for the gratification of my senses or my passions, but have retired from the world for the sake of the supreme and absolute enlightenment."

"Verily," said the king, when his repeated offers had all been refused, "you are sure to become a Buddha; but when that happens, your first journey must be to my kingdom."

The above is an abridgment, but the full account, beginning with the lines, —

> "I sing the man of insight keen,
> And his retirement from the world,"

can be found by referring to the "Discourse on Retirement from the World," and its commentary.

Then the Future Buddha, having made the king the required promise, proceeded on his way; and coming to Ālāra Kālāma and Uddaka, the disciple of Rāma, he acquired from them the eight stages of meditation. But becoming convinced that they did not lead to enlightenment,[1] he ceased to practise them. And being desirous of making the Great Struggle, so as to show the world of gods and men his fortitude and heroism, he went to Uruvelā, and saying, "Truly, delightful is this spot," he there took up his abode, and began the Great Struggle.

And those five persons, Koṇḍañña and the others,[2] who since their retirement from the world, were wandering about for alms through villages, market-towns, and royal cities, here met with the Future Buddha. And during the six

---

[1] See pages 334–8.   [2] See pages 52–3.

years of the Great Struggle, they swept his cell, and did all
manner of service for him, and kept constantly at his beck
and call, all the time saying, "Now he will become a Buddha,
now he will become a Buddha."

And the Future Buddha, thinking, "I will carry auster-
ity to the uttermost," tried various plans, such as living on one
sesamum seed or on one grain of rice a day, and even ceased
taking nourishment altogether, and moreover rebuffed the
gods when they came and attempted to infuse nourishment
through the pores of his skin. By this lack of nourishment
his body became emaciated to the last degree, and lost its
golden color, and became black, and his thirty-two physical
characteristics as a great being became obscured. Now, one
day, as he was deep in a trance of suppressed breathing, he
was attacked by violent pains, and fell senseless to the
ground, at one end of his walking-place.

And certain of the deities said, "The monk Gotama is
dead;" but others said, "This is a practice of the saints."
Then those who thought he was dead went to king Suddhodana, and announced to him that his son was dead.

"Did he die after becoming a Buddha, or before?" asked
the king.

"He was unable to become a Buddha, but in making the
Struggle, he fell to the ground and died."

When the king heard this, he refused to credit it, saying,
"I do not believe it. Death cannot come to my son before
he attains to enlightenment."

But why would not the king believe it? Because of the
miracles he had seen, — the first when the ascetic Kāladevala
had been compelled to do homage to the Future Buddha, and
the other which happened to the rose-apple tree.

But the Future Buddha recovering his consciousness, and
standing up, the deities went a second time to the king, and
told him that his son was well again.

Said the king, "I knew that my son could not have
died."

Now the six years which the Great Being thus spent in
austerities were like time spent in endeavoring to tie the air

into knots. And coming to the decision, " These austerities
are not the way to enlightenment," he went begging through
villages and market-towns for ordinary material food, and
lived upon it. And his thirty-two physical characteristics as
a great being again appeared, and the color of his body
became like unto gold.

Then the band of five priests thought, "It is now six
years that this man has been performing austerities without
being able to attain to omniscience. And how much less can
he be expected to do so in future, now that he has again taken
to ordinary material food begged from town to town! He
has become luxurious, and given up the Struggle. For us to
look for any benefit to come from that quarter would be as
reasonable as if a man were to imagine he could bathe his
head in a dew-drop. We will have nothing more to do with
him." With that they took their bowls and robes, and left
the Great Being, and going eighteen leagues off, entered
Isipatana.

---

§ 8. THE ATTAINMENT OF BUDDHASHIP.

Translated from the Introduction to the Jātaka (i.68⁵).

Now at that time there lived in Uruvelā a girl named
Sujātā, who had been born in the family of the householder
Senāni, in General's Town. On reaching maturity she made
a prayer to a certain banyan-tree, saying, "If I get a husband of equal rank with myself, and my first-born is a son,
I will make a yearly offering to you of the value of a hundred thousand pieces of money." And her prayer had been
successful.

And wishing to make her offering on the day of full
moon of the month Visākhā, full six years after the Great
Being commenced his austerities, she first pastured a thousand cows in Latthimadhu Wood, and fed their milk to five
hundred cows, and the milk of these five hundred cows to
two hundred and fifty, and so on down to feeding the milk

of sixteen cows to eight. This "working the milk in and
in," as it is called, was done to increase the thickness and
the sweetness and the strength-giving properties of the milk.
And when it came to be the full-moon day of Visākhā, she
resolved to make her offering, and rose up early in the morning, just when night was breaking into day, and gave orders
to milk the eight cows. The calves had not come at the
teats of the cows; yet as soon as new pails were put under
the udders, the milk flowed in streams of its own accord.
When she saw this miracle, Sujātā took the milk with her
own hands and placed it in a new vessel, and herself made a
fire and began to cook it. While the milk-rice was cooking,
immense bubbles arose, and turning to the right, went round
together; but not a single drop ran over the edge, and not a
particle of smoke went up from the fireplace. On this occasion the four guardian angels were present, and stood guard
over the fireplace; Mahā-Brahma bore aloft the canopy of
state, and Sakka raked the fire-brands together and made the
fire blaze up brightly. And just as a man crushes honey out
of a honey-comb that has formed around a stick, so the
deities by their superhuman power collected an amount of
vital sap sufficient for the sustenance of the gods and men of
all the four great continents and their two thousand attendant
isles, and infused it into the milk-rice. At other times, to be
sure, the deities infuse this sap into each mouthful; but on
the day of the attainment of the Buddhaship, and on the
day of decease, they place it in the kettle itself.

When Sujātā had seen so many miracles appear to her in
one day, she said to her slave-girl Puṇṇā, —

"Puṇṇā, dear girl, the deity is very graciously disposed
to us to-day. I have never before seen so many marvellous
things happen in so short a time. Run quickly, and get
everything ready at the holy place."

"Yes, my lady," replied the slave-girl, and ran in great
haste to the foot of the tree.

Now that night the Future Buddha had five great dreams,
and on considering their meaning reached the conclusion,
"Without doubt I shall become a Buddha this very day."

And when night was over, and he had cared for his person, he came early in the morning to that tree, to await the
hour to go begging. And when he sat down he illumined
the whole tree with his radiance.

Then came Puṇṇā, and saw the Future Buddha sitting at
the foot of the tree, contemplating the eastern quarter of the
world. And when she beheld the radiance from his body
lighting up the whole tree with a golden color, she became
greatly excited, saying to herself, " Our deity, methinks, has
come down from the tree to-day, and has seated himself,
ready to receive our offering in person." And she ran in
great haste, and told Sujātā of the matter.

When Sujātā heard this news, she was overjoyed; and
saying, "From this day forth be to me in the room of an
eldest daughter," she decked Puṇṇā with all the ornaments
appropriate to that position. And since a Future Buddha
on the day he attains the Buddhaship must needs receive a
golden dish worth a hundred thousand pieces of money,
therefore the idea occurred to her of putting the milk-rice in
a golden dish. And bringing out a golden dish that was
worth a hundred thousand, she took up the cooking-vessel
and began to pour out the milk-rice. All the milk-rice
rolled off like water from a lotus-leaf, and exactly filled the
dish. Then, covering the dish with another, which was also
made of gold, and wrapping it in a cloth, she adorned herself
in all her ornaments, and with the dish on her head proceeded
in state to the foot of the banyan-tree. As soon as she caught
sight of the Future Buddha she was exceedingly overjoyed,
supposing him to be the tree-god; and as she advanced she kept
constantly bowing. And taking the pot from her head, she
uncovered it, and with some flower-scented water in a golden
vase, drew near and took up a position close to the Future
Buddha. The earthenware bowl which the Future Buddha
had kept so long, and which had been given him by Ghaṭīkāra,
the Mahā-Brahma god, at that instant disappeared; and
the Future Buddha, stretching out his right hand in an
attempt to find his bowl, grasped the vase of water. Next
Sujātā placed the dish of milk-rice in the hand of the Great

Being.   Then the Great Being looked at Sujātā; and she
perceived that he was a holy man, and did obeisance, and
said, —

"Lord, accept my donation, and go whithersoever it
seemeth to you good."   And adding, "May your wishes
prosper like mine own," she departed, caring no more for her
golden dish worth a hundred thousand pieces of money than
if it had been a dead leaf.

The Future Buddha rose from his seat and walked round
the tree with his right side towards it; and taking the dish,
he proceeded to the banks of the Nerañjarā and descended
into its waters, just as many thousands of Future Buddhas
before him had descended on the day of their complete
enlightenment. — The spot where he bathed is now a place
of pilgrimage named Suppatiṭṭhita, and here he deposited the
dish on the bank before descending into the water. — After
bathing he dressed himself in that garb of saintship which
had been the dress of many hundreds of thousands of Future
Buddhas before him; and sitting down with his face to the
east, he made the whole of the thick, sweet milk-rice into
forty-nine pellets of the size of the fruit of the single-seeded
palmyra-tree, and ate it.   And he took no further nourishment until the end of the seven weeks, or forty-nine days,
which he spent on the throne of wisdom after he had become
a Buddha.   During all that time he had no other nourishment; he neither bathed, nor rinsed his mouth, nor did he
ease himself; but was wholly taken up by the delights of
the Trances, of the Paths, and of the Fruits.

Now when he had consumed the milk-rice, he took the
golden dish; and saying, "If I am to succeed in becoming a
Buddha to-day, let this dish go up-stream; but if not, let it
go down-stream," he threw it into the water.   And it swam,
cleaving the stream, until it came to the middle of the river,
and then, like a fleet horse, it ran up-stream for a distance of
eighty cubits, keeping all the while in the middle of the
stream.   Then it dived into a whirlpool and went to the palace of the black snake-king, and hit, "click! click!" against
the dishes that had been used by the last three Buddhas, and

took its place at the end of the row. When the black snake-king heard the noise, he exclaimed, —

> "But yesterday a Buddha lived,
> And now another has been born."

and so on, through several hundred laudatory verses. As a matter of only yesterday and to-day did the times of the snake-king's appearance above ground seem to him; and his body at such times towered up into the sky to a height of one and three quarters leagues.

Then the Future Buddha took his noonday rest on the banks of the river, in a grove of sal-trees in full bloom. And at nightfall, at the time the flowers droop on their stalks, he rose up, like a lion when he bestirs himself, and went towards the Bo-tree, along a road which the gods had decked, and which was eight usabhas wide.

The snakes, the fairies, the birds, and other classes of beings did him homage with celestial perfumes, flowers, and other offerings, and celestial choruses poured forth heavenly music; so that the ten thousand worlds were filled with these perfumes, garlands, and shouts of acclaim.

Just then there came from the opposite direction a grass-cutter named Sotthiya, and he was carrying grass. And when he saw the Great Being, that he was a holy man, he gave him eight handfuls of grass. The Future Buddha took the grass, and ascending the throne of wisdom, stood on the southern side and faced the north. Instantly the southern half of the world sank, until it seemed to touch the Avīci hell, while the northern half rose to the highest of the heavens.

"Methinks," said the Future Buddha, "this cannot be the place for the attainment of the supreme wisdom;" and walking round the tree with his right side towards it, he came to the western side and faced the east. Then the western half of the world sank, until it seemed to touch the Avīci hell, while the eastern half rose to the highest of the heavens. Wherever, indeed, he stood, the broad earth rose and fell, as though it had been a huge cart-wheel lying on its hub, and some one were treading on the rim.

"Methinks," said the Future Buddha, "this also cannot be the place for the attainment of supreme wisdom;" and walking round the tree with his right side towards it, he came to the northern side and faced the south. Then the northern half of the world sank, until it seemed to touch the Avīci hell, while the southern half rose to the highest of the heavens.

"Methinks," said the Future Buddha, "this also cannot be the place for the attainment of supreme wisdom;" and walking round the tree with his right side towards it, he came to the eastern side and faced the west. Now it is on the eastern side of their Bo-trees that all The Buddhas have sat cross-legged, and that side neither trembles nor quakes.

Then the Great Being, saying to himself, "This is the immovable spot on which all The Buddhas have planted themselves! This is the place for destroying passion's net!" took hold of his handful of grass by one end, and shook it out there. And straightway the blades of grass formed themselves into a seat fourteen cubits long, of such symmetry of shape as not even the most skilful painter or carver could design.

Then the Future Buddha turned his back to the trunk of the Bo-tree and faced the east. And making the mighty resolution, "Let my skin, and sinews, and bones become dry, and welcome! and let all the flesh and blood in my body dry up! but never from this seat will I stir, until I have attained the supreme and absolute wisdom!" he sat himself down cross-legged in an unconquerable position, from which not even the descent of a hundred thunder-bolts at once could have dislodged him.

At this point the god Māra, exclaiming, "Prince Siddhattha is desirous of passing beyond my control, but I will never allow it!" went and announced the news to his army, and sounding the Māra war-cry, drew out for battle. Now Māra's army extended in front of him for twelve leagues, and to the right and to the left for twelve leagues, and in the rear as far as to the confines of the world, and it was nine leagues high. And when it shouted, it made an earthquake-

like roaring and rumbling over a space of a thousand leagues.
And the god Māra, mounting his elephant, which was a hundred and fifty leagues high, and had the name " Girded-with-
mountains," caused a thousand arms to appear on his body,
and with these he grasped a variety of weapons.   Also in the
remainder of that army, no two persons carried the same
weapon; and diverse also in their appearances and counte-
nances, the host swept on like a flood to overwhelm the
Great Being.

Now deities throughout the ten thousand worlds were
busy singing the praises of the Great Being. Sakka, the
king of the gods, was blowing the conch-shell Vijayuttara.
(This conch, they say, was a hundred and twenty cubits
long, and when once it had been filled with wind, it would
sound for four months before it stopped.) The great black
snake-king sang more than a hundred laudatory verses. And
Mahā-Brahma stood holding aloft the white umbrella. But
as Māra's army gradually drew near to the throne of wisdom,
not one of these gods was able to stand his ground, but each
fled straight before him. The black snake-king dived into
the ground, and coming to the snake-abode, Mañjerika, which
was five hundred leagues in extent, he covered his face with
both hands and lay down. Sakka slung his conch-shell Vijayuttara over his back, and took up his position on the rim of
the world. Mahā-Brahma left the white umbrella at the end
of the world, and fled to his Brahma-abode. Not a single
deity was able to stand his ground, and the Great Being was
left sitting alone.

Then said Māra to his followers, —

"My friends, Siddhattha, the son of Suddhodana, is far
greater than any other man, and we shall never be able to
fight him in front. We will attack him from behind."

All the gods had now disappeared, and the Great Being
looked around on three sides, and said to himself, "There is
no one here." Then looking to the north, he perceived
Māra's army coming on like a flood, and said, —

"Here is this multitude exerting all their strength and
power against me alone. My mother and father are not here,

nor my brother, nor any other relative.   But I have these
Ten Perfections, like old retainers long cherished at my board.
It therefore behooves me to make the Ten Perfections my
shield and my sword, and to strike a blow with them that
shall destroy this strong array."   And he remained sitting,
and reflected on the Ten Perfections.

Thereupon the god Māra caused a whirlwind, thinking,
"By this will I drive away Siddhattha." Straightway the
east wind and all the other different winds began to blow;
but although these winds could have torn their way through
mountain-peaks half a league, or two leagues, or three leagues
high, or have uprooted forest-shrubs and trees, or have reduced to powder and scattered in all directions, villages and
towns, yet when they reached the Future Buddha, such was
the energy of the Great Being's merit, they lost all power
and were not able to cause so much as a fluttering of the
edge of his priestly robe.

Then he caused a great rain-storm, saying, "With water
will I overwhelm and drown him." And through his mighty
power, clouds of a hundred strata, and clouds of a thousand
strata arose, and also the other different kinds. And these
rained down, until the earth became gullied by the torrents
of water which fell, and until the floods had risen over the
tops of every forest-tree. But on coming to the Great Being,
this mighty inundation was not able to wet his priestly robes
as much as a dew-drop would have done.

Then he caused a shower of rocks, in which immense
mountain-peaks flew smoking and flaming through the sky.
But on reaching the Future Buddha they became celestial
bouquets of flowers.

Then he caused a shower of weapons, in which single-
edged, and double-edged swords, spears, and arrows flew
smoking and flaming through the sky. But on reaching the
Future Buddha they became celestial flowers.

Then he caused a shower of live coals, in which live coals
as red as kiṁsuka flowers flew through the sky. But they
scattered themselves at the Future Buddha's feet as a shower
of celestial flowers.

Then he caused a shower of hot ashes, in which ashes that glowed like fire flew through the sky. But they fell at the Future Buddha's feet as sandal-wood powder.

Then he caused a shower of sand, in which very fine sand flew smoking and flaming through the sky. But it fell at the Future Buddha's feet as celestial flowers.

Then he caused a shower of mud, in which mud flew smoking and flaming through the sky. But it fell at the Future Buddha's feet as celestial ointment.

Then he caused a darkness, thinking, " By this will I frighten Siddhattha, and drive him away." And the darkness became fourfold, and very dense. But on reaching the Future Buddha it disappeared like darkness before the light of the sun.

Māra, being thus unable with these nine storms of wind, rain, rocks, weapons, live coals, hot ashes, sand, mud, and darkness, to drive away the Future Buddha, gave command to his followers, " Look ye now ! Why stand ye still? Seize, kill, drive away this prince ! " And, arming himself with a discus, and seated upon the shoulders of the elephant " Girded-with-mountains," he drew near the Future Buddha, and said, —

" Siddhattha, arise from this seat ! It does not belong to you, but to me."

When the Great Being heard this he said, —

" Māra, you have not fulfilled the Ten Perfections in any of their three grades ; nor have you made the five great donations ;[1] nor have you striven for knowledge, nor for the welfare of the world, nor for enlightenment. This seat does not belong to you, but to me."

Unable to restrain his fury, the enraged Māra now hurled his discus. But the Great Being reflected on the Ten Perfections, and the discus changed into a canopy of flowers,

---

[1] These are the five donations great:
The gift of treasure, gift of child,
The gift of wife, of royal rule,
And last, the gift of life and limb.

From the *Abhidhānappadīpikā,* 421.

and remained suspended over his head. Yet they say that
this keen-edged discus, when at other times Māra hurled it
in anger, would cut through solid stone pillars as if they had
been the tips of bamboo shoots. But on this occasion it
became a canopy of flowers. Then the followers of Māra
began hurling immense mountain-crags, saying, "This will
make him get up from his seat and flee." But the Great
Being kept his thoughts on the Ten Perfections, and the
crags also became wreaths of flowers, and then fell to the
ground.

Now the gods meanwhile were standing on the rim of
the world, and craning their necks to look, saying, —

"Ah, woe the day! The handsome form of prince
Siddhattha will surely be destroyed! What will he do to
save himself?"

Then the Great Being, after his assertion that the seat
which Future Buddhas had always used on the day of their
complete enlightenment belonged to him, continued, and
said, —

"Māra, who is witness to your having given donations?"

Said Māra, "All these, as many as you see here, are my
witnesses;" and he stretched out his hand in the direction of
his army. And instantly from Māra's army came a roar, "I
am his witness! I am his witness!" which was like to the
roar of an earthquake.

Then said Māra to the Great Being, —

"Siddhattha, who is witness to your having given
donations?"

"Your witnesses," replied the Great Being, "are animate
beings, and I have no animate witnesses present. However,
not to mention the donations which I gave in other existences, the great seven-hundred-fold donation which I gave in
my Vessantara existence shall now be testified to by the solid
earth, inanimate though she be." And drawing forth his
right hand from beneath his priestly robe, he stretched it out
towards the mighty earth, and said, "Are you witness, or are
you not, to my having given a great seven-hundred-fold
donation in my Vessantara existence?"

And the mighty earth thundered, "I bear you witness!" with a hundred, a thousand, a hundred thousand roars, as if to overwhelm the army of Māra.

Now while the Great Being was thus calling to mind the donation he gave in his Vessantara existence, and saying to himself, "Siddhattha, that was a great and excellent donation which you gave," the hundred-and-fifty-league-high elephant "Girded-with-mountains" fell upon his knees before the Great Being. And the followers of Māra fled away in all directions. No two went the same way, but leaving their head-ornaments and their cloaks behind, they fled straight before them.

Then the hosts of the gods, when they saw the army of Māra flee, cried out, "Māra is defeated! Prince Siddhattha has conquered! Let us go celebrate the victory!" And the snakes egging on the snakes, the birds the birds, the deities the deities, and the Brahma-angels the Brahma-angels, they came with perfumes, garlands, and other offerings in their hands to the Great Being on the throne of wisdom. And as they came, —

274.   "The victory now hath this illustrious Buddha won!
       The Wicked One, the Slayer, hath defeated been!"
       Thus round the throne of wisdom shouted joyously
       The bands of snakes their songs of victory for the Sage;

275.   "The victory now hath this illustrious Buddha won!
       The Wicked One, the Slayer, hath defeated been!"
       Thus round the throne of wisdom shouted joyously
       The flocks of birds their songs of victory for the Sage;

276.   "The victory now hath this illustrious Buddha won!
       The Wicked One, the Slayer, hath defeated been!"
       Thus round the throne of wisdom shouted joyously
       The bands of gods their songs of victory for the Sage;

277.   "The victory now hath this illustrious Buddha won!
       The Wicked One, the Slayer, hath defeated been!"
       Thus round the throne of wisdom shouted joyously
       The Brahma-angels songs of victory for the Saint.

And the remaining deities, also, throughout the ten thousand worlds, made offerings of garlands, perfumes, and ointments, and in many a hymn extolled him.

It was before the sun had set that the Great Being thus vanquished the army of Māra. And then, while the Bo-tree in homage rained red, coral-like sprigs upon his priestly robes, he acquired in the first watch of the night the knowledge of previous existences; in the middle watch of the night, the divine eye; and in the last watch of the night, his intellect fathomed Dependent Origination.

Now while he was musing on the twelve terms of Dependent Origination, forwards and backwards, round and back again, the ten thousand worlds quaked twelve times, as far as to their ocean boundaries. And when the Great Being, at the dawning of the day, had thus made the ten thousand worlds thunder with his attainment of omniscience, all these worlds became most gloriously adorned. Flags and banners erected on the eastern rim of the world let their streamers fly to the western rim of the world; likewise those erected on the western rim of the world, to the eastern rim of the world; those erected on the northern rim of the world, to the southern rim of the world; and those erected on the southern rim of the world, to the northern rim of the world; while those erected on the level of the earth let theirs fly until they beat against the Brahma-world; and those of the Brahma-world let theirs hang down to the level of the earth. Throughout the ten thousand worlds the flowering trees bloomed; the fruit trees were weighted down by their burden of fruit; trunk-lotuses bloomed on the trunks of trees; branch-lotuses on the branches of trees; vine-lotuses on the vines; hanging-lotuses in the sky; and stalk-lotuses burst through the rocks and came up by sevens. The system of ten thousand worlds was like a bouquet of flowers sent whirling through the air, or like a thick carpet of flowers; in the intermundane spaces the eight-thousand-league-long hells, which not even the light of seven suns had formerly been able to illumine, were now flooded with radiance; the eighty-four-thousand-league-deep ocean became sweet to the taste; the rivers checked their flowing; the blind from birth received their sight; the deaf from birth their hearing; the cripples from birth the use of their limbs; and the bonds and fetters of captives broke and fell off.

When thus he had attained to omniscience, and was the centre of such unparalleled glory and homage, and so many prodigies were happening about him, he breathed forth that solemn utterance which has never been omitted by any of The Buddhas: —

> 278. "Through birth and rebirth's endless round,
>   Seeking in vain, I hastened on,
>   To find who framed this edifice.
>   What misery! — birth incessantly!
>
> 279. "O builder! I've discovered thee!
>   This fabric thou shalt ne'er rebuild!
>   Thy rafters all are broken now,
>   And pointed roof demolished lies!
>   This mind has demolition reached,
>   And seen the last of all desire!"

The period of time, therefore, from the existence in the Tusita Heaven to this attainment of omniscience on the throne of wisdom, constitutes the Intermediate Epoch.

---

§ 9. FIRST EVENTS AFTER THE ATTAINMENT OF BUDDHASHIP.

Translated from the Mahā-Vagga, and constituting the opening sections.

Hail to that Blessed One, that Saint, and Supreme Buddha!

AT that time The Buddha, The Blessed One, was dwelling at Uruvelā at the foot of the Bo-tree on the banks of the river Nerañjarā, having just attained the Buddhaship. Then The Blessed One sat cross-legged for seven days together at the foot of the Bo-tree experiencing the bliss of emancipation.

Then The Blessed One, during the first watch of the night, thought over Dependent Origination both forward and back : —

> On ignorance depends karma ;
> On karma depends consciousness ;
> On consciousness depend name and form ;
> On name and form depend the six organs of sense ;
> On the six organs of sense depends contact ;
> On contact depends sensation ;
> On sensation depends desire ;
> On desire depends attachment ;
> On attachment depends existence ;
> On existence depends birth ;
> On birth depend old age and death, sorrow, lamentation, misery, grief, and despair.

Thus does this entire aggregation of misery arise. But on the complete fading out and cessation of ignorance ceases karma ; on the cessation of karma ceases consciousness ; on the cessation of consciousness cease name and form ; on the cessation of name and form cease the six organs of sense ; on the cessation of the six organs of sense ceases contact ; on the cessation of contact ceases sensation ; on the cessation of sensation ceases desire ; on the cessation of desire ceases attachment ; on the cessation of attachment ceases existence ; on the cessation of existence ceases birth ; on the cessation of birth cease old age and death, sorrow, lamentation, misery, grief, and despair. Thus does this entire aggregation of misery cease.

Then The Blessed One, concerning this, on that occasion, breathed forth this solemn utterance, —

> " When to the strenuous, meditative Brahman
> There come to light the elements of being,
> Then vanish all his doubts and eager questions,
> What time he knows THE ELEMENTS HAVE CAUSES."

Then The Blessed One, during the middle watch of the

night, thought over Dependent Origination both· forward and
back : — On ignorance depends karma. . . . Thus does this
entire aggregation of misery arise. But on the complete fading out and cessation of ignorance ceases karmá. . . . Thus
does this entire aggregation of misery cease.

Then The Blessed One, concerning this, on that occasion,
breathed forth this solemn utterance, —

> " When to the strenuous, meditative Brahman
> There come to light the elements of being,
> Then vanish all his doubts and eager questions,
> What time he knows How Causes have an Ending."

Then The Blessed One, during the last watch of the
night, thought over Dependent Origination both forward
and back : — On ignorance depends karma. . . . Thus does
this entire aggregation of misery arise. But on the complete
fading out and cessation of ignorance ceases karma. . . . Thus
does this entire aggregation of misery cease.

Then The Blessed One, concerning this, on that occasion,
breathed forth this solemn utterance, —

> " When to the strenuous, meditative Brahman
> There come to light the elements of being,
> Then scattereth he the hordes of Mára's army ;
> Like to the sun that lightens all the heavens."

End of the account of what took place under the Bo-tree.

Then The Blessed One, after the lapse of seven days,
arose from that state of exalted calm, and leaving the
foot of the Bo-tree, drew near to where the Ajapála (that
is, the Goatherd's) banyan-tree was ; and having drawn
near, he sat cross-legged at the foot of the Ajapála banyan-
tree for seven days together, experiencing the bliss of
emancipation.

Then a certain Brahman, who was of a proud and con-
temptuous disposition, drew near to where The Blessed One

was; and having drawn near, he exchanged greetings with
The Blessed One. And having passed with him the greetings of friendship and civility, he stood respectfully at one
side. And standing respectfully at one side, the Brahman
spoke to The Blessed One as follows: —

"Gotama, what is it constitutes a Brahman? and what
are the Brahman-making qualities?"

Then The Blessed One, concerning this, on that occasion,
breathed forth this solemn utterance, —

> "The Brahman who his evil traits hath banished,
> Is free from pride, is self-restrained and spotless,
> Is learnèd, and the holy life hath followed,
> 'T is he alone may claim the name of Brahman;
> With things of earth he hath no point of contact."

End of the account of what took place under the Ajapāla-tree.

Then The Blessed One, after the lapse of seven days, arose
from that state of exalted calm, and leaving the foot of the
Ajapāla banyan-tree, drew near to where the Mucalinda tree
was; and having drawn near, he sat cross-legged at the foot
of the Mucalinda tree for seven days together, experiencing
the bliss of emancipation.

Now at that time a great cloud appeared out of season,
and for seven days it was rainy, cloudy weather, with a cold
wind. Then issued Mucalinda, the serpent-king, from his
abode, and enveloping the body of The Blessed One seven
times with his folds, spread his great hood above his head,
saying, —

"Let neither cold nor heat, nor gnats, flies, wind, sun-
shine, nor creeping creatures come near The Blessed
One!"

Then, when seven days had elapsed, and Mucalinda, the
serpent-king, knew that the storm had broken up, and that
the clouds had gone, he unwound his coils from the body of
The Blessed One. And changing his natural appearance into
that of a young man, he stood before The Blessed One, and
with his joined hands to his forehead did reverence to The
Blessed One.

Then The Blessed One, concerning this, on that occasion, breathed forth this solemn utterance, —

> "How blest the happy solitude
> Of him who hears and knows the truth!
> How blest is harmlessness towards all,
> And self-restraint towards living things!
> How blest from passion to be free,
> All sensuous joys to leave behind!
> Yet far the highest bliss of all
> To leave the pride which says, ' I am.' "

> End of the account of what took place under the Mucalinda-tree.

§ 10. THE CONVERSION OF SĀRIPUTTA AND MOGGALLĀNA.[1]

Translated from the Mahā-Vagga (i.23¹).

Now at that time, Sañjaya, the wandering ascetic, was dwelling at Rājagaha in company with a large following of wandering ascetics, two hundred and fifty in number; and at that time Sāriputta and Moggallāna were leading the religious life under Sañjaya, the wandering ascetic. And they had made this compact: " That one of us who shall first attain to the deathless is to tell it to the other."

Then the venerable Assaji, having put on his tunic in the morning and taken his bowl and his robes, entered Rājagaha for alms, winning the minds of men with his advancing and his retiring, with his looking and his gazing, with his drawing in his arms and his stretching out his arms, and having his eyes cast down, and perfect in his deportment. And Sāriputta, the wandering ascetic, saw the venerable Assaji going the rounds of Rājagaha for alms, winning the minds of men with his advancing and his retiring, with his looking and

---

[1] Sāriputta and Moggallāna after their conversion became the two chief disciples of The Buddha. See page 16, Story of Sumedha, verse 77.

his gazing, with his drawing in his arms and his stretching out his arms, and having his eyes cast down, and perfect in his deportment. And when he had seen him, it occurred to him as follows : —

" This must be a priest who is either a saint already, or has entered the path which conducts to saintship. What if now I draw near to this priest, and ask him, ' To follow whom, brother, did you retire from the world ? Who is your teacher ? and whose doctrine do you approve ? ' "

Then it occurred to Sāriputta, the wandering ascetic, as follows : —

" It is not a fit time to ask this priest questions while he is inside the city, and going the rounds for alms. What if now I follow in the wake of this priest in the manner approved of for those who have requests to prefer ? "

Then the venerable Assaji, after he had gone the rounds of Rājagaha and obtained alms, issued from the city ; and Sāriputta, the wandering ascetic, drew near to where the venerable Assaji was ; and having drawn near, he exchanged greetings with the venerable Assaji ; and having passed with him the greetings of friendship and civility, he stood respectfully at one side. And standing respectfully at one side, Sāriputta, the wandering ascetic, spoke to the venerable Assaji as follows : —

" Placid, brother, are all your organs of sense ; clear and bright is the color of your skin. To follow whom, brother, did you retire from the world ? Who is your teacher ? and whose doctrine do you approve ? "

" Brother, there is a great Sakyaputta monk, one who has retired from the world out of the Sakya clan. To follow this Blessed One have I retired from the world, and this Blessed One is my teacher, and the Doctrine of this Blessed One do I approve."

" But what, venerable sir, is your teacher's doctrine ? and what does he proclaim ? "

" Brother, I am a novice and a new-comer, and the time is but short since I retired from the world under this Doctrine and Discipline. I am not able to expound to you the Doc-

trine at any great length, but I can tell you the substance of
it in brief."

Then Sāriputta, the wandering ascetic, spoke to the venerable Assaji as follows : —

" So be it, brother. Whether little or much, tell it me.
Tell me only the substance ; it is the substance I want.
Why should you make a long matter of it ? "

Then the venerable Assaji recited to Sāriputta, the wandering ascetic, the following exposition of the Doctrine : —

> " The Buddha hath the causes told
> Of all things springing from a cause ;
> And also how things cease to be —
> 'T is this the Mighty Monk proclaims."

On hearing this exposition of the Doctrine, there arose in
the mind of Sāriputta, the wandering ascetic, a clear and distinct perception of the Doctrine that whatever is subject to
origination is subject also to cessation. " If this is the Doctrine," said he, " then, indeed, have you reached the sorrowless state lost sight of and neglected for many myriads of
world-cycles."

Then Sāriputta, the wandering ascetic, drew near to where
Moggallāna, the wandering ascetic, was. And Moggallāna,
the wandering ascetic, saw Sāriputta, the wandering ascetic,
approaching from afar ; and when he had seen him, he spoke
to Sāriputta, the wandering ascetic, as follows : —

" Placid, brother, are all your organs of sense ; clear and
bright is the color of your skin. Brother, have you attained
to the deathless ? "

" Yea, brother, I have attained to the deathless."

" But how, brother, did you attain to the deathless ? "

" Brother, just now I saw Assaji the priest going the
rounds of Rājagaha for alms, winning the minds of men with
his advancing and his retiring, with his looking and his gazing, with his drawing in his arms and his stretching out his
arms, and having his eyes cast down, and perfect in his
deportment ; and when I had seen him, it occurred to me as
follows : —

" This must be a priest who is either a saint already, or has entered the path which conducts to saintship. What if now I were to draw near to this priest, and ask him, ' To follow whom, brother, did you retire from the world ? Who is your teacher ? and whose doctrine do you approve ?' Then, brother, it occurred to me as follows : ' It is not a fit time to ask this priest questions while he is inside the city and going the round for alms. What if now I follow in the wake of this priest in the manner approved of for those who have requests to prefer ?' Then, brother, Assaji the priest, after he had gone the rounds of Rājagaha and obtained alms, issued from the city ; and I, brother, drew near to where Assaji the priest was ; and having drawn near, I exchanged greetings with the venerable Assaji ; and having passed with him the greetings of friendship and civility, I stood respectfully at one side. And standing respectfully at one side, I spoke, brother, to the venerable Assaji as follows : ' Placid, brother, are all your organs of sense ; clear and bright is the color of your skin. To follow whom, brother, did you retire from the world ? Who is your teacher ? and whose doctrine do you approve ?' ' Brother, there is a great Sakyaputta monk, one who has retired from the world out of the Sakya clan. To follow this Blessed One have I retired from the world, and this Blessed One is my teacher, and the Doctrine of this Blessed One do I approve.' ' But what, venerable sir, is your teacher's doctrine ? and what does he proclaim ?' ' Brother, I am a novice and a new-comer, and the time is but short since I retired from the world under the Doctrine and Discipline. I am not able to expound to you the Doctrine at any great length, but I can tell you the substance of it in brief.' ' So be it, brother. Whether little or much, tell it me. Tell me only the substance ; it is the substance I want. Why should you make a long matter of it ?' Then, brother, Assaji the priest recited to me the following exposition of the Doctrine : —

> " ' The Buddha hath the causes told
> Of all things springing from a cause ;
> And also how things cease to be —
> 'T is this the Mighty Monk proclaims.' "

On hearing this exposition of the Doctrine, there arose in the mind of Moggallāna, the wandering ascetic, a clear and distinct perception of the Doctrine that whatever is subject to origination is subject also to cessation. " If this is the Doctrine," said he, " then, indeed, have you reached the sorrowless state lost sight of and neglected for many myriads of world-cycles."

---

§ 11. THE BUDDHA'S DAILY HABITS.

Translated from the Sumaṅgala-Vilāsinī (i.45[10]), Buddhaghosa's Commentary on the Dīgha-Nikāya.

HABITS are of two kinds, the profitable, and the unprofitable. Of these, the unprofitable habits of The Blessed One had been extirpated by his attainment of saintship at the time he sat cross-legged under the Bo-tree. Profitable habits, however, remained to The Blessed One.

These were fivefold: his before-breakfast habits; his after-breakfast habits; his habits of the first watch of the night; his habits of the middle watch of the night; his habits of the last watch of the night.

His before-breakfast habits were as follows : —

The Blessed One would rise early in the morning, and when, out of kindness to his body-servant[1] and for the sake of bodily comfort, he had rinsed his mouth and otherwise cared for his person, he would sit retired until it was time to go begging. And when it came time, he would put on his tunic, girdle, and robes, and taking his bowl, he would enter the village or the town for alms. Sometimes he went alone, sometimes surrounded by a congregation of priests ; sometimes without anything especial happening, sometimes with the accompaniment of many prodigies.

While, namely, the Lord of the World is entering for

---

[1] In order to give him a chance to acquire merit by waiting on a Buddha: compare page 99d.

alms, gentle winds clear the ground before him; the clouds let fall drops of water to lay the dust in his pathway, and then become a canopy over him; other winds bring flowers and scatter them in his path; elevations of ground depress themselves, and depressions elevate themselves; wherever he places his foot, the ground is even and pleasant to walk upon,[1] or lotus-flowers receive his tread. No sooner has he set his right foot within the city-gate than the rays of six different colors which issue from his body race hither and thither over palaces and pagodas, and deck them, as it were, with the yellow sheen of gold, or with the colors of a painting. The elephants, the horses, the birds, and other animals give forth melodious sounds; likewise the tom-toms, lutes, and other musical instruments, and the ornaments worn by the people.

By these tokens the people would know, "The Blessed One has now entered for alms;" and in their best tunics and best robes, with perfumes, flowers, and other offerings, they issue forth from their houses into the street. Then, having zealously paid homage to The Blessed One with the perfumes, flowers, and other offerings, and done him obeisance, some would implore him, "Reverend Sir, give us ten priests to feed;" some, "Give us twenty;" and some, "Give us a hundred priests." And they would take the bowl of The Blessed One, and prepare a seat for him, and zealously show their reverence for him by placing food in the bowl.

When he had finished his meal, The Blessed One, with due consideration for the different dispositions of their minds, would so teach them the Doctrine that some would become established in the refuges, some in the five precepts, some would become converted, some would attain to the fruit of either once returning, or of never returning, while some would become established in the highest fruit, that of saint-ship, and would retire from the world. Having shown this kindness to the multitude, he would rise from his seat, and return to the monastery.

---

[1] Compare Isaiah xl. 4: Every valley shall be exalted, and every mountain and hill shall be made low: . . . and the rough places plain.

On his arrival there, he would take his seat in a pavilion, on the excellent Buddha-mat which had been spread for him, where he would wait for the priests to finish their meal. When the priests had finished their meal, the body-servant would announce the fact to The Blessed One. Then The Blessed One would enter the perfumed chamber.

These, then, were his before-breakfast habits.

Then The Blessed One, having thus finished his before-breakfast duties, would first sit in the perfumed chamber, on a seat that had been spread for him by his body-servant, and would wash his feet. Then, taking up his stand on the landing of the jewelled staircase which led to the perfumed chamber, he would exhort the congregation of the priests, saying, —

" O priests, diligently work out your salvation; for not often occur the appearance of a Buddha in the world and existence among men[1] and the propitious moment and retirement from the world and the opportunity to hear the true Doctrine."

At this point some would ask The Blessed One for exercises in meditation, and The Blessed One would assign them exercises suited to their several characters. Then all would do obeisance to The Blessed One, and go to the places where they were in the habit of spending the night or the day — some to the forest, some to the foot of trees, some to the hills, and so on, some to the heaven of the four great kings, . . . and some to Vasavatti's heaven.

Then The Blessed One, entering the perfumed chamber, would, if he wished, lie down for a while, mindful and conscious, and on his right side after the manner of a lion. And secondly, his body being now refreshed, he would rise, and gaze over the world. And thirdly, the people of the village or town near which he might be dwelling, who had given him breakfast, would assemble after breakfast at the monastery, again in their best tunics and their best robes, and with perfumes, flowers, and other offerings.

---

[1] It is necessary to be a human being in order to attain to saintship, though gods can become converted and animals can keep the precepts. See pages 302, 279.

Thereupon The Blessed One, when his audience had assembled, would approach in such miraculous manner as was fitting; and taking his seat in the lecture-hall, on the excellent Buddha-mat which had been spread for him, he would teach the Doctrine, as suited the time and occasion. And when he perceived it was time, he would dismiss the audience, and the people would do obeisance to The Blessed One, and depart.

These were his after-breakfast habits.

When he had thus finished his after-breakfast duties, he would rise from the excellent Buddha-seat, and if he desired to bathe, he would enter the bath-house, and cool his limbs with water made ready by his body-servant. Then the body-servant would fetch the Buddha-seat, and spread it in the perfumed chamber. And The Blessed One, putting on a tunic of double red cloth, and binding on his girdle, and throwing his upper robe over his right shoulder, would go thither and sit down, and for a while remain solitary, and plunged in meditation. After that would come the priests from here and from there to wait on The Blessed One. And some would propound questions, some would ask for exercises in meditation, and some for a sermon; and in granting their desires The Blessed One would complete the first watch of the night.

These were his habits of the first watch of the night.

And now, when The Blessed One had finished his duties of the first watch of the night, and when the priests had done him obeisance and were departing, the deities throughout the entire system of ten thousand worlds would seize the opportunity to draw near to The Blessed One and ask him any questions that might occur to them, even such as were but four syllables long. And The Blessed One in answering their questions would complete the middle watch of the night.

These were his habits of the middle watch of the night.

The last watch of the night he would divide into three parts, and as his body would be tired from so much sitting since the morning, he would spend one part in pacing up

and down to free himself from the discomfort.   In the second
part he would enter the perfumed chamber, and would lie
down mindful and conscious, and on his right side after the
manner of a lion.   In the third part he would rise, and
taking his seat, he would gaze over the world with the eye
of a Buddha, in order to discover any individual who, under
some former Buddha, with alms-giving, or keeping the precepts, or other meritorious deeds, might have made the
earnest wish.

These were his habits of the last watch of the night.

---

§ 12. THE DEATH OF THE BUDDHA.

Translated from the Mahā-Parinibbāna-Sutta (v. and vi.) of the
Dīgha-Nikāya.

THEN The Blessed One addressed the venerable Ānanda : —
"Let us go hence, Ānanda.   To the further bank of the
Hiraññavatī river, and to the city of Kusinārā and the sal-
tree grove Upavattana of the Mallas will we draw near."

"Yes, Reverend Sir," said the venerable Ānanda to The
Blessed One in assent.

Then The Blessed One, accompanied by a large congregation of priests, drew near to the further bank of the Hiraññavatī river, and to the city of Kusinārā and the sal-tree
grove Upavattana of the Mallas ; and having drawn near, he
addressed the venerable Ānanda : —

"Be so good, Ānanda, as to spread me a couch with its
head to the north between twin sal-trees.   I am weary,
Ānanda, and wish to lie down."

"Yes, Reverend Sir," said the venerable Ānanda to The
Blessed One in assent, and spread the couch with its head to
the north between twin sal-trees.   Then The Blessed One
lay down on his right side after the manner of a lion, and
placing foot on foot, remained mindful and conscious.

Now at that time the twin sal-trees had completely burst
forth into bloom, though it was not the flowering season ;

and the blossoms scattered themselves over the body of The Tathāgata,[1] and strewed and sprinkled themselves in worship of The Tathāgata. Also heavenly Erythrina flowers fell from the sky; and these scattered themselves over the body of The Tathāgata, and strewed and sprinkled themselves in worship of The Tathāgata. Also heavenly sandal-wood powder fell from the sky; and this scattered itself over the body of The Tathāgata, and strewed and sprinkled itself in worship of The Tathāgata. And music sounded in the sky in worship of The Tathāgata, and heavenly choruses were heard to sing in worship of The Tathāgata.

Then The Blessed One addressed the venerable Ānanda: —

" The twin sal-trees, Ānanda, have completely burst forth into bloom, though it is not the flowering season; and the blossoms have scattered themselves over the body of The Tathāgata, and have strewn and sprinkled themselves in worship of The Tathāgata. Also heavenly Erythrina flowers have fallen from the sky; and these have scattered themselves over the body of The Tathāgata, and have strewn and sprinkled themselves in worship of The Tathāgata. Also heavenly sandal-wood powder has fallen from the sky; and this has scattered itself over the body of The Tathāgata, and has strewn and sprinkled itself in worship of The Tathāgata. Also music is sounding in the sky in worship of The Tathāgata, and heavenly choruses are heard to sing in worship of The Tathāgata. But it is not by all this, Ānanda, that The Tathāgata is honored, esteemed, revered, worshiped, or venerated; but the priest, Ānanda, or the priestess, or the lay disciple, or the female lay disciple, who shall fulfil all the greater and lesser duties, conducting himself with propriety and in accordance with the precepts, by him is The Tathāgata honored, esteemed, revered, and worshiped with the best of worship. Accordingly, Ānanda, train yourselves,

---

[1] Tathāgata is a term most commonly used by The Buddha in referring to himself. Its meaning, like that of its Jaina equivalent *Tatthagaya*, possibly is, " He who has arrived there (*tatra* or *tattha*), *i.e.* to emancipation *or* Nirvana." See " Sacred Books of the East," vol. xiii. p. 82.

and fulfil all the greater and lesser duties, and conduct yourselves with propriety and in accordance with the precepts."

Now at that time the venerable Upavāna was standing
in front of The Blessed One, and fanning him. Then The
Blessed One was harsh to the venerable Upavāna, saying, —

"Step aside, O priest; stand not in front of me."

Then it occurred to the venerable Ānanda as follows: —

" Here, this venerable Upavāna has for a long time been
the body-servant of The Blessed One, and kept himself at
his beck and call; yet, although his last moments are near,
The Blessed One is harsh to the venerable Upavāna, saying,
'Step aside, O priest; stand not in front of me.' What,
pray, was the reason, and what was the cause, that The
Blessed One was harsh to the venerable Upavāna, saying,
'Step aside, O priest; stand not in front of me'?"

Then the venerable Ānanda spoke to The Blessed One
as follows: —

" Reverend Sir, here this venerable Upavāna has for a
long time been the body-servant of The Blessed One, and
kept himself at his beck and call; yet, although his last moments are near, The Blessed One is harsh to the venerable
Upavāna, saying, 'Step aside, O priest; stand not in front
of me.' Reverend Sir, what, pray, was the reason, and what
was the cause, that The Blessed One was harsh to the venerable Upavāna, saying, 'Step aside, O priest; stand not in
front of me'?"

" Ānanda, almost all the deities throughout ten worlds
have come together to behold The Tathāgata. For an extent,
Ānanda, of twelve leagues about the city Kusinārā and the
sal-tree grove Upavattana of the Mallas, there is not a spot
of ground large enough to stick the point of a hair into,
that is not pervaded by powerful deities. And these deities,
Ānanda, are angered, saying, 'From afar have we come to
behold The Tathāgata, for but seldom, and on rare occasions,
does a Tathāgata, a saint, and Supreme Buddha arise in the
world; and now, to-night, in the last watch, will The Tathāgata pass into Nirvana; but this powerful priest stands in
front of The Blessed One, concealing him, and we have no

chance to see The Tathāgata, although his last moments are
near.' Thus, Ānanda, are these deities angered."

"What are the deities doing, Reverend Sir, whom The
Blessed One perceives?"

"Some of the deities, Ānanda, are in the air with their
minds engrossed by earthly things, and they let fly their hair
and cry aloud, and stretch out their arms and cry aloud, and
fall headlong to the ground and roll to and fro, saying, 'All
too soon will The Blessed One pass into Nirvana; all too
soon will The Happy One pass into Nirvana; all too soon
will The Light of the World vanish from sight!' Some of
the deities, Ānanda, are on the earth with their minds
engrossed by earthly things, and they let fly their hair and
cry aloud, and stretch out their arms and cry aloud, and fall
headlong on the ground and roll to and fro, saying, 'All too
soon will The Blessed One pass into Nirvana; all too soon
will The Happy One pass into Nirvana; all too soon will
The Light of the World vanish from sight.' But those
deities which are free from passion, mindful and conscious,
bear it patiently, saying, 'Transitory are all things. How is
it possible [that whatever has been born, has come into being,
and is organized and perishable, should not perish? That
condition is not possible.]'"

. . . .

(Chapter v., page 53¹⁶.)

Then the venerable Ānanda entered the monastery, and,
leaning against the bolt of the door, he wept, saying, —

"Behold, I am but a learner and not yet perfect, and my
Teacher is on the point of passing into Nirvana, he who was
so compassionate to me."

Then The Blessed One addressed the priests: —

"Where, O priests, is Ānanda?"

"Reverend Sir, the venerable Ānanda has entered the
monastery, and leaning against the bolt of the door, he weeps,
saying, 'Behold, I am but a learner, and not yet perfect, and
my Teacher is on the point of passing into Nirvana, he who
was so compassionate to me.'"

Then The Blessed One addressed a certain priest, saying, —

" Go, O priest, and say to the venerable Ānanda from me, ' The Teacher calleth thee, brother Ānanda.' "

" Yes, Reverend Sir," said the priest to The Blessed One in assent, and drew near to where the venerable Ānanda was; and having drawn near, he spoke to the venerable Ānanda as follows : —

" The Teacher calleth thee, brother Ānanda."

" Yes, brother," said the venerable Ānanda to the priest in assent, and drew near to where The Blessed One was; and having drawn near and greeted The Blessed One, he sat down respectfully at one side. And the venerable Ānanda being seated respectfully at one side, The Blessed One spoke to him as follows : —

" Enough, Ānanda, do not grieve, nor weep. Have I not already told you, Ānanda, that it is in the very nature of all things near and dear unto us that we must divide ourselves from them, leave them, sever ourselves from them ? How is it possible, Ānanda, that whatever has been born, has come into being, is organized and perishable, should not perish ? That condition is not possible. For a long time, Ānanda, have you waited on The Tathāgata with a kind, devoted, cheerful, single-hearted, unstinted service of body, with a kind, devoted, cheerful, single-hearted, unstinted service of voice, with a kind, devoted, cheerful, single-hearted, unstinted service of mind. You have acquired much merit, Ānanda ; exert yourself, and soon will you be free from all depravity."

Then The Blessed One addressed the priests : —

" Priests, of all those Blessed Ones who aforetime were saints and Supreme Buddhas, all had their favorite body-servants, just as I have now my Ānanda. And, priests, of all those Blessed Ones who in the future shall be saints and Supreme Buddhas, all will have their favorite body-servants, just as I have now my Ānanda. Wise, O priests, is Ānanda — he knows when it is a fit time to draw near to see The Tathāgata, whether for the priests, for the priestesses, for the lay disciples, for the female lay disciples, for the king, for the king's courtiers, for the leaders of heretical sects, or for their adherents.

"Ānanda, O priests, has four wonderful and marvellous qualities. And what are the four? O priests, if an assembly of priests draw near to behold Ānanda, it is delighted with beholding him; and if then Ānanda hold a discourse on the Doctrine, it is also delighted with the discourse; and when Ānanda, O priests, ceases to speak, the assembly of priests is still unsated. O priests, if an assembly of priestesses . . . an assembly of lay disciples . . . an assembly of female lay disciples draw near to behold Ānanda, it is delighted with beholding him; and if then Ānanda hold a discourse on the Doctrine, it is also delighted with the discourse; and when Ānanda, O priests, ceases to speak, the assembly of female lay disciples is still unsated.

"A Universal Monarch, O priests, has four wonderful and marvellous qualities. And what are the four? O priests, if an assembly of men of the warrior caste . . . an assembly of men of the Brahman caste . . . an assembly of householders . . . an assembly of monks draw near to behold the Universal Monarch, it is delighted with beholding him; and if then the Universal Monarch hold a discourse, it is also delighted with the discourse; and when the Universal Monarch, O priests, ceases to speak, the assembly of monks is still unsated.

"In exactly the same way, O priests, Ānanda has four wonderful and marvellous qualities. O priests, if an assembly of priests . . . an assembly of priestesses . . . an assembly of lay disciples . . . an assembly of female lay disciples draw near to behold Ānanda, it is delighted with beholding him; and if then Ānanda hold a discourse on the Doctrine, it is also delighted with the discourse; and when Ānanda, O priests, ceases to speak, the assembly of female lay disciples is still unsated. These, O priests, are the four wonderful and marvellous qualities possessed by Ānanda."

When The Blessed One had thus spoken, the venerable Ānanda spoke to him as follows: —

"Reverend Sir, let not The Blessed One pass into Nirvana

in this wattle-and-daub town, this town of the jungle, this branch village. For there are other great cities, Reverend Sir, to wit, Campā, Rājagaha, Sāvatthi, Sāketa, Kosaṁbī, and Benares. Let The Blessed One pass into Nirvana in one of them. In them are many wealthy men of the warrior caste, many wealthy men of the Brahman caste, and many wealthy householders who are firm believers in The Tathāgata, and they will perform the funeral rites for The Tathāgata."

"O Ānanda, say not so! O Ānanda, say not so, that this is a wattle-and-daub town, a town of the jungle, a branch village. There was once, Ānanda, a king called Sudassana the Great, who was a Universal Monarch, a virtuous king of justice, a victorious ruler of the four quarters of the earth, possessing a secure dominion over his territory and owning the seven precious gems.[1] This city Kusinārā, Ānanda, was the capital of king Sudassana the Great, and had then the name of Kusāvatī. From the east to the west it was twelve leagues in length, and from the north to the south it was seven leagues in breadth. Kusāvatī, the capital, Ānanda, was prosperous and flourishing, populous and thronging with people, and well provided with food. As Ālakamandā, the capital of the gods, Ānanda, is prosperous and flourishing, populous and thronging with gods, and is well provided with food, in exactly the same way, Ānanda, Kusāvatī, the capital, was prosperous and flourishing, populous and thronging with people, and well provided with food. Kusāvatī, the capital, Ānanda, was neither by day nor night without the ten noises, — to wit, the noise of elephants, the noise of horses, the noise of chariots, the noise of drums, the noise of tabors, the noise of lutes, the noise of song, the noise of cymbals, the noise of gongs, and the tenth noise of people crying, 'Eat ye, and drink!'

"Go thou, Ānanda, and enter the city Kusinārā, and announce to the Kusinārā-Mallas: —

"'To-night, O ye Vāseṭṭhas, in the last watch, The

---

[1] The wheel of empire, the elephant, the horse, the gem, the empress, the treasurer, and the crown-prince.

Tathāgata will pass into Nirvana. Be favorable, be favorable, O ye Vāseṭṭhas, and suffer not that afterwards ye feel remorse, saying, " The Tathāgata passed into Nirvana while in our borders, but we did not avail ourselves of the opportunity of being present at the last moments of The Tathāgata." ' "

" Yes, Reverend Sir," said the venerable Ānanda to The Blessed One in assent; and putting on his tunic, and taking his bowl and his robes, he went to Kusinārā with another member of the Order.

Now at that time the Kusinārā-Mallas were assembled together in the town-hall on some matter of business. And the venerable Ānanda drew near to the town-hall of the Kusinārā-Mallas; and having drawn near, he made announcement to the Kusinārā-Mallas, as follows : —

" To-night, O ye Vāseṭṭhas, in the last watch, The Tathāgata will pass into Nirvana. Be favorable, be favorable, O ye Vāseṭṭhas, and suffer not that afterwards ye feel remorse, saying, ' The Tathāgata passed into Nirvana while in our borders, but we did not avail ourselves of the opportunity of being present at the last moments of The Tathāgata.' "

The Mallas, on hearing this speech of the venerable Ānanda, and their children and their daughters-in-law and their wives were grieved and sorrowful and overwhelmed with anguish of mind, and some let fly their hair and cried aloud, and stretched out their arms and cried aloud, and fell headlong to the ground and rolled to and fro, saying, " All too soon will The Blessed One pass into Nirvana; all too soon will The Happy One pass into Nirvana ; all too soon will The Light of the World vanish from sight." Then the Mallas and their children and their daughters-in-law and their wives, being grieved and sorrowful and overwhelmed with anguish of mind, drew near to the sal-tree grove Upavattana of the Mallas, and to where the venerable Ānanda was.

Then it occurred to the venerable Ānanda as follows : —

" If I shall cause the Kusinārā-Mallas one by one to do reverence to The Blessed One, the day will dawn ere they have finished. What if now I marshal the Mallas by families, and cause them by families to do reverence to The Blessed One, and say, ' Reverend Sir, a Malla named so-and-so, with his children, his wife, his following, and his friends, bows low in reverence at the feet of The Blessed One.' "

And the venerable Ānanda marshalled the Mallas by families, and caused them by families to do reverence to The Blessed One, saying, " Reverend Sir, a Malla named so-and-so, with his children, his wife, his following, and his friends, bows low in reverence at the feet of The Blessed One." And the venerable Ānanda by this device succeeded in causing all the Kusinārā-Mallas to do reverence to The Blessed One before the end of the first watch of the night.

Now at that time Subhadda, a wandering ascetic, was dwelling at Kusinārā. And Subhadda, the wandering ascetic, heard the report : —

" To-night, in the last watch, the monk Gotama will pass into Nirvana."

Then it occurred to Subhadda, the wandering ascetic, as follows : —

" I have heard wandering ascetics, that were old men, advanced in years, teachers, and teachers' teachers, declare, ' But seldom, and on rare occasions, does a Tathāgata, a saint, and Supreme Buddha arise in the world.' And to-night, in the last watch, the monk Gotama will pass into Nirvana. And a certain question has arisen in my mind, and I am persuaded of the monk Gotama that he can so teach me the Doctrine that I shall be relieved of this my doubt."

Then Subhadda, the wandering ascetic, drew near to the sal-tree grove Upavattana of the Mallas, and to where the venerable Ānanda was, and having drawn near, he spoke to the venerable Ānanda as follows : —

" Ānanda, I have heard wandering ascetics, that were old men, advanced in years, teachers, and teachers' teachers, declare, ' But seldom, and on rare occasions, does a Tathāgata, a saint, and Supreme Buddha arise in the world.' And to-night, in the last watch, the monk Gotama will pass into Nirvana. And a certain doubt has arisen in my mind, and I am persuaded of the monk Gotama that he can so teach

me the Doctrine that I shall be relieved of this my doubt.
Let me, then, Ānanda, have an opportunity of seeing the
monk Gotama."

When Subhadda, the wandering ascetic, had so spoken,
the venerable Ānanda spoke to him as follows: —

"Enough of that, brother Subhadda; trouble not The
Tathāgata. The Blessed One is weary."

And a second time Subhadda, the wandering ascetic, . . .

And a third time Subhadda, the wandering ascetic, spoke
to the venerable Ānanda as follows: —

"Ānanda, I have heard wandering ascetics, old men,
advanced in years, teachers, and teachers' teachers, when
they said, 'But seldom, and on rare occasions, does a Tathāgata, a saint, and Supreme Buddha arise in the world.' And
to-night, in the last watch, the monk Gotama will pass into
Nirvana. And a certain doubt has arisen in my mind, and
I am persuaded of the monk Gotama that he can so teach
me the Doctrine that I shall be relieved of this my doubt.
Let me, then, Ānanda, have an opportunity of seeing the
monk Gotama."

And a third time the venerable Ānanda spoke to Subhadda, the wandering ascetic, as follows: —

"Enough of that, brother Subhadda; trouble not The
Tathāgata. The Blessed One is weary."

Now The Blessed One chanced to hear the conversation
between the venerable Ānanda and the wandering ascetic
Subhadda. And The Blessed One called to the venerable
Ānanda: —

"Enough, Ānanda; hinder not Subhadda. Let Subhadda,
Ānanda, have an opportunity of beholding The Tathāgata.
Whatever Subhadda shall ask of me, he will ask for the sake
of information, and not for the sake of troubling me, and he
will quickly understand my answers to his questions."

Then the venerable Ānanda spoke to Subhadda, the
wandering ascetic, as follows: —

"You may come, brother Subhadda; The Blessed One
grants you an audience."

Then Subhadda, the wandering ascetic, drew near to

where The Blessed One was; and having drawn near, he exchanged greetings with The Blessed One; and having passed with him the greetings of friendship and civility, he sat down respectfully at one side. And seated respectfully at one side, Subhadda, the wandering ascetic, spoke to The Blessed One as follows: —

" Gotama, all those monks and Brahmans who possess a large following and crowds of hearers and disciples, and who are distinguished, renowned leaders of sects, and highly esteemed by the multitudes, — to wit, Pūraṇa Kassapa, Makkhali Gosāla, Ajita Kesakambali, Pakudha Kaccāyana, Sañjaya Belaṭṭhiputta, Nigaṇṭha Nāthaputta, — have they all done as they maintain, discovered the truth, or have they not? or have some of them done so, and others not? "

" Enough, O Subhadda; let us leave the question, ' Have they all done as they maintain, discovered the truth, or have they not? or have some of them done so, and others not? ' The Doctrine will I teach you, Subhadda. Listen to me, and pay strict attention, and I will speak."

" Yes, Reverend Sir," said Subhadda, the wandering ascetic, to The Blessed One in assent. And The Blessed One spoke as follows: —

"Subhadda, in whatever doctrine and discipline the noble eightfold path is not found, therein also is not found the monk of the first degree, nor the monk of the second degree, nor the monk of the third degree, nor the monk of the fourth degree; and in whatever doctrine and discipline, O Subhadda, the noble eightfold path is found, therein also are found the monk of the first degree, and the monk of the second degree, and the monk of the third degree, and the monk of the fourth degree. Now in this Doctrine and Discipline, O Subhadda, the noble eightfold path is found: and therein alone, O Subhadda, are found the monk of the first degree, and the monk of the second degree, and the monk of the third degree, and the monk of the fourth degree. Destitute of true monks are all other creeds. But let these my priests, O Subhadda, live rightly, and the world will not be destitute of saints.

" What time my age was twenty-nine, Subhadda,
I left the world to seek the summum bonum.
Now fifty years and more have passed, Subhadda,
Since I renounced the world and lived ascetic
Within the Doctrine's pale, that rule of conduct
Outside of which no genuine monk existeth,

nor the monk of the second degree, nor the monk of the
third degree, nor the monk of the fourth degree. Destitute
of monks are all other creeds. But let these my priests, O
Subhadda, live rightly, and the world will not be destitute of
saints."

When The Blessed One had thus spoken, Subhadda, the
wandering ascetic, spoke to him as follows : —

" O wonderful is it, Reverend Sir! O wonderful is it,
Reverend Sir! It is as if, Reverend Sir, one were to set up
that which was overturned, or were to disclose that which
was hidden, or were to point out the way to a lost traveller,
or were to carry a lamp into a dark place that they who had
eyes might see forms. Even so has The Blessed One expounded the Doctrine in many different ways. Reverend
Sir, I betake myself to The Blessed One for refuge, to the
Doctrine, and to the Congregation of the priests. Suffer me
to retire from the world under The Blessed One ; suffer me
to receive ordination."

" Subhadda, any one who aforetime has been an adher-
ent of another sect and afterwards desires to retire from the
world and receive ordination under this Doctrine and Discipline, must first spend four months on probation ; and after
the lapse of four months, strenuous-minded priests receive him
into the Order and confer on him the priestly ordination.
Nevertheless, in this matter of probation I recognize a difference in persons."

" Reverend Sir, if all they who aforetime have been adherents of other sects and afterwards desire to retire from the
world and receive ordination under this Doctrine and Discipline, must first spend four months on probation, and after the
lapse of four months strenuous-minded priests receive them
into the Order, and confer on them the priestly ordination,

then am I ready to spend four years on probation, and after the lapse of four years, let strenuous-minded priests᾽receive me into the Order and confer on me the priestly ordination."

Then The Blessed One said to the venerable Ānanda,

" Well, then, Ānanda, receive Subhadda into the Order."

" Yes, Reverend Sir," said the venerable Ānanda to The Blessed One in assent.

Then Subhadda, the wandering ascetic, spoke to the venerable Ānanda as follows : —

" How fortunate you priests are, brother Ānanda ! How supremely fortunate, brother Ānanda, that you all have been sprinkled with the sprinkling of discipleship at the hands of The Teacher himself."

And Subhadda, the wandering ascetic, retired from the world under The Blessed One, and received ordination. And without delay, after he had received ordination, the venerable Subhadda began to live solitary and retired, vigilant, strenuous, and zealous ; and in no long time, and while yet alive, he came to learn for himself, and to realize, and to live in the possession of that highest good to which the holy life conducts, and for the sake of which youths of good family so nobly retire from the household life to the houseless one. And he knew that for him rebirth was exhausted, that he had lived the holy life, that he had done what it behooved him to do, and that he was no more for this world.   So the venerable Subhadda became of the number of the saints, and he was the last disciple made by The Blessed One himself.

End of the Hiraññavatī Recitation, which is the Fifth.

Then The Blessed One addressed the venerable Ānanda : —

" It may be, Ānanda, that some of you will think, ' The word of The Teacher is a thing of the past ; we have now no Teacher.'   But that, Ānanda, is not the correct view.   The Doctrine and Discipline, Ānanda, which I have taught and enjoined upon you is to be your teacher when I am gone. But whereas now, Ānanda, all the priests address each other with the title of ' brother,' not so must they address each other after I am gone.   A senior priest, Ānanda, is to address a junior priest either by his given name, or by his family name, or by the title of 'brother;' a junior priest is to address a senior priest with the title 'reverend sir,' or 'venerable.' If the Order, Ānanda, wish to do so, after I am gone they may abrogate all the lesser and minor precepts. On Channa,[1] Ānanda, after I am gone, the higher penalty is to be inflicted."

"Reverend Sir, what is this higher penalty?"

"Let Channa, Ānanda, say what he likes, he is not to be spoken to nor admonished nor instructed by the priests."

Then The Blessed One addressed the priests : —

"It may be, O priests, that some priest has a doubt or perplexity respecting either The Buddha or the Doctrine or the Order or the Path or the course of conduct. Ask any questions, O priests, and suffer not that afterwards ye feel remorse, saying, 'Our Teacher was present with us, but we failed to ask him all our questions.'"

When he had so spoken, the priests remained silent.

And a second time The Blessed One, and a third time The Blessed One addressed the priests : —

"It may be, O priests, that some priest has a doubt or perplexity respecting either The Buddha or the Doctrine or the Order or the Path or the course of conduct. Ask any question, O priests, and suffer not that afterwards ye feel remorse, saying, 'Our Teacher was present with us, but we failed to ask him all our questions.'"

And a third time the priests remained silent.

Then The Blessed One addressed the priests : —

"It may be, O priests, that it is out of respect to The Teacher that ye ask no questions. Then let each one speak to his friend."

And when he had thus spoken, the priests remained silent.

Then the venerable Ānanda spoke to The Blessed One as follows : —

"It is wonderful, Reverend Sir! It is marvellous, Rev-

---

[1] Not the Channa who had been the Future Buddha's charioteer.

erend Sir! Reverend Sir, I have faith to believe that in this
congregation of priests not a single priest has a doubt or
perplexity respecting either The Buddha or the Doctrine or
the Order or the Path or the course of conduct."

"With you, Ānanda, it is a matter of faith, when you say
that; but with The Tathāgata, Ānanda, it is a matter of
knowledge that in this congregation of priests not a single
priest has a doubt or perplexity respecting either The Buddha
or the Doctrine or the Order or the Path or the course of
conduct. For of all these five hundred priests, Ānanda, the
most backward one has become converted, and is not liable
to pass into a lower state of existence, but is destined necessarily to attain supreme wisdom."

Then The Blessed One addressed the priests : —

"And now, O priests, I take my leave of you; all the
constituents of being are transitory; work out your salvation
with diligence."

And this was the last word of The Tathāgata.

Thereupon The Blessed One entered the first trance; and
rising from the first trance, he entered the second trance;
and rising from the second trance, he entered the third
trance; and rising from the third trance, he entered the
fourth trance; and rising from the fourth trance, he entered
the realm of the infinity of space ; and rising from the realm
of the infinity of space, he entered the realm of the infinity
of consciousness ; and rising from the realm of the infinity of
consciousness, he entered the realm of nothingness; and
rising from the realm of nothingness, he entered the realm of
neither perception nor yet non-perception ; and rising from
the realm of neither perception nor yet non-perception, he
arrived at the cessation of perception and sensation.

Thereupon the venerable Ānanda spoke to the venerable
Anuruddha as follows : —

"Reverend Anuruddha, The Blessed One has passed into
Nirvana."

"Nay, brother Ānanda, The Blessed One has not passed
into Nirvana; he has arrived at the cessation of perception
and sensation."

Thereupon The Blessed One rising from the cessation of his perception and sensation, entered the realm of neither perception nor yet non-perception; and rising from the realm of neither perception nor yet non-perception, he entered the realm of nothingness; and rising from the realm of nothingness, he entered the realm of the infinity of consciousness; and rising from the realm of the infinity of consciousness, he entered the realm of the infinity of space; and rising from the realm of the infinity of space, he entered the fourth trance; and rising from the fourth trance, he entered the third trance; and rising from the third trance, he entered the second trance; and rising from the second trance, he entered the first trance; and rising from the first trance, he entered the second trance; and rising from the second trance, he entered the third trance; and rising from the third trance, he entered the fourth trance; and rising from the fourth trance, immediately The Blessed One passed into Nirvana.

CHAPTER II.

SENTIENT EXISTENCE.

INTRODUCTORY DISCOURSE.

THE word Ego, when it occurs in this book, usually translates Pāli *attan*, Sanskrit *ātman*. It is more literally rendered Self; but I have preferred the word Ego, as the reader is not thereby led astray into thinking of the Brahmanical Universal Self and kindred doctrines. Buddhist doctrine is quite different and negative, as the reader will see. In selection § 15 *a*, however, Ego represents Pāli *puggala*, a word I sometimes render by 'individual,' as, for example, throughout selection § 40 *b*.

In the first two selections of this chapter occurs a list of ten theories which have caused considerable trouble, not merely, as may be supposed, to their original propounders, but to modern students of Pāli Buddhism. This latter-day anxiety, however, concerns itself not so much with their truth, as with the question, what was really the precise attitude of The Buddha with respect to them. Did he claim to know the truth concerning them, but refuse to tell; or did they lie entirely outside of the scope of his philosophy; or what other reason could he have for refusing to discuss them? Now I think that all these questions are left unanswered for the same reasons. If the reader will compare these two selections with selection § 15 *d*, and in particular note the next to the last paragraph on page 141, I think that he will see that The Buddha considered all such questions to be out of court.

All the questions (even perhaps the two concerning the finiteness or the infinity of the world) take for granted what he denies. Hence he refuses to give a Yes or No answer, just as any one of us might be excused for doing, in case any one were to be so impolite as to ask, " Have you left off beating your mother?" The truth of no one of these theories could be allowed. They were one and all heretical and incompatible with his doctrine. In proof of this, see selection § 15 *d* and page 167. But The Buddha also objected to these questions as being metaphysical ones and betraying a speculative spirit on the part of those who asked them. His was a purely practical aim, and his arguments *à posteriori*. If he taught his disciples the truth concerning misery and how misery could be made to cease, he thought that should suffice, and cared not to go deeper into ultimate questions than was sufficient for that end. This, I take it, is the reason why at the end of § 67 The Buddha objected to the form of the priest's question concerning the four elements. For The Buddha's way of putting the question does not appear to me so very different; but he added to it so as to make it apply to the living being.

The Buddha's system was a religious one, his philosophy an applied philosophy; and in the sermons and sayings attributed directly to The Buddha there is but little metaphysics that does not have a direct and practical bearing. Hence it is that I have given to this chapter the caption Sentient Existence. By this phrase, I in no way intend to imply that the doctrines herein advanced have no application to the inanimate world, but as The Buddha in his teachings kept constantly in mind the welfare of what had the capability of suffering, of undergoing rebirth, I find but little to insert concerning inorganic nature. Section 24, which bears directly on the subject, is not taken from the Tipiṭaka, but from the Visuddhi-Magga, a work that endeavors to be systematically complete.

Here I would call the reader's attention to the Three Characteristics which I have placed at the head of this book, as giving the Buddhist pessimistic analysis of the universe. The Three Characteristics are applicable to inanimate as well as to animate nature. This makes it hard to translate the third Characteristic, as what is translated by Ego in the case of sentient beings cannot so be rendered in the case of life-less things, but some such phrase as an underlying persistent reality (*substantia*) must be employed. This question of an Ego in sentient beings or of an underlying persistent reality in inanimate matter is of the last importance in Buddhism. Unless the thesis of this chapter be true, the scheme of salva-tion elaborated in the fourth chapter is impossible. Hence the reader will find this subject taken up in this and the two following chapters with perhaps wearying iteration. A very curious and instructive parallel can here be drawn between Buddhism and the teachings of modern science. All evolu-tion of animate nature can be characterized as a process of self-integration or assertion of self through countless genera-tions. The Buddhists make a similar statement; only they say that a man inherits from himself, and do not bring in the scientific doctrine of heredity, or inheritance from others. If such is the origin of the sentient being, then, naturally, the disintegration of self will cause dissolution, as the fourth chapter will explain.

I hope that the reader will be able to make out the Bud-dhist theory of existence. It does not appear to me that it corresponds to either τὸ ὄν or τὸ γιγνόμενον, nor yet is it nihil-ism, that is to say, a doctrine of unreality. The human being is composed of five groups, so-called because they each consist of many independent elements. In the case of the

sensation-group, these elements of being are said to be consecutive in time, but in other cases many members of one
group can occur at the same time; for instance, it is stated in
the Visuddhi-Magga that over thirty predispositions occur in
conjunction with the first of the eighty-nine consciousnesses.
Now each of the elements that together form a group is an
independent existence, and is real enough while it lasts.
All things we know of are formed from one or more of
these groups. When milk changes to sour cream, Buddhist
doctrine does not say that an underlying substance has entered on a new mode or phase of being, but that we have a
new existence, or rather, perhaps, a new existence-complex,
— that is to say, that the elements of the form-group that
now compose the sour cream are not the same as those that
composed the milk, the elements that composed the milk
having passed away and new ones having come into being.
This is what is intended in § 24, when it says, " This form
in the series of forms belonging to its own nature." It
would appear from page 151 that the form-group contains
tolerably persistent elements, while those of the mental
groups are momentary and more easily overcome. So far as
the mental groups are concerned, Nirvana can be obtained in
the present life, but from the form-group deliverance can
only be attained at death, because, as stated on page 156,
" whereas there are sensations, perceptions, etc. [i. e. predispositions and consciousnesses] which are not subject to
depravity, it is not so with form."

Having explained the nature of the human being as consisting of the five groups, the next thing to be done is to
show the causes of these five groups and how their several
series are perpetuated. All this, too, must be done without
recourse being had to what we call a First Cause. This gives
occasion for an elaborate theory which is expressed in the

formula of Dependent Origination (Pāli paṭiccasamuppāda), also called the middle doctrine, as avoiding the doctrine of τὸ ὄν on the one hand, and of nihilism or the denial of the reality of existence on the other. The Buddhist Sacred Books seem to claim Dependent Origination as the peculiar discovery of The Buddha, and I suppose they would have us understand that he invented the whole formula from beginning to end. But it is to be observed that the formula repeats itself, that the human being is brought into existence twice — the first time under the name of consciousness and name and form and by means of ignorance and karma, the second time in birth and by means of desire (with its four branches called attachments) and karma again, this time called existence. See § 35. Therefore, though Buddhaghosa, as the reader will see, is at great pains to explain this repetition as purposely intended for practical ends, yet one is much inclined to surmise that the full formula in its present shape is a piece of patchwork put together of two or more that were current in The Buddha's time and by him — perhaps expanded, perhaps contracted, but at any rate — made into one. If The Buddha added to the formula of Dependent Origination, it would appear that the addition consisted in the first two propositions. For ignorance, of course, is the opposite of wisdom, and wisdom, or the third discipline, that is to say, the method for getting rid of ignorance, is, as the reader will see in the Introductory Discourse to the fourth chapter and elsewhere in this book, The Buddha's particular contribution to the science of meditation; whereas concentration, or the second discipline, the method for opposing desire, he had learnt from his teachers. In § 37 these first two propositions are omitted, and consciousness and name-and-form of the third proposition are made mutually dependent.

The same antithesis of ignorance and desire appears also to

be present in the threefold fire of lust, hatred, and infatuation, where lust and hatred can be viewed as but the two opposite poles of the same feeling and will then together stand for desire, while infatuation will represent ignorance.

In addition to my remarks on *attan* and *puggala* above, it may be well to say a few words in regard to my translations of some other Pāli terms. "Elements of being" (*dhamma*) and "constituents of being" (*sankhāra*) are often used synonymously to mean the individual components of the Five Groups; but when *dhamma* refers to the twelve terms of the formula, Dependent Origination, I have sometimes used the phrase "factors of being." The two terms *dhamma* and *sankhāra* are very troublesome to render into English, both because they each of them mean so many things and because their ground meaning is not translatable into English, being expressive of a different philosophy. *Sankhāra* means what makes or what is made, fashioned, or put together: we should naturally with our different beliefs say, creator and created things. Everything except Nirvana and space is *sankhāra*. *Sankhāra* as a name for the fourth group, I translate by predispositions; as the second term in Dependent Origination, by karma. *Dhamma* means any established law, condition, or fact, either of nature or of human institutions. It is the word I render by Doctrine when it signifies The Buddha's teachings. This word *dhamma* occasioned me especial difficulty when used in § 74 to characterize the subjects of the Fourth Contemplation. But although "elements of being" is a bad rendering, the reader need not be led astray, as all the different things denoted by it are there enumerated.

§ 13.   QUESTIONS WHICH TEND NOT TO EDIFICATION.

Sermon Number 1.

§ 13 *a*. — Translated from the Majjhima-Nikāya, and constituting Sutta 63.

Thus have I heard.

On a certain occasion The Blessed One was dwelling at Sāvatthi in Jetavana monastery in Anāthapiṇḍika's Park. Now it happened to the venerable Māluṅkyāputta, being in seclusion and plunged in meditation, that a consideration presented itself to his mind, as follows : —

"These theories which The Blessed One has left elucidated, has set aside and rejected, — that the world is eternal, that the world is not eternal, that the world is finite, that the world is infinite, that the soul and the body are identical, that the soul is one thing and the body another, that the saint exists after death, that the saint does not exist after death, that the saint both exists and does not exist after death, that the saint neither exists nor does not exist after death, — these The Blessed One does not elucidate to me. And the fact that The Blessed One does not elucidate them to me does not please me nor suit me. Therefore I will draw near to The Blessed One and inquire of him concerning this matter. If The Blessed One will elucidate to me, either that the world is eternal, or that the world is not eternal, or that the world is finite, or that the world is infinite, or that the soul and the body are identical, or that the soul is one thing and the body another, or that the saint exists after death, or that the saint does not exist after death, or that the saint both exists and does not exist after death, or that the saint neither exists nor does not exist after death, in that case will I lead the religious life under The Blessed One. If The Blessed One will not elucidate to me, either that the world is eternal, or that the world is not eternal, . . . or that the saint neither exists

nor does not exist after death, in that case will I abandon
religious training and return to the lower life of a layman."

Then the venerable Māluṅkyāputta arose at eventide from
his seclusion, and drew near to where The Blessed One was;
and having drawn near and greeted The Blessed One, he sat
down respectfully at one side. And seated respectfully at
one side, the venerable Māluṅkyāputta spoke to The Blessed
One as follows: —

"Reverend Sir, it happened to me, as I was just now in
seclusion and plunged in meditation, that a consideration presented itself to my mind, as follows: 'These theories which
The Blessed One has left unelucidated, has set aside and rejected, — that the world is eternal, that the world is not eternal, . . . that the saint neither exists nor does not exist
after death, — these The Blessed One does not elucidate to
me. And the fact that The Blessed One does not elucidate
them to me does not please me nor suit me. I will draw near
to The Blessed One and inquire of him concerning this matter.
If The Blessed One will elucidate to me, either that the world
is eternal, or that the world is not eternal, . . . or that the
saint neither exists nor does not exist after death, in that case
will I lead the religious life under The Blessed One. If The
Blessed One will not elucidate to me, either that the world is
eternal, or that the world is not eternal, . . . or that the saint
neither exists nor does not exist after death, in that case
will I abandon religious training and return to the lower life
of a layman.'

"If The Blessed One knows that the world is eternal, let
The Blessed One elucidate to me that the world is eternal;
if The Blessed One knows that the world is not eternal, let
The Blessed One elucidate to me that the world is not eternal. If The Blessed One does not know either that the world
is eternal or that the world is not eternal, the only upright
thing for one who does not know, or who has not that insight,
is to say, 'I do not know; I have not that insight.'

"If The Blessed One knows that the world is finite, . . . '

"If The Blessed One knows that the soul and the body
are identical, . . . '

" If The Blessed One knows that the saint exists after death, . . . '

" If The Blessed One knows that the saint both exists and does not exist after death, let The Blessed One elucidate to me that the saint both exists and does not exist after death ; if The Blessed One knows that the saint neither exists nor does not exist after death, let The Blessed One elucidate to me that the saint neither exists nor does not exist after death. If The Blessed One does not know either that the saint both exists and does not exist after death, or that the saint neither exists nor does not exist after death, the only upright thing for one who does not know, or who has not that insight, is to say, ' I do not know ; I have not that insight.' "

" Pray, Māluṅkyāputta, did I ever say to you, ' Come, Māluṅkyāputta, lead the religious life under me, and I will elucidate to you either that the world is eternal, or that the world is not eternal, . . . or that the saint neither exists nor does not exist after death ' ? "

" Nay, verily, Reverend Sir."

" Or did you ever say to me, ' Reverend Sir, I will lead the religious life under The Blessed One, on condition that The Blessed One elucidate to me either that the world is eternal, or that the world is not eternal, . . . or that the saint neither exists nor does not exist after death ' ? "

" Nay, verily, Reverend Sir."

" So you acknowledge, Māluṅkyāputta, that I have not said to you, ' Come, Māluṅkyāputta, lead the religious life under me and I will elucidate to you either that the world is eternal, or that the world is not eternal, . . . or that the saint neither exists nor does not exist after death ; ' and again that you have not said to me, ' Reverend Sir, I will lead the religious life under The Blessed One, on condition that The Blessed One elucidate to me either that the world is eternal, or that the world is not eternal, . . . or that the saint neither exists nor does not exist after death.' That being the case, vain man, whom are you so angrily denouncing ?

" Māluṅkyāputta, any one who should say, ' I will not lead the religious life under The Blessed One until The

Blessed One shall elucidate to me either that the world is eternal, or that the world is not eternal, . . . or that the saint neither exists nor does not exist after death;' — that person would die, Mālunkyāputta, before The Tathāgata had ever elucidated this to him.

"It is as if, Mālunkyāputta, a man had been wounded by an arrow thickly smeared with poison, and his friends and companions, his relatives and kinsfolk, were to procure for him a physician or surgeon; and the sick man were to say, 'I will not have this arrow taken out until I have learnt whether the man who wounded me belonged to the warrior caste, or to the Brahman caste, or to the agricultural caste, or to the menial caste.'

"Or again he were to say, 'I will not have this arrow taken out until I have learnt the name of the man who wounded me, and to what clan he belongs.'

"Or again he were to say, 'I will not have this arrow taken out until I have learnt whether the man who wounded me was tall, or short, or of the middle height.'

"Or again he were to say, 'I will not have this arrow taken out until I have learnt whether the man who wounded me was black, or dusky, or of a yellow skin.'

"Or again he were to say, 'I will not have this arrow taken out until I have learnt whether the man who wounded me was from this or that village, or town, or city.'

"Or again he were to say, 'I will not have this arrow taken out until I have learnt whether the bow which wounded me was a cāpa, or a kodanda.'

"Or again he were to say, 'I will not have this arrow taken out until I have learnt whether the bow-string which wounded me was made from swallow-wort, or bamboo, or sinew, or maruva, or from milk-weed.'

"Or again he were to say, 'I will not have this arrow taken out until I have learnt whether the shaft which wounded me was a kaccha or a ropima.'

"Or again he were to say, 'I will not have this arrow taken out until I have learnt whether the shaft which wounded me was feathered from the wings of a vulture, or of a heron, or of a falcon, or of a peacock, or of a sithilahanu.'

" Or again he were to say, 'I will not have this arrow taken out until I have learnt whether the shaft which wounded me was wound round with the sinews of an ox, or of a buffalo, or of a ruru deer, or of a monkey.'

" Or again he were to say, 'I will not have this arrow taken out until I have learnt whether the arrow which wounded me was an ordinary arrow, or a claw-headed arrow, or a vekaṇḍa, or an iron arrow, or a calf-tooth arrow, or a karavīrapatta.' That man would die, Māluṅkyāputta, without ever having learnt this.

" In exactly the same way, Māluṅkyāputta, any one who should say, 'I will not lead the religious life under The Blessed One until The Blessed One shall elucidate to me either that the world is eternal, or that the world is not eternal, . . . or that the saint neither exists nor does not exist after death;'—that person would die, Māluṅkyāputta, before The Tathāgata had ever elucidated this to him.

" The religious life, Māluṅkyāputta, does not depend on the dogma that the world is eternal; nor does the religious life, Māluṅkyāputta, depend on the dogma that the world is not eternal. Whether the dogma obtain, Māluṅkyāputta, that the world is eternal, or that the world is not eternal, there still remain birth, old age, death, sorrow, lamentation, misery, grief, and despair, for the extinction of which in the present life I am prescribing.

" The religious life, Māluṅkyāputta, does not depend on the dogma that the world is finite; . . .

" The religious life, Māluṅkyāputta, does not depend on the dogma that the soul and the body are identical; . . .

" The religious life, Māluṅkyāputta, does not depend on the dogma that the saint exists after death; . . .

" The religious life, Māluṅkyāputta, does not depend on the dogma that the saint both exists and does not exist after death; nor does the religious life, Māluṅkyāputta, depend on the dogma that the saint neither exists nor does not exist after death. Whether the dogma obtain, Māluṅkyāputta, that the

saint both exists and does not exist after death, or that the
saint neither exists nor does not exist after death, there still
remain birth, old age, death, sorrow, lamentation, misery,
grief, and despair, for the extinction of which in the present
life I am prescribing.

"Accordingly, Māluṅkyāputta, bear always in mind what
it is that I have not elucidated, and what it is that I have elucidated. And what, Māluṅkyāputta, have I not elucidated?
I have not elucidated, Māluṅkyāputta, that the world is eternal; I have not elucidated that the world is not eternal; I
have not elucidated that the world is finite; I have not elucidated that the world is infinite; I have not elucidated that
the soul and the body are identical; I have not elucidated that
the soul is one thing and the body another; I have not elucidated that the saint exists after death; I have not elucidated
that the saint does not exist after death; I have not elucidated
that the saint both exists and does not exist after death; I
have not elucidated that the saint neither exists nor does not
exist after death. And why, Māluṅkyāputta, have I not
elucidated this? Because, Māluṅkyāputta, this profits not,
nor has to do with the fundamentals of religion, nor tends to
aversion, absence of passion, cessation, quiescence, the supernatural faculties, supreme wisdom, and Nirvana; therefore
have I not elucidated it.

"And what, Māluṅkyāputta, have I elucidated? Misery,
Māluṅkyāputta, have I elucidated; the origin of misery have
I elucidated; the cessation of misery have I elucidated; and
the path leading to the cessation of misery have I elucidated.
And why, Māluṅkyāputta, have I elucidated this? Because, Māluṅkyāputta, this does profit, has to do with the
fundamentals of religion, and tends to aversion, absence of
passion, cessation, quiescence, knowledge, supreme wisdom,
and Nirvana; therefore have I elucidated it. Accordingly,
Māluṅkyāputta, bear always in mind what it is that I have
not elucidated, and what it is that I have elucidated."

Thus spake The Blessed One; and, delighted, the venerable Māluṅkyāputta applauded the speech of The Blessed
One.

The Lesser Māluṅkyāputta Sermon.

SERMON NUMBER 2.

§ 13 *b.* — Translated from the Majjhima-Nikāya, and constituting Sutta 72.

Thus have I heard.

On a certain occasion The Blessed One was dwelling at Sāvatthi in Jetavana monastery in Anāthapiṇḍika's Park. Then drew near Vaccha, the wandering ascetic, to where The Blessed One was; and having drawn near, he greeted The Blessed One ; and having passed the compliments of friendship and civility, he sat down respectfully at one side. And seated respectfully at one side, Vaccha, the wandering ascetic, spoke to The Blessed One as follows : —

" How is it, Gotama ? Does Gotama hold that the world is eternal, and that this view alone is true, and every other false ? "

" Nay, Vaccha. I do not hold that the world is eternal, and that this view alone is true, and every other false."

" But how is it, Gotama ? Does Gotama hold that the world is not eternal, and that this view alone is true, and every other false ? "

" Nay, Vaccha. I do not hold that the world is not eternal, and that this view alone is true, and every other false."

" How is it, Gotama ? Does Gotama hold that the world is finite, . . ."

" How is it, Gotama ? Does Gotama hold that the soul and the body are identical, . . ."

" How is it, Gotama ? Does Gotama hold that the saint exists after death, . . ."

" How is it, Gotama ? Does Gotama hold that the saint both exists and does not exist after death, and that this view alone is true, and every other false ? "

" Nay, Vaccha. I do not hold that the saint both exists and does not exist after death, and that this view alone is true, and every other false."

" But how is it, Gotama? Does Gotama hold that the saint neither exists nor does not exist after death, and that this view alone is true, and every other false ? "

"Nay, Vaccha.   I do not hold that the saint neither exists nor does not exist after death, and that this view alone is true, and every other false."

"How is it, Gotama, that when you are asked, 'Does the monk Gotama hold that the world is eternal, and that this view alone is true, and every other false?' you reply, 'Nay, Vaccha.   I do not hold that the world is eternal, and that this view alone is true, and every other false'?

"But how is it, Gotama, that when you are asked, 'Does the monk Gotama hold that the world is not eternal, and that this view alone is true, and every other false?' you reply, 'Nay, Vaccha.   I do not hold that the world is not eternal, and that this view alone is true, and every other false'?

"How is it, Gotama, that when you are asked, 'Does Gotama hold that the world is finite, . . .'?

"How is it, Gotama, that when you are asked, 'Does Gotama hold that the soul and the body are identical, . . .'?

"How is it, Gotama, that when you are asked, 'Does Gotama hold that the saint exists after death, . . .'?

"How is it, Gotama, that when you are asked, 'Does the monk Gotama hold that the saint both exists and does not exist after death, and that this view alone is true, and every other false?' you reply, 'Nay, Vaccha.   I do not hold that the saint both exists and does not exist after death, and that this view alone is true, and every other false'?

"But how is it, Gotama, that when you are asked, 'Does the monk Gotama hold that the saint neither exists nor does not exist after death, and that this view alone is true, and every other false?' you reply, 'Nay, Vaccha.   I do not hold that the saint neither exists nor does not exist after death, and that this view alone is true, and every other false'?   What objection does Gotama perceive to these theories that he has not adopted any one of them?"

"Vaccha, the theory that the world is eternal, is a jungle, a wilderness, a puppet-show, a writhing, and a fetter, and is coupled with misery, ruin, despair, and agony, and does not tend to aversion, absence of passion, cessation, quiescence, knowledge, supreme wisdom, and Nirvana.

. . . .

" Vaccha, the theory that the saint neither exists nor does not exist after death, is a jungle, a wilderness, a puppet-show, a writhing, and a fetter, and is coupled with misery, ruin, despair, and agony, and does not tend to aversion, absence of passion, cessation, quiescence, knowledge, supreme wisdom, and Nirvana.

" This is the objection I perceive to these theories, so that I have not adopted any one of them."

" But has Gotama any theory of his own? "

" The Tathāgata, O Vaccha, is free from all theories; but this, Vaccha, does The Tathāgata know, — the nature of form, and how form arises, and how form perishes; the nature of sensation, and how sensation arises, and how sensation perishes; the nature of perception, and how perception arises, and how perception perishes; the nature of the predispositions, and how the predispositions arise, and how the predispositions perish; the nature of consciousness, and how consciousness arises, and how consciousness perishes. Therefore say I that The Tathāgata has attained deliverance and is free from attachment, inasmuch as all imaginings, or agitations, or proud thoughts concerning an Ego or anything pertaining to an Ego, have perished, have faded away, have ceased, have been given up and relinquished."

" But, Gotama, where is the priest reborn who has attained to this deliverance for his mind? "

" Vaccha, to say that he is reborn would not fit the case."

" Then, Gotama, he is not reborn."

" Vaccha, to say that he is not reborn would not fit the case."

" Then, Gotama, he is both reborn and is not reborn."

" Vaccha, to say that he is both reborn and not reborn would not fit the case."

" Then, Gotama, he is neither reborn nor not reborn."

" Vaccha, to say that he is neither reborn nor not reborn would not fit the case."

" When I say to you, ' But, Gotama, where is the priest reborn who has attained to this deliverance for his mind?' you reply, ' Vaccha, to say that he is reborn would not fit the case.' And when I say to you, 'Then, Gotama, he is not reborn,' you reply, 'Vaccha, to say that he is not reborn would not fit the case.' And when I say to you, 'Then, Gotama, he is both reborn and not reborn, ' you reply, 'Vaccha, to say that he is both reborn and not reborn would not fit the case.' And when I say to you, 'Then, Gotama, he is neither reborn nor not reborn,' you reply, 'Vaccha, to say that he is neither reborn nor not reborn would not fit the case.' Gotama, I am at a loss what to think in this matter, and I have become greatly confused, and the faith in Gotama inspired by a former conversation has now disappeared."

"Enough, O Vaccha! Be not at a loss what to think in this matter, and be not greatly confused. Profound, O Vaccha, is this doctrine, recondite, and difficult of comprehension, good, excellent, and not to be reached by mere reasoning, subtile, and intelligible only to the wise; and it is a hard doctrine for you to learn, who belong to another sect, to another faith, to another persuasion, to another discipline, and sit at the feet of another teacher. Therefore, Vaccha, I will now question you, and do you make answer as may seem to you good. What think you, Vaccha? Suppose a fire were to burn in front of you, would you be aware that the fire was burning in front of you?"

"Gotama, if a fire were to burn in front of me, I should be aware that a fire was burning in front of me."

"But suppose, Vaccha, some one were to ask you, 'On what does this fire that is burning in front of you depend?' what would you answer, Vaccha?"

"Gotama, if some one were to ask me, 'On what does this fire that is burning in front of you depend?' I would answer, Gotama, 'It is on fuel of grass and wood that this fire that is burning in front of me depends.'"

"But, Vaccha, if the fire in front of you were to become extinct, would you be aware that the fire in front of you had become extinct?"

"Gotama, if the fire in front of me were to become extinct, I should be aware that the fire in front of me had become extinct."

"But, Vaccha, if some one were to ask you, 'In which direction has that fire gone, — east, or west, or north, or south?' what would you say, O Vaccha?"

"The question would not fit the case, Gotama. For the fire which depended on fuel of grass and wood, when that fuel has all gone, and it can get no other, being thus without nutriment, is said to be extinct."

"In exactly the same way, Vaccha, all form by which one could predicate the existence of the saint, all that form has been abandoned, uprooted, pulled out of the ground like a palmyra-tree, and become non-existent and not liable to spring up again in the future. The saint, O Vaccha, who has been released from what is styled form, is deep, immeasurable, unfathomable, like the mighty ocean. To say that he is reborn would not fit the case. To say that he is not reborn would not fit the case. To say that he is both reborn and not reborn would not fit the case. To say that he is neither reborn nor not reborn would not fit the case.

"All sensation . . .

"All perception . . .

"All the predispositions . . .

"All consciousness by which one could predicate the existence of the saint, all that consciousness has been abandoned, uprooted, pulled out of the ground like a palmyra-tree, and become non-existent and not liable to spring up again in the future. The saint, O Vaccha, who has been released from what is styled consciousness, is deep, immeasurable, unfathomable, like the mighty ocean. To say that he is reborn would not fit the case. To say that he is not reborn would not fit the case. To say that he is both reborn and not reborn would not fit the case. To say that he is neither reborn nor not reborn would not fit the case."

When The Blessed One had thus spoken, Vaccha, the wandering ascetic, spoke to him as follows:

"It is as if, O Gotama, there were a mighty sal-tree near to some village or town, and it were to lose its dead branches and twigs, and its loose shreds of bark, and its unsound wood, so that afterwards, free from those branches and twigs, and the loose shreds of bark, and the unsound wood, it were to stand neat and clean in its strength. In exactly the same way doth the word of Gotama, free from branches and twigs, and from loose shreds of bark, and from unsound wood, stand neat and clean in its strength. O wonderful is it, Gotama! O wonderful is it, Gotama! It is as if, O Gotama, one were to set up that which was overturned; or were to disclose that which was hidden; or were to point out the way to a lost traveller; or were to carry a lamp into a dark place, that they who had eyes might see forms. Even so has Gotama expounded the Doctrine in many different ways. I betake myself to Gotama for refuge, to the Doctrine, and to the Congregation of the priests. Let Gotama receive me who have betaken myself to him for refuge, and accept me as a disciple from this day forth as long as life shall last."

The Aggi-Vacchagotta Sermon.

---

§ 14. KING MILINDA AND NĀGASENA COME TO AN UNDERSTANDING.

Translated from the Milindapañha (28²⁸).

Said the king, "Bhante Nāgasena, will you converse with me?"

"Your majesty, if you will converse with me as the wise converse, I will; but if you converse with me as kings converse, I will not."

"Bhante Nāgasena, how do the wise converse?"

"Your majesty, when the wise converse, whether they become entangled by their opponents' arguments or extricate themselves, whether they or their opponents are convicted of error, whether their own superiority or that of their opponents is established, nothing in all this can make them angry. Thus, your majesty, do the wise converse."

"And how, bhante, do kings converse?"

"Your majesty, when kings converse, they advance a proposition, and whoever opposes it, they order his punishment, saying, ' Punish this fellow ! ' Thus, your majesty, do kings converse."

"Bhante, I will converse as the wise converse, not as kings do. Let your worship converse in all confidence. Let your worship converse as unrestrainedly as if with a priest or a novice or a lay disciple or a keeper of the monastery grounds. Be not afraid ! "

" Very well, your majesty," said the elder in assent.

---

§ 15. THERE IS NO EGO.

§ 15 *a*. — Translated from the Milindapañha (25¹).

Then drew near Milinda the king to where the venerable Nāgasena was; and having drawn near, he greeted the venerable Nāgasena ; and having passed the compliments of friendship and civility, he sat down respectfully at one side. And the venerable Nāgasena returned the greeting ; by which, verily, he won the heart of king Milinda.

And Milinda the king spoke to the venerable Nāgasena as follows : —

"How is your reverence called ? Bhante, what is your name ? "

" Your majesty, I am called Nāgasena ; my fellow-priests, your majesty, address me as Nāgasena : but whether parents give one the name Nāgasena, or Sūrasena, or Vīrasena, or Sīhasena, it is, nevertheless, your majesty, but a way of counting, a term, an appellation, a convenient designation, a mere name, this Nāgasena ; for there is no Ego here to be found."

Then said Milinda the king, —

"Listen to me, my lords, ye five hundred Yonakas, and ye eighty thousand priests ! Nāgasena here says thus : ' There is no Ego here to be found.' Is it possible, pray, for me to assent to what he says ? "

And Milinda the king spoke to the venerable Nāgasena as follows : —

"Bhante Nāgasena, if there is no Ego to be found, who is it then furnishes you priests with the priestly requisites, — robes, food, bedding, and medicine, the reliance of the sick? who is it makes use of the same? who is it keeps the precepts? who is it applies himself to meditation? who is it realizes the Paths, the Fruits, and Nirvana? who is it destroys life? who is it takes what is not given him? who is it commits immorality? who is it tells lies? who is it drinks intoxicating liquor? who is it commits the five crimes that constitute 'proximate karma'?[1] In that case, there is no merit; there is no demerit; there is no one who does or causes to be done meritorious or demeritorious deeds; neither good nor evil deeds can have any fruit or result. Bhante Nāgasena, neither is he a murderer who kills a priest, nor can you priests, bhante Nāgasena, have any teacher, preceptor, or ordination. When you say, 'My fellow-priests, your majesty, address me as Nāgasena,' what then is this Nāgasena? Pray, bhante, is the hair of the head Nāgasena?"

"Nay, verily, your majesty."

"Is the hair of the body Nāgasena?"

"Nay, verily, your majesty."

"Are nails . . . teeth . . . skin . . . flesh . . . sinews . . . bones . . . marrow of the bones . . . kidneys . . . heart . . . liver . . . pleura . . . spleen . . . lungs . . . intestines . . . mesentery . . . stomach . . . faeces . . . bile . . . phlegm . . . pus . . . blood . . . sweat . . . fat . . . tears . . . lymph . . . saliva . . . snot . . . synovial fluid . . . urine . . . brain of the head Nāgasena?"

"Nay, verily, your majesty."

---

[1] Translated from the Sārasaṅgaha, as quoted in Trenckner's note to this passage:

"By *proximate karma* is meant karma that ripens in the next existence. To show what this is, I [the author of the Sārasaṅgaha] give the following passage from the Aṭṭhānasutta of the first book of the Aṅguttara-Nikāya: — 'It is an impossibility, O priests, the case can never occur, that an individual imbued with the correct doctrine should deprive his mother of life, should deprive his father of life, should deprive a saint of life, should in a revengeful spirit cause a bloody wound to a Tathāgata, should cause a schism in the church. This is an impossibility.'"

" Is now, bhante, form Nāgasena ? "

" Nay, verily, your majesty."

" Is sensation Nāgasena ? "

" Nay, verily, your majesty."

" Is perception Nāgasena ? "

" Nay, verily, your majesty."

" Are the predispositions Nāgasena ? "

" Nay, verily, your majesty."

" Is consciousness Nāgasena ? "

" Nay, verily, your majesty."

" Are, then, bhante, form, sensation, perception, the pre-dispositions, and consciousness unitedly Nāgasena ? "

" Nay, verily, your majesty."

" Is it, then, bhante, something besides form, sensation, perception, the predispositions, and consciousness, which is Nāgasena ? "

" Nay, verily, your majesty."

" Bhante, although I question you very closely, I fail to discover any Nāgasena. Verily, now, bhante, Nāgasena is a mere empty sound. What Nāgasena is there here ? Bhante, you speak a falsehood, a lie : there is no Nāgasena."

Then the venerable Nāgasena spoke to Milinda the king as follows : —

" Your majesty, you are a delicate prince, an exceedingly delicate prince ; and if, your majesty, you walk in the middle of the day on hot sandy ground, and you tread on rough grit, gravel, and sand, your feet become sore, your body tired, the mind is oppressed, and the body-consciousness suffers. Pray, did you come afoot, or riding ? "

" Bhante, I do not go afoot : I came in a chariot."

" Your majesty, if you came in a chariot, declare to me the chariot. Pray, your majesty, is the pole the chariot ? "

" Nay, verily, bhante."

" Is the axle the chariot ? "

" Nay, verily, bhante."

" Are the wheels the chariot ? "

" Nay, verily, bhante."

" Is the chariot-body the chariot ? "

" Nay, verily, bhante."

" Is the banner-staff the chariot?"

" Nay, verily, bhante."

" Is the yoke the chariot?"

" Nay, verily, bhante."

" Are the reins the chariot?"

" Nay, verily, bhante."

" Is the goading-stick the chariot?"

" Nay, verily, bhante."

" Pray, your majesty, are pole, axle, wheels, chariot-body, banner-staff, yoke, reins, and goad unitedly the chariot?"

" Nay, verily, bhante."

" Is it, then, your majesty, something else besides pole, axle, wheels, chariot-body, banner-staff, yoke, reins, and goad which is the chariot?"

" Nay, verily, bhante."

" Your majesty, although I question you very closely, I fail to discover any chariot. Verily now, your majesty, the word chariot is a mere empty sound. What chariot is there here? Your majesty, you speak a falsehood, a lie: there is no chariot. Your majesty, you are the chief king in all the continent of India; of whom are you afraid that you speak a lie? Listen to me, my lords, ye five hundred Yonakas, and ye eighty thousand priests! Milinda the king here says thus: 'I came in a chariot;' and being requested, 'Your majesty, if you came in a chariot, declare to me the chariot,' he fails to produce any chariot. Is it possible, pray, for me to assent to what he says?"

When he had thus spoken, the five hundred Yonakas applauded the venerable Nāgasena and spoke to Milinda the king as follows:—

" Now, your majesty, answer, if you can."

Then Milinda the king spoke to the venerable Nāgasena as follows:—

" Bhante Nāgasena, I speak no lie: the word 'chariot' is but a way of counting, term, appellation, convenient designation, and name for pole, axle, wheels, chariot-body, and banner-staff."

"Thoroughly well, your majesty, do you understand a chariot. In exactly the same way, your majesty, in respect of me, Nāgasena is but a way of counting, term, appellation, convenient designation, mere name for the hair of my head, hair of my body . . . brain of the head, form, sensation, perception, the predispositions, and consciousness. But in the absolute sense there is no Ego here to be found. And the priestess Vajirā, your majesty, said as follows in the presence of The Blessed One : —

> " ' Even as the word of " chariot " means
> That members join to frame a whole ;
> So when the Groups appear to view,
> We use the phrase, " A living being.[1]" ' "

"It is wonderful, bhante Nāgasena ! It is marvellous, bhante Nāgasena ! Brilliant and prompt is the wit of your replies. If The Buddha were alive, he would applaud. Well done, well done, Nāgasena ! Brilliant and prompt is the wit of your replies."

§ 15 *b*. — Translated from the Visuddhi-Magga (chap. xviii.).

Just as the word " chariot " is but a mode of expression for axle, wheels, chariot-body, pole, and other constituent members, placed in a certain relation to each other, but when we come to examine the members one by one, we discover that in the absolute sense there is no chariot ; and just as the word " house " is but a mode of expression for wood and other constituents of a house, surrounding space in a certain relation, but in the absolute sense there is no house ; and just as the word " fist " is but a mode of expression for the fingers, the thumb, etc., in a certain relation ; and the word " lute " for the body of the lute, strings, etc. ; " army " for elephants, horses, etc. ; " city " for fortifications, houses, gates, etc. ; " tree " for trunk, branches, foliage, etc., in a certain relation, but when we come to examine the parts one by one, we discover that in the absolute sense there is no tree ; in exactly the same way the words " living entity " and " Ego " are but

---

[1] That is, " a living entity."

a mode of expression for the presence of the five attachment
groups, but when we come to examine the elements of being
one by one, we discover that in the absolute sense there is no
living entity there to form a basis for such figments as " I
am," or " I "; in other words, that in the absolute sense there
is only name and form. The insight of him who perceives
this is called knowledge of the truth.

He, however, who abandons this knowledge of the truth
and believes in a living entity must assume either that this living entity will perish' or that it will not perish. If he assume
that it will not perish, he falls into the heresy of the persistence of existences; or if he assume that it will perish, he
falls into that of the annihilation of existences. And why do
I say so? Because, just as sour cream has milk as its antecedent, so nothing here exists but what has its own ante-
cedents.[1] To say, " The living entity persists," is to fall
short of the truth; to say, " It is annihilated," is to outrun
the truth. Therefore has The Blessed One said : —

" There are two heresies, O priests, which possess both
gods and men, by which some fall short of the truth, and
some outrun the truth; but the intelligent know the truth.

" And how, O priests, do some fall short of the truth?

" O priests, gods and men delight in existence, take
pleasure in existence, rejoice in existence, so that when the
Doctrine for the cessation of existence is preached to them,
their minds do not leap toward it, are not favorably disposed
toward it, do not rest in it, do not adopt it.

" Thus, O priests, do some fall short of the truth.

" And how, O priests, do some outrun the truth ?

" Some are distressed at, ashamed of, and loathe existence, and welcome the thought of non-existence, saying, ' See
here ! When they say that on the dissolution of the body this
Ego is annihilated, perishes, and does not exist after death,
that is good, that is excellent, that is as it should be.'

" Thus, O priests, do some outrun the truth.

" And how, O priests, do the intelligent know the
truth ?

------

[1] See pages 239-40.

"We may have, O priests, a priest who knows things as they really are, and knowing things as they really are, he is on the road to aversion for things, to absence of passion for them, and to cessation from them.

"Thus, O priests, do the intelligent know the truth."

§ 15 *c.* — Translated from the Mahā-Nidāna-Sutta (256[21]) of the Dīgha-Nikāya.

"In regard to the Ego, Ānanda, what are the views held concerning it?

"In regard to the Ego, Ānanda, either one holds the view that sensation is the Ego, saying, 'Sensation is my Ego;'

"Or, in regard to the Ego, Ānanda, one holds the view, 'Verily, sensation is not my Ego; my Ego has no sensation;'

"Or, in regard to the Ego, Ānanda, one holds the view, 'Verily, neither is sensation my Ego, nor does my Ego have no sensation. My Ego has sensation; my Ego possesses the faculty of sensation.'[1]

"In the above case, Ānanda, where it is said, 'Sensation is my Ego,' reply should be made as follows: 'Brother, there are three sensations: the pleasant sensation, the unpleasant sensation, and the indifferent sensation. Which of these three sensations do you hold to be the Ego?'

"Whenever, Ānanda, a person experiences a pleasant sensation, he does not at the same time experience an unpleasant sensation, nor does he experience an indifferent sensation; only the pleasant sensation does he then feel. Whenever, Ānanda, a person experiences an unpleasant sensation, he does not at the same time experience a pleasant sensation, nor does he experience an indifferent sensation; only the un-

---

[1] From the commentary on the Mahā-Nidāna-Sutta, Providence Manuscript, folio *ghāu,* b, lines 4 and 5 : — *Sensation is my Ego* gives the heresy of individuality as based on the sensation-group; *My Ego has no sensation,* as based on the form-group; and *My Ego has sensation; my Ego possesses a faculty of sensation,* as based on the perception-group, the predisposition-group, and the consciousness-group. For these three groups have sensation through union with sensation, and possess a faculty of sensation on account of the inseparability of this union.

pleasant sensation does he then feel. Whenever, Ānanda, a person experiences an indifferent sensation, he does not at the same time experience a pleasant sensation, nor does he experience an unpleasant sensation; only the indifferent sensation does he then feel.

"Now pleasant sensations, Ānanda, are transitory, are due to causes, originate by dependence, and are subject to decay, disappearance, effacement, and cessation; and unpleasant sensations, Ānanda, are transitory, are due to causes, originate by dependence, and are subject to decay, disappearance, effacement, and cessation; and indifferent sensations, Ānanda, are transitory, are due to causes, originate by dependence, and are subject to decay, disappearance, effacement, and cessation. While this person is experiencing a pleasant sensation, he thinks, 'This is my Ego.' And after the cessation of this same pleasant sensation, he thinks, 'My Ego has passed away.' While he is experiencing an unpleasant sensation, he thinks, 'This is my Ego.' And after the cessation of this same unpleasant sensation, he thinks, 'My Ego has passed away.' And while he is experiencing an indifferent sensation, he thinks, 'This is my Ego.' And after the cessation of this same indifferent sensation, he thinks, 'My Ego has passed away.' So that he who says, 'Sensation is my Ego,' holds the view that even during his lifetime his Ego is transitory, that it is pleasant, unpleasant, or mixed, and that it is subject to rise and disappearance.

"Accordingly, Ānanda, it is not possible to hold the view, 'Sensation is my Ego.'

"In the above case, Ānanda, where it is said, 'Verily sensation is not my Ego; my Ego has no sensation,' reply should be made as follows: 'But, brother, where there is no sensation, is there any "I am"?'"

"Nay, verily, Reverend Sir."

"Accordingly, Ānanda, it is not possible to hold the view, 'Verily, sensation is not my Ego; my Ego has no sensation.'

"In the above case, Ānanda, where it is said, 'Verily, neither is sensation my Ego, nor does my Ego have no sensa-

tion.   My Ego has sensation ; my Ego possesses the faculty
of sensation,' reply should be made as follows : 'Suppose,
brother, that utterly and completely, and without remainder,
all sensation were to cease — if there were nowhere any sensation, pray, would there be anything, after the cessation of
sensation, of which it could be said, " This am I "?'"

"Nay, verily, Reverend Sir."

"Accordingly, Ānanda, it is not possible to hold the view,
'Verily, neither is sensation my Ego, nor does my Ego have
no sensation.   My Ego has sensation ; my Ego possesses the
faculty of sensation.'

"From the time, Ānanda, a priest no longer holds the
view that sensation is the Ego, no longer holds the view that
the Ego has no sensation, no longer holds the view that the
Ego has sensation, possesses the faculty of sensation, he ceases
to attach himself to anything in the world, and being free
from attachment, he is never agitated, and being never agitated, he attains to Nirvana in his own person ; and he knows
that rebirth is exhausted, that he has lived the holy life, that
he has done what it behooved him to do, and that he is no
more for this world.

"Now it is impossible, Ānanda, that to a mind so freed
a priest should attribute the heresy that the saint exists after
death, or that the saint does not exist after death, or that the
saint both exists and does not exist after death, or that the
saint neither exists nor does not exist after death.

"And why do I say so ?

"Because, Ānanda, after a priest has been freed by
a thorough comprehension of affirmation and affirmation's
range, of predication and predication's range, of declaration
and declaration's range, of knowledge and knowledge's field
of action, of rebirth and what rebirth affects, it is impossible
for him to attribute such a heretical lack of knowledge and
perception to a priest similarly freed."

§ 15 *d.* — Translated from the Samyutta-Nikāya (xxii. 85¹).

Thus have I heard.

On a certain occasion the venerable Sāriputta was dwelling at Sāvatthi in Jetavana monastery in Anāthapiṇḍika's Park.

Now at that time the following wicked heresy had sprung up in the mind of a priest named Yamaka: "Thus do I understand the doctrine taught by The Blessed One, that on the dissolution of the body the priest who has lost all depravity is annihilated, perishes, and does not exist after death."

And a number of priests heard the report: "The following wicked heresy has sprung up in the mind of a priest named Yamaka: 'Thus do I understand the doctrine taught by The Blessed One, that on the dissolution of the body the priest who has lost all depravity is annihilated, perishes, and does not exist after death.'"

Then drew near these priests to where the venerable Yamaka was; and having drawn near, they greeted the venerable Yamaka; and having passed the compliments of friendship and civility, they sat down respectfully at one side. And seated respectfully at one side, these priests spoke to the venerable Yamaka as follows: "Is the report true, brother Yamaka, that the following wicked heresy has sprung up in your mind: 'Thus do I understand the doctrine taught by The Blessed One, that on the dissolution of the body the priest who has lost all depravity is annihilated, perishes, and does not exist after death'?"

"Even so, brethren, do I understand the doctrine taught by The Blessed One, that on the dissolution of the body the saint who has lost all depravity is annihilated, perishes, and does not exist after death."

"Say not so, brother Yamaka. Do not traduce The Blessed One; for it is not well to traduce The Blessed One. The Blessed One would never say that on the dissolution of the body the saint who has lost all depravity is annihilated, perishes, and does not exist after death."

Nevertheless, in spite of all these priests could say, the venerable Yamaka persisted obstinately to adhere to his pestiferous delusion : " Thus do I understand the doctrine taught by The Blessed One, that on the dissolution of the body the priest who has lost all depravity is annihilated, perishes, and does not exist after death."

And when these priests found themselves unable to detach the venerable Yamaka from this wicked heresy, then these priests arose from their seats and drew near to where the venerable Sāriputta was. And having drawn near they spoke to the venerable Sāriputta as follows : —

" Brother Sāriputta, the following wicked heresy has sprung up in the mind of a priest named Yamaka : ' Thus do I understand the doctrine taught by The Blessed One, that on the dissolution of the body the priest who has lost all depravity is annihilated, perishes, and does not exist after death.' Pray, let the venerable Sāriputta be so kind as to draw near to where the priest Yamaka is."

And the venerable Sāriputta consented by his silence.

Then the venerable Sāriputta in the evening of the day arose from meditation, and drew near to where the venerable Yamaka was ; and having drawn near, he greeted the venerable Yamaka ; and having passed the compliments of friendship and civility, he sat down respectfully at one side. And seated respectfully at one side, the venerable Sāriputta spoke to the venerable Yamaka as follows : " Is the report true, brother Yamaka, that the following wicked heresy has sprung up in your mind : ' Thus do I understand the doctrine taught by The Blessed One, that on the dissolution of the body the priest who has lost all depravity is annihilated, perishes, and does not exist after death ' ? "

" Even so, brother, do I understand the doctrine taught by The Blessed One, that on the dissolution of the body the priest who has lost all depravity is annihilated, perishes, and does not exist after death."

" What think you, brother Yamaka ? Is form permanent, or transitory ? "

" It is transitory, brother."

" And that which is transitory — is it evil, or is it good?"

" It is evil, brother."

" And that which is transitory, evil, and liable to change — is it possible to say of it: ' This is mine; this am I; this is my Ego'?"

" Nay, verily, brother."

" Is sensation . . . perception . . . the predispositions . . . consciousness permanent, or transitory?"

" It is transitory, brother."

" And that which is transitory — is it evil, or is it good?"

" It is evil, brother."

" And that which is transitory, evil, and liable to change — is it possible to say of it: ' This is mine; this am I; this is my Ego'?"

" Nay, verily, brother."

" Accordingly, brother Yamaka, as respects all form whatsoever, past, future, or present, be it subjective or existing outside, gross or subtile, mean or exalted, far or near, the correct view in the light of the highest knowledge is as follows: ' This is not mine; this am I not; this is not my Ego.'

" As respects all sensation whatsoever, . . . as respects all perception whatsoever, . . . as respects all predispositions whatsoever, . . . as respects all consciousness whatsoever, past, future, or present, be it subjective or existing outside, gross or subtile, mean or exalted, far or near, the correct view in the light of the highest knowledge is as follows: ' This is not mine; this am I not; this is not my Ego.'

" Perceiving this, brother Yamaka, the learned and noble disciple conceives an aversion for form, conceives an aversion for sensation, conceives an aversion for perception, conceives an aversion for the predispositions, conceives an aversion for consciousness. And in conceiving this aversion he becomes divested of passion, and by the absence of passion he becomes free, and when he is free he becomes aware that he is free; and he knows that rebirth is exhausted, that he has lived the holy life, that he has done what it behooved him to do, and that he is no more for this world.

"What think you, brother Yamaka? Do you consider form as the saint?"

"Nay, verily, brother."

"Do you consider sensation . . . perception . . . the predispositions . . . consciousness as the saint?"

"Nay, verily, brother."

"What think you, brother Yamaka? Do you consider the saint as comprised in form?"

"Nay, verily, brother."

"Do you consider the saint as distinct from form?"

"Nay, verily, brother."

"Do you consider the saint as comprised in sensation? . . . as distinct from sensation? . . . as comprised in perception? . . . as distinct from perception? . . . as comprised in the predispositions? . . . as distinct from the predispositions? . . . as comprised in consciousness?"

"Nay, verily, brother."

"Do you consider the saint as distinct from consciousness?"

"Nay, verily, brother."

"What think you, brother Yamaka? Are form, sensation, perception, the predispositions, and consciousness unitedly the saint?"

"Nay, verily, brother."

"What think you, brother Yamaka? Do you consider the saint as a something having no form, sensation, perception, predispositions, or consciousness?"

"Nay, verily, brother."

"Considering now, brother Yamaka, that you fail to make out and establish the existence of the saint in the present life, is it reasonable for you to say: 'Thus do I understand the doctrine taught by The Blessed One, that on the dissolution of the body the priest who has lost all depravity is annihilated, perishes, and does not exist after death'?"

"Brother Sāriputta, it was because of my ignorance that I held this wicked heresy; but now that I have listened to the doctrinal instruction of the venerable Sāriputta, I have abandoned that wicked heresy and acquired the true doctrine."

" But if others were to ask you, brother Yamaka, as follows : ' Brother Yamaka, the priest who is a saint and has lost all depravity, what becomes of him on the dissolution of the body, after death ? ' what would you reply, brother Yamaka, if you were asked that question ? "

" Brother, if others were to ask me as follows : ' Brother Yamaka, the priest who is a saint and has lost all depravity, what becomes of him on the dissolution of the body, after death ? ' I would reply, brother, as follows, if I were asked that question : ' Brethren, the form was transitory, and that which was transitory was evil, and that which was evil has ceased and disappeared. The sensation . . . perception . . . predispositions . . . consciousness was transitory, and that which was transitory was evil, and that which was evil has ceased and disappeared.' Thus would I reply, brother, if I were asked that question."

" Well said ! well said ! brother Yamaka. Come now, brother Yamaka, I will give you an illustration that you may still better comprehend this matter.

" Suppose, brother Yamaka, there were a householder, or a son of a householder, rich, wealthy, and affluent, and thoroughly well guarded, and some man were to become unfriendly, inimical, and hostile to him, and were to wish to kill him. And suppose it were to occur to this man as follows : ' This householder, or son of a householder, is rich, wealthy, and affluent, and thoroughly well-guarded. It would not be easy to kill him by violence. What if now I were to ingratiate myself with him and then kill him.' And suppose he were to draw near to that householder, or son of a householder, and say as follows : ' Lord, I would fain enter your service.' And suppose the householder, or son of a householder, were to admit him into his service ; and the man were to be his servant, rising before him and retiring after him, willing and obliging and pleasant-spoken. And suppose the householder, or son of a householder, were to treat him as a friend, were to treat him as a comrade, and repose confidence in him. And suppose then, brother, that when that man judged that the householder, or son of a householder, had

acquired thorough confidence in him, he were to get him into
some secluded spot and kill him with a sharp weapon.

"What think you, brother Yamaka? When that man
drew near to that householder, or son of a householder, and
said as follows : 'Lord, I would fain enter your service,' was
he not a murderer, though not recognized as such?

"And also when he was his servant, rising before him and
retiring after him, willing and obliging and pleasant-spoken,
was he not a murderer, though not recognized as such?

"And also when he got him into a secluded spot and
killed him with a sharp weapon, was he not a murderer,
though not recognized as such?"

"Even so, brother."

"In exactly the same way, brother, the ignorant, unconverted man, who is not a follower of noble disciples, not
conversant with the Noble Doctrine, not disciplined in the
Noble Doctrine, not a follower of good people, not conversant with the Doctrine held by good people, not trained in
the Doctrine held by good people, not disciplined in the Doctrine held by good people, considers form in the light of an
Ego — either the Ego as possessing form, or form as comprised in the Ego, or the Ego as comprised in form. Considers sensation . . . perception . . . the predispositions . . .
consciousness in the light of an Ego — either the Ego as
possessing consciousness, or consciousness as comprised in the
Ego, or the Ego as comprised in consciousness.

"He does not recognize the fact that form is transitory. He does not recognize the fact that sensation . . . perception . . . the predispositions . . . consciousness is transitory.

"He does not recognize the fact that form . . . sensation . . . perception . . . the predispositions . . . consciousness is evil.

"He does not recognize the fact that form . . . sensation . . . perception . . . the predispositions . . . consciousness
is not an Ego.

"He does not recognize the fact that form . . . sensation . . . perception . . . the predispositions . . . consciousness
is due to causes.

" He does not recognize the fact that form . . . sensation . . . perception . . . the predispositions . . . consciousness is a murderer.

" And he seeks after form, attaches himself to it, and makes the affirmation that it is his Ego. And he seeks after sensation, . . . perception, . . . the predispositions, . . . consciousness, attaches himself to it, and makes the affirmation that it is his Ego. And these five attachment-groups, sought after and become attached, long inure to his detriment and misery.

" But the learned and noble disciple, brother, who is a follower of noble disciples, conversant with the Noble Doctrine, disciplined in the Noble Doctrine, a follower of good people, conversant with the Doctrine held by good people, disciplined in the Doctrine held by good people, does not consider form in the light of an Ego — neither the Ego as possessing [form, nor form as comprised in the Ego, nor the Ego as comprised in form. Does not consider sensation . . . perception . . . the predispositions . . . consciousness in the light of an Ego — neither the Ego as possessing consciousness, nor consciousness as comprised in the Ego, nor the Ego as comprised in consciousness.

" He recognizes the fact that form . . . sensation . . . perception . . . the predispositions . . . consciousness is transitory.

" He recognizes the fact that form . . . sensation . . . perception . . . the predispositions . . . consciousness is evil.

" He recognizes the fact that form . . . sensation . . . perception . . . the predispositions . . . consciousness is not an Ego.

" He recognizes the fact that form . . . sensation . . . perception . . . the predispositions . . . consciousness is due to causes.

" He recognizes the fact that form . . . sensation . . . perception . . . the predispositions . . . consciousness is a murderer.

" And he does not seek after form, . . . sensation, . . .

perception, . . . the predispositions, . . . consciousness, nor attach himself to it, nor make the affirmation that it is his Ego. And these five attachment-groups, not sought after and not become attached, long inure to his welfare and happiness."

"Even so, brother Sāriputta, is it with those venerable persons who have for co-religionists such compassionate and benevolent exhorters and instructors as you. And now that I have listened to the doctrinal instruction of the venerable Sāriputta my mind has lost all attachment and become released from the depravities."

Thus spake the venerable Sāriputta, and, delighted, the venerable Yamaka applauded the speech of the venerable Sāriputta.

§ 15 *e*. — Translated from the Visuddhi-Magga (chap. xxi.).

He grasps the fourfold emptiness disclosed in the words: " I am nowhere a somewhatness for any one, and nowhere for me is there a somewhatness of any one." And how?

I am nowhere: — He sees that he has no Ego anywhere.

A somewhatness[1] *for any one:* — He sees that he has no Ego to bring forward to be a somewhatness for any one else. The sense is, he sees that he has none to bring forward to play the rôle of a brother, or of a friend, or of a follower.

And nowhere for me: — Here we must disregard for the present the words "*for me,*" and the sense then is, he sees that nowhere has any one an Ego.

Is there a somewhatness of any one: — We must now bring in the words "*for me*" and understand a somewhatness in any rôle assumed towards himself. He sees that no one has any Ego to be a somewhatness to him. The sense is, he sees that no one else has an Ego to bring forward to be a somewhatness in any rôle, either of a brother, or of a friend, or of a follower.

Thus, inasmuch as he sees that there is no Ego anywhere,

---

[1] That is, somethingness, the opposite of nothingness.

and that he has none to bring forward to be a somewhatness to any one else, and that no one else has an Ego to bring forward to be a somewhatness to himself, he has grasped the fourfold emptiness.

§ 15 *f.* — Translated from the Visuddhi-Magga (chap. xvi.).

Therefore has it been said as follows : —

> " Misery only doth exist, none miserable.
> No doer is there; naught save the deed is found.
> Nirvana is, but not the man who seeks it.
> The Path exists, but not the traveler on it."

---

§ 16.   ALL SIGNS OF AN EGO ARE ABSENT.

Translated from the Mahā-Vagga (i. 6[88]).

Then The Blessed One addressed the band of five priests : —

"Form, O priests, is not an Ego. For if now, O priests, this form were an Ego, then would not this form tend towards destruction, and it would be possible to say of form, 'Let my form be this way; let not my form be that way!' But inasmuch, O priests, as form is not an Ego, therefore does form tend towards destruction, and it is not possible to say of form, 'Let my form be this way; let not my form be that way!'

"Sensation . . . perception . . . the predispositions . . . consciousness, is not an Ego. For if now, O priests, this consciousness were an Ego, then would not this consciousness tend towards destruction, and it would be possible to say of consciousness, 'Let my consciousness be this way; let not my consciousness be that way!' But inasmuch, O priests, as consciousness is not an Ego, therefore does consciousness tend towards destruction, and it is not possible to say of consciousness, 'Let my consciousness be this way; let not my consciousness be that way!'

"What think you, O priests? Is form permanent, or transitory?"

" It is transitory, Reverend Sir."

" And that which is transitory — is it evil, or is it good?"

" It is evil, Reverend Sir."

" And that which is transitory, evil, and liable to change — is it possible to say of it: ' This is mine ; this am I ; this is my Ego'?"

" Nay, verily, Reverend Sir."

" Is sensation . . . perception . . . the predispositions . . . consciousness, permanent, or transitory?"

" It is transitory, Reverend Sir."

" And that which is transitory — is it evil, or is it good?"

" It is evil, Reverend Sir."

" And that which is transitory, evil, and liable to change — is it possible to say of it: ' This is mine ; this am I ; this is my Ego'?"

" Nay, verily, Reverend Sir."

" Accordingly, O priests, as respects all form whatsoever, past, future, or present, be it subjective or existing outside, gross or subtile, mean or exalted, far or near, the correct view in the light of the highest knowledge is as follows : ' This is not mine ; this am I not ; this is not my Ego.'

" As respects all sensation whatsoever . . . as respects all perception whatsoever . . . as respects all predispositions whatsoever . . . as respects all consciousness whatsoever, past, future, or present, be it subjective or existing outside, gross or subtile, mean or exalted, far or near, the correct view in the light of the highest knowledge is as follows : ' This is not mine ; this am I not ; this is not my Ego.'

" Perceiving this, O priests, the learned and noble disciple conceives an aversion for form, conceives an aversion for sensation, conceives an aversion for perception, conceives an aversion for the predispositions, conceives an aversion for consciousness. And in conceiving this aversion he becomes divested of passion, and by the absence of passion he becomes free, and when he is free he becomes aware that he is free ; and he knows that rebirth is exhausted, that he has lived the holy life, that he has done what it behooved him to do, and that he is no more for this world."

Thus spake The Blessed One, and the delighted band of five priests applauded the speech of The Blessed One. Now while this exposition was being delivered, the minds of the five priests became free from attachment and delivered from the depravities.

Now at that time there were six saints in the world.

---

§ 17. NO CONTINUOUS PERSONAL IDENTITY.

§ 17 *a*. — Translated from the Milindapañha (40¹).

"Bhante Nāgasena," said the king, "is a person when just born that person himself, or is he some one else?"

"He is neither that person," said the elder, "nor is he some one else."

"Give an illustration."

"What do you say to this, your majesty? When you were a young, tender, weakly infant lying on your back, was that your present grown-up self?"

"Nay, verily, bhante. The young, tender, weakly infant lying on its back was one person, and my present grown-up self is another person."

"If that is the case, your majesty, there can be no such thing as a mother, or a father, or a teacher, or an educated man, or a righteous man, or a wise man. Pray, your majesty, is the mother of the *kalala* ¹ one person, the mother of the *abbuda* ¹ another person, the mother of the *pesī* ¹ another person, the mother of the *ghana* ¹ another person, the mother of the little child another person, and the mother of the grown-up man another person? Is it one person who is a student, and another person who has finished his education? Is it one person who commits a crime, and another person whose hands and feet are cut off?"

"Nay, verily, bhante. But what, bhante, would you reply to these questions?"

Said the elder, "It was I, your majesty, who was a young,

---

¹ Various stages of the embryo.

tender, weakly infant lying on my back, and it is I who am
now grown up. It is through their connection with the em-
bryonic body that all these different periods are unified."

"Give an illustration."

"It is as if, your majesty, a man were to light a light; —
would it shine all night?"

"Assuredly, bhante, it would shine all night."

"Pray, your majesty, is the flame of the first watch the
same as the flame of the middle watch?"

"Nay, verily, bhante."

"Is the flame of the middle watch the same as the flame of
the last watch?"

"Nay, verily, bhante."

"Pray, then, your majesty, was there one light in the first
watch, another light in the middle watch, and a third light in
the last watch?"

"Nay, verily, bhante. Through connection with that
first light there was light all night."

"In exactly the same way, your majesty, do the elements
of being join one another in serial succession : one element
perishes, another arises, succeeding each other as it were
instantaneously. Therefore neither as the same nor as a
different person do you arrive at your latest aggregation of
consciousnesses."

"Give another illustration."

"It is as if, your majesty, new milk were to change in
process of time into sour cream, and from sour cream into
fresh butter, and from fresh butter into clarified butter. And
if any one, your majesty, were to say that the sour cream,
the fresh butter, and the clarified butter were each of them
the very milk itself — now would he say well, if he were to
say so?"

"Nay, verily, bhante. They came into being through
connection with that milk."

"In exactly the same way, your majesty, do the elements
of being join one another in serial succession : one element
perishes, another arises, succeeding each other as it were
instantaneously. Therefore neither as the same nor as a

different person do you arrive at your latest aggregation of consciousnesses."

" You are an able man, bhante Nāgasena."

§ 17 b. — Translated from the Visuddhi-Magga (chap. viii.).

Strictly speaking, the duration of the life of a living being is exceedingly brief, lasting only while a thought lasts.   Just as a chariot-wheel in rolling rolls only at one point of the tire, and in resting rests only at one point; in exactly the same way, the life of a living being lasts only for the period of one thought.   As soon as that thought has ceased the being is said to have ceased.   As it has been said : —

" The being of a past moment of thought has lived, but does not live, nor will it live.

" The being of a future moment of thought will live, but has not lived, nor does it live.

" The being of the present moment of thought does live, but has not lived, nor will it live."

---

§ 18. THE MIND LESS PERMANENT THAN THE BODY.

Translated from the Samyutta-Nikāya (xii. 62¹).

Thus have I heard.

On a certain occasion The Blessed One was dwelling at Sāvatthi in Jetavana monastery in Anāthapindika's Park. And there The Blessed One addressed the priests.

" Priests," said he.

" Lord," said the priests to The Blessed One in reply.

And The Blessed One spoke as follows : —

" Even the ignorant, unconverted man, O priests, may conceive an aversion for this body which is composed of the four elements, may divest himself of passion for it, and attain to freedom from it.   And why do I say so ?   Because, O priests, the increase and the wasting away of this body which is composed of the four elements are evident, and the way in which it is obtained and afterwards laid away again.[1] Therefore here the ignorant, unconverted man may conceive aversion, divest himself of passion, and attain to freedom. But that, O priests, which is called mind, intellect, consciousness, — here the ignorant, unconverted man is not equal to conceiving aversion, is not equal to divesting himself of passion, is not equal to attaining freedom. And why do I say so? Because, O priests, from time immemorial the ignorant, unconverted man has held, cherished, and affected the notion, ' This is mine ; this am I ; this is my Ego.' Therefore here the ignorant, unconverted man is not equal to conceiving aversion, is not equal to divesting himself of passion, is not equal to attaining freedom. But it were better, O priests, if the ignorant, unconverted man regarded the body which is composed of the four elements as an Ego, rather than the mind. And why do I say so? Because it is evident, O priests, that this body which is composed of the four elements lasts one year, lasts two years, lasts three years, lasts four years, lasts five years, lasts ten years, lasts twenty years, lasts thirty years, lasts forty years, lasts fifty years, lasts a hundred years, and even more. But that, O priests, which is called mind, intellect, consciousness, keeps up an incessant round by day and by night of perishing as one thing and springing up as another.

" Here the learned and noble disciple, O priests, attentively considers Dependent Origination — Behold this exists when that exists, this originates from the origination of the other ; this does not exist when that does not exist, this ceases from the cessation of the other. O priests, a pleasant sensation originates in dependence on contact with pleasant objects ; but when that contact with pleasant objects ceases, the feeling sprung from that contact, the pleasant sensation that originated in dependence on contact with pleasant objects ceases and comes to an end. O priests, an unpleasant sensa-

---

[1] Visuddhi-Magga, chap. xx. : By " The way in which it is obtained " is meant conception ; by " The way in which it is laid away again " is meant death.

tion . . . an indifferent sensation originates in dependence on contact with indifferent objects; but when that contact with indifferent objects ceases, the feeling sprung from that contact, the indifferent sensation that originated in dependence on contact with indifferent objects ceases and comes to an end.

" Just as, O priests, heat comes into existence and flame into being from the friction and concussion of two sticks of wood, but on the separation and parting of these two sticks of wood the heat sprung from those two sticks of wood ceases and comes to an end: in exactly the same way, O priests, a pleasant sensation originates in dependence on contact with pleasant objects; but when that contact with pleasant objects ceases, the feeling sprung from that contact, the pleasant sensation that originated in dependence on contact with pleasant objects ceases and comes to an end. An unpleasant sensation . . . an indifferent sensation originates in dependence on contact with indifferent objects; but when that contact with indifferent objects ceases, the feeling sprung from that contact, the indifferent sensation that originated in dependence on contact with indifferent objects ceases and comes to an end.

Perceiving this, O priests, the learned and noble disciple conceives an aversion for contact, conceives an aversion for sensation, conceives an aversion for perception, conceives an aversion for the predispositions, conceives an aversion for consciousness. And in conceiving this aversion he becomes divested of passion, and by the absence of passion he becomes free, and when he is free he becomes aware that he is free; and he knows that rebirth is exhausted, that he has lived the holy life, that he has done what it behooved him to do, and that he is no more for this world.

§ 19. WHAT IS UNITY OR ONE?

Translated from the Jātaka (ii.257^18), and constituting Birth-Story 244.

"*What he sees he does not wish for.*" This was related by The Teacher while dwelling in Jetavana monastery, and it was concerning a certain wandering ascetic who ran away.

It seems this ascetic had not found any one throughout the whole continent of India to refute his propositions; and coming to Sāvatthi, he inquired, "Who is able to debate with me?" On hearing it said, "The Supreme Buddha is able," he went to Jetavana monastery, surrounded by a crowd of people. There he saw The Blessed One in the midst of the four classes of his disciples teaching them the Doctrine; and he propounded to him his questions.

Then The Teacher answered him, and in return asked, "What constitutes a unit?" And he, being unable to reply, rose up and ran away.

And they of the assembly said, —

"Reverend Sir, you silenced the wandering ascetic with the question concerning the unit."

Said The Teacher, —

"Not now for the first time, O lay disciples, have I silenced him with the question concerning the unit; formerly also did I do so."

So saying, he related the by-gone occurrence : —

Once upon a time, when Brahmadatta was ruling at Benares, the Future Buddha was born in the family of a Brahman of that kingdom. When he was come of age, he renounced pleasures and adopted the life of a holy recluse, and dwelt for a long time in the Himalaya Mountains. And descending from the hills, he made his abode in a leaf-hut close by a market-village, at a bend of the Ganges.

And a certain wandering ascetic who had not found any one throughout the whole continent of India to refute his propositions, came to that market-village, and inquired, "Is there any one here able to debate with me?" And hearing that the Future Buddha was able, he went to his dwelling-place, surrounded by a crowd of people, and greeting him politely, sat down.

And the Future Buddha said to him, —

"Will you have a drink of Ganges water, fragrant with the scent of the forest?"

Thereupon the wandering ascetic began volubly to debate, saying, —

"What is the Ganges? Is the sand the Ganges? Is the water the Ganges? Is the hither bank the Ganges? Is the further bank the Ganges?"

But the Future Buddha said to him, —

"If you except the water, the sand, the hither bank, and the further bank, where can you find any Ganges?"

The wandering ascetic was confounded, and rose up and ran away.

When he was gone, the Future Buddha began teaching the Doctrine to the assembly that was seated about, and spoke the following stanzas : —

> "What he sees he does not wish for,
> But something that he does not see;
> Methinks that he will wander long,
> And what he wishes, not obtain.

> "He is not pleased with what he gets;
> No sooner gained, it meets his scorn.
> Insatiate are wishes all!
> The wish-free, therefore, we adore!"

Here : —

What he sees : — The water etc. which he sees, he does not wish to regard as the Ganges.

But something that he does not see : — But he wishes for a Ganges he does not see, for one abstracted from water etc.

Methinks that he will wander long : — Methinks thus: "This wandering ascetic, in his search for such a Ganges, will wander long; or if, in the same manner as for this Ganges abstracted from water etc., he is in search of an Ego abstracted from form etc., he will wander a long time in the round of rebirth."

And what he wishes, not obtain : — Although he wander a long time, he will not find such a Ganges or Ego as he is looking for.

What he gets : — He is not pleased with the water, or the form etc., which he gets.

No sooner gained, it meets his scorn : — Being thus not pleased with what he gets, any longed-for success which he gains, this he scorns and despises, saying, "What do I care for this?"

Insatiate are wishes all : — Wish or desire is insatiate, as it continually seeks for a fresh object which it scorns as soon as obtained.

The wish-free, therefore, we adore : — Therefore we adore The Buddhas and all others who are free from wishes.

When The Teacher had given this instruction, he identified the characters in the Birth-Story: "The wandering
ascetic of that existence was the wandering ascetic of this.
The anchorite was I myself."

The Wish-free Birth-Story.

---

§ 20. ANALYSIS OF THE HUMAN BEING.

Translated from the Visuddhi-Magga (chap. xiv.).

According to their difference : — According to whether they are groups or attachment-groups.

And what is this difference?

"Groups" is a general term; while the term "attachment-groups" specifies those which are coupled with depravity
and attachment. As it has been said: —

"I will teach you, O priests, the five groups, and the five
attachment-groups. Listen to me and pay attention, and I
will speak."

"Even so," said the priests to The Blessed One in reply.

And The Blessed One spoke as follows: —

"And what, O priests, are the five groups?

"All form whatsoever, O priests, past, future, or present,
be it subjective or existing outside, gross or subtile, mean or
exalted, far or near, belongs to the form-group.

"All sensation whatsoever, . . . all perception whatsoever, . . . all predispositions whatsoever, . . . all consciousness whatsoever, past, future, or present, be it subjective or
existing outside, gross or subtile, mean or exalted, far or near,
belongs to the consciousness-group.

"These, O priests, are called the five groups.

"And what, O priests, are the five attachment-groups?

"All form whatsoever, O priests, past, future, or present,
be it subjective or existing outside, gross or subtile, mean or
exalted, far or near, which is coupled with depravity and
attachment, belongs to the form-attachment-group.

"All sensation whatsoever, . . . all perception whatsoever, . . . all predispositions whatsoever, . . . all consciousness whatsoever, past, future, or present, be it subjective or
existing outside, gross or subtile, mean or exalted, far or near,
which is coupled with depravity and attachment, belongs to
the consciousness-attachment-group.

"These, O priests, are called the five attachment-groups."

Now, whereas there are sensations, perceptions, etc., which
are not subject to depravity, it is not so with form. But
inasmuch as form from its numerousness constitutes a group,
it is reckoned among the groups; and inasmuch as from its
numerousness and from its being coupled with depravity, it
constitutes an attachment-group, it is reckoned among the
attachment-groups. But only those sensations, perceptions,
etc., which are not coupled with depravity are reckoned
among the groups; while those coupled with depravity are
assigned to the attachment-groups. Here those groups which
are in the grasp of attachment are attachment-groups. This
is the way the matter should be viewed. In the present case,
however, under the term groups I include both classes.

No less and no more : — Why did The Blessed One say
there were five groups, no less and no more?

Because these sum up and classify, according to their
affinities, all the constituents of being; because it is only
these that can afford a basis for the figment of an Ego or of
anything related to an Ego; and because these include all
other classifications.

For in classifying, according to their affinities, the many different constituents of being, form constitutes one group, and comprises everything that has any affinity to form; sensation constitutes another group, and comprises everything that has any affinity to sensation. Similarly with respect to perception and the rest. Accordingly he laid down only five groups, because these sum up and classify, according to their affinities, all the constituents of being.

The basis for the figment of an Ego or of anything related to an Ego, is afforded only by these, namely form and the rest. For it has been said as follows: —

" When there is form, O priests, then through attachment to form, through engrossment in form, the persuasion arises, ' This is mine; this am I; this is my Ego.'

" When there is sensation, . . . when there is perception, . . . when there are predispositions, . . . when there is consciousness, O priests, then through attachment to consciousness, through engrossment in consciousness, the persuasion arises, ' This is mine; this am I; this is my Ego.' "

Accordingly he laid down only five groups, because it is only these that can afford a basis for the figment of an Ego or of anything related to an Ego.

As to other groups which he lays down, such as the five of conduct and the rest, these are included, for they are comprised in the predisposition-group. Accordingly he laid down only five groups, because these include all other classifications.

After this manner, therefore, is the conclusion reached that there are no less and no more.

§ 21.   THE COMPOSITION OF THE BODY.

Translated from the Visuddhi-Magga (chap. xi.).

The amount of the earthy element in the body of a man of medium size is about a bushel, and consists of an exceedingly fine and impalpable powder. This is prevented from being dispersed and scattered abroad, because it is held together by about half a bushel of the watery element and is preserved by the fiery element and is propped up by the windy element. And thus prevented from being dispersed and scattered abroad, it masquerades in many different disguises, such as the various members and organs of women and men, and gives the body its thinness, thickness, length, shortness, firmness, solidity, etc.

The watery element is of a juicy nature and serves to hold the body together. It is prevented from trickling or flowing away, because it rests in the earthy element and is preserved by the fiery element and is propped up by the windy element. And thus prevented from trickling or flowing away, it gives the body its plumpness or leanness.

The fiery element has heat as its characteristic, and has a vaporous nature, and digests what is eaten and drunk. Resting in the earthy element and held together by the watery element and propped up by the windy element, it cooks the body and gives it its beauty of complexion. And the body thus cooked is kept free from decay.

The windy element is characterized by its activeness and its ability to prop up, and courses through every member of the body. Resting in the earthy element and held together by the watery element and preserved by the fiery element, it props up the body. And it is because the body is thus propped up that it does not fall over, but stands upright. And it is when the body is impelled by the windy element that it performs its four functions of walking, standing, sitting, or lying-down, or draws in and stretches out its arms, or moves its hands and its feet.

Thus does this machine made of the four elements move like a puppet, and deceives all foolish people with its femininity, masculinity, etc.

§ 22.   ON GETTING ANGRY.

Translated from the Visuddhi-Magga (chap. ix.).

" My friend, who hast retired from the world and art angry
with this man, tell me what it is you are angry with ?   Are
you angry with the hair of the head, or with the hair of the
body, or with the nails, etc. ?   Or are you angry with the
earthy element in the hair of the head and the rest ?   Or are
you angry with the watery element, or with the fiery element,
or with the windy element in them ?   What is meant by the
venerable N. N. is only the five groups, the six organs of sense,
the six objects of sense, and the six sense-consciousnesses.
With which of these are you angry ?   Is it with the form-
group ?   Or is it with the sensation-group, perception-group,
predisposition-group, or consciousness-group ?   Or are you
angry with an organ of sense, or an object of sense, or a
sense-consciousness ? "

For a person who has made the above analysis, there is no
hold for anger, any more than there is for a grain of mustard-
seed on the point of an awl, or for a painting in the sky.

------

§ 23.   THE ORIGIN AND CESSATION OF THE
HUMAN BEING.

§ 23 *a.* — Translated from the Saṁyutta-Nikāya (xxii. 22¹).

Thus have I heard.

On a certain occasion The Blessed One was dwelling at
Sāvatthi in Jetavana monastery in Anāthapiṇḍika's Park.
And there The Blessed One addressed the priests.

" Priests," said he.

" Lord," said the priests to The Blessed One in reply.

And The Blessed One spoke as follows : —

" I will teach you, O priests, the burden, the bearer of the burden, the taking up of the burden, and the laying down of the burden.

"And what, O priests, is the burden?

"Reply should be made that it is the five attachment-groups. And what are the five? They are: the form-attachment-group, the sensation-attachment-group, the perception-attachment-group, the predisposition-attachment-group, the consciousness-attachment-group. These, O priests, are called the burden.

"And who, O priests, is the bearer of the burden?

"Reply should be made that it is the individual; the venerable So-and-so of such-and-such a family. He, O priests, is called the bearer of the burden.

"And what, O priests, is the taking up of the burden?

"It is desire leading to rebirth, joining itself to pleasure and passion, and finding delight in every existence, — desire, namely, for sensual pleasure, desire for permanent existence, desire for transitory existence.[1] This, O priests, is called the taking up of the burden.

"And what, O priests, is the laying down of the burden?

"It is the complete absence of passion, the cessation, giving up, relinquishment, forsaking, and non-adoption of desire. This, O priests, is called the laying down of the burden."

Thus spake The Blessed One; and when The Happy One had so spoken, The Teacher afterwards spoke as follows: —

> "The five groups form the heavy load,
> And man this heavy load doth bear;
> This load 't is misery to take up,
> The laying down thereof is bliss.

> "He who this heavy load lays down,
> Nor any other taketh up,
> By extirpating all desire
> Shall hunger lose, Nirvana gain."

---

[1] For these three desires see p. 188.

§ 23 *b*. — Translated from the Saṁyutta-Nikāya (xxii. 35¹).

Thus have I heard.

On a certain occasion The Blessed One was dwelling at Sāvatthi in Jetavana monastery in Anāthapiṇḍika's Park.

Then drew near a certain priest to where The Blessed One was; and having drawn near and greeted The Blessed One, he sat down respectfully at one side. And seated respectfully at one side, the priest spoke to The Blessed One as follows:

"Pray, Reverend Sir, let The Blessed One teach me the Doctrine in brief, so that when I have listened to the Doctrine of The Blessed One I may dwell solitary, retired, vigilant, strenuous, and earnest."

"By cleaving to anything, O priest, thus does one come to be; by not cleaving to anything, thus does one not come to be."

"I understand, O Blessed One! I understand, O Happy One!"

"But what, O priest, do you understand is the full meaning of what I said in brief?"

"By cleaving to form, Reverend Sir, thus does one come to be. By cleaving to sensation, . . . perception, . . . the predispositions, . . . consciousness, thus does one come to be. By not cleaving to form, Reverend Sir, thus does one not come to be. By not cleaving to sensation, . . . perception, . . . the predispositions, . . . consciousness, thus does one not come to be. This is what I understand to be the full meaning of what The Blessed One said in brief."

"Well said, well said, O priest! Well do you understand the full meaning of what I said in brief. By cleaving to form, O priest, thus does one come to be. By cleaving to sensation, . . . perception, . . . the predispositions, . . . consciousness, thus does one come to be. By not cleaving to form, O priest, thus does one not come to be. By not cleaving to sensation, . . . perception, . . . the predispositions, . . . consciousness, thus does one not come to be. This, O priest, is the full meaning of what I said in brief."

Then that priest, having applauded the speech of The

Blessed One and returned thanks, rose from his seat, and saluting The Blessed One and keeping his right side towards him, he departed.

Then that priest, solitary, retired, vigilant, strenuous, and earnest, in no long time, and in his life-time, came to learn for himself, realize, and live in the possession of that highest good to which the holy life conducts, and for the sake of which youths of good family so nobly retire from the household life to the houseless one.   And he became conscious that rebirth was exhausted, that he had lived the holy life, that he had done what it behooved him to do, and that he was no more for this world.

And that priest was of the number of the saints.

§ 23 *c.* — Translated from the Saṁyutta-Nikāya (xxii. 53¹).

Thus have I heard.

On a certain occasion The Blessed One was dwelling at Sāvatthi in Jetavana monastery in Anāthapiṇḍika's Park. And there The Blessed One addressed the priests.

"Priests," said he.

"Lord," said the priests to The Blessed One in reply.

And The Blessed One spoke as follows : —

"Not to seek for anything, O priests, is to be free ; to seek for anything is not to be free.

"If consciousness abide, O priests, it is because of a seeking for form that it abides, and supported by form, and resting in form, and taking delight therein, it attains to growth, increase, and development.   When consciousness abides, O priests, it is because of a seeking for sensation, . . . perception, . . . the predispositions, that it abides, and supported by the predispositions, and resting in the predispositions, and taking delight therein, it attains to growth, increase, and development.

"It is impossible, O priests, for any one to say that he can declare either the coming, or the going, or the passing out of an existence, or the springing up into an existence, or the growth, or the increase, or the development of consciousness apart from form, apart from sensation, apart from perception, apart from the predispositions.

" If passion for form, O priests, is abandoned, then through the abandonment of passion the support is cut off, and there is no resting-place for consciousness. If passion for sensation, . . . for perception, . . . for the predispositions is abandoned, then through the abandonment of passion the support is cut off, and there is no resting-place for consciousness.

" When that consciousness has no resting-place, does not increase, and no longer accumulates karma, it becomes free; and when it is free, it becomes quiet; and when it is quiet, it is blissful; and when it is blissful, it is not agitated; and when it is not agitated, it attains Nirvana in its own person; and it knows that rebirth is exhausted, that it has lived the holy life, that it has done what it behooved it to do, and that it is no more for this world."

§ 23 *d.* — Translated from the Saṁyutta-Nikāya (xxii. 112).

Thus have I heard.

On a certain occasion The Blessed One was dwelling at Sāvatthi in Jetavana monastery in Anāthapiṇḍika's Park. And there The Blessed One addressed the priests.

"Priests," said he.

"Lord," said the priests to The Blessed One in reply.

And The Blessed One spoke as follows: —

" O priests, abandon all wish, passion, delight, desire, seeking, attachment, mental affirmation, proclivity, and pre-judice in respect of form. Thus will form be abandoned, uprooted, pulled out of the ground like a palmyra-tree, and become non-existent and not liable to spring up again in the future.

" Abandon all wish, passion, delight, desire, seeking, attachment, mental affirmation, proclivity, and prejudice in respect of sensation, . . . perception, . . . the predisposi-tions, . . . consciousness. Thus will consciousness be aban-doned, uprooted, pulled out of the ground like a palmyra-tree, and become non-existent and not liable to spring up again in the future."

What is it causeth man to be?
What has he, will not be controlled?
Who are they that rebirth endure?
From what can respite ne'er be found?

Desire ay causeth man to be.
Man's thoughts refuse to be controlled.
All sentient life rebirth endures.
From misery no release is found.

---

§ 24. INANIMATE NATURE.

Translated from the Visuddhi-Magga (chap. xx.).

The forms of Nature are forms which have been coming into being since the renovation of the world-cycle and exist without organs of sense or mental faculties outside of ourselves, such as: iron, copper, tin, lead, gold, silver, pearls, gems, cat's-eyes, shells, rocks, coral, rubies, sapphires, earth, stones, mountains, grass, trees, vines, etc. This will be made plain by instancing the bud of an Asoka tree. For the form of an Asoka bud is at first of a delicate red; after the lapse of two or three days, of a deep red; after the lapse of two or three more, of a dull red; then of the color of a tender shoot, then of a mature twig, then of a green leaf, and then of the color of a dark green leaf. In the course of a year from the time of its being the color of a dark green leaf, this form, in the series of forms belonging to its own nature, becomes a yellow leaf, and breaking loose from its stalk falls to the ground. When the meditative priest has grasped all this, he applies the Three Characteristics, as follows:

"The form that was in existence at the time of the delicate red color perished without attaining to the time of the deep red color; the form that was in existence at the time of the deep red color, without attaining to the time of the dull red color; the form that was in existence at the time of the

dull red color, without attaining to the time of the tender-
shoot color; the form that was in existence at the time of
the tender-shoot color, without attaining to the time of the
mature-twig color; the form that was in existence at the
time of the mature-twig color, without attaining to the time
of the green-leaf color; the form that was in existence at the
time of the green-leaf color, without attaining to the time of
the dark-green-leaf color; the form that was in existence at
the time of the dark-green-leaf color, without attaining to the
time of the yellow-leaf color; the form that was in existence
at the time of the yellow leaf perished without attaining to
the time of breaking loose from the stalk and falling to the
ground. Therefore is it transitory, evil, and without substantive reality."

Having thus applied the Three Characteristics in this particular instance, he then in the same way reflects on all other
forms of Nature.

---

§ 25. THE MIDDLE DOCTRINE.

§ 25 *a.* — Translated from the Saṁyutta-Nikāya (xxii. 90[16]).

The world, for the most part, O Kaccāna, holds either to
a belief in being or to a belief in non-being. But for one
who in the light of the highest knowledge, O Kaccāna, considers how the world arises, belief in the non-being of the
world passes away. And for one who in the light of the
highest knowledge, O Kaccāna, considers how the world
ceases, belief in the being of the world passes away. The
world, O Kaccāna, is for the most part bound up in a seeking,
attachment, and proclivity [for the groups], but a priest does
not sympathize with this seeking and attachment, nor with
the mental affirmation, proclivity, and prejudice which affirms
an Ego. He does not doubt or question that it is only evil
that springs into existence, and only evil that ceases from
existence, and his conviction of this fact is dependent on no
one besides himself. This, O Kaccāna, is what constitutes
Right Belief.

That things have being, O Kaccāna, constitutes one extreme of doctrine; that things have no being is the other extreme. These extremes, O Kaccāna, have been avoided by The Tathāgata, and it is a middle doctrine he teaches: —

On ignorance depends karma;
On karma depends consciousness;
On consciousness depend name and form;
On name and form depend the six organs of sense;
On the six organs of sense depends contact;
On contact depends sensation;
On sensation depends desire;
On desire depends attachment;
On attachment depends existence;
On existence depends birth;
On birth depend old age and death, sorrow, lamentation, misery, grief, and despair. Thus does this entire aggregation of misery arise.

But on the complete fading out and cessation of ignorance ceases karma;
On the cessation of karma ceases consciousness;
On the cessation of consciousness cease name and form;
On the cessation of name and form cease the six organs of sense;
On the cessation of the six organs of sense ceases contact;
On the cessation of contact ceases sensation;
On the cessation of sensation ceases desire;
On the cessation of desire ceases attachment;
On the cessation of attachment ceases existence;
On the cessation of existence ceases birth;
On the cessation of birth cease old age and death, sorrow, lamentation, misery, grief, and despair. Thus does this entire aggregation of misery cease.

§ 25 *b.* — Translated from the Saṃyutta-Nikāya (xii. 35¹).

Thus have I heard.

On a certain occasion The Blessed One was dwelling at Sāvatthi in Jetavana monastery in Anāthapiṇḍika's Park. And there The Blessed One addressed the priests.

" Priests," said he.

" Lord," said the priests to The Blessed One in reply.

And The Blessed One spoke as follows :

" O priests, on ignorance depends karma. . . . Thus does this entire aggregation of misery arise."

" Reverend Sir, what are old age and death? and what is it has old age and death ? "

" The question is not rightly put," said The Blessed One. " O priest, to say: ' What are old age and death? and what is it has old age and death?' and to say: ' Old age and death are one thing, but it is another thing which has old age and death,' is to say the same thing in different ways. If, O priest, the dogma obtain that the soul and the body are identical, then there is no religious life; or if, O priest, the dogma obtain that the soul is one thing and the body another, then also there is no religious life. Both these extremes, O priest, have been avoided by The Tathāgata, and it is a middle doctrine he teaches: ' On birth depend old age and death.' "

" Reverend Sir, what is birth? and what is it has birth ? "

" The question is not rightly put," said The Blessed One. " O priest, to say : ' What is birth? and what is it has birth?' and to say: ' Birth is one thing, but it is another thing which has birth,' is to say the same thing in different ways. If, O priest, the dogma obtain that the soul and the body are identical, then there is no religious life ; or if, O priest, the dogma obtain that the soul is one thing and the body another, then also there is no religious life. Both these extremes, O priest, have been avoided by The Tathāgata, and it is a middle doctrine he teaches : ' On existence depends birth.' "

" Reverend Sir, what is existence? . . . attachment? . . . desire? . . . sensation? . . . contact? . . . the six organs of sense? . . . name and form? . . . consciousness? . . . karma? and what is it has karma?"

" The question is not rightly put," said The Blessed One. " O priest, to say: ' What is karma? and what is it has karma?' and to say: ' Karma is one thing, but it is another thing which has karma,' is to say the same thing in different

ways. If, O priest, the dogma obtain that the soul and the
body are identical, then there is no religious life; or if, O
priest, the dogma obtain that the soul is one thing and the
body another, then also there is no religious life.   Both these
extremes, O priest, have been avoided by The Tathāgata, and
it is a middle doctrine he teaches: 'On ignorance depends
karma.'

"But on the complete fading out and cessation of ignorance, O priest, all these refuges, puppet-shows, resorts, and
writhings, — to wit: What are old age and death? and
what is it has old age and death? or, old age and death are
one thing, but it is another thing which has old age and
death; or, the soul and the body are identical, or the soul is
one thing, and the body another, — all such refuges of whatever kind are abandoned, uprooted, pulled out of the ground
like a palmyra-tree, and become non-existent and not liable
to spring up again in the future.

"But on the complete fading out and cessation of ignorance, O priest, all these refuges, puppet-shows, resorts, and
writhings, — to wit: What is birth? . . . existence? . . .
attachment? . . . desire? . . . sensation? . . . contact? . . .
the six organs of sense? . . . name and form? . . . consciousness? . . . karma? and what is it has karma? or, karma is one
thing, but it is another thing which has karma; or, the soul
and the body are identical, or the soul is one thing and the
body another, — all such refuges are abandoned, uprooted,
pulled out of the ground like a palmyra-tree, and become
non-existent and not liable to spring up again in the future."

§ 25 c. — Translated from the Visuddhi-Magga (chap. xvii.).

Inasmuch as it is dependently on each other and in unison
and simultaneously that the factors which constitute dependence originate the elements of being, therefore did The Sage
call these factors Dependent Origination.

For the ignorance etc. which have been enumerated as
constituting dependence, when they originate any of the elements of being, namely, karma and the rest, can only do so
when dependent on each other and in case none of their num-

ber is lacking. Therefore it is dependently on each other and
in unison and simultaneously that the factors which constitute dependence originate the elements of being, not by a
part of their number nor by one succeeding the other.   Accordingly The Sage, skilful in the art of discovering the
signification of things, calls this dependence by the name of
Dependent Origination.

And in so doing, by the first of these two words is shown
the falsity of such heresies as that of the persistence of existences, and by the second word, a rejection of such heresies as
that existences cease to be, while by both together is shown
the truth.

By the first : — The word " Dependent," as exhibiting a
full complement of dependence and inasmuch as the elements
of being are subject to that full complement of dependence,
shows an avoidance of such heresies as that of the persistence
of existences, the heresies, namely, of the persistence of existences, of uncaused existences, of existences due to an overrul-
ing power, of self-determining existences. For what have
persistent existences, uncaused existences, etc., to do with
a full complement of dependence ?

By the second word : — The word " Origination," as exhibiting an origination of the elements of being and inasmuch
as the elements of being originate by means of a full complement of dependence, shows a rejection of such heresies as
that of the annihilation of existences, the heresies, namely,
of the annihilation of existences, of nihilism, of the inefficacy
of karma. For if the elements of being are continually originating by means of an antecedent dependence, whence can
we have annihilation of existence, nihilism, and an inefficacy
of karma ?

By both together : — By the complete phrase " Dependent
Origination," inasmuch as such and such elements of being
come into existence by means of an unbroken series of their
full complement of dependence, the truth, or middle course,
is shown. This rejects the heresy that he who experiences
the fruit of the deed is the same as the one who performed
the deed, and also rejects the converse one that he who

experiences the fruit of a deed is different from the one who performed the deed, and leaning not to either of these popular hypotheses, holds fast by nominalism.

---

§ 26. IGNORANCE.

§ 26 a. — Translated from the Visuddhi-Magga (chap. xvii.).

According to the Sutta-Piṭaka, ignorance is want of knowledge concerning four matters, namely, misery etc.; according to the Abhidhamma-Piṭaka, concerning eight, namely, in addition to the above, anteriority etc.

For it has been said as follows:

"What is ignorance? Want of knowledge concerning misery, want of knowledge concerning the origin of misery, want of knowledge concerning the cessation of misery, want of knowledge concerning the path leading to the cessation of misery, want of knowledge concerning anteriority, want of knowledge concerning posteriority, want of knowledge concerning anteriority and posteriority, want of knowledge concerning definite dependence and of the elements of being sprung from dependence."

In the above quotation ignorance is only considered in its aspect as a concealer of the verities cited, although, except in the case of the two transcendent truths [*i. e.* the truth concerning the cessation of misery and the truth concerning the path leading to the cessation of misery], it also comes into being with reference to objects of sense. Having come into being, it conceals the truth concerning misery, and does not allow of the comprehension of its essential elements and characteristics, as also it conceals the origin of misery, the cessation of misery, the path, the five groups of the past, otherwise called anteriority, the five groups of the future otherwise called posteriority, both sets of groups otherwise called anteriority and posteriority, and both definite dependence and the elements of being sprung from dependence, and does not allow of the comprehension of their essential elements and characteristics, so that one can discriminate and say, "This is ignorance; this is karma," and so on. Thus is it said to be "want of knowledge concerning misery, . . . want of knowledge concerning both definite dependence and the elements of being sprung from dependence."

§ 26 *b.* — Translated from the Visuddhi-Magga (chap. xvii.).

But why is ignorance put at the beginning? Is it because ignorance, like the *natura naturans* of the Sankhya philosophers, is the causeless primary cause of the world? It is not causeless. For in the quotation, "On the arising of the depravities depends the arising of ignorance," the cause of ignorance is declared. But there is an occasion when ignorance may be said to be a primary cause. What is that occasion? When it is made the starting-point of a discourse concerning the round of rebirth.

For The Blessed One in his discourses on the round of rebirth was accustomed to choose from Dependent Origination two of the factors of being as his starting-points: either, on the one hand, ignorance, as when he says, "As I have told you, O priests, the first beginning of ignorance cannot be discerned, nor can one say, 'Before a given point of time there was no ignorance, it came into being afterwards.' Nevertheless, O priests, it can be discerned that ignorance possesses a definite dependence;" or, on the other hand, desire for existence, as when he says, "As I have told you, O priests, the first beginning of desire for existence cannot be discerned, nor can one say, 'Before a given point of time there was no desire for existence, it came into being afterwards.' Nevertheless, O priests, it can be discerned that desire for existence possesses a definite dependence."

But why was The Blessed One in his discourses on the round of rebirth accustomed to choose these two factors of being as his starting-points? Because they constitute the difference between the karma which conducts to blissful states of existence and the karma which conducts to unhappy states of existence. For the cause of the karma which conducts to unhappy states of existence is ignorance. And why do I say so? Because, just as a cow about to be slaughtered, overcome by weariness due to fiery heat and to blows of the stick, will, as the result of that exhaustion, drink water that is hot, although it is unpleasant and does her harm; so the unconverted man, overcome by ignorance, will take life and perform many other kinds of karma which conduct to unhappy states of existence, although such karma is unpleasant on account of the fiery heat of the corruptions, and does him harm by casting him into unhappy states of existence.

But the cause of the karma which conducts to blissful states of existence is desire for existence. And why do I say so? Because, just as the cow described above will thirstily drink cold water, and the drink will be pleasant to her and remove her weariness; so the unconverted man, overcome by desire for existence, ridding himself of the fiery heat of the corruptions, will cease from taking life and perform many other kinds of karma which conduct to blissful states of existence, and such karma will be pleasant, as it conducts to blissful states of existence and removes the weariness of the misery of unhappy states of existence.

Now in his discourses on the round of rebirth The Blessed One sometimes sets out from only one of these factors, as when he says, " Thus, O priests, ignorance causes karma; karma causes consciousness," etc.; or, " When a man lives, O priests, absorbed in the fascinations of objects of attachment, then does desire increase, and on desire depends attachment," etc.; sometimes from both, as when he says, " O priests, it is because the fool is blinded by ignorance and joined to desire that thus his body has come to be. Such is the origin not merely of one's own body, but also of name and form existing outside. Verily it is in dependence on these two, ignorance and desire, that arise contact and the six organs of sense, and that the fool experiences happiness and misery," etc.

§ 26 *c.* — Translated from the Visuddhi-Magga (chap. xvii.).

Whereas, however, sorrow etc. are mentioned last, they constitute the fruition of the ignorance mentioned in the

Wheel of Existence's opening phrase, " On ignorance depends karma." And it is to be understood that this Wheel of Existence constantly and continuously rolls onward, without known beginning, without a personal cause or passive recipient and empty with a twelvefold emptiness.

If it be asked: How do sorrow etc. constitute the fruition of ignorance? How is the Wheel of Existence without known beginning? How is it without a personal cause or passive recipient? How is it empty with a twelvefold emptiness ? — we reply: —

Of him who is not free from ignorance there is sorrow, grief, and despair, and of him who is infatuated there is lamentation. Thus it is when sorrow etc. have ripened that ignorance attains to fruition.

Moreover, it has been said, " Ignorance springs from the depravities." Sorrow etc. also spring from the depravities. And how? Sorrow springs from the depravity of sensual pleasure as soon as the object of sensual desire is removed. As it is said:

> " The man who lives for sensual joys,
> And findeth his delight therein,
> When joys of sense have taken flight,
> Doth smart as if with arrows pierced."

And as it is said :

> " From sensual pleasure sorrow springs."

Also sorrow etc. all spring from the depravity of heresy. As it is said :

" When he has become possessed with the notion, ' I am form; form belongs to the I,' then through the changing and alteration of form arise sorrow, misery, grief, and despair."

And just as they spring from the depravity of heresy, so also do they spring from the depravity of desire for existence, as occurs in the case of the gods when frightened by the fear of death on perceiving the five omens. As it is said:

" Also the gods long-lived, handsome, and dwelling long ages in lofty palaces in a plenitude of bliss, they also on hearing the doctrinal instruction of The Tathāgata become afraid, alarmed, and agitated."

And just as they spring from the depravity of desire for existence, so also do they spring from the depravity of ignorance. As it is said:

" The foolish man, O priests, experiences even in the present life a threefold misery and grief."

Thus, inasmuch as sorrow etc. spring from the depravities, therefore in ripening they accomplish the fruition of the depravities, which are the causes of ignorance. Thus it is when the depravities have ripened that ignorance attains to fruition, as it is one of them.

After this manner, therefore, is to be understood the clause: *Ignorance attains to fruition in sorrow etc.*

Inasmuch, however, as when ignorance has thus attained to fruition in sorrow etc., as being one of their causes, there is then no end to the succession of cause and effect, " On ignorance depends karma; on karma depends consciousness," etc.; therefore we have a twelve-membered Wheel of Existence without known beginning, continuing to exist by virtue of a concatenation of cause and effect.

If it be objected — " In that case it is contradictory to say, ' On ignorance depends karma,' and to call this the beginning," — we reply — " This is not the beginning; this merely enunciates the chief of the elements of being." For ignorance is chief in the three rounds. For when the fool seizes hold of it, then the rounds of corruption, of karma, and of the fruition of karma, coil themselves about him; just as when a man seizes the head of a serpent all the rest of the body coils itself about his arm. But when the annihilation of ignorance has been effected, deliverance is thereby gained; just as when the serpent's head has been cut off the arm becomes delivered of the coils. As it is said:

" On the complete fading out and cessation of ignorance ceases karma; " and so forth.

Thus, inasmuch as ignorance is the imprisonment of him who seizes it, and the deliverance of him who lets it go, it is the chief but not the beginning.

Thus is to be understood the clause: *The Wheel of Existence is without known beginning.*

Now inasmuch as the factors of being, karma etc., exist
by reason of their own causes, ignorance etc., therefore is
this same Wheel of Existence wanting in any other cause for
the round of rebirth, such as Brahma etc., conceived of under
the names of Brahma, Great Brahma, The Chief, The Victorious One, and is also wanting in any Ego passively recipient
of happiness and misery, conceived of as " This I that talks
and feels." Thus is to be understood the phrase: *Without a
personal cause or passive recipient.*

Inasmuch, however, as ignorance is empty of stability
from being subject to a coming into existence and a disappearing from existence, and is empty of loveliness from being
corrupted and one of the corruptions, and is empty of happiness from being harassed by coming into existence and disappearing from existence, and is empty of a self-determining
Ego from being subject to dependence, — and similarly with
reference to karma and the remaining terms; or, in other
words, inasmuch as ignorance is not an Ego, belongs to no
Ego, is comprised in no Ego, possesses no Ego, and similarly
with reference to karma and the rest, — therefore is it to be
understood of the Wheel of Existence that it is *empty with a
twelvefold emptiness.*

When he has learned this, he next perceives that ignorance and desire are its root; that the past etc. are its three
times; and that these contain two, eight, and two members
respectively.

Respecting this Wheel of Existence it is to be understood
that the two factors *ignorance and desire are its root;* and that
this root is twofold: the root ignorance, deriving from the
past and ending with sensation; and the root desire, continuing into the future and ending with old age and death. Here
the first of these two roots is specified with reference to him
who is inclined to heresy, the latter with reference to him
who is inclined to desire. For the ignorance of those who
are inclined to heresy, and the desire of those who are
inclined to desire, conduct to the round of rebirth. Or again,

the first is designed to destroy the heresy of the annihilation
of existences, by showing that the causes for the springing
up of fruit are never annihilated; the second to destroy the
heresy of the persistence of existences, by showing that those
causes which have sprung up are subject to old age and
death.   Or again, the first is to show the gradual coming into
existence of such beings as are born from the womb, the
latter the instantaneous coming into complete existence of
apparitional existences.

The past, the present, and the future *are its three times.*
As touching the question which those members are which are
stated by the text to occur in each of these *respectively,* —
ignorance and karma are the *two* which belong to past time;
those which belong to present time are the *eight* which begin
with consciousness and end with existence; while birth and
old-age-and-death are the *two* which belong to future time.

Again it is to be understood that this Wheel of Existence
has three connections of cause and effect and of cause and a
predecessor: that it has four divisions, twenty component
spokes, three rounds, and incessantly revolves.

Here between karma and rebirth-consciousness is one connection of cause and effect; between sensation and desire is
a connection of effect and cause; and between existence and
birth a connection of cause and effect.   Thus is to be understood the phrase *this Wheel of Existence has three connections
of cause and effect and of cause and a predecessor.*

Its four divisions begin and end at these connections,
namely: ignorance and karma form one division; consciousness, name-and-form, the six organs of sense, contact, and
sensation, the second; desire, attachment, and existence, the
third; birth and old age the fourth.   Thus is to be understood the statement that this Wheel of Existence *has four
divisions.*

> Five causes are there in the past
> And five fruitions now at hand.
> Five causes are there now at hand
> And five fruitions yet to come.

With these twenty spokes called component is to be understood that it has twenty component spokes. Of the causes mentioned in the phrase *five causes are there in the past*, two, ignorance and karma, have been mentioned above; but inasmuch as the ignorant man has strong desires and having strong desires attaches himself, and on attachment depends existence, therefore desire, attachment, and existence are also included. Therefore has it been said,

"In a former-karma-existence, infatuation-ignorance, initiatory karma, longing desire, approximating attachment, and thought-existence, these five factors were the dependence for conception into this existence."

Here by the phrase *in a former-karma-existence* is meant a former karma-existence;[1] the sense is a karma-existence taking place in a previous birth.

Infatuation-ignorance means the ignorance belonging to that previous birth which consists of infatuation in respect of the truths concerning misery etc., under the influence of which the infatuated man produces karma.

Initiatory karma consists of the antecedent thoughts of the one who performs that karma, as for instance the antecedent thoughts of him who gets ready objects to give away in alms, in order that he may give them away a month or a year later. The thoughts, however, of him who places a gift in the hands of a recipient is thought-existence. Or again, thought in the six swiftnesses containing one contemplation is initiatory karma. The seventh thought is existence. Or again, any thought is existence; the conjoined thought is initiatory karma.

Longing desire is that desire on the part of him who performs karma which consists in a longing or aspiration for its fruition in a rebirth-existence.

Approximating attachment: — This attachment is any approximating, seizing hold of, or affectation that has become the dependence of karma-existence, as, for instance, "This action will yield sensual pleasure in such and such a grade of being;" or again, "I shall be annihilated."

---

[1] That is, *not* former-karma existence.

Thought-existence is thought-existence as explained at the end of Initiatory Karma. Thus are these expressions to be understood.

Now as to the phrase, *and five fruitions now at hand*, these are the five beginning with consciousness and ending with sensation. As it has been said,

" Rebirth-consciousness, the descent of name and form, the sensitiveness of the organs of sense, the contact experienced, the sensation felt, these five factors belonging to the originating-existence of the present time depend on the karma of a previous existence."

Here by *rebirth-consciousness* is meant the consciousness called rebirth, inasmuch as it springs into being by a process of rebirth into another existence.

The descent of name and form consists in the descent of the elements of being into the womb not only of those with form but also of those without, as it were, their coming and entering.

The sensitiveness of the senses : — By this are meant the five organs of sense, eye etc.

The contact experienced : — The contact which arises from contact experienced when in contact with an object of sense.

The sensation felt consists in the fruition-sensation that springs into being in company with either the rebirth-consciousness or the contact which depends on the six organs of sense. Thus are these expressions to be understood.

Five causes are there now at hand : — These are desire, attachment, and existence as mentioned in the text above; but when existence has been obtained, then karma, either that which is antecedent to existence or conjoined with it, is included ; and that ignorance which, in the taking up of desire and attachment, is conjoined with these two factors, or that whereby the infatuated man performs karma, that also is included. Thus there are five.

Therefore has it been said,

" When the senses have matured, then infatuation-ignorance, initiatory karma, longing desire, approximating attachment, and thought-existence, these five factors of a

present karma-existence are the dependence of rebirth in the
future."

Here by the phrase *when the senses have matured* is shown
the infatuation which occurs at the time of the performance
of karma in the case of one who has his senses matured.
The meaning of the rest is plain.

By *five fruitions yet to come* are meant the five, consciousness etc. These are all included in speaking of birth; and
old age and death are the old age and death of them alone.
Therefore has it been said,

"The rebirth-consciousness, the descent of name and
form, the sensitiveness of the organs of sense, the contact
experienced, the sensation felt, these five factors belonging
to the originating-existence of a future life depend on the
karma performed in this one."

After this manner, therefore, has this Wheel of Existence
twenty component spokes.

And incessantly revolves : — Here it is to be understood
that karma and existence form the round of karma; ignorance, desire, and attachment form the round of the corruptions; and consciousness, name and form, the six organs of
sense, contact, and sensation form the round of fruition. And
it is through these three that this Wheel of Existence is said
to have three rounds; and as long as the round of corruptions is uninterrupted, because its dependence has not been
cut off, the Wheel of Existence is *incessant ;* and inasmuch
as it turns over and over again, it *revolves.*

---

§ 27.   KARMA.

Translated from the Visuddhi-Magga (chap. xvii.).

The kinds of karma are those already briefly mentioned,
as consisting of the triplet beginning with meritorious karma
and the triplet beginning with bodily karma, making six
in all.

To give them here in full, however, meritorious karma
consists of the eight meritorious thoughts which belong to

the realm of sensual pleasure and show themselves in alms-
giving, keeping the precepts, etc., and of the five meritorious
thoughts which belong to the realm of form and show themselves in ecstatic meditation, — making thirteen thoughts;
demeritorious karma consists of the twelve demeritorious
thoughts which show themselves in the taking of life etc.;
and karma leading to immovability consists of the four meritorious thoughts which belong to the realm of formlessness and show themselves in ecstatic meditation. Accordingly these three karmas consist of twenty-nine thoughts.

As regards the other three, bodily karma consists of the
thoughts of the body, vocal karma of the thoughts of the
voice, mental karma of the thoughts of the mind. The object
of this triplet is to show the avenues by which meritorious
karma etc. show themselves at the moment of the initiation
of karma.

For bodily karma consists of an even score of thoughts,
namely, of the eight meritorious thoughts which belong to
the realm of sensual pleasure and of the twelve demeritorious
ones. These by exciting gestures show themselves through
the avenue of the body.

Vocal karma is when these same thoughts by exciting
speech show themselves through the avenue of the voice.
The thoughts, however, which belong to the realm of form,
are not included, as they do not form a dependence for subsequent consciousness. And the case is the same with the
thoughts which belong to the realm of formlessness. Therefore they also are to be excluded from the dependence of
consciousness. However, all depend on ignorance.

Mental karma, however, consists of all the twenty-nine
thoughts, when they spring up in the mind without exciting
either gesture or speech.

Thus, when it is said that ignorance is the dependence of
the karma-triplet consisting of meritorious karma etc., it
is to be understood that the other triplet is also included.

But it may be asked, " How can we tell that these
karmas are dependent on ignorance?" Because they exist
when ignorance exists.

For, when a person has not abandoned the want of
knowledge concerning misery etc., which is called ignorance, then by that want of knowledge concerning misery
and concerning anteriority etc. he seizes on the misery of
the round of rebirth with the idea that it is happiness and
hence begins to perform the threefold karma which is its
cause; by that want of knowledge concerning the origin of
misery and by being under the impression that thus happiness is secured, he begins to perform karma that ministers
to desire, though such karma is really the cause of misery;
and by that want of knowledge concerning cessation and the
path and under the impression that some particular form of
existence will prove to be the cessation of misery, although
it really is not so, or that sacrifices, alarming the gods by
the greatness of his austerities, and other like procedures
are the way to cessation, although they are not such a way,
he begins to perform the threefold karma.

Moreover, through this non-abandonment of ignorance in
respect of the Four Truths, he does not know the fruition of
meritorious karma to be the misery it really is, seeing that it
is completely overwhelmed with the calamities, birth, old age,
disease, death, etc.; and so to obtain it he begins to perform
meritorious karma in its three divisions of bodily, vocal, and
mental karma, just as a man in love with a heavenly nymph
will throw himself down a precipice. When he does not perceive that at the end of that meritorious fruition considered
to be such happiness comes the agonizing misery of change
and disappointment, he begins to perform the meritorious
karma above described, just as a locust will fly into the flame
of a lamp, or a man that is greedy after honey will lick the
honey-smeared edge of a knife. When he fails to perceive
the calamities due to sensual gratification and its fruition,
and, being under the impression that sensuality is happiness, lives enthralled by his passions, he then begins to perform demeritorious karma through the three avenues, just as
a child will play with filth, or one who wishes to die will eat
poison. When he does not perceive the misery of the change
that takes place in the constituents of being, even in the

realm of formlessness, but has a perverse belief in persistence etc., he begins to perform mental karma that leads to immovability, just as a man who has lost his way will go after a mirage.

As, therefore, karma exists when ignorance exists but not when it does not exist, it is to be understood that this karma depends on ignorance. And it has been said as follows:

" O priests, the ignorant, uninstructed man performs meritorious karma, demeritorious karma, and karma leading to immovability. But whenever, O priests, he abandons his ignorance and acquires wisdom, he through the fading out of ignorance and the coming into being of wisdom does not even perform meritorious karma."

---

§ 28. CONSCIOUSNESS.

§ 28 *a.* — Translated from the Milindapañha (62⁸).

"Bhante Nāgasena, what is consciousness?"

"Your majesty, consciousness is the act of being conscious."

"Give an illustration."

"It is as if, your majesty, the city watchman were to take his seat at the cross-roads in the middle of the city and were to behold every man who approached from the eastern quarter, were to behold every man who approached from the southern quarter, were to behold every man who approached from the western quarter, were to behold every man who approached from the northern quarter: in exactly the same way, your majesty, whatever form a man beholds with the eye, of that he is conscious with the consciousness; whatever sound he hears with the ear, of that he is conscious with the consciousness; whatever odor he smells with the nose, of that he is conscious with the consciousness; whatever taste he tastes with the tongue, of that he is conscious with the consciousness; whatever tangible thing he touches with the body, of that he is conscious with the consciousness; whatever idea he is conscious of with the mind, of that he is conscious with the consciousness. Thus, your majesty, is consciousness the act of being conscious."

" You are an able man, bhante Nāgasena."

§ 28 *b.* — Translated from the Majjhima-Nikāya (Sutta 38).

O priests, consciousness is named from that in dependence on which it comes into being. The consciousness which comes into being in respect of forms in dependence on the eye is called eye-consciousness. The consciousness which comes into being in respect of sounds in dependence on the ear is called ear-consciousness. The consciousness which comes into being in respect of odors in dependence on the nose is called nose-consciousness. The consciousness which comes into being in respect of tastes in dependence on the tongue is called tongue-consciousness. The consciousness which comes into being in respect of things tangible in dependence on the body is called body-consciousness. The consciousness which comes into being in respect of ideas in dependence on the mind is called mind-consciousness.

Just as, O priests, fire is named from that in dependence on which it burns. The fire which burns in dependence on logs of wood is called a log-fire. The fire which burns in dependence on chips is called a chip-fire. The fire which burns in dependence on grass is called a grass-fire. The fire which burns in dependence on cow-dung is called a cow-dung fire. The fire which burns in dependence on husks is called a husk-fire. The fire which burns in dependence on rubbish is called a rubbish-fire. In exactly the same way, O priests, consciousness is named from that in dependence on which it comes into being. The consciousness which comes into being in respect of forms in dependence on the eye is called eye-consciousness. The consciousness which comes into being in respect of sounds in dependence on the ear is called ear-consciousness. The consciousness which comes into being in respect of odors in dependence on the nose is called nose-con-sciousness. The consciousness which comes into being in respect of tastes in dependence on the tongue is called

tongue-consciousness. The consciousness which comes into
being in respect of things tangible in dependence on the body
is called body-consciousness. The consciousness which comes
into being in respect of ideas in dependence on the mind is
called mind-consciousness.

§ 28 c. — Translated from the Visuddhi-Magga (chap. xvii.).

In the proposition, *On karma depends consciousness*, consciousness is sixfold, eye-consciousness etc.

Here eye-consciousness is twofold, being either a meritorious or a demeritorious fruition—likewise ear-consciousness,
nose-consciousness, tongue-consciousness, and body-consciousness. Mind-consciousness is the two minds, namely, the meritorious fruition-mind as well as the demeritorious fruition-
mind, the three mind-consciousnesses without a cause, the
eight fruition-thoughts belonging to the realm of sensual
pleasure and possessing a cause, the five thoughts belonging
to the realm of form, and the four belonging to the realm of
formlessness, making twenty-two divisions. Thus in the six
consciousnesses are included all the thirty-two worldly fruition-consciousnesses. The consciousnesses, however, which
transcend the world are not included as they are not
pertinent in a discussion of rebirth.

---

§ 29. NAME AND FORM.

§ 29 a. — Translated from the Visuddhi-Magga (chap. xvii.).

By "Name" are meant the three Groups beginning with
Sensation [*i. e.*, Sensation, Perception, and the Predisposi-
tions]; by "Form," the four elements and form derivative
from the four elements.

§ 29 b. — Translated from the Visuddhi-Magga (chap. xviii.).

Name has no power of its own, nor can it go on of its
own impulse, either to eat, or to drink, or to utter sounds, or
to make a movement. Form also is without power and can-

not go on of its own impulse. It has no desire to eat, or to drink, or to utter sounds, or to make a movement. But Form goes on when supported by Name, and Name when supported by Form. When Name has a desire to eat, or to drink, or to utter sounds, or to make a movement, then Form eats, drinks, utters sounds, makes a movement.

To make this matter clear they give the following illustration:

It is as if two men, the one blind from birth and the other a cripple, were desirous of going traveling. And the man blind from birth were to say to the cripple as follows: "See here! I am able to use my legs, but I have no eyes with which to see the rough and the smooth places in the road." And the cripple were to say to the man blind from birth as follows: "See here! I am able to use my eyes, but I have no legs with which to go forward and back." And the man blind from birth, pleased and delighted, were to mount the cripple on his shoulders. And the cripple sitting on the shoulders of the man blind from birth were to direct him, saying, "Leave the left and go to the right; leave the right and go to the left."

Here the man blind from birth is without power of his own, and weak, and cannot go of his own impulse or might. The cripple also is without power of his own, and weak, and cannot go of his own impulse or might. Yet when they mutually support one another it is not impossible for them to go.

In exactly the same way Name is without power of its own, and cannot spring up of its own might, nor perform this or that action. Form also is without power of its own, and cannot spring up of its own might, nor perform this or that action. Yet when they mutually support one another it is not impossible for them to spring up and go on.

§ 29 c. — Translated from the Visuddhi-Magga (chap. xx.).

And he knows as follows:

" No heap or collection of material exists for the production of Name and Form; nor are Name and Form sprung

from any such heap or collection of material; and when
Name and Form cease, they do not go to any of the cardinal
or intermediate points of the compass; and after Name and
Form have ceased, they do not exist anywhere in the shape
of heaped-up material. But, just as when a lute is played
upon, there is no previous store of sound; and when the
sound comes into existence, it does not come from any such
store; and when it ceases, it does not go to any of the cardinal or intermediate points of the compass; and when it has
ceased, it exists nowhere in a stored-up state; but having previously been non-existent, it came into existence in dependence on the body and neck of the lute and the exertions of
the performer; and having come into existence passes away:
in exactly the same way, all the elements of being, both those
with form and those without, come into existence after having
previously been non-existent; and having come into existence
pass away.

---

§ 30. THE SIX ORGANS OF SENSE.

Translated from the Saṃyutta-Nikāya (xii. 2[11]).

And what, O priests, are the six organs of sense?

Eye, ear, nose, tongue, body, and mind — these, O priests,
are called the six organs of sense.

---

§ 31. CONTACT.

Translated from the Milindapañha (60[10]).

"Bhante Nāgasena, what is contact?"

"Your majesty, contact is the act of coming in contact."

"Give an illustration."

"It is as if, your majesty, two rams were to fight one
another. The eye is comparable to one of these rams, form
to the other, and contact to their collision with each other."

"Give another illustration."

"It is as if, your majesty, the two hands were to be clapped together. The eye is comparable to one hand, form to the other, and contact to their collision with each other."

"Give another illustration."

"It is as if, your majesty, two cymbals were to be clapped together. The eye is comparable to one cymbal, form to the other, and contact to their collision with each other."

"You are an able man, bhante Nāgasena."

§ 32. SENSATION.

Translated from the Majjhima-Nikāya (Sutta 44 or i.302²⁸).

"My lady [Dhammadinnā], how many sensations are there?"

"Brother Visākha, there are three sensations; the pleasant sensation, the unpleasant sensation, and the indifferent sensation."

"But what, my lady, is the pleasant sensation, what the unpleasant sensation, and what the indifferent sensation?"

"Brother Visākha, whatever pleasant or joyous sensation is felt by the body or by the mind, that is pleasant sensation. Brother Visākha, whatever unpleasant or joyless sensation is felt by the body or by the mind, that is unpleasant sensation. Brother Visākha, whatever sensation that is neither joyous nor joyless is felt by the body or by the mind, that is indifferent sensation."

§ 33. DESIRE.

Translated from the Visuddhi-Magga (chap. xvii.).

In the proposition, *On sensation depends desire,*

> Desire for forms and all the rest
> Make up a list of six desires;
> And each of these is then perceived
> To triply manifest itself.

For the Vibhaṅga shows that in this proposition there are
six desires, named *desire for forms,* desire for sounds, . . .
odors, . . . tastes, . . . things tangible, . . . ideas, according to the designation of the object; just as a son is named
the treasurer's son, the Brahman's son, according to the
designation of his father. But it *is then perceived* that *each
of these* is *triple* according to the way it *manifests itself,*
namely, whether as desire for sensual pleasure, as desire for
permanent existence, or as desire for transitory existence.

When desire for, forms manifests itself in a sensual relish
for some form-object that may be within the field of vision, it
is then called desire for sensual pleasure.

When it is coupled with a heretical belief in the persistence of existences, and considers that its object is stable and
persistent, it is then called desire for permanent existence.
For passion when coupled with a heretical belief in the
persistence of existences is called desire for permanent
existence.

But when this desire for forms is coupled with a heretical belief in the annihilation of existences, and considers that
its object will be annihilated and perish, it is then called
desire for transitory existence. For passion when coupled
with a heretical belief in the annihilation of existences is
called desire for transitory existence. Similarly in regard to
sounds and the rest. This makes eighteen desires.

Eighteen desires for subjective forms etc., together with
eighteen for those existing outside, make thirty-six desires;
and thirty-six in the past, thirty-six in the future, and thirty-
six in the present make one hundred and eight desires. And
these can be reduced again to six, according to their objects,
forms etc., or to three only, desire for sensual pleasure etc.

Now just as we honour a nurse because of our love and
devotion to our children, so living beings, on account of their
love and devotion to the sensations excited by forms and the
other objects of sense, give high honour to painters, musicians,
perfumers, cooks, weavers, elixir-prescribing physicians, and
other like persons who furnish us with objects of sense.
Therefore all these desires are included in the proposition,
" On sensation depends desire."

> But inasmuch as here is meant
> Sensation that hath happy fruit,
> And that is one, it thus gives rise
> By one dependence to desire.

By one. It is its dependence by the proximate dependence alone.

And moreover, inasmuch as

> Th' unhappy happy seek to be,
> The happy seek still greater joy,
> And since indifference is bliss,
> And happiness is likewise called,

> Therefore these three sensations form
> Dependence threefold for desire.
> Now as The Sage hath said, " Upon
> Sensation doth depend desire,"

> And since desire can ne'er exist
> And baleful karma not produce,
> Therefore no lodgment can it find
> In mind of any Brahman wise.

This is the full discussion of the proposition, " On sensation depends desire."

---

§ 34. ATTACHMENT.

§ 34 *a*. — Translated from the Visuddhi-Magga (chap. xiv.).

In looking upon Form and the other Groups as having a
nature resembling bubbles of foam and the like, the meditative priest ceases to look upon the unsubstantial as substan-
tiality. To particularize : —

In looking upon subjective Form as impure, he comes
thoroughly to understand material food, abandons the perverse mistaking of the impure for the pure, crosses the torrent
of sensual pleasure, breaks loose from the yoke of sensual
pleasure, is freed from the depravity of sensual pleasure,

severs the myriad bonds of covetousness, and does not attach
himself by the Attachment of Sensual Pleasure ;

In looking upon Sensation as misery, he comes thoroughly
to understand the nutriment called contact, abandons the
perverse mistaking of misery for happiness, crosses the torrent
of existence, breaks loose from the yoke of existence, is freed
from the depravity of passion for existence, severs the myriad
bonds of malevolence, and does not attach himself by the
Attachment of Fanatical Conduct;

In looking upon Perception and the Predispositions as
not an Ego, he comes thoroughly to understand the nutriment called karma, abandons the perverse mistaking of
what is no Ego for an Ego, crosses the torrent of heresy,
breaks loose from the yoke of heresy, is freed from the depravity of heresy, severs the myriad bonds of dogmatism, and does
not attach himself by the Attachment of the Assertion of
an Ego ;

In looking upon Consciousness as transitory, he comes
thoroughly to understand the nutriment called consciousness,
abandons the perverse mistaking of the transitory for the permanent, crosses the torrent of ignorance, breaks loose from
the yoke of ignorance, is freed from the depravity of ignorance, severs the myriad bonds of an affectation of fanatical
conduct, and does not attach himself by the Attachment of
Heresy.

§ 34 *b.* — Translated from the Visuddhi-Magga (chap. xvii.).

In the proposition, *On desire depends attachment,*

> Attachments are in number four :
> Whose definition various,
> Their short description, and their long,
> And sequence must one seek to show.

The following is the *showing :* —

The following are the *four attachments ;* the attachment
of sensual pleasure, the attachment of heresy, the attachment
of fanatical conduct, the attachment of the assertion of
an Ego.

The following is the *definition various.*

The attachment of sensual pleasure is attachment with some form of sensual pleasure as its object. Or, again, it is the attachment of sensual pleasure because it is at the same time attachment and sensual pleasure. The word attachment [1] means a tenacious grasp. The syllables *u-pa* strengthen the word, just as in *upāyāsa, upakkuṭṭha,* etc.

In like manner the attachment of heresy is heresy and attachment; or it is attachment to some form of heresy, whether concerning the past or the future, as when one says, " The Ego and the world are persistent," etc.

In like manner the attachment of fanatical conduct is attachment to some mode of fanatical conduct; or it is attachment and fanatical conduct. Cattle-conduct, cattle-behavior, and the like are attachments because they involve the belief that thus purity can be obtained.

In like manner assertion is what people assert; attachment is that by which they attach themselves. What do they assert? and to what do they attach themselves ? The Ego. The attachment of the assertion of an Ego is the attachment to the assertion of an Ego, or it is the simple assertion of an Ego. The attachment of the assertion of an Ego is when people attach themselves by the assertion of an Ego.

The above, then, is the *definition various.*

Their short description, and their long.

First in regard to the attachment of sensual pleasure.

" What is the attachment of sensual pleasure ? Sensual craving, sensual passion, sensual delight, sensual desire, sensual affection, sensual torment, sensual infatuation, sensual cleaving, this is called the attachment of sensual pleasure." In short, in this quotation, attachment is described as tenacity of desire. Tenacious desire is when an earlier desire has become tenacious by the proximate dependence. Some, however, say, " Desire is the quest of an object before it is obtained, as when a robber gropes about in the dark ; attachment is the seizing hold of an object within reach, as when the robber gets

---

[1] In Pāli upādāna, i. e. upa + ādāna.

hold of his booty.   And both are inimical to moderation and
contentment and are the roots out of which grow seeking and
guarding.

The short description of the other three attachments is that
they are heresy.

In their long description, however, the attachment of sensual pleasure is tenacity of the aforesaid one-hundred-and-
eight-fold desire for forms and other objects of sense.

The attachment of heresy consists of heretical views
regarding ten different subjects.

" What is the attachment of heresy? ' There is no such
thing as a gift, a sacrifice, an offering, a fruition or result of
good or evil deeds, a present life, a future life, a mother,
a father, apparitional existence, or any monk or Brahman
having found the right road and correct line of conduct who
can proclaim of his own knowledge and perception either
this world or the next!' any such heresy, heretical belief,
heretical jungle, heretical wilderness, heretical puppet-show,
heretical writhing, heretical fetter, figment, notion, persuasion, affectation, byway, false way, falsity, schismatic doctrine, or error is called the attachment of heresy."

The heresy of fanatical conduct is the affectation of the
belief that purity is by fanatical conduct.   As it is said :

" What is the attachment of fanatical conduct? Purity is
by conduct; purity is by fanaticism ; purity is by fanatical
conduct, — any such heresy, heretical belief, heretical jungle,
heretical wilderness, heretical puppet-show, heretical writhing,
heretical fetter, figment, notion, persuasion, affectation, byway, false way, falsity, schismatic doctrine, or error is called
the attachment of fanatical conduct."

The attachment of the assertion of an Ego is the twenty-
fold heresy of individuality.   As it is said :

" What is the heresy of the assertion of an Ego? Here an
ignorant, unconverted man, who is not a follower of noble
disciples, not conversant with the Noble Doctrine, not disciplined in the Noble Doctrine, not a follower of good people,
not conversant with the doctrine held by good people, not
disciplined in the doctrine of good people, considers form in

the light of an Ego — either the Ego as possessing form, or
form as comprised in the Ego, or the Ego as comprised in
form; considers sensation . . . perception . . . the predispositions . . . consciousness as the Ego, or the Ego as possessing consciousness, or consciousness as comprised in the
Ego, or the Ego as comprised in consciousness, — any such
heresy, heretical belief, heretical jungle, heretical wilderness,
heretical puppet-show, heretical writhing, heretical fetter,
figment, notion, persuasion, affectation, byway, false way,
falsity, schismatic doctrine, or error is called the attachment
of the assertion of the Ego." [1]

The above is *their short description, and their long.*

And sequence: — That sequence is threefold; sequence
in originating, sequence in abandoning, sequence in teaching.

Now, as the round of rebirth is without known beginning
and it is impossible to say which corruption first arises, no
absolute order of sequence can be laid down; but in any particular existence the order most commonly followed is for the
heresy of the assertion of an Ego to come first and be followed
by a heretical belief either in the persistence of existences or
in their annihilation.   Then he who believes that the Ego is
persistent adopts the attachment of the heresy of fanatical
conduct to purify his Ego, and he who believes that the Ego
is annihilated, being reckless of a future life, adopts the
attachment of sensual pleasure.   Thus the sequence of originating in any particular existence is for the attachment of the
heresy of the assertion of an Ego to come first, and after it
the attachments of heresy, fanatical conduct, and sensual
pleasure.

The attachment of heresy, the attachment of fanatical conduct, and the attachment of the assertion of an Ego are first
abandoned, as they are destroyed by the Path of Conversion;
the attachment of sensual pleasure afterwards by the Path of
Arhatship.   This is the sequence in abandonment.

The attachment of sensual pleasure is first taught both on
account of its extent and of its conspicuousness.   For as it

---

[1] See Dhammasaṅgani, §§ 1214 to 1217.

occurs in conjunction with eight of the consciousnesses it has a large extent; the others have but little, being conjoined with only four. And as mankind is for the most part given over to its lusts, the attachment of sensual pleasure is conspicuous; not so the others. Or, the attachment of sensual pleasure is for the purpose of obtaining objects of lust, and the attachment of heresy in the form of belief in the persistence of the Ego comes next as being more a question of speculative curiosity and the like. This has two divisions, the attachment of fanatical conduct, and the attachment of the assertion of an Ego. Of these two, the attachment of fanatical conduct is first taught from its grossness as one can see cattle-practices and dog-practices with one's own eyes; the attachment of the assertion of an Ego comes last on account of its subtileness. This is the sequence in teaching.

---

§ 35. EXISTENCE.

Translated from the Visuddhi-Magga (chap. xvii.).

In the proposition, *On attachment depends existence,*

> The sense, the different elements,
> The use, divisions, summings up,
> And which the dependence makes of which,
> Must now be understood in full.

"Existence" is so called because it is an existing. It is twofold; karma-existence, and originating-existence. As it has been said: "Existence is twofold: there is a karma-existence, and there is an originating-existence." Here *karma-existence* is equivalent to karma; and in like manner *originating-existence* is equivalent to originating. Originating is called existence because it is an existing; but karma is called existence because it causes existence, just as the birth of a Buddha is called happy because it results in happiness.

This, then, is the full understanding of *the sense*.

The different elements : — Karma-existence is in brief thought and the elements covetousness etc., which go under the name of karma and exist conjoined with thought.   As it has been said,

"What is karma-existence?   Meritorious karma, demeritorious karma, and karma leading to immovability, all these are called karma-existence, whether they be of little or great extent.   Moreover all karma conducive to existence is karma-existence."

In the above, the term meritorious karma includes thirteen thoughts, demeritorious karma includes twelve, and the term, karma leading to immovability, includes four thoughts. Also, by the phrase, "Whether of little or great extent," is meant the slight or large amount of fruition of these same thoughts, and, by the phrase, "And all karma conducive to existence," are meant covetousness and so on conjoined with thought.

Originating-existence, however, is in brief the groups which have come into existence through karma, and it has a ninefold division.   As it is said,

"What is originating-existence?   Existence in the realm of sensual pleasure, existence in the realm of form, existence in the realm of formlessness, existence in the realm of perception, existence in the realm of non-perception, existence in the realm of neither perception nor yet non-perception, existence once infected, existence four times infected, existence five times infected, all these are originating-existence."

In the above, existence in the realm of sensual pleasure is the existence called sensual pleasure, and similarly in respect of existence in the realm of form, and of existence in the realm of formlessness.   Existence in the realm of perception is so called either because perception constitutes that existence, or because there is perception in that existence. The converse is the case with existence in the realm of non-perception.   Existence in the realm of neither perception nor yet non-perception is so called because, as there is no gross perception there, but only a subtile one, there is neither perception nor yet non-perception in that existence.   Existence

once infected is existence infected with the form-group alone,
or it is called existence once infected because there is but one
infection to that existence, and similarly in regard to existences four times and five times infected.

Existence in the realm of sensual pleasure is the five
attachment-groups, and existence in the realm of form is
the same. Existence in the realm of formlessness is four
attachment-groups. Existence in the realm of perception is
five attachment-groups, and existence in the realm of non-
perception is one attachment-group. Existence in the realm
of neither perception nor yet non-perception is four attachment-groups, and existence once infected etc., is one, four, or
five attachment-groups.

This, then, is the full understanding of *the different
elements.*

The use : — It is true that the meritorious and the other
karmas have been already spoken of in the exposition of
karma. However, this karma was the karma of a previous
existence and hence given as constituting the dependence for
conception into this one, — while in the present case they are
present karma and given as constituting the dependence for
conception into a future existence. Thus the repetition is of
use. Or again, when it was said, " What is meritorious
karma? It is meritorious thoughts in the realm of sensual
pleasure," and so on, only thoughts were included in the term
karma, while in the present instance where it is said, " And
all karma conducive to existence," there are also included
the elements of being which are conjoined with thoughts.
Or again, only that karma which is the dependence of consciousness was in the first instance intended by the term
karma, but now that also which gives rise to an existence in
the realm of non-perception. But why make a long story
of it? By the meritorious karma etc. intended in the proposition, " On ignorance depends karma," meritorious and
demeritorious factors of being only are meant ; but in the
present case, in the proposition, " On attachment depends
existence," inasmuch as originating-existence is included, all
elements of being, whether meritorious or demeritorious or

indeterminate are intended.   Accordingly the repetition is
useful from every point of view.

This, then, is the full understanding of *the use.*

Divisions, summings up : — The divisions and summings up
of an existence dependent on attachment. For, whatever
karma depends on the attachment of sensual pleasure and
produces existence in the realm of sensual pleasure, this is
karma-existence, and the groups that spring from it are originating-existence.   Similarly in regard to existence in the
realm of form and existence in the realm of formlessness.
This makes two existences in the realm of sensual pleasure
besides the therewith included existence in the realm of perception and existence five times infected; two existences in
the realm of form besides the therewith included existence
in the realm of perception, existence in the realm of non-perception, existence once infected, and existence five times
infected; and two existences in the realm of formlessness
besides the therewith included existence in the realm of
perception, existence in the realm of neither perception nor
yet non-perception, and existence four times infected, all of
which depend on the attachment of sensual pleasure — six
existences besides the therewith included existences.   And
just as six existences and the therewith included existences
depend on the attachment of sensual pleasure, so also do six
existences depend on each of the other three attachments.
Thus in respect of their divisions there are twenty-four existences besides the therewith included existences, all of which
depend on attachment.

In regard to their summings up, however, by putting
karma-existence and originating-existence together we have
existence in the realm of sensual pleasure and the therewith
included existences, existence in the realm of form, and existence in the realm of formlessness, making three existences
which depend on the attachment of sensual pleasure; and
similarly in regard to the remaining attachments. Thus there
sum up twelve existences besides the therewith included
existences, all of which depend on attachment. Moreover, to
speak absolutely, karma-existence is karma which leads to

existence in the realm of sensual pleasure and is dependent on attachment, and the groups which spring from it are originating-existence. And it is the same in regard to existence in the realm of form and existence in the realm of formlessness. This makes two existences in the realm of sensual pleasure, two existences in the realm of form, and two existences in the realm of formlessness besides the therewith included existences, all of which depend on attachment. By another method of computation, the six existences, by not dividing into karma-existence and originating-existence, sum up as three existences, namely, existence in the realm of sensual pleasure etc., besides the existences therewith included. Also by not dividing into existence in the realm of sensual pleasure etc., karma-existence and originating-existence become two existences; and again, by not dividing into karma-existence and originating-existence, there remains in the proposition, "On attachment depends existence," only existence.

This, then, is the full understanding of *the divisions* and *summings up* of existence dependent on attachment.

And which the dependence makes of which : — The sense is, it must be fully understood which attachment is the dependence of which? But which is the dependence of which? Every one is the dependence of every one else. For the unconverted are like madmen, and fail to reflect on what is suitable and what is unsuitable. As the result of any and every attachment, they long for any and every existence and perform any and every karma. Therefore the view of those who say that existence in the realm of form and existence in the realm of formlessness do not come about by the attachment of fanatical conduct is not to be accepted. But on the contrary, any and every existence comes about by any and every attachment. As follows : —

We may have one who, because of what he hears reported or by inference from what he sees, reflects as follows: "Sensual pleasures obtain in the world of men in wealthy families of the warrior caste and so forth and so on, and also in the six heavens of sensual pleasures." Then he becomes deceived

by listening to false doctrine and takes a wrong way to attain
them, and thinking, " By this kind of karma I shall obtain
sensual pleasures," he adopts the attachment of sensual
pleasure and does evil with his body, evil with his voice, and
evil with his mind, and when he has fulfilled his wickedness
he is reborn in a lower state of existence. Or again, he
adopts the attachment of sensual pleasure through being desirous of sensual pleasure and of protecting that which he
has already obtained, and does evil with his body, evil with
his voice, and evil with his mind, and when he has fulfilled
his wickedness he is reborn in a lower state of existence.
Here the karma that was the cause of his rebirth is karma-
existence. The groups which sprang from that karma were
originating-existence. Existence in the realm of perception
and existence five times infected are therewith included.

Another, however, strengthens his knowledge by listening to the Good Doctrine, and thinking, " By this kind
of karma I shall obtain sensual pleasures," adopts the attachment of sensual pleasure and does good with his body, good
with his voice, and good with his mind; and when he has
fulfilled his righteousness he is reborn either among the
gods or among men. Here the karma that was the cause of
his rebirth is karma-existence. The groups which sprang
from that karma were originating-existence. Existence in
the realm of form and existence five times infected are therewith included. Accordingly the attachment of sensual pleasure is the dependence of existence in the realm of sensual
pleasure together with its divisions and whatever existences
are therewith included.

Another, having heard or come to the conclusion that
there are superior sensual pleasures in the realm of form and
in the realm of formlessness, adopts the attachment of sensual pleasure and achieves the trances of the realm of form
and of the realm of formlessness, and by the might of these
trances is reborn in a Brahma-heaven. Here the karma that
was the cause of his rebirth was karma-existence. The
groups which sprang from that karma were originating-existence. Existence in the realm of perception, existence in the

realm of non-perception, existence in the realm of neither perception nor yet non-perception, existence once infected, and
existence five times infected, are therewith included. Accordingly the attachment of sensual pleasure is the dependence of existence in the realm of form and existence in the
realm of formlessness, together with their divisions and the
existences therewith included.

Another adopts the heresy of the annihilation of existences and thinking either that it would be a good plan to
have his Ego undergo annihilation while in the realm of
sensual pleasure or else while in the realm of form or else
while in the realm of formlessness, performs karma leading
to those existences. This karma of his is karma-existence
and the groups that spring from it are originating-existence.
Existence in the realm of perception etc. are therewith
included. Accordingly the attachment of heresy is the
dependence of all three modes of existence, viz., of existence
in the realm of sensual pleasure, existence in the realm of
form, and existence in the realm of formlessness, together
with their divisions and the existences therewith included.

Another, thinking either that his Ego is happy when in
the realm of sensual pleasure, or else when in the realm of
form, or else when in the realm of formlessness, by the
attachment of the assertion of an Ego performs karma leading to those existences. This karma of his is karma-existence
and the groups that spring from it are originating-existence.
Existence in the realm of perception etc. are therewith
included. Accordingly the attachment of the assertion of
an Ego is the dependence for the three modes of existence
together with their divisions and the existences therewith
included.

Another, thinking that fanatical conduct attains to a
happy fulfilment either in the realm of sensual pleasure, or
else in the realm of form, or else in the realm of formlessness, adopts the attachment of fanatical conduct and performs the karma leading to those existences. This karma
of his is karma-existence and the groups that spring from it
are originating-existence. Existence in the realm of percep-

tion etc. are therewith included. Accordingly the attachment of fanatical conduct is the dependence for the three
modes of existence together with their divisions and the
existences therewith included.

This, then, is the full understanding of *and which the
dependence makes of which.*

Now if it be asked, " But how is which the dependence
of which existence?" we answer that attachment is to be
understood as the proximate dependence of existence in the
realm of form and in the realm of formlessness, and the
connate etc. dependence of existence in the realm of sensual
pleasure.

For when a being is in the realm of sensual pleasure,
then the four attachments are the dependence of meritorious karma and of originating-existence in the realm of form
and in the realm of formlessness by the proximate dependence alone. When conjoined with demeritorious karma they
are the dependence by the connate dependence etc., that is,
by the connate, the mutual, the basal, the conjoined, the
actual, the abiding, and the causal dependence; but when
not so conjoined, by the proximate dependence alone.

This is the full discussion of the proposition " On attachment depends existence."

---

§ 36. BIRTH ETC.

Translated from the Visuddhi-Magga (chap. xvii.).

The definitions of birth etc. in the last two propositions
of Dependent Origination are to be understood as above
expounded in the Exposition of the Four Truths; but by
existence is here meant only karma-existence. For that and
not originating-existence is the dependence of birth. Moreover it is its dependence in only one of two ways, namely, as
karma-dependence or as proximate dependence.

If it be asked in this connection, " But how do we know
that existence is the dependence of birth?" we answer, "Be-

cause differences in respect of meanness, greatness, etc. are apparent, even when the external dependence remains the same. For even when the external dependence, such as the seed, blood, food, etc., of father and mother are the same, differences of meanness, greatness, etc. in the progeny are observable, and that even in the case of twins. And these differences are due to a cause, for some do not have these differences; but these differences can have no other cause than karma, from the non-existence of any other instrumentality for the purpose in the sequence of beings who show these differences. Thus they have only karma-existence as their cause. Karma is indeed the cause for the difference in beings as regards meanness, greatness, etc. Therefore has The Blessed One said: — "Karma allots beings to meanness or greatness." Therefore is it to be understood that existence is the dependence of birth.

But inasmuch as when there is no birth there is no old age or death, nor those other elements of being, sorrow and the rest; and on the other hand when there is birth, then, to the fool who is afflicted with the misery called old age and death, occur the sorrow and the rest that are associated with old age and death; and also to the fool who is afflicted with this or that other misery do they occur, but not so associated; therefore is it to be understood of birth that it is the dependence both of old age and death and of sorrow etc. But it is their dependence by the proximate dependence alone.

This is the full discussion of the propositions, "On existence depends birth," etc.

---

§ 37. DISCUSSION OF DEPENDENT ORIGINATION.

Translated from the Mahā-Nidāna-Sutta of the Dīgha-Nikāya (Grimblot's edition, p. 245[1]).

Thus have I heard.

On a certain occasion The Blessed One was dwelling among the Kurus where was the Kuru-town named Kammā-sadhamma.

Then drew near the venerable Ānanda to where The Blessed One was; and having drawn near and greeted The Blessed One, he sat down respectfully at one side. And seated respectfully at one side, the venerable Ānanda spoke to The Blessed One as follows:

"O wonderful is it, Reverend Sir! O marvellous is it, Reverend Sir! How profound, Reverend Sir, is Dependent Origination, and of how profound an appearance! To me, nevertheless, it is as clear as clear can be."

"O Ānanda, say not so! O Ānanda, say not so! Profound, Ānanda, is Dependent Origination, and profound of appearance. It is through not understanding this doctrine, Ānanda, through not penetrating it, that thus mankind is like to an entangled warp, or to an ensnarled web, or to muñja-grass and pabbaja-grass, and fails to extricate itself from punishment, suffering, perdition, rebirth.

"Ānanda, if it be asked, 'Do old age and death depend on anything?' the reply should be, ' They do.' And if it be asked, 'On what do old age and death depend?' the reply should be, ' Old age and death depend on birth.'

"Ānanda, if it be asked, 'Does birth depend on anything?' the reply should be, 'It does.' And if it be asked, 'On what does birth depend?' the reply should be, 'Birth depends on existence.'

"Ānanda, if it be asked, 'Does existence depend on anything?' the reply should be, 'It does.' And if it be asked, 'On what does existence depend?' the reply should be, 'Existence depends on attachment.'

"Ānanda, if it be asked, 'Does attachment depend on anything?' the reply should be, 'It does.' And if it be asked, 'On what does attachment depend?' the reply should be, 'Attachment depends on desire.'

"Ānanda, if it be asked, 'Does desire depend on anything?' the reply should be, 'It does.' And if it be asked, 'On what does desire depend?' the reply should be, 'Desire depends on sensation.'

"Ānanda, if it be asked, 'Does sensation depend on anything?' the reply should be, 'It does.' And if it be asked,

'On what does sensation depend?' the reply should be, 'Sensation depends on contact.'

"Ānanda, if it be asked, 'Does contact depend on anything?' the reply should be, 'It does.' And if it be asked, 'On what does contact depend?' the reply should be, 'Contact depends on name and form.'

"Ānanda, if it be asked, 'Do name and form depend on anything?' the reply should be, 'They do.' And if it be asked, 'On what do name and form depend?' the reply should be, 'Name and form depend on consciousness.'

"Ānanda, if it be asked, 'Does consciousness depend on anything?' the reply should be, 'It does.' And if it be asked, 'On what does consciousness depend?' the reply should be, 'Consciousness depends on name and form.'

"Thus, Ānanda, on name and form depends consciousness;

"On consciousness depend name and form;

"On name and form depends contact;

"On contact depends sensation;

"On sensation depends desire;

"On desire depends attachment;

"On attachment depends existence;

"On existence depends birth;

"On birth depend old age and death, sorrow, lamentation, misery, grief, and despair. Thus does this entire aggregation of misery arise.

"I have said that on birth depend old age and death. This truth, Ānanda, that on birth depend old age and death, is to be understood in this way. Suppose, Ānanda, there were utterly and completely no birth at all for any one into any world, as, namely, for gods into the world of gods; for genii into the world of genii; for ogres into the world of ogres; for demons into the world of demons; for men into the world of men; for quadrupeds into the world of quadrupeds; for winged creatures into the world of winged creatures; for creeping things into the world of creeping things; — suppose, Ānanda, there were no birth for any of these beings into their several worlds: if there were nowhere any birth, pray, on the cessation of birth would there be any old age and death ? "

" Nay, verily, Reverend Sir."

" Accordingly, Ānanda, here we have in birth the cause, the occasion, the origin, and the dependence of old age and death.

" I have said that on existence depends birth. This truth, Ānanda, that on existence depends birth, is to be understood in this way. Suppose, Ānanda, there were utterly and completely no existence at all for any one in any mode, as, namely, existence in the realm of sensual pleasure, existence in the realm of form, existence in the realm of formlessness ; — if there were nowhere any existence, pray, on the cessation of existence would there be any birth ? "

" Nay, verily, Reverend Sir."

" Accordingly, Ānanda, here we have in existence the cause, the occasion, the origin, and the dependence of birth.

" I have said that on attachment depends existence. This truth Ānanda, that on attachment depends existence, is to be understood in this way. Suppose, Ānanda, there were utterly and completely no attachment at all of any one to anything, as, namely, the attachment of sensual pleasure, the attachment of heresy, the attachment of fanatical conduct, the attachment of the assertion of an Ego ; — if there were nowhere any attachment, pray, on the cessation of attachment would there be any existence ? "

" Nay, verily, Reverend Sir."

" Accordingly, Ānanda, here we have in attachment the cause, the occasion, the origin, and the dependence of existence.

" I have said that on desire depends attachment. This truth, Ānanda, that on desire depends attachment, is to be understood in this way. Suppose, Ānanda, there were utterly and completely no desire at all on the part of any one for anything, as, namely, desire for forms, desire for sounds, desire for odors, desire for tastes, desire for things tangible, desire for ideas ; — if there were nowhere any desire, pray, on the cessation of desire would there be any attachment ? "

" Nay, verily, Reverend Sir."

" Accordingly, Ānanda, here we have in desire the cause, the occasion, the origin, and the dependence of attachment.

" I have said that on sensation depends desire. This truth, Ānanda, that on sensation depends desire, is to be understood in this way. Suppose, Ānanda, there were utterly and completely no sensation at all on the part of any one for anything, as, namely, sensation sprung from contact of the eye, sensation sprung from contact of the ear, sensation sprung from contact of the nose, sensation sprung from contact of the tongue, sensation sprung from contact of the body, sensation sprung from contact of the mind; — if there were nowhere any sensation, pray, on the cessation of sensation would there be any desire ? "

" Nay, verily, Reverend Sir."

" Accordingly, Ānanda, here we have in sensation the cause, the occasion, the origin, and the dependence of desire."

.   .   .   .   .   [Grimblot 253⁴]   .   .   .   .   .

" I have said that on contact depends sensation. This truth, Ānanda, that on contact depends sensation, is to be understood in this way. Suppose, Ānanda, there were utterly and completely no contact at all of any organ with any object, as, namely, contact of the eye, contact of the ear, contact of the nose, contact of the tongue, contact of the body, contact of the mind; — if there were nowhere any contact, pray, on the cessation of contact would there be any sensation ? "

" Nay, verily, Reverend Sir."

" Accordingly, Ānanda, here we have in contact the cause, the occasion, the origin, and the dependence of sensation.

" I have said that on name and form depends contact. This truth, Ānanda, that on name and form depends contact, is to be understood in this way. Suppose, Ānanda, there were not these different traits, peculiarities, signs, and indications by which are made manifest the multitude of elements of being constituting name ; — if there were not these different traits, peculiarities, signs, and indications, pray, would there be any designative contact appearing in form?"

"Nay, verily, Reverend Sir."

"Suppose, Ānanda, there were not these different traits, peculiarities, signs, and indications by which are made manifest the multitude of elements of being constituting form; — if there were not these different traits, peculiarities, signs, and indications, pray, would there be any inertia-contact appearing in name?"

"Nay, verily, Reverend Sir."

"Suppose, Ānanda, there were not these different traits, peculiarities, signs, and indications by which are made manifest the multitude of elements of being constituting name and the multitude of elements of being constituting form; — if there were not these different traits, peculiarities, signs, and indications, pray, would there be any contact?"

"Nay, verily, Reverend Sir."

"Accordingly, Ānanda, here we have in name and form the cause, the occasion, the origin, and the dependence of contact.

"I have said that on consciousness depend name and form. This truth, Ānanda, that on consciousness depend name and form, is to be understood in this way. Suppose, Ānanda, consciousness were not to descend into the maternal womb, pray, would name and form consolidate in the maternal womb?"

"Nay, verily, Reverend Sir."

"Suppose, Ānanda, consciousness, after descending into the maternal womb, were then to go away again, pray, would name and form be born to life in the world?"

"Nay, verily, Reverend Sir."

"Suppose, Ānanda, consciousness were to be severed from a child, either boy or girl, pray, would name and form attain to growth, increase, and development?"

"Nay, verily, Reverend Sir."

"Accordingly Ānanda, here we have in consciousness the cause, the occasion, the origin, and the dependence of name and form.

"I have said that on name and form depends consciousness. This truth, Ānanda, that on name and form depends consciousness, is to be understood in this way. Suppose, Ānanda, that name and form were not to become established, pray, would there, in the future, be birth, old age and death, and the coming into existence of misery's host?"

"Nay, verily, Reverend Sir."

"Accordingly, Ānanda, here we have in name and form the cause, the occasion, the origin, and the dependence of consciousness.

"Verily, Ānanda, this name and form coupled with consciousness is all there is to be born, or to grow old, or to die, or to leave one existence, or to spring up in another. It is all that is meant by any affirmation, predication, or declaration we may make concerning anybody. It constitutes knowledge's field of action. And it is all that is reborn to appear in its present shape."

CHAPTER III.

KARMA AND REBIRTH.

Introductory Discourse.

Perhaps one of the hardest of the Buddhist doctrines is that of Karma. It is a doctrine, not only hard in itself, but it seems to contradict their other tenets. The Buddhists, as we have seen, resolve the human being into a number of elements called *dhammas* which possess no permanent existence, and they say that on account of this transitoriness no one of these can be considered as the individual, the Ego, the "self." There is therefore here nothing to be reborn — nothing to transmigrate. How then is it, that when he has thus denied all substantive existence to everything which to the Occidental thinker appears to possess the greatest reality, the Oriental should attribute to karma this faculty of being reborn indefinitely?

The word *karma* means 'deeds,' or, as it is often used in the singular, it might perhaps be translated by 'performance' or 'action.' How can substantive reality be attributed to a mere conception of the mind like that of deed or performance, when it is denied of all those components of the human being of which we are cognizant by means of our senses and our self-consciousness? How can any deed be said to be immortal, except in a purely figurative sense, meaning that the memory or else the objective effect of it persists? Now if we look at this doctrine of Karma a little more closely, we may see that it is not so very unlike Christian ideas. If we were to translate the word *karma* somewhat freely, we might call it 'character.' And what, indeed, do we ordinarily mean when we speak of personal immortality, unless it be that the characters of our friends are reborn in heaven? It is evidently not the body that is reborn, for that is left behind with us. And what do we know of the spirit except simply its manifestations, and what we may argue from our own self-consciousness? Our knowledge of our friend is composed of what our senses tell us of his body and what we observe of his deeds. It is his character, his particular set of deeds, or karma, that we think of as surviving death; and this is exactly what the Buddhists do, — the only difference being that we claim the existence of an Ego. This we claim to know by self-inspection; and therefore, when we speak metaphysically, we say that it is our friend's Ego, or soul, that is reborn, and that our friend's character, which is really all we directly know of our friend, is simply the manifestation of that Ego. But as the Buddhists deny the existence of any soul, it is only observed character, or karma, that is left to be reborn. The reader will see, I think, that the two doctrines are really very similar, if we but leave the postulation of an Ego out of the question.

But the question still remains: How can character that is no entity in itself be reborn? Now here it is to be noted that the word 'karma' covers two distinct ideas; namely, the deed itself, and the effects of that deed in modifying the subsequent character and fortunes of the doer. The Buddhists say that this subjective effect continues after death into the next life. The following illustration may tend to make the general idea of the perpetuation of character without identity of substance seem more reasonable. Why cannot a swallow's egg hatch out a lark? or a lark's a swallow? Is there any difference perceptible between the two eggs in respect of composition or structure, adequate to account for the difference in the result? If not, how is it that the egg of the lark will never hatch out into any other kind of a bird than a lark, and that a swallow's egg must always yield a swallow? Now although it is true that if we take the eggs before the first sign of an embryo has appeared we may not be able to detect any physical or chemical difference that would seem to account for the difference in the result, yet we know the why and wherefore of that difference. A swallow's egg cannot hatch out a lark because of the difference in heredity. The countless influences that affected the ancestors of that egg, and the numberless actions performed under those influences are in some mysterious way stored up in that egg, and must bear their own fruit and none other. Therefore a swallow's egg cannot hatch out a lark, because a lark is the result of an entirely different set of conditions; as we might say, its karma is different. But of course the Buddhists do not mean heredity when they use the word *karma*. 'Karma' expresses, not that which a man inherits from his ancestors, but that which he inherits from himself in some previous state of existence. But with this difference the Buddhist doctrine and the scientific doctrine of heredity seem very similar.

Not all deeds, however, are fruitful and perpetuate existence. Karma is like heredity in that it is an informing principle which must have an embodiment. Just as the informing principle of an egg would never find expression without the accompaniment of yolk, albumen, and other material constituents, so karma embeds itself in objects of desire in order to form that factitious entity which goes by the name of man. If karma be performed in a state of pure passionlessness, that is, without attachment to anything, then it is barren. The fruitful karma will be quickly undermined and not suffered to bear the full fruit it otherwise would have done. Like a tree whose nourishment has been poisoned, the being who performs such karma will cease to be. See § 40, § 76 in Chapter IV, and § 41, which last is given by way of illustration of § 40 *b*. Thus a being without karma is as arbitrary a conception as a chicken without heredity, that is, one formed by creative fiat independent of antecedent conditions.

In illustration of the doctrine of repeated existence I give at the end of this chapter a number of "Birth-Stories," as they are called; namely, stories concerning the anterior "births" or existences of The Buddha. There is a separate work in the Buddhist Scriptures called the "Jātaka," or "Book of Birth-Stories," containing several hundred such tales. They form a mine of folk-lore, and, though credited to The Buddha, can hardly have been original with him. The ancient Buddhists, like other Orientals, appear to have been fond of gathering together in little companies and listening while some one of their number related a tale or fable; and ancient Buddhist sculptures have come down to the present day representing scenes taken out of these same stories that fill the Jātaka. Some of these tales are much traveled ones, and are to be found in Æsop's Fables, and in La Fontaine, and other European works. As a sample I give "The Ass in the Lion's Skin." Another instance of folk-lore common to both the Orient and the Occident, but not given as a Birth-Story, occurs in this chapter. The Pāli version is entitled "Death's Messengers," while "The Three Warnings" gives the same general idea in English dress. There are other English versions extant, and German, French, and Latin ones, so that this is an interesting instance of how a fable will travel about from country to country and from clime to clime, varying in dress to suit the habits, customs, and ways of thinking of the different peoples who adopt it into their literatures and then often forget its alien origin.

§ 38. BE A FRIEND TO YOURSELF.

Translated from the Saṁyutta-Nikāya (iii. 1.4¹).

Thus have I heard.

On a certain occasion The Blessed One was dwelling at Sāvatthi, in Jetavana monastery in Anāthapiṇḍika's Park.

Then drew near king Pasenadi the Kosalan to where The Blessed One was; and having drawn near and greeted The Blessed One, he sat down respectfully at one side. And seated respectfully at one side, king Pasenadi the Kosalan spoke to The Blessed One as follows:—

"Reverend Sir, it happened to me, as I was just now in seclusion and plunged in meditation, that a consideration presented itself to my mind, as follows: 'Who are those who love themselves? and who do not love themselves?' And, Reverend Sir, it occurred to me as follows: 'All they who do evil with their body, who do evil with their voice, who do evil with their mind, they do not love themselves.' And although they should say thus: 'We love ourselves,' nevertheless, they do not love themselves. And why do I say so? Because, whatever a man would do to one whom he did not love, that they do to themselves. Therefore, they do not love themselves.

"But all they who do good with their body, who do good with their voice, who do good with their mind, they love themselves. And although they should say thus: 'We do not love ourselves,' nevertheless, they do love themselves. And why do I say so? Because, whatever a man would do to one whom he loved, that they do to themselves. Therefore, they love themselves."

"Thus it is, great king! Thus it is! Certainly, great king, all they who do evil with their body, who do evil with their voice, who do evil with their mind, they do not love themselves. And although they should say thus: 'We love ourselves,' nevertheless, they do not love themselves. And why do I say so? Because, whatever a man would do to one whom he did not love, that they do to themselves. Therefore, they do not love themselves.

"But all they, great king, who do good with their body, who do good with their voice, who do good with their mind, they love themselves. And although they should say thus: 'We do not love ourselves,' nevertheless, they do love themselves. And why do I say so? Because, whatever a man would do to one he loved, that they do to themselves. Therefore, they love themselves.

> "Let any one who holds self dear,
> That self keep free from wickedness;
> For happiness can ne'er be found
> By any one of evil deeds.

> "Assailed by death, in life's last throes,
> At quitting of this human state,
> What is it one can call his own?
> What with him take as he goes hence?
> What is it follows after him,
> And like a shadow ne'er departs?

> "His good deeds and his wickedness,
> Whate'er a mortal does while here;
> 'T is this that he can call his own,
> This with him take as he goes hence.
> This is what follows after him,
> And like a shadow ne'er departs.

> "Let all, then, noble deeds perform,
> A treasure-store for future weal;
> For merit gained this life within,
> Will yield a blessing in the next."

§ 39. THE CAUSE OF INEQUALITY IN THE WORLD.

Translated from the Milindapañha (65¹¹).

Said the king, "Bhante Nāgasena, what is the reason that men are not all alike, but some long-lived and some short-lived, some healthy and some sickly, some handsome and some ugly, some powerful and some weak, some rich and some poor, some of high degree and some of low degree, some wise and some foolish?"

Said the elder, "Your majesty, why are not trees all alike, but some sour, some salt, some bitter, some pungent, some astringent, some sweet?"

"I suppose, bhante, because of a difference in the seed."

"In exactly the same way, your majesty, it is through a difference in their karma that men are not all alike, but some long-lived and some short-lived, some healthy and some sickly, some handsome and some ugly, some powerful and some weak, some rich and some poor, some of high degree and some of low degree, some wise and some foolish. Moreover, your majesty, The Blessed One has said as follows : ' All beings, O youth, have karma as their portion ; they are heirs of their karma ; they are sprung from their karma ; their karma is their kinsman ; their karma is their refuge ; karma allots beings to meanness or greatness.' "

"You are an able man, bhante Nāgasena."

---

§ 40. FRUITFUL AND BARREN KARMA.

§ 40 *a.* — Translated from the Añguttara-Nikāya (iii. 33¹).

[I. FRUITFUL KARMA.]

There are three conditions, O priests, under which deeds are produced. And what are the three? Covetousness is a condition under which deeds are produced ; hatred is a condition under which deeds are produced ; infatuation is a condition under which deeds are produced.

When a man's deeds, O priests, are performed through covetousness, arise from covetousness, are occasioned by covetousness, originate in covetousness, wherever his personality may be, there those deeds ripen, and wherever they ripen, there he experiences the fruition of those deeds, be it in the present life, or in some subsequent one.

When a man's deeds, O priests, are performed through hatred, . . . are performed through infatuation, arise from infatuation, are occasioned by infatuation, originate in infatuation, wherever his personality may be, there those deeds ripen, and wherever they ripen, there he experiences the fruition of those deeds, be it in the present life, or in some subsequent one.

It is like seed, O priests, that is uninjured, undecayed, unharmed by wind or heat, and is sound, and advantageously sown in a fertile field on well-prepared soil; if then rain falls in due season, then, O priests, will that seed attain to growth, increase, and development. In exactly the same way, O priests, when a man's deeds are performed through covetousness, arise from covetousness, are occasioned by covetousness, originate in covetousness, wherever his personality may be, there those deeds ripen, and wherever they ripen, there he experiences the fruition of those deeds, be it in the present life, or in some subsequent one; when a man's deeds are performed through hatred, . . . are performed through infatuation, arise from infatuation, are occasioned by infatuation, originate in infatuation, wherever his personality may be, there those deeds ripen, and wherever they ripen, there he experiences the fruition of those deeds, be it in the present life, or in some subsequent one.

These, O priests, are the three conditions under which deeds are produced.

[II. Barren Karma.]

There are three conditions, O priests, under which deeds are produced. And what are the three? Freedom from covetousness is a condition under which deeds are produced; freedom from hatred is a condition under which deeds are produced; freedom from infatuation is a condition under which deeds are produced.

When a man's deeds, O priests, are performed without covetousness, arise without covetousness, are occasioned without covetousness, originate without covetousness, then, inasmuch as covetousness is gone, those deeds are abandoned, uprooted, pulled out of the ground like a palmyra-tree, and become non-existent and not liable to spring up again in the future.

When a man's deeds, O priests, are performed without hatred, . . . are performed without infatuation, arise without infatuation, are occasioned without infatuation, originate without infatuation, then, inasmuch as infatuation is gone, those deeds are abandoned, uprooted, pulled out of the ground like a palmyra-tree, and become non-existent and not liable to spring up again in the future.

It is like seed, O priests, that is uninjured, undecayed, unharmed by wind or heat, and is sound, and advantageously sown; if some one then burn it with fire and reduce it to soot, and having reduced it to soot were then to scatter it to the winds, or throw it into a swift-flowing river, then, O priests, will that seed be abandoned, uprooted, pulled out of the ground like a palmyra-tree, and become non-existent and not liable to spring up again in the future. In exactly the same way, O priests, when a man's deeds are performed without covetousness, arise without covetousness, are occasioned without covetousness, originate without covetousness, then, inasmuch as covetousness is gone, those deeds are abandoned, uprooted, pulled out of the ground like a palmyra-tree, and become non-existent and not liable to spring up again in the future; when a man's deeds are performed without hatred, . . . without infatuation, arise without infatuation, are occasioned without infatuation, originate without infatuation, then, inasmuch as infatuation is gone, those deeds are abandoned, uprooted, pulled out of the ground like a palmyra-tree, and become non-existent and not liable to spring up again in the future.

These, O priests, are the three conditions under which deeds are produced.

> A wise priest knows he now must reap
> The fruits of deeds of former births.
> For be they many or but few,
> Deeds done in cov'tousness or hate,
> Or through infatuation's power,
> Must bear their needful consequence.

Hence not to cov'tousness, nor hate,
Nor to infatuation's power
The wise priest yields, but knowledge seeks
And leaves the way to punishment.

§ 40 b. — Translated from the Aṅguttara-Nikāya (iii. 99¹).

" O priests, if any one says that a man must reap according to his deeds, in that case, O priests, there is no religious
life, nor is any opportunity afforded for the entire extinction
of misery. But if any one says, O priests, that the reward a
man reaps accords with his deeds, in that case, O priests, there
is a religious life, and opportunity is afforded for the entire
extinction of misery.

" We may have the case, O priests, of an individual who
does some slight deed of wickedness which brings him to hell;
or, again, O priests, we may have the case of another individual who does the same slight deed of wickedness, and
expiates it in the present life, though it may be in a way
which appears to him not slight but grievous.

" What kind of individual, O priests, is he whose slight
deed of wickedness brings him to hell? — Whenever, O
priests, an individual is not proficient in the management of
his body, is not proficient in the precepts, is not proficient in
concentration, is not proficient in wisdom, and is limited and
bounded, and abides in what is finite and evil: such an individual, O priests, is he whose slight deed of wickedness brings
him to hell.

" What kind of individual, O priests, is he who does the
same slight deed of wickedness, and expiates it in the present
life, though it may be in a way which appears to him not
slight but grievous? — Whenever, O priests, an individual is
proficient in the management of his body, is proficient in the
precepts, is proficient in concentration, is proficient in wisdom,
and is not limited, nor bounded, and abides in the universal: such an individual, O priests, is he who does the same
slight deed of wickedness, and expiates it in the present life,
though it may be in a way which appears to him not slight
but grievous.

"It is as if, O priests, a man were to put a lump of salt into a small cup of water. What think ye, O priests? Would now the small amount of water in this cup be made salt and undrinkable by the lump of salt?"

"Yes, Reverend Sir."

"And why?"

"Because, Reverend Sir, there was but a small amount of water in the cup, and so it was made salt and undrinkable by the lump of salt."

"It is as if, O priests, a man were to throw a lump of salt into the river Ganges. What think ye, O priests? Would now the river Ganges be made salt and undrinkable by the lump of salt?"

"Nay, verily, Reverend Sir."

"And why not?"

"Because, Reverend Sir, the mass of water in the river Ganges is great, and so is not made salt and undrinkable by the lump of salt."

"In exactly the same way, O priests, we may have the case of an individual who does some slight deed of wickedness which brings him to hell; or, again, O priests, we may have the case of another individual who does the same slight deed of wickedness, and expiates it in the present life, though it may be in a way which appears to him not slight but grievous.

[Repetition of paragraphs 3 and 4, above.]

"We may have, O priests, the case of one who is cast into prison for a half-penny, for a penny, or for a hundred pence; or, again, O priests, we may have the case of one who is not cast into prison for a half-penny, for a penny, or for a hundred pence.

"Who, O priests, is cast into prison for a half-penny, for a penny, or for a hundred pence?

"Whenever, O priests, any one is poor, needy, and indigent: he, O priests, is cast into prison for a half-penny, for a penny, or for a hundred pence.

"Who, O priests, is not cast into prison for a half-penny, for a penny, or for a hundred pence?

" Whenever, O priests, any one is rich, wealthy, and affluent: he, O priests, is not cast into prison for a half-penny, for
a penny, or for a hundred pence.

" In exactly the same way, O priests, we may have the
case of an individual who does some slight deed of wickedness which brings him to hell; or, again, O priests, we may
have the case of another individual who does the same slight
deed of wickedness, and expiates it in the present life, though
it may be in a way which appears to him not slight but
grievous.

[Repetition of paragraphs 3 and 4, above.]

" Just as, O priests, a butcher and killer of rams will smite
one man if he steal a ram, and will bind him, and burn him,
and wreak his pleasure on him; and another who steals a
ram, he will not attack, nor bind him, nor burn him, nor
wreak his pleasure on him.

" Who is he, O priests, whom a butcher and killer of rams
will smite if he steal a ram, and will bind him, and burn him,
and wreak his pleasure on him?

" Whenever, O priests, the robber is poor, needy, and indigent: him, O priests, a butcher and killer of rams will smite
if he steal a ram, and will bind him, and burn him, and wreak
his pleasure on him.

" Who is he, O priests, whom a butcher and killer of rams
will not smite if he steal a ram, nor bind him, nor burn him,
nor wreak his pleasure on him?

" Whenever, O priests, the robber is rich, wealthy, and
affluent, a king, or a king's minister: him, O priests, a butcher
and killer of rams will not smite if he steal a ram, nor bind
him, nor burn him, nor wreak his pleasure on him. On the
contrary, he will stretch out his joined palms, and make sup-
plication, saying, ' Sir, give me the ram, or the price of the
ram.'

" In exactly the same way, O priests, we may have the
case of an individual who does some slight deed of wickedness which brings him to hell; or, again, O priests, we may
have the case of another individual who does the same slight
deed of wickedness, and expiates it in the present life, though

it may be in a way which appears to him not slight but grievous.

[Repetition of paragraphs 3 and 4, above.]

"O priests, if any one were to say that a man must reap according to his deeds, in that case, O priests, there is no religious life, nor is any opportunity afforded for the entire extinction of misery.   But if any one says, O priests, that the reward a man reaps accords with his deeds, in that case, O priests, there is a religious life, and opportunity is afforded for the entire extinction of misery."

§ 41. THE DEATH OF MOGGALLĀNA.[1]

Translated from the Dhammapada, and from Buddhaghosa's commentary
on stanza 137.

137. " Who striketh him that striketh not,
          And harmeth him that harmeth not,
          Shall quickly punishment incur,
          Some one among a list of ten.

138. " Or cruel pain, or drear old age
          And failure of the vital powers,
          Or some severe and dread disease,
          Or madness him shall overtake.

139. " Or from the king calamity,
          Or calumny shall be his lot;
          Or he shall see his kinsfolk die,
          Or all his wealth shall disappear.

140. " Or conflagrations shall arise
          And all his houses sweep away;
          And when his frame dissolves in death,
          In hell the fool shall be reborn."

---

[1] Aṅguttara-Nikāya, i. 14[1]: "O priests, the chief of my disciples who possess magical power is Moggallāna the Great."

"*Who striketh him.*"   This doctrinal instruction was given
by The Teacher while dwelling at Bamboo Grove; and it was
concerning the elder, Moggallāna the Great.

For on a certain occasion those who were members of
other sects held a meeting, and took counsel as follows:

"Brethren, do you know the reason why the alms and the
honor given to the monk Gotama have increased?"

"No: we do not. Do you?"

"Yes, truly: we know. It is solely due to Moggallāna
the Great. For he goes to heaven and questions the deities
concerning their previous karma, and then he returns and
tells it to men: 'It is by having done thus and so that they
now enjoy so great glory.' Also, he asks those who have
been born in hell concerning their karma, and returning, he
tells it to men: 'It is by having done such and such evil deeds
that they now experience so great misery.' And the people,
when they have heard him, shower alms and attentions upon
him. If we can only kill him, the alms and the honor that
now go to him will be ours."

The suggestion met with universal favor, and it was
unanimously agreed that in some way or other he should be
killed. Then they stirred up their supporters and obtained
from them a thousand pieces of money, and summoning some
red-handed highwaymen, they said,

"An elder, called Moggallāna the Great, is dwelling at
Black Rock. Go thither and kill him." And they gave them
the money.

The highwaymen greedily took the money, and went and
surrounded the elder's house in order to kill him.

The elder, perceiving that he was surrounded, got out
through the key-hole and escaped. Having failed that day to
find the elder, they came again on another day and surrounded him again. Then the elder pierced the peaked roof
and sprang into the sky. In this manner, neither during the
fore part nor during the middle of the month, were they able
to capture the elder. But when it drew towards the latter
part of the month, the elder found himself held back by his
previous karma, and could not flee. Then the highwaymen

captured him, and broke his bones into bits of the size of rice-grains.[1] And when they supposed he was dead, they threw him into a thicket, and departed.

But the elder thought, "I will see The Teacher before I pass into Nirvana." And swathing himself about with meditation, as with a bandage, and thus stiffening his body, he went to The Teacher by way of the air. And having done obeisance, he said:

"Reverend Sir, I am about to pass into Nirvana."

"You are about to pass into Nirvana, Moggallāna?"

"Yes, Reverend Sir."

"From where?"

"From Black Rock."

"In that case, Moggallāna, recite to me the Doctrine, before you go: for I have no other such disciple as you."

"I will do so, Reverend Sir." And having done obeisance to The Teacher, he sprang into the sky. And when he had performed various miracles, such as the elder Sāriputta did on the day he passed into Nirvana, he recited the Doctrine. And having done obeisance to The Teacher, he went to the forest of Black Rock and passed into Nirvana.

Now the report that the elder had been murdered by highwaymen spread over all the continent of India, and king Ajātasattu dispatched spies to hunt for them. And as the highwaymen happened to be drinking together in a tavern, one of them struck his comrade, and threw filth into his hand.

"How now, you ill-mannered dog!" said the other, threateningly; "Why did you throw filth into my hand?"

"And why, you rascally highwayman, did you give the first blow to Moggallāna the Great?"

"And how do you know I hit him?"

While they were thus quarreling, the spies heard and arrested them, and informed the king. And the king had the highwaymen summoned into his presence and said to them:

"Did you kill the elder?"

"Yes, sire."

---

[1] See the *Straw-Bolster* torture as described on page 440.

" Who instigated you ? "

" The naked ascetics, sire."

Then the king seized five hundred naked ascetics, and buried them together with five hundred highwaymen up to their navels in pits dug in the royal court. Then he covered them with straw, and set fire; and after thus burning them, he took iron plows and plowed them into bits.

In the lecture-hall the priests raised a discussion, saying,

" Moggallāna the Great met with a death unworthy of him."

Then came The Teacher, and inquired,

" Priests, what is the subject of your present discussion ? "

And they told him.

" Priests, the death of Moggallāna the Great was unsuited to his present existence, but suited to his karma of a previous existence."

" Reverend Sir, what was this karma of his ? "

And he told the whole story, as follows :

There was once upon a time at Benares a certain high-caste youth who took care of his father and his mother, him-self grinding and cooking their food, and performing all the other work of the house. And they said to him,

" Child, you are tiring yourself out with trying single-handed to do the work of the house in addition to your work in the forest. We will get you a wife."

" Mother, father ! I do not need anything of that sort. As long as you live, I will take care of you with my own hands."

But in spite of his repeated refusals, they insisted, and got him a wife. The girl waited on the old people for a few days, but finally got so that she could not bear the sight of them, and angrily said to her husband :

" It is impossible to stay in the same house with your parents."

But when she found that he would not listen to her, she chose a time when he was out of the house to scatter the floor over with rubbish and the scum of rice-gruel. And on his coming home and asking her, " What means all this ? " she said,

" It is the work of these blind old people. They do nothing but make the house dirty. It is impossible to get on with them."

And so, as the result of her incessant talk, this great soul, although he had fulfilled the perfections, broke with his parents, and said to her,

" Very well ! I know what to do with them."

Then he fed them, and said,

" Mother, father ! Your relatives are expecting you in such and such a place. We will go to meet them."

Then placing them in a cart, he went along with them until he had come to the heart of the forest. On arriving there, he put the reins into the hands of his father, and said,

" Father, take the reins: the oxen will follow the track. I will get down on the ground, for there are highwaymen hereabouts."

And going off a little way, he altered the tones of his voice and uttered a cry like highwaymen when they make an attack. And while his mother and father, who heard the cry and supposed it came from robbers, were calling out, " Child, you are young: leave us, and save yourself ! " he pounded them, and slew them, all the time uttering the robber yell. Then leaving their bodies in the forest, he returned home.

When The Teacher had related this by-gone occurrence, he continued and said,

" Priests, the fruit of this one deed of Moggallāna's was torment in hell for many hundreds of thousands of years, and death by pounding, in a hundred existences, as suited the nature of his crime. Moggallāna's death is, therefore, suited to his karma. Also the five hundred highwaymen, and the five hundred heretics, have met with a suitable death for doing harm to my innocent son. For they who harm innocent persons are liable to calamities and misfortunes of ten different sorts."

Having thus shown the connection, he taught them the Doctrine by means of the stanzas: —

> " Who striketh him that striketh not,
> And harmeth him that harmeth not,
> Shall quickly punishment incur,
> Some one among a list of ten.

> " Or cruel pain, or drear old age
> And failure of the vital powers,
> Or some severe and dread disease,
> Or madness him shall overtake.

> " Or from the king calamity,
> Or calumny, shall be his lot ;
> Or he shall see his kinsfolk die,
> Or all his wealth shall disappear.

> " Or conflagrations shall arise
> And all his houses sweep away ;
> And when his frame dissolves in death,
> In hell the fool shall be reborn."

§ 42. GOOD AND BAD KARMA.

Translated from the Saṁyutta-Nikāya (iii. 2. 10[1]).

Thus have I heard.

On a certain occasion The Blessed One was dwelling at Sāvatthi, in Jetavana monastery in Anāthapiṇḍika's Park.

Then drew near king Pasenadi the Kosalan, at an unusual time of day, to where The Blessed One was; and having drawn near and greeted The Blessed One, he sat down respectfully at one side. And king Pasenadi the Kosalan being seated respectfully at one side, The Blessed One spoke to him as follows :

" Pray, whence have you come, great king, at this unusual time of day?"

" Reverend Sir, a householder who was treasurer in Sāvatthi has just died leaving no son, and I have come from transferring his property to my royal palace; and, Reverend

Sir, he had ten million pieces of gold, and silver beyond all reckoning. But this householder, Reverend Sir, would eat sour gruel and kaṇājaka, and the clothes he wore were made of hemp . . . , and the conveyance in which he rode was a broken-down chariot with an umbrella of leaves."

"Even so, great king! Even so, great king! Formerly, great king, that householder and treasurer gave food in alms to a Private Buddha named Tagarasikkhi. But after he had given the order, saying, ' Give food to this monk,' and had risen from his seat and departed, he repented him of the gift and said to himself, ' It would have been better if my slaves or my servants had had this food.' And, moreover, he murdered his brother's only son for the sake of the inheritance. Now whereas, great king, that householder and treasurer gave food in alms to the Private Buddha Tagarasikkhi, as the fruit of this deed he was born seven times in a higher state of existence, into a heavenly world; and as a further result of this deed he has held the treasurership seven times here in Sāvatthi. And whereas, great king, that householder and treasurer repented him of the gift, and said to himself, ' It would have been better if my slaves or my servants had had this food,' as the result of this sinful thought his mind has been averse to sumptuous food, to sumptuous clothing, to sumptuous equipages, to a sumptuous gratification of the five senses. And whereas, great king, the treasurer murdered his brother's only son for the sake of the inheritance, as a result of this deed he has suffered in hell for many years, for many hundreds of years, for many thousands of years, for many hundreds of thousands of years; and as a further result of this deed he has now for the seventh time died without leaving any son and forfeited his property into the royal treasury. But now, great king, the former merit of this treasurer has become exhausted, and no new merit has been accumulated, and at the present time, great king, the treasurer is suffering in the Mahā-Roruva hell."

"Reverend Sir, has the treasurer been reborn in the Mahā-Roruva hell?"

"Yes, great king. The treasurer has been reborn in the Mahā-Roruva hell."

" Nor grain, nor wealth, nor store of gold and silver,
Not one amongst his women-folk and children,
Nor slave, domestic, hirèd man,
Nor any one that eats his bread,
Can follow him who leaves this life,
But all things must be left behind.

" But every deed a man performs,
With body, or with voice, or mind,
' T is this that he can call his own,
This with him take as he goes hence.
This is what follows after him,
And like a shadow ne'er departs.

" Let all, then, noble deeds perform,
A treasure-store for future weal;
For merit gained this life within,
Will yield a blessing in the next."

§ 43. HOW TO OBTAIN WEALTH, BEAUTY, AND SOCIAL POSITION.

Translated from the Aṅguttara-Nikāya (iv. 197¹).

On a certain occasion The Blessed One was dwelling at Sāvatthi, in Jetavana monastery in Anāthapiṇḍika's Park. Then drew near Mallikā the queen to where The Blessed One was; and having drawn near and greeted The Blessed One, she sat down respectfully at one side. And seated respectfully at one side, Mallikā the queen spoke to The Blessed One as follows:

" Reverend Sir, what is the reason, and what is the cause, when a woman is ugly, of a bad figure, and horrible to look at, and indigent, poor, needy, and low in the social scale?

" Reverend Sir, what is the reason, and what is the cause, when a woman is ugly, of a bad figure, and horrible to look at, and rich, wealthy, affluent, and high in the social scale?

" Reverend Sir, what is the reason, and what is the cause,

when a woman is beautiful, attractive, pleasing, and possessed of surpassing loveliness, and indigent, poor, needy, and low in the social scale?

"Reverend Sir, what is the reason, and what is the cause, when a woman is beautiful, attractive, pleasing, and possessed of surpassing loveliness, and rich, wealthy, affluent, and high in the social scale?"

"Mallikā, when a woman has been irascible and violent, and at every little thing said against her has felt spiteful, angry, enraged, and sulky, and manifested anger, hatred, and heart-burning; when she has given no alms to monk or Brahman, of food, drink, building-sites, carriages, garlands, scents, ointments, bedding, dwelling-houses, and lamps, but has been of an envious disposition, and felt envy at the gains, honor, reverence, respect, homage, and worship that came to others, and been furious and envious thereat; then, when she leaves that existence and comes to this one, wherever she may be born, she is ugly, of a bad figure, and horrible to look at, and indigent, poor, needy, and low in the social scale.

"And, again, Mallikā, when a woman has been irascible and violent, and at every little thing said against her has felt spiteful, angry, enraged, and sulky, and manifested anger, hatred, and heart-burning; but has given alms to monks and Brahmans, of food, drink, building-sites, carriages, garlands, scents, ointments, bedding, dwelling-houses, and lamps, and has not been of an envious disposition, nor felt envy at the gains, honor, reverence, respect, homage, and worship that came to others, nor been furious and envious thereat; then, when she leaves that existence and comes to this one, wherever she may be born, she is ugly, of a bad figure, and horrible to look at, and rich, wealthy, affluent, and high in the social scale.

"And, again, Mallikā, when a woman has not been irascible or violent, and though much had been said against her, has not felt spiteful, angry, enraged, or sulky, nor manifested anger, hatred, and heart-burning; when she has given no alms to monk or Brahman, of food, drink, building-sites, carriages, garlands, scents, ointments, bedding, dwelling-houses, and lamps, but has been of an envious disposition, and felt envy at the gains, honor, reverence, respect, homage, and worship that came to others, and been furious and envious thereat; then, when she leaves that existence and comes to this one wherever she may be born, she is beautiful, attractive, pleasing, and possessed of surpassing loveliness, and indigent, poor needy, and low in the social scale.

"And, again, Mallikā, when a woman has not been irascible or violent, and though much had been said against her, has not felt spiteful, angry, enraged, or sulky, nor manifested anger, hatred, and heart-burning; when she has given alms to monks and Brahmans, of food, drink, building-sites, carriages, garlands, scents, ointments, bedding, dwelling-houses, and lamps, and has not been of an envious disposition, nor felt envy at the gains, honor, reverence, respect, homage, and worship that came to others, nor been furious and envious thereat; then, when she leaves that existence and comes to this one, wherever she may be born, she is beautiful, attractive, pleasing, and possessed of surpassing loveliness, and rich, wealthy, affluent, and high in the social scale.

"This, Mallikā, is the reason, this is the cause, when a woman is ugly, of a bad figure, and horrible to look at, and indigent, poor, needy, and low in the social scale.

"This, Mallikā, is the reason, this is the cause, when a woman is ugly, of a bad figure, and horrible to look at, and rich, wealthy, affluent, and high in the social scale.

"This, Mallikā, is the reason, this is the cause, when a woman is beautiful, attractive, pleasing, and possessed of surpassing loveliness, and indigent, poor, needy, and low in the social scale.

"This, Mallikā, is the reason, this is the cause, when a woman is beautiful, attractive, pleasing, and possessed of surpassing loveliness, and rich, wealthy, affluent, and high in the social scale."

When he had thus spoken, Mallikā the queen replied to The Blessed One as follows:

"Since, now, Reverend Sir, in a former existence I was irascible and violent, and at every little thing said against me felt spiteful, angry, enraged, and sulky, and manifested anger, hatred, and heart-burning, therefore am I now ugly, of a bad figure, and horrible to look at. Since, now, Reverend Sir, in a former existence I gave alms to monks and Brahmans, of food, drink, building-sites, carriages, garlands, scents, ointments, bedding, dwelling-houses, and lamps, therefore am I now rich, wealthy, and affluent. Since, now, Reverend Sir, in a former existence I was not of an envious disposition, nor felt envy at the gains, honor, reverence, respect, homage, and worship that came to others, nor was furious and envious thereat, therefore am I now high in the social scale.

"Now, in this royal family, Reverend Sir, there are maidens of the warrior caste, maidens of the Brahman caste, and maidens of the householder caste, and I bear rule over them. From this day forth I will not be irascible nor violent, and, though much be said against me, I will not feel spiteful, angry, enraged, or sulky, nor manifest anger, hatred, and heart-burning; I will give alms to monks and Brahmans, of food, drink, building-sites, carriages, garlands, scents, ointments, bedding, dwelling-houses, and lamps; and I will not be of an envious disposition, nor feel envy at the gains, honor, reverence, respect, homage, and worship that shall come to others, nor be furious and envious thereat.

"O wonderful is it, Reverend Sir! O wonderful is it, Reverend Sir! It is as if, Reverend Sir, one were to set up that which was overturned; or were to disclose that which was hidden; or were to point out the way to a lost traveller; or were to carry a lamp into a dark place that they who had eyes might see forms. Even so has The Blessed One expounded the Doctrine in many different ways. I betake myself to The Blessed One for refuge, to the Doctrine, and to the Congregation of the priests. Let The Blessed One receive me, who have come to him for refuge, and accept me as a disciple from this day forth as long as life shall last."

§ 44. THE ROUND OF EXISTENCE.

Translated from the Milindapañha (77⁸).

"Bhante Nāgasena," said the king, "when you say 'round of existence,' what is that?"

"Your majesty, to be born here and die here, to die here and be born elsewhere, to be born there and die there, to die there and be born elsewhere, — this, your majesty, is the round of existence."

"Give an illustration."

"It is as if, your majesty, a man were to eat a ripe mango, and plant the seed; and from that a large mango-tree were to spring and bear fruit; and then the man were to eat a ripe mango from that tree also and plant the seed; and from that seed also a large mango-tree were to spring and bear fruit; thus of these trees there is no end discernible. In exactly the same way, your majesty, to be born here and die here, to die here and be born elsewhere, to be born there and die there, to die there and be born elsewhere, this, your majesty, is the round of existence."

"You are an able man, bhante Nāgasena."

—————

§ 45. CAUSE OF REBIRTH.

Translated from the Milindapañha (32¹²).

"Bhante Nāgasena," said the king, "are there any who die without being born into another existence?"

"Some are born into another existence," said the elder, "and some are not born into another existence."

"Who is born into another existence, and who is not born into another existence?"

"Your majesty, he that still has the corruptions is born into another existence; he that no longer has the corruptions is not born into another existence."

"But will you, bhante, be born into another existence?"

" Your majesty, if there shall be in me any attachment, I shall be born into another existence; if there shall be in me no attachment, I shall not be born into another existence."

" You are an able man, bhante Nāgasena."

---

§ 46. IS THIS TO BE MY LAST EXISTENCE ?

Translated from the Milindapañha (41¹¹).

" Bhante Nāgasena," said the king, " does a man know when he is not to be born into another existence ? "

" Assuredly, your majesty, a man knows when he is not to be born into another existence."

" Bhante, how does he know it ? "

" He knows it from the cessation of all cause or reason for being born into another existence."

" Give an illustration."

" It is as if, your majesty, a house-holding farmer were to plow and sow and fill his granary; and then were neither to plow nor sow, and were to use the grain previously stored up, or give it away, or do with it however else might suit him: your majesty, would this house-holding farmer know that his granary would not become filled up again ? "

" Assuredly, bhante, would he know it."

" How would he know it ? "

" He would know it from the cessation of all cause or reason for the filling up of the granary."

" In exactly the same way, your majesty, a man knows when he is not to be born into another existence, from the cessation of all cause or reason for being born into another existence."

" You are an able man, bhante Nāgasena."

§ 47. REBIRTH IS NOT TRANSMIGRATION.

§ 47 *a.* — Translated from the Milindapañha (71¹⁶).

Said the king: "Bhante Nāgasena, does rebirth take place without anything transmigrating [passing over]?"

"Yes, your majesty. Rebirth takes place without anything transmigrating."

"How, bhante Nāgasena, does rebirth take place without anything transmigrating? Give an illustration."

"Suppose, your majesty, a man were to light a light from another light; pray, would the one light have passed over [transmigrated] to the other light?"

"Nay, verily, bhante."

"In exactly the same way, your majesty, does rebirth take place without anything transmigrating."

"Give another illustration."

"Do you remember, your majesty, having learnt, when you were a boy, some verse or other from your professor of poetry?"

"Yes, bhante."

"Pray, your majesty, did the verse pass over [transmigrate] to you from your teacher?"

"Nay, verily, bhante."

"In exactly the same way, your majesty, does rebirth take place without anything transmigrating."

"You are an able man, bhante Nāgasena."

§ 47 *b.* — Translated from the Milindapañha (46⁵).

"Bhante Nāgasena," said the king, "what is it that is born into the next existence?"

"Your majesty," said the elder, "it is name and form that is born into the next existence."

"Is it this same name and form that is born into the next existence?"

"Your majesty, it is not this same name and form that is born into the next existence; but with this name and form, your majesty, one does a deed — it may be good, or it may be wicked — and by reason of this deed another name and form is born into the next existence."

"Bhante, if it is not this same name and form that is born into the next existence, is one not freed from one's evil deeds?"

"If one were not born into another existence," said the elder, "one would be freed from one's evil deeds; but, your majesty, inasmuch as one is born into another existence, therefore is one not freed from one's evil deeds."

"Give an illustration."

"Your majesty, it is as if a man were to take away another man's mangoes, and the owner of the mangoes were to seize him, and show him to the king, and say, 'Sire, this man hath taken away my mangoes;' and the other were to say, 'Sire, I did not take away this man's mangoes. The mangoes which this man planted were different mangoes from those which I took away. I am not liable to punishment.' Pray, your majesty, would the man be liable to punishment?"

"Assuredly, bhante, would he be liable to punishment."

"For what reason?"

"Because, in spite of what he might say, he would be liable to punishment for the reason that the last mangoes derived from the first mangoes."

"In exactly the same way, your majesty, with this name and form one does a deed — it may be good, or it may be wicked — and by reason of this deed another name and form is born into the next existence. Therefore is one not freed from one's evil deeds."

"Give another illustration."

"Your majesty, it is as if a man were to take away the rice of another man, . . . were to take away the sugar-cane, . . . Your majesty, it is as if a man were to light a fire in the winter-time and warm himself, and were to go off without putting it out. And then the fire were to burn another man's field, and the owner of the field were to seize him, and show him to the king, and say, 'Sire, this man has burnt up my field; ' and the other were to say, 'Sire, I did not set this man's field on fire. The fire which I failed to put out was a different one from the one which has burnt up this man's field. I am not liable to punishment.' Pray, your majesty, would the man be liable to punishment?"

"Assuredly, bhante, would he be liable to punishment."

"For what reason?"

"Because, in spite of what he might say, the man would be liable to punishment for the reason that the last fire derived from the first fire."

"In exactly the same way, your majesty, with this name and form one does a deed — it may be good, or it may be wicked — and by reason of this deed another name and form is born into the next existence. Therefore is one not freed from one's evil deeds."

"Give another illustration."

"Your majesty, it is as if a man were to ascend to the top storey of a house with a light, and eat there; and the light in burning were to set fire to the thatch; and the thatch in burning were to set fire to the house; and the house in burning were to set fire to the village; and the people of the village were to seize him, and say, 'Why, O man, did you set fire to the village?' and he were to say, 'I did not set fire to the village. The fire of the lamp by whose light I ate was a different one from the one which set fire to the village;' and they, quarreling, were to come to you. Whose cause, your majesty, would you sustain?"

"That of the people of the village, bhante."

"And why?"

"Because, in spite of what the man might say, the latter fire sprang from the former."

"In exactly the same way, your majesty, although the name and form which is born into the next existence is different from the name and form which is to end at death, nevertheless, it is sprung from it. Therefore is one not freed from one's evil deeds."

"Give another illustration."

"Your majesty, it is as if a man were to choose a young

girl in marriage, and having paid the purchase-money, were
to go off; and she subsequently were to grow up and become
marriageable ; and then another man were to pay the purchase-money for her, and marry her; and the first man were
to return, and say, ' O man, why did you marry my wife ? '
and the other were to say, ' I did not marry your wife.   The
young, tender girl whom you chose in marriage, and for
whom you paid purchase-money, was a different person from
this grown-up and marriageable girl whom I have chosen in
marriage, and for whom I have paid purchase-money;' and
they, quarreling, were to come to you.   Whose cause, your
majesty, would you sustain ? "

" That of the first man."

" And why ? "

" Because, in spite of what the second man might say, the
grown-up girl sprang from the other."

" In exactly the same way, your majesty, although the
name and form which is born into the next existence is different from the name and form which is to end at death,
nevertheless, it is sprung from it.   Therefore is one not freed
from one's evil deeds."

" Give another illustration."

" Your majesty, it is as if a man were to buy from a cowherd a pot of milk, and were to leave it with the cowherd,
and go off, thinking he would come the next day and take it.
And on the next day it were to turn into sour cream; and
the man were to come back, and say, ' Give me the pot of
milk.'   And the other were to show him the sour cream; and
the first man were to say, ' I did not buy sour cream from
you.   Give me the pot of milk.'   And the cowherd were to
say, ' While you were gone, your milk turned into sour
cream;' and they, quarreling, were to come to you.   Whose
cause, your majesty, would you sustain ? "

" That of the cowherd, bhante."

" And why ? "

" Because, in spite of what the man might say, the one
sprang from the other."

" In exactly the same way, your majesty, although the

name and form which is born into the next existence is different from the name and form which is to end at death, nevertheless, it is sprung from it. Therefore is one not freed from one's evil deeds."

"You are an able man, bhante Nāgasena."

§ 47 c. — Translated from the Visuddhi-Magga (chap. xvii.).

It is only elements of being possessing a dependence that arrive at a new existence: none transmigrated from the last existence, nor are they in the new existence without causes contained in the old. By this is said that it is only elements of being, with form or without, but possessing a dependence, that arrive at a new existence. There is no entity, no living principle; no elements of being transmigrated from the last existence into the present one; nor, on the other hand, do they appear in the present existence without causes in that one. This we will now make plain by considering birth and death as they occur every day among men.

For when, in any existence, one arrives at the gate of death, either in the natural course of things or through violence; and when, by a concourse of intolerable, death-dealing pains, all the members, both great and small, are loosened and wrenched apart in every joint and ligament; and the body, like a green palm-leaf exposed to the sun, dries up by degrees; and the eye-sight and the other senses fail; and the power of feeling, and the power of thinking, and vitality are making the last stand in the heart — then consciousness residing in that last refuge, the heart, continues to exist by virtue of karma, otherwise called the predispositions. This karma, however, still retains something of what it depends on, and consists of such former deeds as were weighty, much practised, and are now close at hand; or else this karma creates a reflex of itself or of the new mode of life now being entered upon, and it is with this as its object that consciousness continues to exist.

Now while the consciousness still subsists, inasmuch as

desire and ignorance have not been abandoned and the evil
of the object is hidden by that ignorance, desire inclines the
consciousness to the object; and the karma that sprang up
along with the consciousness impels it toward the object.
This consciousness being in its series thus inclined toward
the object by desire, and impelled toward it by karma, like
a man who swings himself over a ditch by means of a rope
hanging from a tree on the hither bank, quits its first resting-
place and continues to subsist in dependence on objects of
sense and other things, and either does or does not light on
another resting-place created by karma. Here the former
consciousness, from its passing out of existence, is called
passing away, and the latter, from its being reborn into a
new existence, is called rebirth. But it is to be understood
that this latter consciousness did not come to the present
existence from the previous one, and also that it is only to
causes contained in the old existence, — namely, to karma
called the predispositions, to inclination, an object, etc., — that
its present appearance is due.

> As illustrations here may serve
> Echoes and other similes.
> Nor sameness, nor diversity,
> Can from that series take their rise.

As illustrations of how consciousness does not come over
from the last existence into the present, and how it springs
up by means of causes belonging to the former existence,
here may serve echoes, light, the impressions of a seal, and
reflections in a mirror. For as echoes, light, the impressions of a seal, and shadows have sound etc. for their causes,
and exist without having come from elsewhere, just so is it
with this mind.
    Moreover

> *Nor sameness, nor diversity,*
> *Can from that series take their rise.*

For if, in a continuous series, an absolute sameness obtained,
then could sour cream not arise from milk; while, on the

other hand, if there were an absolute diversity, then could not a milk-owner obtain sour cream. The same argument holds good in regard to all causes and effects. This being so, it would be more correct not to use the popular mode of stating the case, but that would not be desirable. Therefore, we must merely guard ourselves from supposing that there is here either an absolute sameness or an absolute diversity. Here some one will say,

" This explanation is not a good one. For is it not true that if there be no transmigration, and both the Groups and the fruitful karma which belong to this existence in the world of men cease, nor arrive in the new existence, the fruit of this karma would then be borne by a different thing from that which produced the karma itself? If the reaper ceased to exist, it would not be he experienced the fruit. Therefore this position is not good."

The following quotation will answer this :

> " The series which doth bear a fruit,
> Is not the same nor something else.
> The fabricating power in seeds
> Will show the meaning of this word."

For when the *fruit* arises in a *series*, as absolute sameness and absolute diversity are both excluded, it cannot be said that the fruit is borne by the *same* thing *nor* yet by *something else*.

The fabricating power in seeds will show this. For when the fabricating power in the seed of mangoes and other plants operate, inasmuch as any particular kind of fruit is dependent on the previous part of its series, it cannot come from other seeds, nor in dependence on other fabricating powers ; nor yet is it those other seeds, or those other fabricating powers, which arrive at fruition. Such is to be understood to be the nature of the present case. Also when education, training, and medicaments have been applied to the body of a young person, the fruit will appear in after time in the mature body etc. Thus is the sense to be understood.

Now as to what was said, "If the reaper ceased to exist, it would not be he experienced the fruit," consider the following:

> " As when 't is said, ' The tree bears fruit,'
> As soon as fruit on it appears;
> Just so the Groups are reapers called,
> As soon as karma's fruit springs up."

Just as in the case of those elements of being which go under the name of tree, as soon as at any point the fruit springs up, *it is* then *said,* "*The tree bears fruit,*" or, "The tree has fructified" — so also in the case of those *Groups* which go under the name of " god " or " man," when a fruition of happiness or misery springs up at any point, then it is said, "That god or man is happy or miserable." Therefore is it that we have here no need of any other *reaper*.

§ 47 *d.* — Translated from the Visuddhi-Magga (chap. xvii.).

He, then, that has no clear idea of death and does not master the fact that death everywhere consists in the dissolution of the Groups, he comes to a variety of conclusions, such as, "A living entity dies and transmigrates into another body."

He that has no clear idea of rebirth and does not master the fact that the appearance of the Groups everywhere constitutes rebirth, he comes to a variety of conclusions, such as, "A living entity is born and has obtained a new body."

§ 47 *e.* — Translated from the Visuddhi-Magga (chap. xxi.).

Therefore have the ancients said:

> " ' The Groups break up, and only they,' the wise say,
> ' And death consisteth in their dissolution.'
> The thoughtful man of insight sees them vanish;
> They 're like the jewel shattered by the diamond."

§ 48. REFLECTIONS ON EXISTENCE.

Translation of the nineteenth chapter of the Visuddhi-Magga.

The knowledge, however, of the dependence of name and
form and the consequent removal of doubt in the three divisions of time is called the Purity Ensuing on the Removal
of Doubt.

The priest who is desirous of this knowledge enters on a
search for the causes and dependence of name and form, just
as a skilful physician seeing a disease will search to find how
it arose, or just as a compassionate man seeing a small,
weakly, helpless boy-baby lying on its back in the middle of
the road will try to discover its parents.

And at first he reflects as follows: " Name and form cannot be without a cause, as they are not the same everywhere,
at all times, and for all people; nor yet are they caused by
any personal power or the like, for there is no such power
behind name and form; nor, again, are they right who say
that name and form themselves constitute such a power, as
the name and form thus called a personal power or the like
are not a cause.   Therefore it must needs be that name and
form have causes and a dependence.   And what are they?

Having made these reflections, he begins to investigate
the causes and dependence of form, as follows: When this
body comes into existence, it does not arise in the midst of
nymphaeas, nelumbiums, lotuses, and water-lilies, etc., nor of
jewels, pearl-necklaces, etc.; but ill-smelling, disgusting, and
repulsive, it arises between the stomach and the lower intestines, with the belly-wall behind and the back-bone in front,
in the midst of the entrails and mesentery, in an exceedingly
contracted, ill-smelling, disgusting, and repulsive place, like a
worm in rotten fish, carrion, or rancid gruel, or in a stagnant
or dirty pool or the like.   As it thus comes into being, these
four — ignorance, desire, attachment, and karma — are the
cause of it, inasmuch as they produce it; food is its dependence, inasmuch as it supports it.   These five are its causes

and dependence.   Three of these — ignorance etc. — are the
basis for this body, as is the mother for the child; karma is
the begetter, as is the father of the son; food is the sustainer,
like the nurse."

Having thus grasped the dependence of form, he then
grasps the dependence of name, as follows: "In dependence on the eye and in respect to form, eye-consciousness
arises," etc.

When he has thus perceived the dependent manner of
existence of name and form, he reaches the insight: "As
name and form have at the present time a dependent manner
of existence, so also had they in the past time, and so will
they have in the future."   In reaching this insight, that
which is called the fivefold questioning concerning the
past, namely:

" Did I exist in past time?

" Did I not exist in past time?

" What was I in past time?

" How was I in past time?

" Did I in past time change from one existence to another?" and that called the fivefold questioning concerning
the future, namely:

" Shall I exist in future time?

" Shall I not exist in future time?

" What shall I be in future time?

" How shall I be in future time?

" Shall I in the future change from one existence to
another?" and that called the sixfold questioning concerning the present, throwing doubt on his present existence, namely:

" Am I?

" Am I not?

" What am I?

" How am I?

" Whence came this existing being?

" Whither is it to go?" —
are all abandoned.

Another observes the twofold dependence of name as

general and specific, and the fourfold one of form as karma etc.

For the dependence of name is twofold, general and specific. The six sense-apertures, eye etc., and the six objects of sense, form etc., are the general dependence of name in respect of giving rise to any kind of name whether meritorious or not; but attention etc. are special. For philosophic attention, listening to the Good Doctrine etc. are the dependence of only meritorious name. Their opposites are the dependence of that which is demeritorious; karma etc. of fruition; existence-substratum etc. of action.

Of form, however, karma etc., *i. e.*, karma, thoughts, the seasons, and nutriment constitute the fourfold dependence.

Of these four, it is past *karma* which is the dependence of form springing from karma; present *thoughts* of that springing from thoughts; *the seasons and nutriment* are the dependence for the continuance of that springing from the seasons and from nutriment.

Thus does one priest grasp the dependence of name and form. And when he has perceived their dependent manner of existence he reaches the insight: "As name and form have at the present time a dependent manner of existence, so also had they in past time, and so will they have in the future." And when he reaches this insight, the questioning concerning the three divisions of time is abandoned as aforesaid.

Another observes in respect of these constituents of being, called name and form, their growing old and their subsequent dissolution, as follows: "The old age and death of the constituents of being exist when birth exists, birth when existence exists, existence when attachment exists, attachment when desire exists, desire when sensation exists, sensation when contact exists, contact when the six organs of sense exist, the six organs of sense when name and form exist, name and form when consciousness exists, consciousness when karma exists, karma when ignorance exists." Thus does he grasp the dependence of name and form by considering Dependent Origination in the reverse direction. And his questioning is abandoned as aforesaid.

Another grasps the dependence of name and form by first considering the formula of Dependent Origination in the forward direction, in full, "Behold! On ignorance depends karma," etc. And his questioning is abandoned as aforesaid.

Another grasps the dependence of name and form by considering the round of karma and the round of its fruit as follows:

"Behold! in a former karma-existence, infatuation-ignorance, initiatory karma, longing desire, approximating attachment, and thought-existence, these five factors were the dependence for conception into this existence; rebirth-consciousness, the descent of name and form, the sensitiveness of the organs of sense, the contact experienced, the sensation felt, these five factors belonging to the originating-existence of the present life depend on the karma of a previous existence; when the senses have matured, then infatuation-ignorance, . . . thought-existence, these five factors of a present karma-existence are the dependence of rebirth in the future."

Now karma is fourfold:

That which bears fruit in the present existence;
That which bears fruit in rebirth;
That which bears fruit at no fixed time; and
By-gone karma.

The karma *which bears fruit in the present existence* is the meritorious or demeritorious thoughts constituting the first swiftness in the seven thoughts of a stream of swiftnesses. That brings forth fruit in this existence. But if it fail to do so, then it is *by-gone karma*, and it is to be said of it in respect to the three divisions of time, as follows: "That karma has gone by: there was no fruit from it, nor will there be, nor is there."

The karma *which bears fruit in rebirth* is the efficacious thought which constitutes the seventh swiftness. That bears fruit in the next existence. But if it fail to do so, it is by-gone karma, as described above.

The karma *which bears fruit at no fixed time* is the thoughts constituting the five intermediate swiftnesses. That bears fruit in the future whenever it may find opportunity, and as long as the round of rebirth continues there is no by-gone karma.

There is another fourfold division of karma:

The weighty;

The abundant;

The close at hand; and

The habitual.

Weighty karma — whether meritorious or demeritorious, such as matricide and other serious crimes of the sort, or lofty deeds — bears fruit before that which is not weighty.

That which is *abundant*, whether good conduct or bad conduct, bears fruit before that which is not abundant.

That which is *close at hand* is karma remembered at the moment of death. For the karma which a man remembers at the point of death springs up with him in rebirth.

But distinct from all these three is karma that has become *habitual* through much repetition. This brings on rebirth when the other three are absent.

There is another fourfold division of karma:

Productive;

Supportive;

Counteractive; and

Destructive.

Productive karma may be either meritorious or demeritorious. It produces both form and the other fruition-groups, not only at the time of conception but as long as they continue.

Supportive karma cannot produce fruit, but when rebirth has been given by other karma, and fruit has been produced, it supports the ensuing happiness or misery, and brings about its continuance.

Counteractive karma, when rebirth has been given by other karma, and fruit has been produced, counteracts the ensuing happiness or misery, suppresses it, and does not suffer it to continue.

Destructive karma, whether meritorious or demeritorious, destroys other weak karma, and, preventing it from bearing

fruit, makes room for its own fruition. The fruit which
thus arises is called apparitional.

The distinctions between these twelve different karmas
and their fruits have their inner nature plainly revealed to
the insight into karma and its fruit possessed by the
Buddhas, but this insight is not shared in by their disciples. The man of insight, however, should know the
general distinction between karma and the fruit of karma.
Therefore it is that these distinctions of karma are only
explained in rough outline.

Thus does this one, in merging these twelve karmas together in the round of karma, grasp the dependence of name
and form by considering the round of karma and the round
of its fruit.

He who, by thus considering the round of karma and the
round of fruit, grasps the dependent manner of existence of
name and form, reaches the insight: "As name and form
have in the present time a dependent manner of existence
by means of a round of karma and a round of fruit, so also
had they in past time, and so will they have in the future."

Thus does he have karma and fruit, a round of karma
and a round of fruit, karma's manner of existing and the
fruit's manner of existing, the karma-series and the fruit-
series, action and the effect of action. And he attains to the
insight:

> " A round of karma and of fruit;
> The fruit from karma doth arise,
> From karma then rebirth doth spring ;
> And thus the world rolls on and on."

When he has attained this insight, the sixteen above-
mentioned doubts concerning the past, present, and future,
"Did I exist?" etc., are all abandoned. And it becomes
evident to him that it is merely name and form which passes
through the various modes, classes, stages, grades, and forms
of existence by means of a connection of cause and effect.
He sees that behind the action there is no actor, and that,
although actions bear their fruit, there is no one that experiences that fruit. He then sees clearly, in the light of the

highest knowledge, that when a cause is acting, or the fruit
of an action ripens, it is merely by a conventional form of
speech that the wise speak of an actor or of any one as
experiencing the fruit of an action. Therefore have the
ancients said,

> " No doer is there does the deed,
>   Nor is there one who feels the fruit;
>   Constituent parts alone roll on;
>   This view alone is orthodox.

> " And thus the deed, and thus the fruit
>   Roll on and on, each from its cause;
>   As of the round of tree and seed,
>   No one can tell when they began.

> " Nor is the time to be perceived
>   In future births when they shall cease.
>   The heretics perceive not this,
>   And fail of mastery o'er themselves.

> " ' An Ego,' say they, ' doth exist,
>   Eternal, or that soon will cease ; '
>   Thus two-and-sixty heresies
>   They 'mongst themselves discordant hold.

> " Bound in the bonds of heresy,
>   By passion's flood they 're borne along ;
>   And borne along by passion's flood,
>   From misery find they no release.

> " If once these facts he but perceive,
>   A priest whose faith on Buddha rests,
>   The subtile, deep, and self-devoid
>   Dependence then will penetrate.

> " Not in its fruit is found the deed,
>   Nor in the deed finds one the fruit;
>   Of each the other is devoid,
>   Yet there 's no fruit without the deed.

> " Just as no store of fire is found
>   In jewel, cow-dung, or the sun,
>   Nor separate from these exists,
>   Yet short of fuel no fire is known ;

" Even so we ne'er within the deed
Can retribution's fruit descry,
Nor yet in any place without;
Nor can in fruit the deed be found.

" Deeds separate from their fruits exist,
And fruits are separate from the deeds:
But consequent upon the deed
The fruit doth into being come.

" No god of heaven or Brahma-world
Doth cause the endless round of birth;
Constituent parts alone roll on,
From cause and from material sprung."

When he has thus grasped the dependence of name and
form by considering the round of karma and the round of
fruit, and has abandoned all questioning in the three divisions of time, he then understands the past, future, and
present elements of being at death and at conception. This
is exact determination. And he knows as follows:

Those groups which came into existence in the past existence in dependence on karma, perished then and there. But
in dependence on the karma of that existence other groups
have come into being in this existence. Not a single element of being has come into this existence from a previous
one. The groups which have come into being in this existence in dependence on karma will perish, and others will
come into being in the next existence, but not a single element of being will go from this existence into the next.
Moreover, just as the words of the teacher do not pass over
into the mouth of the pupil who nevertheless repeats them;
and just as holy water drunk by the messenger sent for the
purpose does not pass into the belly of the sick man and
nevertheless in dependence on this water is the sickness
allayed; and just as the features of the face do not pass
to the reflection in mirrors and the like and nevertheless
in dependence on them does the image appear; and just
as the flame does not pass over from the wick of one lamp to
that of another and nevertheless the flame of the second

lamp exists in dependence on that of the former: in exactly
the same way not a single element of being passes over from
a previous existence into the present existence, nor hence
into the next existence; and yet in dependence on the groups,
organs of sense, objects of sense, and sense-consciousnesses
of the last existence were born those of this one, and from
the present groups, organs of sense, objects of sense, and
sense-consciousnesses will be born the groups, organs of sense,
objects of sense, and sense-consciousnesses of the next
existence.

> Just as, indeed, eye-consciousness
> Doth follow on mentality,
> Yet cometh not from out the same,
> Nor yet doth fail to come to be;
>
> So, when conception comes to pass,
> The thoughts a constant series form;
> The last thought of the old birth dies,
> The first thought of the new springs up.
>
> No interval is 'twixt them found,
> No stop or break to them is known;
> There 's naught that passes on from hence,
> And yet conception comes to pass.

When he thus understands the elements at death and at
conception, and this knowledge gained by grasping the dependence of name and form has become thoroughly established, then the sixteen doubts are still more completely
abandoned. And not merely they, but also the eight doubts
concerning The Teacher etc. are abandoned, and the sixty-
two heresies are estopped.

The knowledge thus gained by this manifold grasping of
the dependence of name and form, and by the ensuing
removal of doubt in the three divisions of time, is what
should be understood by the phrase "the purity ensuing on
the removal of doubt." The knowledge of the continuance
of the factors of being, the knowledge of the truth, and
correct insight, are synonyms of it.

For it has been said as follows:

"The knowledge of the continuance of the factors of being consists of the wisdom gained by grasping their dependence, as, for example, 'On ignorance depends karma, in dependence has it originated. Both of these factors of being have originated by dependence.'"

In considering the factors of being in the light of their transitoriness, what is the knowledge of truth thus achieved? wherein consists correct insight? how does it become plain that all the constituents of being are transitory? where is doubt abandoned?

In considering the factors of being in the light of their misery, . . . in considering the factors of being in the light of their lack of an Ego, . . . where is doubt abandoned?

In considering the factors of being in the light of their transitoriness is achieved the knowledge of the truth of causes; in this knowledge lies what is called correct insight; as the result of this knowledge it becomes plain that all the constituents of being are transitory; here is where doubt is abandoned.

In considering the factors of being in the light of their misery is achieved the knowledge of the truth of what exists; in this knowledge lies what is called correct insight; as the result of this knowledge it becomes plain that all the constituents of being are misery; here is where doubt is abandoned.

In considering the factors of being in the light of their lack of an Ego is achieved the knowledge of the truth both of the causes of existence and of existence; in this knowledge lies what is called correct insight; as the result of this knowledge it becomes plain that all the constituents of being are wanting in an Ego; here is where doubt is abandoned.

Now do the various expressions, "knowledge of the truth," "correct insight," and "removal of doubt," designate various truths, or are they various expressions for one truth? Knowledge of the truth, correct insight, and removal of doubt are various expressions for one truth.

Now the man of insight, having by this knowledge obtained confidence in the dispensation of The Buddha, and a footing in it, and having his destiny established, is called newly converted.

> Therefore should ay a mindful priest,
> Who may desire his doubts removed,
> Search everywhere that he may grasp
> On what his name and form depend.

Thus in the "Way of Purity," composed for the delectation of good people, and in the section on the development of wisdom

The Exposition of the Purity Ensuing on the Removal of Doubt Constitutes the Nineteenth Chapter.

---

§ 49. DIFFERENT KINDS OF DEATH.

Translated from the Visuddhi-Magga (chap. viii.).

By death is meant the cutting off of the vitality comprised in any one existence. Now the death of the saint, which consists in the annihilation of the misery of rebirth; incessant death, which is the incessant breaking up of the constituents of being; and death in popular parlance, as when it is said, "The tree is dead, the iron is dead," — none of these is meant here. But what is meant here is twofold, either natural death, or untimely death.

Natural death occurs either by the exhaustion of merit, or by the exhaustion of the natural term of life, or by the exhaustion of both.

Untimely death occurs by karma cutting off karma.

Death by the exhaustion of merit is death which supervenes when the karma which caused conception has ripened to a termination, although the dependence for continuing the series constituting the term of life be not exhausted. Death by the exhaustion of the natural term of life occurs when the span of life, the nutritive powers, etc., proper to any given grade of existence, come to an end, — in the present race of men on the exhaustion of their natural term of life at the age of only one hundred years.

Untimely death is death like that of Dusī Māra, or of king Kalābu and others, who had their series cut off by karma that carried them off on the spot, or like that of such persons as have their series cut off by a bloody death brought upon them by the karma of a previous existence.

---

§ 50. HOW EXISTENCE IN HELL IS POSSIBLE.

Translated from the Milindapañha (67⁴).

Said the king, " Bhante Nāgasena, you priests say that hell-fire is much hotter than ordinary fire. Also, that if a small stone be thrown into an ordinary fire, though it lie smoking there for a whole day, it is not consumed; but that if a stone as large as a pagoda be cast into hell-fire it is consumed in an instant. This I cannot believe. And again, you say that all those beings that come into existence in hell are not consumed, though they are cooked in hell-fire for many thousands of years. This, also, I cannot believe."

Said the elder, " What do you say to this, your majesty? Do the females of sea-monsters, and of crocodiles, turtles, pea-fowl, and pigeons eat hard stones and gravel?"

" Yes, bhante.   They do."

" But when the hard stones and gravel have arrived in the stomach-cavity of the belly, are they consumed?"

" Yes, bhante.   They are."

" But the embryo that is likewise in the belly, is that also consumed?"

" Nay, verily, bhante."

"And why not?"

" I suppose, bhante, that it is through the superior potency of its former deeds."

" In exactly the same way, your majesty, the inhabitants of hell, through the superior potency of their former deeds, are not consumed, though they are cooked in hell-fire for many thousands of years. Moreover, your majesty, The Blessed One has spoken as follows: ' He does not die so long as that wickedness is unexhausted.' "

" Give another illustration."

" What do you say to this, your majesty ?   Do the
females of lions, tigers, panthers, and dogs eat hard bones
and meat ? "

" Yes, bhante.   They do."

" But when these hard bones and meat have arrived in
the stomach-cavity of the belly, are they consumed ? "

" Yes, bhante.   They are."

" But the embryo that is likewise in the belly, is that also
consumed ? "

" Nay, verily, bhante."

" And why not ? "

" I suppose, bhante, that it is through the superior potency
of its former deeds."

" In exactly the same way, your majesty, the inhabitants
of hell, through the superior potency of their former deeds,
are not consumed, though they are cooked in hell-fire for
many thousands of years."

" Give another illustration."

" What do you say to this, your majesty ?   Do delicate
women of the Yonakas, or of the warrior caste, of the Brahman
caste, of the householder caste eat hard food and meat ? "

" Yes, bhante.   They do."

" But when the hard food and meat have arrived in the
stomach-cavity of the belly, are they consumed ? "

" Yes, bhante.   They are."

" But the embryo that is likewise in the belly, is that also
consumed ? "

" Nay, verily, bhante."

" And why not ? "

" I suppose, bhante, that it is through the superior potency
of its former deeds."

" In exactly the same way, your majesty, the inhabitants
of hell, through the superior potency of their former deeds,
are not consumed, though they are cooked in hell-fire for
many thousands of years.   Moreover, your majesty, The
Blessed One has spoken as follows: ' He does not die so long
as that wickedness is unexhausted.' "

" You are an able man, bhante Nāgasena."

§ 51. DEATH'S MESSENGERS.

§ 51 *a.* — Translated from the Aṅguttara-Nikāya (iii. 35¹).

Death has three messengers, O priests. And what are
the three?

Suppose, O priests, one does evil with his body, does evil
with his voice, does evil with his mind. Having done evil
with his body, done evil with his voice, and done evil with
his mind, he arrives after the dissolution of the body, after
death, at a place of punishment, a place of suffering, perdition, hell. Then, O priests, the guardians of hell seize him
by the arms at every point, and they show him to Yama, the
ruler of the dead, saying,

" Sire, this man did not do his duty to his friends, to his
parents, to the monks, or to the Brahmans, nor did he honor
his elders among his kinsfolk. Let your majesty inflict punishment upon him."

Then, O priests, king Yama questions, sounds, and
addresses him touching the first of death's messengers.

" O man! Did you not see the first of death's messengers visibly appear among men?"

He replies, " Lord, I did not."

Then, O priests, king Yama says to him, " O man! Did
you not see among men a woman or a man, eighty or ninety
or a hundred years of age, decrepit, crooked as the curved
rafter of a gable roof, bowed down, leaning on a staff, trembling as he walked, miserable, with youth long fled, broken-
toothed, gray-haired and nearly bald, tottering, with wrinkled
brow, and blotched with freckles?"

He replies, " Lord, I did."

Then, O priests, king Yama says to him, " O man! Did
it not occur to you, being a person of mature intelligence and
years, ' I also am subject to old age, and in no way exempt.
Come now! I will act nobly with body, voice, and mind'?"

He replies, " Lord, I could not. Lord, I did not think."

Then, O priests, king Yama says to him, " O man!

Through thoughtlessness you failed to act nobly with body, voice, and mind. Verily, it shall be done unto you, O man, in accordance with your thoughtlessness. And it was not your mother who did this wickedness, nor was it your father, nor your brother, nor your sister, nor your friends and companions, nor your relatives and kinsfolk, nor the deities, nor the monks and Brahmans; but it was you yourself who did this wickedness, and you alone shall feel its consequences."

Then, O priests, when king Yama has questioned, sounded, and addressed him touching the first of death's messengers, he questions, sounds, and addresses him touching the second of death's messengers.

"O man! Did you not see the second of death's messengers visibly appear among men?"

He replies, "Lord, I did not."

Then, O priests, king Yama says to him, "O man! Did you not see among men women or men, diseased, suffering, grievously sick, rolling in their own filth, who when lying down had to be lifted up by others, and by others had to be laid down again?"

He replies, "Lord, I did."

Then, O priests, king Yama says to him, "O man! Did it not occur to you, being a person of mature intelligence and years, 'I also am subject to disease, and in no way exempt. Come now! I will act nobly with body, voice, and mind'?"

He replies, "Lord, I could not. Lord, I did not think."

Then, O priests, king Yama says to him, "O man! Through thoughtlessness you failed to act nobly with body, voice, and mind. Verily, it shall be done unto you, O man, in accordance with your thoughtlessness. And it was not your mother who did this wickedness, nor was it your father, nor your brother, nor your sister, nor your friends and companions, nor your relatives and kinsfolk, nor the deities, nor the monks and Brahmans; but it was you yourself who did this wickedness, and you alone shall feel its consequences."

Then, O priests, when king Yama has questioned, sounded, and addressed him touching the second of death's messengers, he questions, sounds, and addresses him touching the third of death's messengers.

"O man! Did you not see the third of death's messengers visibly appear among men?"

He replies, "Lord, I did not."

Then, O priests, king Yama says to him, "O man! Did you not see among men a woman or a man that had been one day dead, or two days dead, or three days dead, and had become swollen, black, and full of putridity?"

He replies, "Lord, I did."

Then, O priests, king Yama says to him, "O man! Did it not occur to you, being a person of mature intelligence and years, 'I also am subject to death, and in no way exempt. Come now! I will act nobly with body, voice, and mind'?"

He replies, "Lord, I could not. Lord, I did not think."

Then, O priests, king Yama says to him, "O man! Through thoughtlessness you failed to act nobly with body, voice, and mind. Verily, it shall be done unto you, O man, in accordance with your thoughtlessness. And it was not your mother who did this wickedness, nor was it your father, nor your brother, nor your sister, nor your friends and companions, nor your relatives and kinsfolk, nor the deities, nor the monks and Brahmans; but it was you yourself who did this wickedness, and you alone shall feel its consequences."

Then, O priests, when king Yama has questioned, sounded, and addressed him touching the third of death's messengers, he becomes silent.

Then, O priests, the guardians of hell inflict on him the torture called the fivefold pinion: they force a heated iron stake through his hand; they force a heated iron stake through his other hand; they force a heated iron stake through his foot; they force a heated iron stake through his other foot; they force a heated iron stake through the middle of his breast. There he experiences grievous, severe, sharp, and bitter pains; but he does not die so long as that wickedness is unexhausted.

Then, O priests, the guardians of hell lay him down, and hack him with axes. There he experiences grievous, severe, sharp, and bitter pains; but he does not die so long as that wickedness is unexhausted.

Then, O priests, the guardians of hell place him feet up, head down, and hack him with hatchets. There he experiences grievous, severe, sharp, and bitter pains; but he does not die so long as that wickedness is unexhausted.

Then, O priests, the guardians of hell harness him to a chariot, and they make him go forward and they make him go back over ground that is blazing, flaming, and glowing. There he experiences grievous, severe, sharp, and bitter pains; but he does not die so long as that wickedness is unexhausted.

Then, O priests, the guardians of hell make him ascend and make him descend an immense, blazing, flaming, and glowing mountain of live coals. There he experiences grievous, severe, sharp, and bitter pains; but he does not die so long as that wickedness is unexhausted.

Then, O priests, the guardians of hell take him feet up, head down, and throw him into a heated iron kettle that is blazing, flaming, and glowing. There he cooks and sizzles. And while he there cooks and sizzles, he goes once upwards, once downwards, and once sideways. There he experiences grievous, severe, sharp, and bitter pains; but he does not die so long as that wickedness is unexhausted.

Then, O priests, the guardians of hell throw him into the chiefest of the hells. Now this chiefest of the hells, O priests, is

> Symmetrical, and square in shape,
> Four-gated, into parts laid off.
> Of iron is its bounding wall,
> An iron roof doth close it in;
> And of its glowing iron floor
> The light with dazzling brilliancy
> Spreads for a hundred leagues around,
> And ever and for ay abides.

In former times, O priests, king Yama thought to himself, "All they, alas, who are guilty of wicked deeds in the

world must suffer such horrible and manifold torture! O
that I may become a man and a Tathāgata arise in the world,
a holy, Supreme Buddha, and that I may sit at the feet of
The Blessed One and The Blessed One teach me the Doctrine, and I come to understand the Doctrine of The Blessed
One!"

Now this, O priests, that I tell you, I did not get from
any one else, be he monk or Brahman; but, O priests, what
I by myself, unassisted, have known, and seen, and learnt,
that I tell you.

> All they who thoughtless are, nor heed,
> What time death's messengers appear,
> Must long the pangs of suffering feel
> In some base body habiting.
> But all those good and holy men,
> What time they see death's messengers,
> Behave not thoughtless, but give heed
> To what the Noble Doctrine says;
> And in attachment frighted see
> Of birth and death the fertile source,
> And from attachment free themselves,
> Thus birth and death extinguishing,
> Secure and happy ones are they,
> Released from all this fleeting show;
> Exempted from all sin and fear,
> All misery have they overcome.

§ 51 *b*. — Reprinted from Mrs. Piozzi's (Thrale's) Autobiography
(ed. Hayward, Ticknor and Fields, Boston (1861), vol. ii. p. 247.

THE THREE WARNINGS.

A TALE.

> The tree of deepest root is found
> Least willing still to quit the ground;
> 'T was therefore said by ancient sages,
> That love of life increased with years.
> So much, that in our latter stages,
> When pains grow sharp and sickness rages,

The greatest love of life appears.
This greatest affection to believe,
Which all confess, but few perceive,
If old affections can't prevail,
Be pleased to hear a modern tale.
When sports went round, and all were gay,
On neighbor Dobson's wedding-day,
Death called aside the jocund groom,
With him into another room;
And looking grave, you must, says he,
Quit your sweet bride, and come with me.
With you, and quit my Susan's side?
With you! the hapless husband cried:
Young as I am; 't is monstrous hard;
Besides, in truth, I 'm not prepared:
My thoughts on other matters go,
This is my wedding night, you know.
What more he urged I have not heard,
His reasons could not well be stronger,
So Death the poor delinquent spared,
And left to live a little longer.
Yet calling up a serious look,
His hour-glass trembled while he spoke,
Neighbor, he said, farewell.   No more
Shall Death disturb your mirthful hour,
And further, to avoid all blame
Of cruelty upon my name,
To give you time for preparation,
And fit you for your future station,
Three several warnings you shall have
Before you 're summoned to the grave:
Willing, for once, I 'll quit my prey,
And grant a kind reprieve;
In hopes you 'll have no more to say
But when I call again this way,
Well pleased the world will leave.
To these conditions both consented,
And parted perfectly contented.
What next the hero of our tale befell,
How long he lived, how wise, how well,
How roundly he pursued his course,
And smoked his pipe, and stroked his horse,
The willing muse shall tell:

He chaffered then, he bought, he sold,
Nor once perceived his growing old,
Nor thought of Death as near;
His friends not false, his wife no shrew,
Many his gains, his children few,
He passed his hours in peace;
But while he viewed his wealth increase,
While thus along life's dusty road
The beaten track content he trod,
Old time whose haste no mortal spares
Uncalled, unheeded, unawares,
Brought him on his eightieth year.
And now one night in musing mood,
As all alone he sate,
Th' unwelcome messenger of fate
Once more before him stood.
Half stilled with anger and surprise,
So soon returned! old Dobson cries.
So soon, d' ye call it!   Death replies:
Surely, my friend, you 're but in jest;
Since I was here before
'T is six-and-thirty years at least,
And you are now fourscore.
So much the worse, the clown rejoined,
To spare the aged would be kind;
However, see your search be legal
And your authority, — Is 't regal?
Else you are come on a fool's errand,
With but a secretary's warrant.
Besides, you promised me three warnings,
Which I have looked for nights and mornings;
But for that loss of time and ease
I can recover damages.
I know, cries Death, that at the best,
I seldom am a welcome guest;
But don't be captious, friend, at least;
I little thought you 'd still be able
To stump about your farm and stable;
Your years have run to a great length,
I wish you joy though of your strength.
Hold, says the farmer, not so fast,
I have been lame these four years past.
And no great wonder, Death replies;

However, you still keep your eyes,
And sure to see one's loves and friends,
For legs and arms would make amends.
Perhaps, says Dobson, so it might,
But, latterly, I 've lost my sight.
This is a shocking story, faith,
Yet there 's some comfort still, says Death;
Each strives your sadness to amuse,
I warrant you have all the news.
There 's none, cries he, and if there were,
I 've grown so deaf, I could not hear.
Nay then, the spectre stern rejoined,
These are unjustifiable yearnings;
If you are lame and deaf and blind,
You 've had your three sufficient warnings
So come along, no more we 'll part:
He said, and touched him with his dart;
And now old Dobson, turning pale,
Yields to his fate, — so ends my tale.

---

§ 52: THE ASS IN THE LION'S SKIN.

Translated from the Jātaka (ii. 109¹⁷), and constituting Birth-Story 189.

" *Nay, this is not a lion's roar.*"   This also was related by
The Teacher concerning Kokālika: and it was while dwelling in Jetavana monastery. Kokālika, at the time, was
desirous of intoning a doctrinal recitation before the congregation of the priests. When The Teacher heard this, he
related the following tale : —

Once upon a time, when Brahmadatta was reigning at
Benares, the Future Buddha, having been born in a farmer's
family, and now come of age, was making his living by hus-
bandry. Now at that time, a certain peddler went about
selling his wares, which he carried on the back of an ass.
And at every place he came to, he would unload the ass, and
dressing him up in the skin of a lion, let him loose in some
field of rice or barley. And the field-watchers did not dare

approach, as they thought it was a lion. Now one day the
peddler took up his abode at the gate of a village, and while
his breakfast was cooking, he dressed up the ass in the lion's
skin, and let him loose in a field of barley. The field-
watchers did not dare approach, as they thought it was a
lion, but went home and announced the news. Then all the
inhabitants of the village took up arms, and blowing conch-
shells, and beating drums, went to the field and shouted, so
that the ass became afraid for his life, and brayed. Then
the Future Buddha knew it was an ass, and pronounced the
first stanza :

> " Nay, this is not a lion's roar,
> Nor tiger, panther, gives its vent;
> But dressed up in a lion's skin,
> It is a wretched ass that brays."

And also the inhabitants of the village knew it was an
ass, and beat him until his bones broke, and took the lion's
skin away with them. Then came the peddler, and seeing
that his ass had come to grief, he pronounced the second
stanza :

> " Long might the ass have lived to eat
> The green and tender barley grain,
> Accoutred in the lion's skin,
> But that he brayed, and ruined all."

And while he was thus speaking, the ass died, whereupon
the peddler left him and went his way.

The Teacher, having given this doctrinal instruction,
identified the characters in the Birth-Story :

" At that time the ass was Kokālika, but the wise farmer
was I myself."

The Lion's-skin Birth-Story.

§ 53. THE DEVOTED WIFE.

Translated from the Dhammapada, and from Buddhaghosa's comment.

48.   While eagerly man culls life's flowers,
With all his faculties intent,
Of pleasure still insatiate —
Death comes and overpowereth him.

" *While eagerly man culls life's flowers.*"   This doctrinal
instruction was given by The Teacher while dwelling at
Sāvatthi, and it was concerning a woman called Husband-
honorer.   The affair began in the Heaven of the Suite of the
Thirty-three.

They say that a god of that heaven named Garland-wearer
went to his pleasure-grounds in company with a thousand
celestial nymphs.   Five hundred of these goddesses ascended
trees and threw down flowers, while five hundred picked up
the flowers that were thrown down and decked the god therewith.   One of these goddesses, while on the bough of a tree,
fell from that existence, her body vanishing like the flame of
a lamp.

Then she was conceived in a high-caste family of Sāvatthi,
and was born with a reminiscence of her previous existences.
And saying to herself, " I am the wife of the god Garland-
wearer," she made offerings of perfumes, garlands, and the
like, with the prayer that in her next rebirth she might again
be with her husband.   And when at the age of sixteen years
she married into another family, with ticket-food, and fortnightly food, she continued to give alms, saying, " May
this prove efficacious in bringing about my rebirth with my
husband."

Thereupon the priests gave her the name of Husband-
honorer, for they said: " She works early and late, and her
only desire is for her husband."

Husband-honorer continually took care of the hall where
the priests sat.   She brought forward the drinking water,

and spread out the mats to sit on. And when other people were desirous of giving ticket-food and other alms, they would bring it to her, and say, " Dear lady, prepare this for the congregation of the priests." And by going to and fro in this manner, she acquired the fifty-six salutary qualities, all at one time.

Then she conceived, and at the end of ten lunar months she brought forth a son; and when he was old enough to walk, another, until she had four sons.

One day, after she had given alms and offerings, and had listened to the Doctrine, and kept the precepts, she died toward night-fall from a sudden disease, and was reborn into the presence of her husband.

The other goddesses had continued to deck the god throughout the whole interval.

" We have not seen you since morning," said the god. " Where have you been ? "

" I fell from this existence, my lord."

" Are you in earnest ? "

" It was precisely so, my lord."

" Where were you born ? "

" At Sāvatthi, in a family of high caste."

" How long were you there ? "

" My lord, at the end of ten months I issued from my mother's womb, and at the age of sixteen years I married into another family; and having borne four sons, and having given gifts and done other meritorious deeds with the prayer that I might again be with you, I have been born into your presence."

" How long is the life of men ? "

" Only a hundred years."

" Is that all ? "

" Yes, my lord."

" If that is the length of life to which men are born, pray, now, do they pass the time asleep and reckless, or do they give gifts and do other meritorious deeds ? "

" Nothing of the kind, my lord. Men are always reckless, as if they were born to a life of an incalculable number of years, and were never to grow old and die."

At this the god Garland-wearer became exceedingly agitated.

"Men, it appears, are born to a life of only one hundred years, yet they recklessly lie down and sleep away their time. When will they ever get free from misery?"

A hundred of our years make one day and night of the Gods of the Suite of the Thirty-three; thirty such days and nights their month; and twelve such months their year. And the length of their lives is a thousand such celestial years, or in human notation thirty-six million years. Thus for that god not one day has passed; but like a moment had the interval seemed to him. And thus he thought, "Recklessness for short-lived men is extremely unsuitable."

On the next day, when the priests entered the village, they found the hall had not been looked after; the mats had not been spread, and the drinking water had not been placed. Then they inquired,

"Where is Husband-honorer?"

"Reverend sirs, how could you expect to see her? Yesterday, after your worships had eaten and departed, she died at even-tide."

When the priests heard this, the unconverted among them, calling to mind her benefactions, were unable to restrain their tears, while those in whom depravity had come to an end had their elements of being agitated.

After breakfast they returned to the monastery, and made inquiry of The Teacher:

"Reverend Sir, Husband-honorer worked early and late doing many kinds of meritorious deeds, and prayed only for her husband. Now she is dead. Where, pray, has she been reborn?"

"With her husband, O priests."

"But, Reverend Sir, she is not with her husband."

"O priests, it was not this husband she was praying for. She had a husband named Garland-wearer, a God of the Suite of the Thirty-three, and fell from that existence while he was decorating himself with flowers. Now she has returned and been born again at his side."

" Reverend Sir, is it really so ? "

" Assuredly, O priests."

" Alas, Reverend Sir, how very short is the life of all creatures ! In the morning she waited on us, and in the evening a disease attacked her, and she died."

" Assuredly, O priests," said The Teacher, " the life of creatures is indeed short. And thus it is that death gets creatures into his power, and drags them away howling and weeping, and still unsated in their senses and lusts."

So saying, he pronounced the following stanza:

> " While eagerly man culls life's flowers,
> With all his faculties intent,
> Of pleasure still insatiate —
> Death comes and overpowereth him."

----

§ 54.   FRIENDSHIP.

Translated from the Jātaka (i. 308²⁴), and constituting Birth-Story 68.

" *On whom the heart instinctive rests.*" This was related by The Teacher while dwelling in Añjana Wood, which is in the vicinity of Sāketa; and it was concerning a certain Brahman.

It appears that, as The Blessed One, surrounded by the congregation of the priests, was about to enter Añjana Wood, which is in the vicinity of Sāketa, a certain aged Brahman, a citizen of Sāketa, came out from that city and saw The One Possessing the Ten Forces in the gate-way. Falling at his feet, the Brahman seized him firmly by the ankles, and said,

" O my dear boy ! Should not parents in their old age be taken care of by their sons ? Why, in all this long time, have you not shown yourself to us ? And now that I have seen you, come and let your mother see you also." And with that he took The Teacher home with him."

When The Teacher arrived there, he sat down with the

congregation of the priests, taking the seat that was spread
for him.

Then came also the Brahman's wife, and fell at The
Teacher's feet.

" O my dear boy ! " said she, weeping. " Where have
you been gone so long ? Should you not have paid your
respects to your aged father and mother? " And she made
her sons and her daughters do him obeisance, saying, " Come,
do obeisance to your brother."

The Brahman and his wife, in great delight, gave a
liberal repast, and at the close of breakfast, The Teacher
preached to these two persons the Discourse on Old Age. At
the close of the discourse, both the Brahman and his wife had
become established in the fruit of never returning. The
Teacher then rose from his seat, and returned to Añjana
Wood.

And it came to pass, that when the priests were convened
in the lecture-hall, they raised a discussion :

" Brethren, the Brahman knows the father of The Tathāgata to be Suddhodana, and his mother Mahā-Māyā. Notwithstanding, both he and his wife call The Tathāgata their son,
and The Teacher consents to it. What now is the reason ? "

When The Teacher heard their discussion, he said,

" Priests, they call me son who am their son." So saying, he related the occurrences of by-gone existences : —

" Priests, in past time this Brahman was for five hundred
successive existences my father, and for five hundred successive existences my uncle, and for five hundred successive
existences my grandfather. And also this Brahman's wife
was for five hundred successive existences my mother, and
for five hundred successive existences my aunt, and for five
hundred successive existences my grandmother. Thus for
fifteen hundred existences was I brought up by this Brahman, and for fifteen hundred existences was I brought up by
this Brahman's wife."

Thus did The Buddha tell of three thousand existences,
and then pronounced the following stanza:

> " On whom the heart instinctive rests,
> In whom the spirit finds delight,
> With him, though one ne'er seen before,
> Safely in friendship one may dwell."

On whom the heart instinctive rests: — On whatever individual the mind rests securely at first sight.

In whom the spirit finds delight: — In whom the spirit delights, for whom it feels tenderness, at first sight.

With him, though one ne'er seen before: — Strictly speaking, one never seen before in this present existence.

Safely in friendship one may dwell: — On account of previous friendship one may have thorough confidence in that individual: in other words, that is the reason one does have confidence in him.

When The Teacher had given this doctrinal instruction, and had applied the moral to the story, he identified the characters of the Birth-Story:

" In those existences the Brahman and the Brahman's wife were the Brahman and the Brahman woman of this existence; the son was I myself."

The Sāketa Birth-Story.

---

§ 55. VIRTUE IS ITS OWN REWARD.

Translated from the Jātaka (ii. 92⁵), and constituting Birth-Story 182.

"*A strider over battle-fields.*" This was related by The Teacher while dwelling at Jetavana monastery; and it was concerning Nanda the elder.

For when The Teacher made his first visit home to Kapilapura, he induced his youngest brother, prince Nanda, to join the Order. Then he departed from Kapilapura, and traveling from place to place, he came and dwelt at Sāvatthi.

Now when the venerable Nanda had taken The Blessed One's bowl, and was leaving home, Belle-of-the-Country heard the report that prince Nanda was going away in company with The Teacher, and with hair half-braided she looked out of the window, and called out to him: "Come back quickly, my love!" And her speech remained in the venerable Nanda's mind, so that he became love-sick, and discontented, and pined away until the net-work of his veins showed on the surface of his body.

When The Teacher heard of all this, he thought: "What if now I were to establish Nanda in saintship." And going to the cell which was Nanda's sleeping-room, and taking his seat on the mat that was offered him, he said:

"Nanda, are you contented under this dispensation?"

"Reverend Sir, I am not contented, for I am exceedingly in love with Belle-of-the-Country."

"Nanda, have you ever taken a trip through the Himalaya Mountains?"

"Reverend Sir, I never have."

"Then let us go now."

"Reverend Sir, I have no magical power. How can I go?"

"I will take you, Nanda," said The Teacher, "by my own magical power."

Then he took the elder by the hand, and sprang into the air. As they passed along he pointed out to him a field that had been burnt over, and on a charred stump was seated a she-monkey with her nose and tail destroyed, her hair singed off, her skin fissured and peeled to the quick, and all smeared with blood.

"Nanda, do you see this she-monkey?"

"Yes, Reverend Sir."

"Take good note of her."

Then he took him and showed him Manosilā table-land, which is sixty leagues in extent, and Anotatta, and the rest of the seven great lakes, and the five great rivers, and the Himalaya range containing many hundred pleasant spots, and graced with Gold Mountain, Silver Mountain, and Jewel Mountain.

Then said he, "Nanda, have you ever seen the Heaven of the Suite of the Thirty-three?"

"Reverend Sir, I never have."

"Come, then, Nanda, and I will show it to you."

And he took him thither, and sat down on Sakka's marble throne.

And Sakka, the king of the gods, came up with the gods of two heavens, and did obeisance, and sat down respectfully at one side.   And his female attendants, twenty-five million in number, and five hundred pink-footed celestial nymphs came up also, and did obeisance, and sat down respectfully at one side.

The Teacher suffered the venerable Nanda to look upon these five hundred celestial nymphs again and again with passion.

"Nanda," said he, "do you see these pink-footed celestial nymphs?"

"Yes, Reverend Sir."

"Pray, now, are these or Belle-of-the-Country the prettier?"

"Reverend Sir, as is the burnt she-monkey compared to Belle-of-the-Country, so is Belle-of-the-Country compared to these."

"Well, Nanda, what then?"

"Reverend Sir, what does one do to obtain these celestial nymphs?"

"By performing the duties of a monk does one obtain these nymphs."

"Reverend Sir, if The Blessed One will be my guarantee that if I perform the duties of a monk, I shall obtain these nymphs, I will perform the duties of a monk."

"Do so, Nanda.   I am your guarantee."

Thus did the elder take The Tathāgata as guarantee in the presence of the assembled gods.   Then he said,

"Reverend Sir, do not delay.   Come, let us go.   I will perform the duties of a monk."

Then The Teacher returned with him to Jetavana monastery; and the elder began to perform the duties of a monk.

"Sāriputta," said then The Teacher, addressing the Captain of the Doctrine, "my youngest brother, Nanda, took me as guarantee for some celestial nymphs in the presence of the gods assembled in the Heaven of the Suite of the Thirty-three."

Thus he told him. And in the same way he told it to Mahā-Moggallāna the elder, to Mahā-Kassapa the elder, to Anuruddha the elder, to Ānanda the elder and Treasurer of the Doctrine, and so on to all the eighty great disciples, and also to the greater part of the other priests.

The Captain of the Doctrine, Sāriputta the elder, then drew near to Nanda the elder, and said,

" Is it true, as they say, brother Nanda, that in the presence of the gods assembled in the Heaven of the Suite of the Thirty-three, you took The One Possessing the Ten Forces as guarantee for some celestial nymphs, if you performed the duties of a monk ? If that be so, is not your chaste religious life all for the sake of women? all for the sake of your passions ? What is the difference between your thus doing the duties of a monk for the sake of women, and a laborer who performs his work for hire ? "

This speech put the elder to shame, and made him quite dispirited. And in the same way all the eighty great disciples, and the remaining priests also, shamed the venerable Nanda. And realizing that he had behaved in an unworthy manner, in shame and remorse he summoned up his heroism, and attained to insight and to saintship; and coming to The Teacher, he said,

" Reverend Sir, I release The Blessed One from his promise."

Said The Teacher, " When you attained to saintship, O Nanda, I became released from my promise."

When the priests heard of this occurrence, they raised a discussion in the lecture-hall :

" Brethren, how amenable to admonition is Nanda the elder ! One admonition was sufficient to arouse in him shame and remorse, so that he performed the duties of a monk, and attained to saintship."

The Teacher came and inquired, " Priests, what now is the subject of your discourse ? "

And they told him.

" Priests, formerly also, and not now for the first time, was Nanda amenable to admonition." So saying, he related the by-gone occurrence : —

Once upon a time, when Brahmadatta was ruling at Benares, the Future Buddha was born in the family of an elephant-trainer; and when he had come of age, and become accomplished as an elephant-trainer, he took service under a king who was hostile to the king of Benares. And he trained the state elephant until it was very well trained.

Then the king resolved to conquer the kingdom of Benares, and taking the Future Buddha with him, and mounting the state elephant, with a mighty army he went to Benares, and surrounded the place. Then he sent a letter to the king, saying, " Give me the kingdom, or give me battle."

Brahmadatta resolved to give battle ; and having manned the walls, the watch-towers, and the gates, he did so.

His enemy had his state elephant armed with a defensive suit of mail, put on armor himself, and mounted on the elephant's shoulders. " I will break into the city, kill my enemy, and take possession of the kingdom." With this thought he seized a sharp goad, and urged the elephant in the direction of the city.

But the elephant, when he saw the hot mud, the stones from the catapults, and the various kinds of missiles thrown by the defenders, did not dare to advance, but retreated in mortal terror.

Then his trainer drew near : " Old fellow," said he, " you are a hero, a strider over battle-fields. Retreat at such a time is not worthy of you." And thus admonishing the elephant, he pronounced the following stanzas : —

> " A strider over battle-fields,
> A hero, strong one, art thou called.
> Why, then, behemoth, dost retreat
> On coming near the gateway arch?

> " Break down in haste the great cross-bar !
> The city-pillars take away !
> And crashing through the gateway arch,
> Enter, behemoth, quickly in ! "

The city-pillars take away : — In front of city gates are pillars buried eight or sixteen feet of their length in the ground to make them immovable : the command is to quickly pull these up.

This one admonition was sufficient. For when the elephant heard it, he turned back, twisted his trunk round the city-pillars, and pulled them up like so many mushrooms. Then, crashing down the gateway arch, and forcing the cross-bar, he broke his way into the city, captured the kingdom, and gave it to his master.

When The Teacher had given this doctrinal instruction, he identified the characters of the Birth-Story :

" In that existence the elephant was Nanda, the king was Ānanda, while the elephant-trainer was I myself."

The Birth-Story of the Strider over Battle-fields.

---

§ 56. THE HARE-MARK IN THE MOON.

Translated from the Jātaka (iii. 51¹⁰), and constituting Birth-Story 316.

" *Some red-fish have I, seven in all.*" This was related by The Teacher while dwelling in Jetavana monastery ; and it was concerning a donation of all the requisites to the congregation of the priests.

It seems that a householder of Sāvatthi prepared a donation of all the requisites for The Buddha and for the Order. At the door of his house he had a pavilion built and gotten ready, and having invited The Buddha and the congregation of the priests, he made them sit down on costly seats which had been spread for them in the pavilion, and gave them an excellent repast of savory dishes. Then he invited them again for the next day, and again for the next, until he had invited them seven times. And on the seventh day he made the donation of all the requisites to The Buddha and to five hundred priests.

At the end of the breakfast The Teacher returned thanks and said,

"Layman, it is fitting that you thus manifest a hearty zeal; for this alms-giving was also the custom of the wise of old time. For the wise of old time surrendered their own lives to chance suppliants, and gave their own flesh to be eaten."

Then, at the request of the householder, he related the by-gone occurrence: —

Once upon a time, when Brahmadatta was ruling at Benares, the Future Buddha was born as a hare, and dwelt in a wood. Now on one side of this wood was a mountain, on another a river, and on another a border village. And there were three other animals that were his comrades — a monkey, a jackal, and an otter. These four wise creatures dwelt together, catching their prey each in his own hunting ground, and at night resorting together. And the wise hare would exhort the other three, and teach them the Doctrine, saying, "Give alms, keep the precepts, and observe fast-days." Then the three would approve of his admonition, and go each to his own lair in the thicket, and spend the night.

Time was going by in this manner, when one day the Future Buddha looked up into the sky and saw the moon, and perceived that the next day would be fast-day. Then said he to the others,

"To-morrow is fast-day. Do you three keep the precepts and observe the day; and as alms given while keeping the precepts bring great reward, if any suppliants present themselves, give them to eat of your own food."

"Very well," said they, and passed the night in their lairs.

On the next day the otter started out early, and went to the banks of the Ganges to hunt for prey. Now a fisherman had caught seven red-fish and strung them on a vine, and

buried them in the sand on the banks of the Ganges, and had
then gone on down-stream catching fish as he went.   The
otter smelt the fishy odor, and scraping away the sand, perceived the fish and drew them out.   Then he called out three
times, " Does any one own these?" and when he saw no
owner, he bit hold of the vine with his teeth, and drew them
to his lair in the thicket.   There he lay down, remembering
that he was keeping the precepts, and thinking, " I will eat
these at the proper time."

And the jackal also went out to hunt for prey, and found
in the hut of a field-watcher two spits of meat, and one
iguana, and a jar of sour cream.   Then he called out three
times, " Does any one own these?" and when he saw no
owner, he placed the cord that served as a handle for the jar
of sour cream about his neck, took hold of the spits of meat
and of the iguana with his teeth, and brought them home,
and placed them in his lair in the thicket.   Then he lay
down, remembering that he was keeping the precepts, and
thinking, " I will eat these at the proper time."

And the monkey also, entering the forest, fetched home a
bunch of mangoes, and placed them in his lair in the thicket.
Then he lay down, remembering that he was keeping the precepts, and thinking, " I will eat these at the proper time."

The Future Buddha, however, remained in his thicket,
thinking, " At the proper time I will go out and eat dabba-[1]
grass."   Then he thought,

" If any suppliants come, they will not want to eat grass,
and I have no sesamum, rice, or other such food.   If any suppliant comes, I will give him of my own flesh."

Such fieriness of zeal in keeping the precepts caused the
marble throne of Sakka to grow hot.   Then, looking carefully, Sakka discovered the cause, and proposed to himself
to try the hare.   And disguised as a Brahman, he went first
to the lair of the otter.

" Brahman, why stand you there?" said the otter.

Said he, " Pandit, if I could but get something to eat, I

---

[1] Name of various kinds of grasses used for sacrificial purposes.

would keep fast-day vows, and perform the duties of a monk."

"Very well," said the otter; "I will give you food." And he addressed him with the first stanza:

> " Some red-fish have I, seven in all,
> Found stranded on the river bank.
> All these, O Brahman, are my own;
> Come eat, and dwell within this wood."

"I will return a little later," said the Brahman; "let the matter rest until to-morrow."

Then he went to the jackal. And the latter also asking, "Why stand you there?" the Brahman answered the same as before.

"Very well," said the jackal; "I will give you some food." And he addressed him with the second stanza:

> " A watchman guards the field close by,
> His supper have I ta'en away;
> Two spits of meat, iguana one,
> One dish of butter clarified.
> All these, O Brahman, are my own;
> Come eat, and dwell within this wood."

"I will return a little later," said the Brahman; "let the matter rest until to-morrow."

Then he went to the monkey. And the latter also asking, "Why stand you there?" the Brahman answered the same as before.

"Very well," said the monkey; "I will give you some food." And he addressed him with the third stanza:

> " Ripe mangoes, water clear and cold,
> And cool and pleasant woodland shade —
> All these, O Brahman, are my own;
> Come eat, and dwell within this wood."

"I will return a little later," said the Brahman; "let the matter rest until to-morrow."

Then he went to the wise hare. And he also asking,

"Why stand you there?" the Brahman answered the same as before.

The Future Buddha was delighted. "Brahman," said he, "you have done well in coming to me for food. To-day I will give alms such as I never gave before; and you will not have broken the precepts by destroying life. Go, my friend, and gather wood, and when you have made a bed of coals, come and tell me. I will sacrifice my life by jumping into the bed of live coals. And as soon as my body is cooked, do you eat of my flesh, and perform the duties of a monk." And he addressed him with the fourth stanza:

> "The hare no seed of sesamum
> Doth own, nor beans, nor winnowed rice.
> But soon my flesh this fire shall roast;
> Then eat, and dwell within this wood."

When Sakka heard this speech, he made a heap of live coals by his superhuman power, and came and told the Future Buddha. The latter rose from his couch of dabba-grass, and went to the spot. And saying, "If there are any insects in my fur, I must not let them die," he shook himself three times. Then throwing his whole body into the jaws of his liberality, he jumped into the bed of coals, as delighted in mind as a royal flamingo when he alights in a cluster of lotuses. The fire, however, was unable to make hot so much as a hair-pore of the Future Buddha's body. He felt as if he had entered the abode of cold above the clouds.

Then, addressing Sakka, he said,

"Brahman, the fire you have made is exceeding cold, and is not able to make hot so much as a hair-pore of my body. What does it mean?"

"Pandit, I am no Brahman; I am Sakka, come to try you."

"Sakka, your efforts are useless; for if all beings who dwell in the world were to try me in respect of my liberality, they would not discover in me any unwillingness to give." Thus the Future Buddha thundered.

"Wise hare," said then Sakka, "let your virtue be proclaimed to the end of this world-cycle." And taking a mountain, he squeezed it, and with the juice drew the outline of a hare in the disk of the moon. Then in that wood, and in that thicket, he placed the Future Buddha on some tender dabba-grass, and taking leave of him, departed to his own celestial abode.

And these four wise creatures lived happily and harmoniously, and kept the precepts, and observed fast-days, and passed away according to their deeds.

When The Teacher had given this instruction, he expounded the truths, and identified the characters of the Birth-Story: [At the close of the exposition of the truths, the householder who had given all the requisites became established in the fruit of conversion.]

"In that existence the otter was Ānanda, the jackal was Moggallāna, the monkey was Sāriputta, while the wise hare was I myself."

The Hare Birth-Story.

CHAPTER IV.

MEDITATION AND NIRVANA.

Introductory Discourse.

Protestant Christianity teaches salvation by faith; while Buddhism places its greatest reliance in meditation. And it is not strange that the methods of the two religions should be so different, when we consider the very different meanings attached by Buddhists and Christians to the word 'salvation,' — the latter wishing to be saved from sin and hell, the former from karma and rebirth.

The Buddha analyzes man and things inanimate, and finds nothing that is permanent, but only the concrete and the perishable. All karma, he says, is performed under the influence of greed after some desired object with hatred of that which is not wanted, and of infatuation or delusion of mind that causes one to believe that satisfaction will result when the object is attained. Now all these objects after which one strives are necessarily more or less concrete and definite, and the concrete and the definite are not satisfying to the reflective mind. Every thinking man endeavors to pass from the things which are seen and temporal to something which is unseen and which he can picture to himself as eternal. Now it is to be observed that when we endeavor to pass in thought from the transitory and the phenomenal to something more permanent and real we try to compass our object by passing from the concrete to the abstract. We try to reduce the multiplicity of phenomena to a few heads, and the more general we can make these heads, the nearer we seem to come to infinite or everlasting verity. But what we gain in extension we lose in intension, and the nearer does our conception approach to being a conception of nothing at all. The Buddha evidently saw this; but as negation was what he was striving for, he considered he had found the way to salvation, and hence we have his elaborate system of meditation. But I ought to say that 'meditation' is here a very clumsy word, and does not properly cover all the ground. The meditations of the Buddhists were not simple reflections on abstract subjects, but trances of self-hypnotism as well, in which they tried to bring, not merely the conceptions of the mind, but also the emotions and feelings of the heart to rarefied generalizations.

The process appears to me to resemble the mathematical one wherein a number of terms plus and minus consisting of a, b, c, and x, y, z, are grouped into one member of an equation and compared to zero in the other, with zero of course as the result. The various activities, or karma, by virtue of which the series composing the supposed Ego, or supposed reality of things, are perpetuated, are the terms consisting of a, b, c, etc. of the mathematical problem. By meditation an equation is made between this karma and nullity whereby subjective terms find themselves wiped out, and only nothingness remains. In other words, if you think of nothing you do not think. This nothingness when temporary is a trance; when permanent, Nirvana. See § 78 b, compared with 388 and 389.

Now the search after a Nirvana, or release from the miseries of rebirth, was not a peculiarity of Gotama, but was a common striving of the age and country in which he lived, and many methods of acquiring the desired end were in vogue. In the selection which I have entitled The Summum Bonum it is described how dissatisfied The Buddha was with what

had been taught him on the subject, the reason being, that
though the forty subjects of meditation and the four trances
were good to diminish passion and to lead one from the dominion of the senses into the realm of form or even to bring
one to the still more abstract realm of formlessness, yet as
long as ignorance was allowed to remain, desire and hence
misery was liable to recur. He therefore superadded an intellectual discipline intended to imbue the minds of his followers, not merely with the persuasion that there is misery in
the world, that this or that thing is evil, but that in the very
nature and constitution of things no good is anywhere possible, inasmuch as the Three Characteristics inhere in all
things. Buddhaghosa, therefore, puts the forty subjects of
meditation and their resulting trances into a category by
themselves, as being all good but not necessarily resulting
in the complete extirpation of desire and release from being.
This discipline he calls Concentration, and the resulting four
trances and the four formless states he calls the eight attainments. But Wisdom, or the intellectual discipline, lies in
the mastery of the Four Noble Truths, of Dependent Origination already discussed, and of much else besides, but above
all in the application of the Three Characteristics to the elements of being. To this discipline belongs one trance, a
ninth attainment or hypnotic state, called the Trance of
Cessation. The whole Visuddhi-Magga (Way of Purity or
Salvation) consists of a consideration of these two disciplines
with Conduct as the foundation. Conduct constitutes Part I,
and comprises the first two chapters; Concentration, Part II,
and comprises chapters III–XII; while Wisdom is treated of
throughout the rest of the book, that is, Part III or Chapters
XIII–XXIII. There are thus nine attainments or hypnotic
states in the Buddhist system of meditation. And these
trances were not merely of importance to learners, as a means

for arriving at Nirvana; but, the temporary release they afforded from the sense-perceptions and the concrete was so highly esteemed, that they were looked upon as luxuries and enjoyed as such by the saints and by The Buddha himself.

The Four Intent Contemplations have always seemed to me to be a sort of compendium or manual of meditation, a *vade-mecum*, as it were. They comprise both meditations belonging to Concentration (thus supplementing what we give under that head) and also to Wisdom. The entire aim of such introspection is to get rid of the idea that any of the bodily or mental functions presuppose an Ego; and the truth thus discovered is then applied to all sentient beings. The Cemeteries, of the First Intent Contemplation, also treated of under the name of the Impurities in " Beauty is but Skin-deep," merit particular notice as they well illustrate the mental attitude that The Buddha inculcates in his disciples. The Buddha teaches that physical beauty is a glamour existing entirely in the mind of the one who sees it. The real truth is that taught by anatomy; namely, that the supposed beautiful object is a congeries of unclean elements. The only reason that we can consider any one as beautiful is to blind our eyes to details and think of the whole; but we are only too prone to forget that there is nothing to be beautiful as a whole.

When a priest by Concentration has etherealized his aspirations, has gotten rid of all desire for any but the more spiritual forms of existence, and has then by Wisdom become convinced that all existence, without exception, no matter how high or abstract, is transitory and evil, he is then prepared to look upon Nirvana as a good. The subject of Nirvana has been much written about and many theories have been advanced as to what was the precise teaching of The Buddha on the subject. Now a large part of the pleasure that I have experienced in the study of Buddhism has arisen from the strangeness of what I may call the intellectual landscape. All the ideas, the modes of argument, even the postulates assumed and not argued about, have always seemed so strange, so different from anything to which I have been accustomed, that I feel all the time as though walking in fairyland. Much of the charm that the Oriental thoughts and ideas have for me appears to be because they so seldom fit into Western categories. Nirvana is an illustration of this; and, therefore, all short and compendious definitions necessarily leave much to be desired. If it be said that Nirvana is a getting rid of the round of rebirth, that is perfectly correct; but then, we do not believe in repeated rebirth. Nor can we call it annihilation; for annihilation implies something to be annihilated, whereas Nirvana occurs when the elements that constitute the stream of any individual existence have their dependence undermined and hence cease to originate. If, again, it be said that it is a getting rid of the threefold fire of lust, hatred, and infatuation, that is also a correct definition; but it is rather an ethical than a philosophical one, and implies a pessimistic view of life of which we Occidentals have but little conception. But I hope that in the two previous chapters and in the present one I have been successful in giving the native point of view of what the religious problem really is of man's relation to the universe; for I conceive that Nirvana can only be properly understood by a tolerably thorough comprehension of the philosophy of which it is the climax and the cap-stone.

§ 57. THE WAY OF PURITY.

Translated from the Visuddhi-Magga (chap. i.).

Therefore has The Blessed One said:

> " What man his conduct guardeth, and hath wisdom,
> And thoughts and wisdom traineth well,
> The strenuous and the able priest,
> He disentangles all this snarl."

When it is said *hath wisdom*, there is meant a wisdom for which he does not need to strive. For it comes to him through the power of his deeds in a former existence.

The strenuous and the able priest. Perseveringly by means of the above-mentioned heroism, and intelligently through the force of his wisdom, should he *guard* his *conduct*, and *train* himself in the quiescence and insight indicated by the words *thoughts* and *wisdom.*

Thus does The Blessed One reveal the Way of Purity under the heads of conduct, concentration, and wisdom. Thus does he indicate the three disciplines, a thrice noble religion, the advent of the threefold knowledge etc., the avoidance of the two extremes and the adoption of the middle course of conduct, the means of escape from the lower and other states of existence, the threefold abandonment of the corruptions, the three hostilities, the purification from the three corruptions, and the attainment of conversion and of the other degrees of sanctification.

And how?

By conduct is indicated the discipline in elevated conduct, by concentration, the discipline in elevated thoughts; and by wisdom, the discipline in elevated wisdom.

By conduct, again, is indicated the nobleness of this religion in its beginning. The fact that conduct is the beginning of this religion appears from the passage, " What is the first of the meritorious qualities? Purity of conduct." And again from that other, which begins by saying, " It is the non-

performance of any wickedness." And it is noble because
it entails no remorse or other like evils.

By concentration is indicated its nobleness in the middle.
The fact that concentration is the middle of this religion
appears from the passage which begins by saying, "It is richness in merit." It is noble because it brings one into the
possession of the magical powers and other blessings.

By wisdom is indicated its nobleness at the end. The
fact that wisdom is the end of this religion appears from the
passage,

> "To cleanse and purify the thoughts,
> 'T is this the holy Buddhas teach,"

and from the fact that there is nothing higher than wisdom.
It is noble because it brings about imperturbability whether
in respect of things pleasant or unpleasant. As it is said:

> "Even as the dense and solid rock
> Cannot be stirred by wind and storm;
> Even so the wise cannot be moved
> By voice of blame or voice of praise."

By conduct, again, is indicated the advent of the threefold
knowledge. For by virtuous conduct one acquires the threefold knowledge, but gets no further. By concentration is
indicated the advent of the Six High Powers. For by concentration one acquires the Six High Powers, but gets no
further. By wisdom is indicated the advent of the four analytical sciences. For by wisdom one acquires the four analytical sciences, and in no other way.

By conduct, again, is indicated the avoidance of the
extreme called sensual gratification; by concentration, the
avoidance of the extreme called self-torture. By wisdom is
indicated the adoption of the middle course of conduct.

By conduct, again, is indicated the means of escape from
the lower states of existence; by concentration, the means of
escape from the realm of sensual pleasure; by wisdom, the
means of escape from every form of existence.

By conduct, again, is indicated the abandonment of the

corruptions through the cultivation of their opposing virtues; by concentration, the abandonment of the corruptions through their avoidance; by wisdom, the abandonment of the corruptions through their extirpation.

By conduct, again, is indicated the hostility to corrupt acts; by concentration, the hostility to corrupt feelings; by wisdom, the hostility to corrupt propensities.

By conduct, again, is indicated the purification from the corruption of bad practices; by concentration, the purification from the corruption of desire; by wisdom, the purification from the corruption of heresy.

And by conduct, again, is indicated the attainment of conversion, and of once returning; by concentration, the attainment of never returning; by wisdom, the attainment of saintship. For the converted are described as "Perfect in the precepts," as likewise the once returning; but the never returning as "Perfect in concentration," and the saint as "Perfect in wisdom."

Thus are indicated the three disciplines, a thrice noble religion, the advent of the threefold knowledge etc., the avoidance of the two extremes and the adoption of the middle course of conduct, the means of escape from the lower and other states of existence, the threefold abandonment of the corruptions, the three hostilities, the purification from the three corruptions, and the attainment of conversion and of the other degrees of sanctification; and not only these nine triplets, but also other similar ones.

Now although this *Way of Purity* was thus taught under the heads of conduct, concentration, and wisdom, and of the many good qualities comprised in them, yet this with excessive conciseness; and as, consequently, many would fail to be benefited, we here give its exposition in detail.

§ 58. CONCENTRATION.

§ 58 *a*. — Translated from the Visuddhi-Magga (chap. iii.).

What is concentration? Concentration is manifold and various, and an answer which attempted to be exhaustive would both fail of its purpose and tend to still greater confusion. Therefore we will confine ourselves to the meaning here intended, and say — Concentration is an intentness of meritorious thoughts.

§ 58 *b*. — Translated from the Aṅguttara-Nikāya (iii. 88).

And what, O priests, is the discipline in elevated concentration?

Whenever, O priests, a priest, having isolated himself from sensual pleasures, having isolated himself from demeritorious traits, and still exercising reasoning, still exercising reflection, enters upon the first trance, which is produced by isolation and characterized by joy and happiness; when, through the subsidence of reasoning and reflection, and still retaining joy and happiness, he enters upon the second trance, which is an interior tranquilization and intentness of thoughts, and is produced by concentration; when, through the paling of joy, indifferent, contemplative, conscious, and in the experience of bodily happiness — that state which eminent men describe when they say, " Indifferent, contemplative, and living happily " — he enters upon the third trance; when, through the abandonment of happiness, through the abandonment of misery, through the disappearance of all antecedent gladness and grief, he enters upon the fourth trance, which has neither misery nor happiness, but is contemplation as refined by indifference, this, O priests, is called the discipline in elevated concentration.

§ 58 *c*. — Translated from the Aṅguttara-Nikāya (ii. 3¹⁰).

What advantage, O priests, is gained by training in quiescence? The thoughts are trained. And what advantage is gained by the training of the thoughts? Passion is abandoned.

§ 59.   THE THIRTY–ONE GRADES OF BEING.

Translated from the Abhidhammattha-Saṅgaha (v. 2–6, and 10).

The realm of punishment, the realm of sensual bliss, the
realm of form, and the realm of formlessness are the four
realms. The realm of punishment is fourfold: hell, the brute
class, the state of the Manes, the Titan host. The realm of
sensual bliss is sevenfold: mankind, the Suite of the Four
Great Kings, the Suite of the Thirty-three, the Yāma Gods,
the Satisfied Gods, the Gods Who Delight in Fashioning, the
Gods Who Have Control of Pleasures Fashioned by Others.
These eleven together are also called the realm of sensual
pleasure. The realm of form is sixteenfold: to the Retinue of
Brahma, to the Priests of Brahma, and to the Great Brahma
Gods access is had through the first trance; to the Gods of
Limited Splendor, to the Gods of Immeasurable Splendor, and
to the Radiant Gods access is had through the second trance;
to the Gods of Limited Lustre, to the Gods of Immeasurable
Lustre, and to the Completely Lustrous Gods access is had
through the third trance; to the Richly Rewarded Gods, to
the Gods without Perception, and to the Pure Abodes access
is had through the fourth trance. There are five of these
Pure Abodes: that of the Aviha [Effortless?] Gods, of the
Untroubled Gods, of the Easily Seen Gods, of the Easily
Seeing Gods, and of the Sublime Gods. The realm of formlessness is fourfold: that of the infinity of space, of the infinity of consciousness, of nothingness, and of neither perception
nor yet non-perception.

> None unconverted e'er are found
> To dwell within the Pure Abodes,
> Nor those who in the holy life
> Are in the first or second path;
>
> No saints 'mongst those perception-reft
> Nor in the realms of punishment;
> But all may reach the other states,
> Be they within the paths or not.

There is no fixed term of life for the four places of punishment, or for mankind, or for those fallen short of heaven,
or for the Titans.   But for the Gods of the Suite of the Four
Great Kings the term of life is five hundred divine years, or,
in human notation, nine million years; for the Gods of the
Suite of the Thirty-three it is four times as long, for the
Yāma Gods four times as long again, for the Satisfied Gods
four times as long again, for the Gods Who Delight in Fashioning four times as long again, and for the Gods Who Have
Control of Pleasures Fashioned by Others four times as long
again.

> Nine hundred and a score and one
> Of twice five times a million years,
> Plus sixty hundred thousand more
> The life of Gods Who Have Control.

. . . .

The term of life for the Gods of the Retinue of Brahma
is the third part of a world-cycle, for the Priests of Brahma
it is half a cycle, for the Great Brahma Gods a whole cycle,
for the Gods of Limited Splendor two cycles, for the Gods of
Immeasurable Splendor four cycles, for the Radiant Gods
eight cycles, for the Gods of Limited Lustre sixteen cycles,
for the Gods of Immeasurable Lustre thirty-two cycles, for
the Completely Lustrous Gods sixty-four cycles, for the
Richly Rewarded Gods and for the Gods without Perception
five hundred cycles, for the Aviha Gods a thousand cycles,
for the Untroubled Gods two thousand cycles, for the Easily
Seen Gods four thousand cycles, for the Easily Seeing Gods
eight thousand cycles, and for the Sublime Gods sixteen
thousand cycles. . . . The length of life of the gods who
make their abode in the realm of the infinity of space is
twenty thousand cycles, of the gods who make their abode
in the realm of the infinity of consciousness forty thousand
cycles, of the gods who make their abode in the realm of
nothingness sixty thousand cycles, and of the gods who make
their abode in the realm of neither perception nor yet non-
perception eighty-four thousand cycles.

. . . .

The first trance, by which access is had to the realm of form, causes, in its lowest exercise, rebirth as one of the Retinue of Brahma; in its mean exercise, as one of the Priests of Brahma; in its highest exercise, as one of the Great Brahma Gods. In like manner, the second and third trances, in their lowest exercise, cause rebirth as one of the Gods of Limited Splendor; in their mean exercise, as one of the Gods of Immeasurable Splendor; in their highest exercise, as one of the Radiant Gods. The fourth trance, in its lowest exercise, as one of the Gods of Limited Lustre; in its mean exercise, as one of the Gods of Immeasurable Lustre; in its highest exercise, as one of the Completely Lustrous Gods; and the fifth trance, as one of the Richly Rewarded Gods; and, if its exercise is accompanied by loss of perception, as one of the Gods without Perception. Those, however, who have attained to never returning are reborn in the Pure Abodes, while the meritorious exercises by which access is had to the realm of formlessness respectively cause rebirth in the four grades of formless gods.

---

§ 60. THE FORTY SUBJECTS OF MEDITATION.

Translated from the Visuddhi-Magga (chap. iii.).

Therefore in respect of what we have said: "Must adopt from the forty subjects of meditation some one adapted to his character" — it is to be understood that these subjects of meditation can be catalogued in ten different ways, namely, in respect to their names, in respect to whether they fall short of the trances or attain them, in respect to the particular trance induced, . . .

In respect to their names. There are forty subjects of meditation. As it has been said:

"The following make forty subjects of meditation: ten kasinas, ten impurities, ten reflections, four sublime states, four formless states, one perception, and one analysis."

Here the ten kasinas are the earth-kasina, the water-kasina, the fire-kasina, the wind-kasina, the dark-blue kasina, the yellow kasina, the blood-red kasina, the white kasina, the light kasina, the limited-aperture kasina.

The ten impurities are: a bloated corpse, a purple corpse, a putrid corpse, a hacked-to-pieces corpse, a gnawed-to-pieces corpse, a scattered-in-pieces corpse, a beaten-and-scattered-in-pieces corpse, a bloody corpse, a worm-infested corpse, a skeleton-corpse.

The ten reflections are: reflection on The Buddha, reflection on the Doctrine, reflection on the Order, reflection on conduct, reflection on liberality, reflection on the gods, the contemplation of death, the contemplation of the body, the contemplation of breathing, reflection on quiescence.

The four sublime states are: friendliness, compassion, joy, and indifference.

The four formless states are: the realm of the infinity of space, the realm of the infinity of consciousness, the realm of nothingness, and the realm of neither perception nor yet non-perception.

The one perception is the perception of the loathsomeness of nutriment.

The one analysis is the analysis into the four elements.

Thus are they to be catalogued in respect to their names.

In respect to whether they fall short of the trances or attain them. With the exception of the contemplation of the body and of the contemplation of breathing, the remaining eight reflections with the perception of the loathsomeness of nutriment and the analysis into the four elements are the ten subjects of meditation which fall short of the trances; all the others attain them. Thus in respect to whether they fall short of the trances or attain them.

In respect to the particular trance induced. Of those that lead to attainment, the ten kasinas and the contemplation of breathing induce all the four trances; the ten impurities and the contemplation of the body, the first trance; the first three sublime states, the first three trances; while the fourth sublime state and the four formless states induce all four. Thus in respect to the particular trance induced.

§ 61.   THE EARTH–KASIṆA.

Translated from the Visuddhi-Magga (chap. iv.).

For it has been said as follows:

" He who adopts the earth-kasiṇa obtains the mental reflex through the instrumentality of earth that is either prepared or else not prepared, and with limits not without limits, with terminations not without terminations, with boundary lines not without boundary lines, with a rim not without a rim, and of the size of a winnowing basket or of a dish. This mental reflex he firmly seizes and carefully examines and defines. And when he has firmly seized and carefully examined and defined that mental reflex, he sees the blessings to be derived from it, and what a valuable thing it is; and holding it in high esteem, and becoming much devoted to it, he fastens his mind firmly to that object, thinking, ' Verily, by this procedure I shall become released from old age and death.' And he ' having isolated himself from sensual pleasures, having isolated himself from demeritorious traits, and still exercising reasoning, still exercising reflection, enters upon the first trance, which is produced by isolation and characterized by joy and happiness.' "

Here the person who in some previous existence retired from the world, either under the religion of a Buddha, or to the life of a seer, and by means of the earth-kasiṇa obtained the four or the five trances, — such a person of merit and potentiality for conversion can obtain the mental reflex by contemplating unprepared earth, either a plowed field or a threshing-floor, as happened in the case of Mallaka the elder. Tradition has it that this venerable person was once gazing at a piece of plowed ground, and obtained a mental reflex of the size of the spot. Generalizing this mental reflex, and obtaining the five trances, he acquired insight based on those trances, and attained to saintship.

He, however, who has not had this initiation, must perform his kasiṇa in accordance with instructions received from

his preceptor who gave him his subject for meditation, taking
care to avoid the four imperfections liable to occur in this
kasina.   The colors dark-blue, yellow, blood-red, and white
are imperfections in this kasina.   Therefore, in practising
this kasina, one must avoid clay of any of these colors, and
use light-red clay, such as is found in the bed of the Ganges.
And it is not to be practised in the middle of the monastery,
where novices and others pass to and fro, but in some concealed spot on the outskirts of the monastery; and there,
either in a cave, or 'in a leaf-hut, a movable or else a fixed
frame must be constructed.

In constructing a movable frame, a piece of cloth or a skin
or a mat is drawn over four sticks, and on this a circle is
made, of the above-described dimensions, of well-kneaded
clay from which all grass, roots, grit, and gravel have been
removed.   This is placed on the ground and gazed at in pre-
paring this kasina.

A fixed frame is made by driving stakes into the ground,
spreading them out so as to make the figure of a lotus-calyx,
and then weaving them together with vines.

If there is not enough clay, other material may be placed
underneath, and the circle then made on top of clean light-
red clay, and one span four inches in diameter.   For this
was the size intended when it was said that it should be of
the size of a winnowing basket or of a dish.   The phrases,
however, "with limits not without limits" etc., were used
with reference to its having an outline.   Having made it of
the above-mentioned size and outline, he must not smooth it
with vegetable juices, as that would discolor it, but must use
water from a rock, and make it as smooth as a drum-head.
Thereupon he must sweep the place, and having gone for a
bath and returned, he must sit on a well-strewn and ready-
prepared seat, of the height of one span and four inches, and
at a distance of two-and-a-half cubits from the kasina-circle.
For if he were to sit further off, the kasina-circle would not
appear plainly; if nearer, the imperfections of the kasina-
circle would be visible ; if too high, he would have to bend
his neck to look; and if too low, his knees would ache.

Having, then, taken his seat as above described, he must first think over the wretchedness of sensual pleasures, with such phrases as, "Sensual pleasures are wanting in savor," etc. And having thus conceived a longing for indifference to sensual pleasures, as being the way of escape from them and the means for passing beyond all misery, he must then incite in himself joy and gladness by reflecting on the virtues of The Buddha, the Doctrine, and the Order; and with the highest respect for this procedure, as being the method employed by all the Buddhas, Private Buddhas, and noble disciples to gain indifference to sensual pleasures, he must put forth a strenuous effort, and say to himself, "Verily, by this method I shall become a partaker of the sweet blessings of isolation," and thus seize and develop the mental reflex with partially and evenly opened eyes. For if he open his eyes too wide, they ache, and the circle appears too plainly, and he consequently fails of the mental reflex. If he open his eyes too little, the circle is not plain enough, and the thoughts are sluggish, and in this way also he fails of the mental reflex. Therefore he must seize and develop the mental reflex with partially and evenly opened eyes, as if looking at his face in a mirror.

He must not consider the color of the mental reflex, nor notice peculiarities, but making its color in no way different from that of the original, he must fix his mind on a predominant characteristic, and attentively consider that. He must repeat over and over some name or epithet of the earth suited to his perception of it, such as, "broad one, big one, fertile one, ground, mine of wealth, container of wealth," etc. However, "broad one" is a well-known name; therefore, on account of its being well-known, let him repeat, "broad one, broad one."

He must contemplate the circle, sometimes with his eyes open, sometimes with them shut; and thus for a hundred times, or for a thousand times, or even more, must he do until the securing of the mental reflex. When in his meditation the circle appears equally visible, whether his eyes are open or shut, that is the securing of the mental reflex. When this occurs, he must no longer remain seated in that spot, but must return and seat himself in his lodging-place, and there go on with his meditation.

In order, however, to avoid being delayed by the necessity of washing his feet, he must endeavor to have on hand some single-soled sandals and a walking-stick. Then, if his feeble concentration is destroyed by some untoward event, he should slip his feet into his sandals, take his walking-stick, and go back to that place, and after obtaining the mental reflex, return and develop it, seated at his ease, and mull it over and again again, and engrain it into his mind.

While doing this, the hindrances are checked, the corruptions become assuaged, the mind concentrates itself by the concentration of the neighborhood degree, and the imitative mental reflex is obtained, all in the order named.

The following is the distinction between this mental reflex and the former, called the securing of the mental reflex. In the securing of the mental reflex any imperfection of the kasiṇa-circle is perceived. The imitative mental reflex, like a mirror taken from one's scrip, or like a polished conch-shell, or like the disk of the moon issuing from the clouds, or like cranes in the clouds, cleaves the securing of the mental reflex, and issues forth a hundred, a thousandfold more clear. But this mental reflex has no color nor shape. If it had, it would be gross and discernible to the eye, tangible, and possessing the Three Characteristics. But no; it is only a reflex existing in the perception of the person practising concentration. From the instant, however, it appears, the hindrances are checked, the corruptions become assuaged, and the mind concentrates itself by the concentration of the neighborhood degree.

For concentration is twofold: neighborhood-concentration, and attainment-concentration. There are two gradations in the achievement of concentration by the mind; that when the mind is in the neighborhood of the trances, and that when it is completely in them.

§ 62. BEAUTY IS BUT SKIN-DEEP.

[The Impurities.]

§ 62 *a.* — Translated from the Visuddhi-Magga (chap. i.).

With his eye he sees forms: — He sees forms with his eye-consciousness, which is able to see forms, and which is called by the name of its instrument, the eye. As the ancients have said, " The eye does not see forms, inasmuch as it is not the mind, and the mind does not see forms, inasmuch as it is not the eye. But when the object of sense meets the organ of sense, a person sees with the mind by means of the sensitiveness of the eye." The phrase to "see with the eye" makes mention only of the instrument, as when it is said, " He wounds with his bow." Accordingly, the sense is, with his eye-consciousness he sees forms.

But takes no note of signs: — Either signs of femininity, or of masculinity, or of sensuous beauty, or of anything else calculated to arouse the passions, but stops short at what he sees.

Nor of minor tokens: — He takes no note of a person's hand, or foot, or smile, or laugh, or conversation, or looking, or gazing, or other personal characteristics called "tokens," because they betoken and reveal the passions. Only that which is real does he note, as did the elder Mahā-Tissa, the hermit of Mt. Cetiya.

The story is that a certain woman had married into a family of rank, but had quarreled with her husband, and, decked and ornamented, until she looked like a goddess, had issued forth from Anurādhapura, early in the morning, and was returning home to her family. On her way she met the elder, as he was on his way from Mt. Cetiya to go on his begging-rounds in Anurādhapura. And no sooner had she seen him, than the perversity of her nature caused her to laugh loudly. The elder looked up inquiringly, and observ-

ing her teeth, realized the impurity of the body,[1] and attained
to saintship.   Therefore was it said:

> "The elder gazed upon her teeth,
> And thought upon impurity;
> And ere that he had left that spot,
> The stage of saintship he attained."

Then came her husband, following in her footsteps, and
seeing the elder, he said:

"Reverend sir, have you seen a woman pass this way?"
And the elder said:

> "Was it a woman, or a man,
> That passed this way? I cannot tell.
> But this I know, a set of bones
> Is traveling on upon this road."

§ 62 b. — Translated from the Visuddhi-Magga (chap. vi.).

For as the body when dead is repulsive, so is it also when
alive; but on account of the concealment afforded by an
adventitious adornment, its repulsiveness escapes notice. The
body is in reality a collection of over three hundred bones,
and is framed into a whole by means of one hundred and
eighty joints. It is held together by nine hundred tendons,
and overlaid by nine hundred muscles, and has an outside
envelope of moist cuticle covered by an epidermis full of
pores, through which there is an incessant oozing and trickling, as if from a kettle of fat. It is a prey to vermin, the seat
of disease, and subject to all manner of miseries. Through
its nine apertures it is always discharging matter, like a ripe
boil. Matter is secreted from the two eyes, wax from the
ears, snot from the nostrils, and from the mouth issue food,
bile, phlegm, and blood, and from the two lower orifices of
the body faeces and urine, while from the ninety-nine thousand pores of the skin an unclean sweat exudes attracting
black flies and other insects.

---

[1] By means of the tenth impurity, the teeth being reckoned as bone.
Compare page 292.

Were even a king in triumphal progress to neglect the use of tooth-sticks, mouth-rinses, anointings of the head, baths and inner and outside garments, and other means for beautifying the person, he would become as uncouth and unkempt as the moment he was born, and would in no wise differ in bodily offensiveness from the low-caste caṇḍāla whose occupation it is to remove dead flowers. Thus in respect of its uncleanness, malodor, and disgusting offensiveness, the person of a king does not differ from that of a caṇḍāla. However, when, with the help of tooth-sticks, mouth-rinses, and various ablutions, men have cleansed their teeth, and the rest of their persons, and with manifold garments have covered their nakedness, and have anointed themselves with many-colored and fragrant unguents, and adorned themselves with flowers and ornaments, they find themselves able to believe in an "I" and a "mine." Accordingly, it is on account of the concealment afforded by this adventitious adornment that people fail to recognize the essential repulsiveness of their bodies, and that men find pleasure in women, and women in men. In reality, however, there is not the smallest just reason for being pleased.

A proof of this is the fact that when any part of the body becomes detached, as, for instance, the hair of the head, hair of the body, nails, teeth, phlegm, snot, faeces, or urine, people are unwilling so much as to touch it, and are distressed at, ashamed of, and loathe it. But in respect of what remains, though that is likewise repulsive, yet men are so wrapped in blindness and infatuated by a passionate fondness for their own selves, that they believe it to be something desirable, lovely, lasting, pleasant, and an Ego.

In this they resemble the old jackal of the forest, who supposes each flower on a kiṁsuka tree to be a piece of meat, until disconcerted by its falling from the tree.

Therefore,

> Even as the jackal, when he sees
> The flowers on a kiṁsuka tree,
> Will hasten on, and vainly think,
> "Lo, I have found a tree with meat!"

But when each several flower that falls
He bites with an exceeding greed,
" Not this is meat; that one is meat
Which in the tree remains," he says;

Even so the sage rejects and loathes
Each fallen particle as vile,
But thinks the same of all the rest
Which in the body still remain.

Yet fools the body pleasant find,
Become therewith infatuate,
And many evil works they do,
Nor find from misery their release.

Let, then, the wise reflect, and see
The body is of grace bereft;
Whether it living be or dead,
Its nature is putridity.

For it has been said,

" The body, loathsome and unclean,
Is carrion-like, resembles dung,
Despised by those whose eyes can see,
Though fools find in it their delight.

" This monstrous wound hath outlets nine,
A damp, wet skin doth clothe it o'er;
At every point the filthy thing
Exudeth nasty, stinking smells.

" If now this body stood revealed,
Were it but once turned inside out,
We sure should need to use a stick
To keep away the dogs and crows." [1]

Therefore the undisciplined priest must acquire the mental reflex wherever he can, wherever an impurity appears, be it in a living body or in one that is dead, and thus bring his meditation to the stage of attainment-concentration.

---

[1] Hampole, *Prick of Conscience*, as quoted in *The Century Dictionary*, s. v. *midding* :

A fouler myddyng sawe thow never nane
Than a man es with flesche and bane.

§ 63. THE CONVERSION OF ANIMALS.

[REFLECTION ON THE BUDDHA.]

Translated from the Visuddhi-Magga (chap. vii.).

The Blessed One, moreover, was The Teacher, because he
gave instruction also to animals. These, by listening to the
Doctrine of The Blessed One, became destined to conversion,
and in the second or third existence would enter the Paths.
The frog who became a god is an illustration.

As tradition relates, The Blessed One was teaching the
Doctrine to the inhabitants of the town of Campā, on the
banks of Lake Gaggarā; and a certain frog, at the sound
of The Blessed One's voice, obtained the mental reflex.
And a certain cowherd, as he stood leaning on his staff,
pinned him down fast by the head. The frog straightway
died, and like a person awaking from sleep, he was reborn in
the Heaven of the Thirty-three, in a golden palace twelve
leagues in length. And when he beheld himself surrounded
by throngs of houris, he began to consider: "To think that I
should be born here ! I wonder what ever I did to bring me
here." And he could perceive nothing else than that he had
obtained the mental reflex at the sound of the voice of The
Blessed One. And straightway he came with his palace,
and worshiped at the feet of The Blessed One. And The
Blessed One asked him: —

> "Who is it worships at my feet,
> And flames with glorious, magic power,
> And in such sweet and winning guise,
> Lights up the quarters all around ?"

> "A frog was I in former times,
> And wandered in the waters free,
> And while I listened to thy Law,
> A cowherd crushed me, and I died."

Then The Blessed One taught him the Doctrine, and the conversion of eighty-four thousand living beings took place. And the frog, who had become a god, became established in the fruit of conversion, and with a pleased smile on his face departed.

§ 64. LOVE FOR ANIMALS.

[Sublime State of Friendliness.]

Translated from the Culla-Vagga (v. 6.)

Now at that time a certain priest had been killed by the bite of a snake, and when they announced the matter to The Blessed One, he said:

"Surely now, O priests, that priest never suffused the four royal families of the snakes with his friendliness. For if, O priests, that priest had suffused the four royal families of the snakes with his friendliness, that priest, O priests, would not have been killed by the bite of a snake. And what are the four royal families of the snakes? The Virū-pakkhas are a royal family of snakes; the Erāpathas are a royal family of snakes; the Chabyāputtas are a royal family of snakes; the Kanhāgotamakas are a royal family of snakes. Surely, now, O priests, that priest did not suffuse the four royal families of the snakes with his friendliness. For surely, O priests, if that priest had suffused the four royal families of the snakes with his friendliness, that priest, O priests, would not have been killed by the bite of a snake. I enjoin, O priests, that ye suffuse these four royal families of the snakes with your friendliness; and that ye sing a song of defence for your protection and safeguard. After this manner, O priests, shall ye sing:

"'Virūpakkhas, I love them all,
The Erāpathas, too, I love,
Chabyāputtas, I love them, too,
And all Kanhāgotamakas.

" ' Creatures without feet have my love,
And likewise those that have two feet,
And those that have four feet I love,
And those, too, that have many feet.

" ' May those without feet harm me not,
And those with two feet cause no hurt;
May those with four feet harm me not,
Nor those who many feet possess.

" ' Let creatures all, all things that live,
All beings of whatever kind,
See nothing that will bode them ill!
May naught of evil come to them!

" ' Infinite is The Buddha, infinite the Doctrine, infinite the Order! Finite are creeping things : snakes, scorpions, centipedes, spiders, lizards, and mice ! I have now made my protection, and sung my song of defence. Let all living beings retreat! I revere The Blessed One, and the seven Supreme Buddhas ! ' "

---

§ 65. THE SIX HIGH POWERS.

Translated from the Ākaṅkheyya-Sutta of the Majjhima-Nikāya (i.34[10]).

" If a priest, O priests, should frame a wish, as follows : ' Let me exercise the various magical powers, — let me being one become multiform, let me being multiform become one, let me become visible, become invisible, go without hindrance through walls, ramparts, or mountains, as if through air, let me rise and sink in the ground as if in the water, let me walk on the water as if on unyielding ground, let me travel cross-legged through the air like a winged bird, let me touch and feel with my hand the moon and the sun, mighty and powerful though they are, and let me go with my body even up to the Brahma-world,' — then must he be perfect in the precepts, bring his thoughts to a state of quiescence,

practise diligently the trances, attain to insight, and be a
frequenter of lonely places.

" If a priest, O priests, should frame a wish, as follows :
' Let me hear with a divinely clear hearing, surpassing that of
men, sounds both celestial and human, far and near,' then
must he be perfect in the precepts, etc.

" If a priest, O priests, should frame a wish, as follows :
' Let me by my own heart investigate and discern the hearts
of other beings, the hearts of other men ; let me discern a
passionate mind to be passionate, let me discern a mind free
from passion to be free from passion, let me discern a mind
full of hatred to be full of hatred, let me discern a mind free
from hatred to be free from hatred, let me discern an infatuated mind to be infatuated, let me discern a mind free from
infatuation to be free from infatuation, let me discern an
intent mind to be intent, let me discern a wandering mind to
be wandering, let me discern an exalted mind to be exalted,
let me discern an unexalted mind to be unexalted, let me discern an inferior mind to be inferior, let me discern a superior
mind to be superior, let me discern a concentrated mind to
be concentrated, let me discern an unconcentrated mind
to be unconcentrated, let me discern an emancipated mind
to be emancipated, let me discern an unemancipated mind to
be unemancipated,' then must he be perfect in the precepts, etc.

" If a priest, O priests, should frame a wish, as follows :
' Let me call to mind many previous states of existence, to wit,
one birth, two births, three births, four births, five births, ten
births, twenty births, thirty births, forty births, fifty births, one
hundred births, one thousand births, one hundred thousand
births, many destructions of a world-cycle, many renovations
of a world-cycle, many destructions and many renovations of
a world-cycle : " I lived in such a place, had such a name,
was of such a family, of such a caste, had such a maintenance, experienced such happinesses and such miseries, had
such a length of life. Then I passed from that existence and
was reborn in such a place. There also I had such a name,
was of such a family, of such a caste, had such a mainten-

ance, experienced such happinesses and such miseries, had
such a length of life.   Then I passed from that existence and
was reborn in this existence."   Thus let me call to mind many
former states of existence, and let me specifically characterize
them,' then must he be perfect in the precepts, etc.

"If a priest, O priests, should frame a wish, as follows :
'Let me with a divinely clear vision, surpassing that of men,
behold beings as they pass from one existence and spring up in
another existence; let me discern the base and the noble, the
handsome and the ugly, those in a higher state of existence
and those in a lower state of existence undergoing the result
of their deeds.   So that I can know as follows : "Alas! these
beings, having been wicked of body, wicked of voice, wicked
of mind, slanderers of noble people, wrong in their views, acquirers of false merit under wrong views, have arrived, after
the dissolution of the body, after death, at a place of punishment, a place of suffering, perdition, hell ; or, again, these other
beings, having been righteous of body, righteous of voice,
righteous of mind, not slanderers of noble people, right in
their views, acquirers of merit under right views, have arrived, after the dissolution of the body, after death, at a place
of happiness, a heavenly world."   Thus let me with a divinely
clear vision, surpassing that of men, discern beings as they
pass from one existence and spring up in another existence ;
let me discern the base and the noble, the handsome and the
ugly, those in a higher state of existence and those in a lower
state of existence undergoing the results of their deeds,' then
must he be perfect in the precepts, etc.

"If a priest, O priests, should frame a wish, as follows :
'Let me, through the destruction of depravity, in the present
life and in my own person, attain to freedom from depravity,
to deliverance of the mind, to deliverance by wisdom,' then
must he be perfect in the precepts, bring his thoughts to a
state of quiescence, practise diligently the trances, attain to
insight, and be a frequenter of lonely places."

§ 66. SPIRITUAL LAW IN THE NATURAL WORLD.

Translated from the Milindapañha (p. 82¹²).

Said the king, "Bhante Nāgasena, how far is it hence to the Brahma-world?"

"Your majesty, it is a long way hence to the Brahma-world. If a rock of the size of a pagoda were to fall thence, and descend forty-eight thousand leagues in a day and a night, it would reach the earth in four months' time."

"Bhante Nāgasena, you priests say as follows: 'As quickly as a strong man might stretch out his bent arm, or might bend his stretched-out arm, even so a priest who possesses magical power and has obtained the mastery over his mind, can disappear from the continent of India and reappear in the Brahma-world.' This I cannot believe, that he should go so very quickly so many hundreds of leagues."

Said the elder, "Your majesty, in what country were you born?"

"Bhante, there is an island named Alexandria, and there was I born."

"Your majesty, how far is it hence to Alexandria?"

"Bhante, it is about two hundred leagues."

"Call to mind, your majesty, something you may have done there."

"Yes, bhante, I am doing so."

"Your majesty, you have gone those two hundred leagues very nimbly."

"You are an able man, bhante Nāgasena."

Said the king, "Bhante Nāgasena, if two men were to die here, and one of them were to be reborn in the Brahma-world and the other in Cashmere, which would arrive first?"

"Your majesty, they would take the same length of time."

"Give an illustration."

" Your majesty, in what city were you born ? "

" Bhante, there is a town called Kalasi, and there was I born."

" Your majesty, how far is it hence to the town of Kalasi ? "

" Bhante, it is about two hundred leagues."

" Your majesty, how far is it hence to Cashmere ? "

" Bhante, it is twelve leagues."

" Be so good, your majesty, as to think of the town of Kalasi."

" Bhante, I have thought of it."

" Your majesty, be so good as to think of Cashmere."

" Bhante, I have thought of it."

" Your majesty, which took the longer to think of ? "

" Bhante, it took the same length of time."

" In exactly the same way, your majesty, if two men were to die here, and one of them were to be reborn in the Brahma-world and the other in Cashmere, it would take them the same length of time."

" Give another illustration."

" What do you say to this, your majesty ? Two birds are flying through the air; one settles on a high tree, and the second on a low one. If now they have alighted at the same time, which one's shadow will first reach the ground ? "

" Bhante, both shadows will reach the ground at the same time."

" In exactly the same way, your majesty, if two men were to die here, and one of them were to be reborn in the Brahma-world and the other in Cashmere, it would take them the same length of time."

" You are an able man, bhante Nāgasena."

§ 67. GOING FURTHER AND FARING WORSE.

[THE FIRST HIGH POWER.]

Translated from the Kevaddha-Sutta of the Dīgha-Nikāya (xi. 67).

Once upon a time, O Kevaddha, a reflection occurred to a certain priest of this very congregation: "Where do these four elements, to wit, the earthy element, the watery element, the fiery element, and the windy element, utterly cease?" Then, O Kevaddha, the priest entered upon a state of trance of such a nature that, his thoughts being in this state of trance, the way to the gods became revealed to him. Then, O Kevaddha, the priest drew near to where the Gods of the Suite of the Four Great Kings were; and having drawn near, he spoke to the Gods of the Suite of the Four Great Kings as follows:

"My friends, where do these four elements, to wit, the earthy element, the watery element, the fiery element, and the windy element, utterly cease?"

When he had thus spoken, O Kevaddha, the Gods of the Suite of the Four Great Kings spoke to the priest as follows:

"We, O priest, do not know where these four elements, to wit, the earthy element, the watery element, the fiery element, and the windy element, utterly cease. However, O priest, there are the Four Great Kings, who are more glorious and more excellent than we, they would know where these four elements, to wit, the earthy element, the watery element, the fiery element, and the windy element, utterly cease."

Then, O Kevaddha, the priest drew near to where the Four Great Kings were; and having drawn near, he spoke to the Four Great Kings as follows:

"My friends, where do these four elements, to wit, the earthy element, the watery element, the fiery element, and the windy element, utterly cease?"

When he had thus spoken, O Kevaddha, the Four Great Kings spoke to the priest as follows:

" We, O priest, do not know where these four elements, to wit, the earthy element, the watery element, the fiery element, and the windy element, utterly cease. However, O priest, there are the Gods of the Suite of the Thirty-three, who are more glorious and more excellent than we, they would know where these four elements, to wit, the earthy element, the watery element, the fiery element, and the windy element, utterly cease."

[The priest then made a visit to the Gods of the Suite of the Thirty-three, and to their ruler, Sakka; to the Yāma gods, and to their ruler, Suyāma; to the Satisfied Gods, and to their ruler, the Satisfied One; to the Gods Who Delight in Fashioning, and to their ruler, the Well-fashioned One; to the Gods Who Have Control of Pleasures Fashioned by Others, and to their ruler, the Controller; in each case putting the same question, and being directed to apply further on. The Controller's speech was as follows :]

" I, O priest, do not know where these four elements, to wit, the earthy element, the watery element, the fiery element, and the windy element, utterly cease. However, O priest, there are the Gods of the Retinue of Brahma, who are more glorious and more excellent than I, they would know where these four elements, to wit, the earthy element, the watery element, the fiery element, and the windy element, utterly cease."

Then, O Kevaddha, the priest entered upon a state of trance of such a nature that, his thoughts being in this state of trance, the way to the Brahma-world became revealed to him. Then, O Kevaddha, the priest drew near to where the Gods of the Retinue of Brahma were; and having drawn near, he spoke to the Gods of the Retinue of Brahma as follows:

" My friends, where do these four elements, to wit, the earthy element, the watery element, the fiery element, and the windy element, utterly cease?"

When he had thus spoken, O Kevaddha, the Gods of the Retinue of Brahma spoke to the priest as follows:

"We, O priest, do not know where these four elements, to wit, the earthy element, the watery element, the fiery element, and the windy element, utterly cease. However, O priest, there is Brahma, Great Brahma, the Supreme Being, the Unsurpassed, the Perceiver of All Things, the Controller, the Lord of All, the Maker, the Fashioner, the Chief, the Victor, the Ruler, the Father of All Beings Who Have Been and Are to Be, who is more glorious and more excellent than we, he would know where these four elements, to wit, the earthy element, the watery element, the fiery element, and the windy element, utterly cease."

"But where, my friends, is Great Brahma at the present moment?"

"We do not know, O priest, where Brahma is, or in what direction Brahma is, or whereabouts Brahma is. But inasmuch, O priest, as signs are seen, and a radiance is noticed, and an effulgence appears, Brahma himself will appear. This is a previous sign of the appearing of Brahma, to wit, that a radiance is noticed, and an effulgence appears."

Then, O Kevaddha, in no long time, Brahma appeared. Then, O Kevaddha, the priest drew near to where Brahma was; and having drawn near, he spoke to Brahma as follows:

"My friend, where do these four elements, to wit, the earthy element, the watery element, the fiery element, and the windy element, utterly cease?"

When he had thus spoken, O Kevaddha, Great Brahma spoke to the priest as follows:

"I, O priest, am Brahma, Great Brahma, the Supreme Being, the Unsurpassed, the Perceiver of All Things, the Controller, the Lord of All, the Maker, the Fashioner, the Chief, the Victor, the Ruler, the Father of All Beings Who Have Been and Are to Be."

And a second time, O Kevaddha, the priest spoke to Brahma as follows:

"My friend, I am not asking you, 'Are you Brahma, Great Brahma, the Supreme Being, the Unsurpassed, the Perceiver of All Things, the Controller, the Lord of All, the Maker, the Fashioner, the Chief, the Victor, the Ruler,

the Father of All Beings Who Have Been and Are to Be?'
But this, my friend, is what I ask you, 'Where do these four
elements, to wit, the earthy element, the watery element, the
fiery element, and the windy element, utterly cease?'"

And a second time, O Kevaddha, Great Brahma spoke to
the priest as follows:

"I, O priest, am Brahma, Great Brahma, the Supreme
Being, the Unsurpassed, the Perceiver of All Things, the
Controller, the Lord of All, the Maker, the Fashioner, the
Chief, the Victor, the Ruler, the Father of All Beings Who
Have Been and Are to Be."

And a third time, O Kevaddha, the priest spoke to Brahma
as follows:

"My friend, I am not asking you, 'Are you Brahma,
Great Brahma, the Supreme Being, the Unsurpassed, the
Perceiver of All Things, the Controller, the Lord of All,
the Maker, the Fashioner, the Chief, the Victor, the Ruler,
the Father of All Beings Who Have Been and Are to Be?'
But this, my friend, is what I ask you, 'Where do these four
elements, to wit, the earthy element, the watery element, the
fiery element, and the windy element, utterly cease?'"

Then, O Kevaddha, Great Brahma took the priest by the
arm, and led him to one side, and spoke to the priest as
follows:

"O priest, these gods of my suite believe as follows:
'Brahma sees all things; knows all things; has penetrated
all things.' Therefore was it that I did not answer you in
their presence. I, O priest, do not know where these four
elements, to wit, the earthy element, the watery element,
the fiery element, and the windy element, utterly cease.
Therefore it was a sin and a crime, O priest, that you left
The Blessed One, and went elsewhere in quest of an answer
to this question. Turn back, O priest, and having drawn
near to The Blessed One, ask him this question, and as The
Blessed One shall explain unto you, so believe."

Then, O Kevaddha, the priest, as quickly as a strong man
might stretch out his bent arm, or might draw in his stretched-
out arm, disappeared from that Brahma-heaven, and appeared

in front of me. Then, O Kevaddha, when the priest had
greeted me, he sat down respectfully at one side; and seated
respectfully at one side, the priest, O Kevaddha, spoke to me
as follows:

"Reverend Sir, where do these four elements, to wit,
the earthy element, the watery element, the fiery element,
and the windy element, utterly cease?"

"When he had thus spoken, O Kevaddha, I spoke to the
priest as follows:

"Once upon a time, O priest, some sea-faring traders,
having a land-sighting bird, sailed out into the sea with their
ship; and when the ship was out of sight of land, they set
free that land-sighting bird. Such a bird flies in an easterly
direction, in a southerly direction, in a westerly direction, in
a northerly direction, towards the zenith, and to the intermediate quarters; and, if it sees land anywhere about, it flies
thither, but if it does not see land anywhere about, it returns
to the ship. In exactly the same way, O priest, when you
had searched as far as to the Brahma-world, and had found
no answer to this question, you returned to me. O priest,
this question ought never to have been put thus, 'Reverend
Sir, where do these four elements, to wit, the earthy element,
the watery element, the fiery element, and the windy element,
utterly cease?' But this, O priest, is how the question
should have been put,

> "O where doth water, where doth earth,
> And fire, and wind no footing find?
> And where doth long, and where doth short,
> And fine and coarse and good and bad,
> And where do name and form both cease,
> And turn to utter nothingness?

"And the answer is,

> "In consciousness invisible
> And infinite, of radiance bright,
> O there doth water, there doth earth,
> And fire and wind no footing find.
> And there doth long, and there doth short,

And fine and coarse and good and bad,
And there do name and form both cease,
And utter nothingness become.
And then, when consciousness hath ceased,
This all hath turned to nothingness."

Thus spake The Blessed One, and the delighted house-holder, Kevaddha, applauded the speech of The Blessed One.

The Kevaddha-Sermon.

---

§ 68.   SĀRIPUTTA AND THE TWO DEMONS.

[THE SECOND AND FIFTH HIGH POWERS.]

Translated from the Udāna (iv. 4).

Thus have I heard.

On a certain occasion The Blessed One was dwelling at Rājagaha, in Bamboo Grove in Kalandakanivāpa. And at that time the venerable Sāriputta and the venerable Moggallāna the Great were dwelling in the monastery called Pigeon Glen. Now it chanced that the venerable Sāriputta, on a moonlight night, was seated under the open sky, with freshly shaven head, and in a state of trance. And it chanced that two demons, who were comrades, were passing on some errand from the northern quarter of the heavens to the southern. And these demons saw the venerable Sāri-putta, on the moonlight night, seated under the open sky, with freshly shaven head. And at sight of him, the first demon spoke to the second demon as follows:

"It occurs to me, comrade, that it would be a fine plan to give this monk a blow on the head."

Hearing this, the second demon replied:

"Enough of that, comrade; do not attack the monk. Great, O comrade, is the monk, of great magical power, and very mighty."

And a second time the first demon spoke to the second demon as follows:

"It occurs to me, comrade, that it would be a fine plan to give this monk a blow on the head."

And a second time the second demon replied:

"Enough of that, comrade; do not attack the monk. Great, O comrade, is the monk, of great magical power, and very mighty."

And a third time the first demon spoke to the second demon as follows:

"It occurs to me, comrade, that it would be a fine plan to give this monk a blow on the head."

And a third time the second demon replied:

"Enough of that, comrade; do not attack the monk. Great, O comrade, is the monk, of great magical power, and very mighty."

Then the first demon, not heeding what the other demon said, gave the venerable Sāriputta a blow on the head. With such a blow one might fell an elephant seven or seven-and-a-half cubits high, or might split a mountain peak. Thereupon, with the cry, "I am burning! I am burning!" the demon fell from where he stood into hell.

And the venerable Moggallāna the Great, with his divinely clear vision surpassing that of men, saw the demon give the venerable Sāriputta the blow on the head. And when he had seen it, he drew near to where the venerable Sāriputta was; and having drawn near, he spoke to the venerable Sāriputta as follows:

"Are you comfortable, brother? Are you doing well? Does nothing trouble you?"

"I am comfortable, brother Moggallāna. I am doing well, brother Moggallāna; but my head troubles me a little."

"O wonderful is it, brother Sāriputta! O marvellous is it, brother Sāriputta! How great is the magical power, and how great is the might of the venerable Sāriputta! Just now, brother Sāriputta, a certain demon gave you a blow on the head. And a mighty blow it was! With such a blow one might fell an elephant seven or seven-and-a-half cubits high, or might split a mountain peak. But the venerable Sāriputta only says thus: 'I am comfortable, brother Moggallāna. I am doing well, brother Moggallāna; but my head troubles me a little.' "

" O wonderful is it, brother Moggallāna! O marvellous is it, brother Moggallāna! How great is the magical power, and how great is the might of the venerable Moggallāna that he should see any demon at all! I, however, have not seen so much as a mud-sprite."

Now The Blessed One, with his divinely clear hearing surpassing that of men, heard the above conversation between these two elephants among men. Then The Blessed One, on learning of this occurrence, on that occasion breathed forth this solemn utterance :

> " The man whose mind, like to a rock,
> Unmovèd stands, and shaketh not;
> Which no delights can e'er inflame,
> Or provocations rouse to wrath —
> O, whence can trouble come to him,
> Who thus hath nobly trained his mind ? "

---

§ 69.   WORLD–CYCLES.

[The Fourth High Power.]

Translated from the Visuddhi-Magga (chap. xiii.).

Can call to mind — Can remember by following either the succession of the groups, or the sequence of births and deaths. For there are six classes of persons who can call to mind former states of existence: members of other sects, ordinary disciples, great disciples, chief disciples, Private Buddhas, and Buddhas. Now members of other sects can call to mind former states of existence for forty world-cycles,[1] and no more.

---

[1] [Samyutta-Nikāya, xv. 5⁶] — "It is as if, O priest, there were a mountain consisting of a great rock, a league in length, a league in width, a league in height, without break, cleft, or hollow, and every hundred years a man were to come and rub it once with a silken garment; that mountain consisting of a great rock, O priest, would more quickly wear away

And why? On account of the weakness of their wisdom.
For their wisdom is weak, as they are unable to define name
and form. Ordinary disciples can call to mind former states
of existence for one hundred or even one thousand world-
cycles, on account of the strength of their wisdom. The
eighty great disciples can call to mind former states of existence for one hundred thousand world-cycles; the two chief
disciples, for one immensity and one hundred thousand world-
cycles; Private Buddhas, for two immensities and one hundred
thousand world-cycles, for such is the limit of their earnest
wish. But The Buddhas have their power unlimited.

Members of other sects follow only the succession of the
groups; they cannot leave the consideration of that succession and follow the sequence of births and deaths, for they
are like blind men, in that they cannot go freely where they
please. Just as the blind cannot walk without a staff, so
they cannot remember if they let go the succession of the
groups. The ordinary disciples can call to mind former states
of existence by following either the succession of the groups,
or they can travel along by the sequence of births and deaths.
So, likewise, the eighty great disciples. But the two chief
disciples do not need to make use of the succession of the
groups; they behold the death of a person in one existence
and his rebirth in another, and again his death in that existence and his rebirth in a third. Thus they travel along
the sequence of births and deaths. So, likewise, the Private
Buddhas. The Buddhas, however, do not need to make use
of the succession of the groups, nor yet of the sequence of

and come to an end than a world-cycle. O priest, this is the length of a
world-cycle. And many such cycles, O priest, have rolled by, and many
hundreds of cycles, and many thousands of cycles, and many hundreds
of thousands of cycles. And why do I say so? Because, O priest, this
round of existence is without known starting-point, and of beings who
course and roll along from birth to birth, blinded by ignorance, and fet-
tered by desire, there is no beginning discernible. Such is the length of
time, O priest, during which misery and calamity have endured, and the
cemeteries have been replenished; insomuch, O priest, that there is every
reason to feel disgust and aversion for all the constituents of being, and
to free oneself from them."

births and deaths. For any point which they choose to remember, throughout many times ten million world-cycles,
becomes plain to them, and that in either direction. Thus
they contract many times ten million world-cycles, as one
would make an abridgment in a Pāli text, arriving at the
desired point with the stride of a lion. Just as an arrow
shot from the bow of a skilled archer, trained like Sarabhaṅga
to shoot at a hair's breadth, goes straight to the mark, and is
not caught in the way by any tree or plant, nor sticks fast,
nor misses its aim, so the intellect of The Buddhas is not
caught by any intervening birth, nor do they miss their aim,
but go straight to the wished-for place.

Now the power possessed by members of other sects to
perceive former states of existence resembles the light of a
glow-worm; that of the ordinary disciples, the light of a
lamp; that of the great disciples, the light of a torch; that of
the chief disciples, the light of the morning star; that of the
Private Buddhas, the light of the moon; that of The Buddhas
resembles the thousand-rayed disk of the autumnal sun.

The power possessed by members of other sects to call to
mind former states of existence is like the groping of a blind
man with the aid of a stick; that of the ordinary disciples,
like walking with the aid of a staff; that of the great disciples, like walking without a staff; that of the chief disciples,
like riding in a cart; that of the Private Buddhas, like riding
on camel-back; that of The Buddhas, like rolling in a chariot
on a great highway.

But our present text concerns itself only with disciples
and their power to call to mind former states of existence.
Therefore was it I said: "'Can call to mind' — Can remember by following either the succession of the groups, or the
sequence of births and deaths."

The priest, then, who tries for the first time to call to mind
former states of existence, should choose a time after breakfast
when he has returned from his begging-rounds, and is alone
and plunged in meditation, and has been absorbed in the four
trances in succession. On rising from the fourth trance, the
one that leads to the High Powers, he should consider the

event which last took place, namely, his sitting down; next the spreading of the mat; the entering of the room; the putting away of bowl and robe; his eating; his leaving the village; his going the rounds of the village for alms; his entering the village for alms; his issuing forth from the monastery; his paying worship in the courts of the shrine and of the Bo-tree; his washing the bowl; his taking the bowl; what he did between his taking the bowl and rinsing his mouth; what he did at dawn; what he did in the middle watch of the night; what he did in the first watch of the night. Thus, in retrograde order, must he consider all that he did for a whole day and night.

As much as this is plain even to the ordinary mind, but it is exceedingly plain to one whose mind is in preliminary concentration. But if there is any one event which is not plain, then he should again enter upon the trance that leads to the High Powers, and when he has risen from it, he must again consider that past event; this will be sufficient to make it as plain as if he had used a lighted lamp. In this retrograde order must he consider what he did the day before, the day before that, up to the fifth day, tenth day, half-month, month, year: and having in the self-same manner considered the previous ten, twenty years, and so on up to the time of his conception in this existence, he must then consider the name and form present at the moment of his death in the previous existence. For a clever priest is able at the first trial to penetrate beyond conception, and to take as his object of thought the name and form present at the moment of his death. But whereas the name and form of the previous existence utterly ceased, and another one came into being, therefore that point of time is like thick darkness, and difficult to be made out by the mind of any stupid person. But even such a one should not despair, and say, " I shall never be able to penetrate beyond conception, and take as my object of thought the name and form present at the moment of my death in the last existence," but he should again and again enter upon the trance that leads to the High Powers, and each time he rises from it, he should again consider that point of time.

Just as a strong man, in cutting down a mighty tree to be used in making the peaked roof of a pagoda, if the edge of his axe become turned in lopping off the branches and twigs, will not despair of cutting down the tree, but will go to a blacksmith's shop, and have his axe made sharp, and return, and go on with the cutting; and if the edge of his axe again become turned, he will again have it sharpened, and return, and go on with the cutting; and inasmuch as nothing that he has chopped needs to be chopped again, he will, in no long time, when there is nothing left to chop, fell that mighty tree. In exactly the same way, the priest, rising from the trance that leads to the High Powers, without considering what he has already considered, and considering only the moment of conception, in no long time will penetrate beyond the moment of conception, and take as his object the name and form present at the moment of his death. This matter can be illustrated by the wood-splitter, extractor of hair, and other similes.

Now the knowledge which has for its object the events from the last sitting down to the moment of conception, is not called the knowledge of former existences, but knowledge belonging to preliminary concentration. Some call it knowledge of past time. This knowledge does not concern itself with the realm of form. When, however, the priest, passing beyond the moment of conception, and taking the name and form present at the moment of his death, considers them with his mind; and when, after he has ceased considering them, the four or the five swiftnesses based on the same object hasten on, of which the first three or four, in the manner aforesaid, are called by such names as preliminary etc., and belong to the realm of sensual pleasure, while the last belongs to the realm of form, and is the attainment-thought belonging to the fourth trance; then the knowledge which accompanies that thought is termed the knowledge which calls to mind former states of existence.

His alert attention, Laving become possessed of this knowledge, *He can call to mind many former states of existence, to wit, one birth, two births, three births, four births, five births, ten*

*births, twenty births, thirty births, forty births, fifty births, one
hundred births, one thousand births, one hundred thousand births,
many destructions of a world-cycle, many renovations of a world-
cycle, many destructions and many renovations of a world-cycle :
" I lived in such a place, had such a name, was of such a family,
of such a caste, had such a maintenance, experienced such happinesses and such miseries, had such a length of life.   Then I
passed from that existence, and was reborn in such a place.
There also I had such a name, was of such a family, of such a
caste, had such a maintenance, experienced such happinesses and
such miseries, had such a length of life.   Then I passed from
that existence, and was reborn in this existence."   Thus he can
call to mind many former states of existence, and can specifically
characterize them.*

Here *one birth* is the series of the groups, beginning at the
moment of conception and ending at the moment of death,
and comprised in one existence.   Similarly as respects *two
births,* and so on.

As respects, however, *many destructions of a world-cycle
etc.,* when a world-cycle is on the wane, that is known as the
destruction of a world-cycle; when it is on the increase, that
is known as the renovation of a world-cycle.   Here destruction includes the continuance of destruction, from being its
beginning, and renovation includes the continuance of renovation.   Accordingly the four immensities of the following
quotation are all included: " There are four immensities, O
priests, to a world-cycle.   And what are the four?   The destruction, continuance of destruction, renovation, and continuance of renovation."

Now there are three destructions: the destruction by water,
the destruction by fire, the destruction by wind.   And there
are three boundaries: the Heaven of the Radiant Gods, the
Heaven of the Completely Lustrous Gods, the Heaven of the
Richly Rewarded Gods.   When a world-cycle is destroyed by
fire, it is consumed by fire from the Heaven of the Radiant
Gods down.   When it is destroyed by water, it is engulfed
by water from the Heaven of the Completely Lustrous Gods
down.   When it is destroyed by wind, it is demolished by

wind from the Heaven of the Richly Rewarded Gods down. In lateral expansion it always perishes to the extent of a Buddha's domain.

Now a Buddha's domain is threefold: birth-domain, authority-domain, knowledge-domain. Birth-domain comprises ten thousand worlds; all these quake at various periods in the life of a Tathāgata, as, for instance, when he is conceived. Authority-domain comprises one hundred thousand times ten million worlds; over all of these extends the protective power of the Ratana-Sutta, of the Khandha-Paritta, of the Dhajagga-Paritta, of the Āṭānāṭiya-Paritta, and of the Mora-Paritta. Knowledge-domain is endless and boundless, and the passage which says, "Or as far as he may wish," means that the knowledge of a Tathāgata extends to any place or to any subject he may wish. Of these three Buddha-domains, it is the authority-domain which perishes; but when that perishes, the birth-domain perishes likewise. They perish coincidently, and they exist coincidently. Now the perishing and the existing of a world-cycle are after the following manner:

When a world-cycle perishes by fire, there arises in the beginning a cycle-destroying great cloud, and a great rain falls throughout one hundred thousand times ten million worlds. The people are delighted and overjoyed, and bring forth seed of all kinds and sow; but when the crops have grown just large enough for cow-fodder, the clouds keep up a braying noise, but do not allow a drop to fall; all rain is utterly cut off. Concerning which the following has been said by The Blessed One:

"There comes a time, O priests, when, for many years, for many hundreds of years, for many thousands of years, for many hundreds of thousands of years, the god does not rain."

Those creatures who depend on rain die, and are reborn in the Brahma-world; likewise the divinities who live on flowers and fruits. When thus a long time has elapsed, here and there the ponds of water dry up. Then, one by one, the fishes and turtles also die and are reborn in the Brahma-world; likewise the inhabitants of the hells. But some say the inhabitants of the hells perish with the appearing of the seventh sun.

But it may be said: "Without the trances, there is no being born into the Brahma-world. Yet some of these beings were overcome by famine, and some were incapable of attaining the trances. How could they be born into that world?" Because of their having attained the trances in the lower heavens.

For when it is known that after the lapse of a hundred thousand years the cycle is to be renewed, the gods called Loka-byūhas, inhabitants of a heaven of sensual pleasure, wander about through the world, with hair let down and flying in the wind, weeping and wiping away their tears with their hands, and with their clothes red and in great disorder. And thus they make announcement:

"Sirs, after the lapse of a hundred thousand years the cycle is to be renewed: this world will be destroyed; also the mighty ocean will dry up; and this broad earth, and Sineru, the monarch of the mountains, will be burnt up and destroyed, — up to the Brahma-world will the destruction of the world extend. Therefore, sirs, cultivate friendliness; cultivate compassion, joy, and indifference; wait on your mothers; wait on your fathers; and honor your elders among your kinsfolk."

When the people and the terrestrial deities hear these words, they, for the most part, become agitated, and their minds soften towards each other, and they cultivate friendliness, and do other meritorious deeds, and are reborn in the world of the gods. There they have heavenly ambrosia for food, and induce the trances by means of the air-kasina. Others, however, are born into the world of the gods by the alternation of the rewards of their good and evil deeds. For there is no being in the round of rebirth but has an alternation of the rewards of his good and evil deeds. Thus do they attain the trances in the world of the gods; and having there attained the trances, all are reborn in the Brahma-world.

When now a long period has elapsed from the cessation of the rains, a second sun appears. Here is to be supplied

in full what was said by The Blessed One in the Discourse
on the Seven Suns, beginning with the words, "There comes,
O priests, a time."

When this second sun has appeared, there is no distinction
of day and night; each sun rises when the other sets, and an
incessant heat beats upon the world. And whereas the ordinary sun is inhabited by its divinity, no such being is to be
found in the cycle-destroying sun. When the ordinary sun
shines, clouds and patches of mist fly about in the air. But
when the cycle-destroying sun shines, the sky is free from
mists and clouds, and as spotless as a mirror, and the water in
all streams dries up, except in the case of the five great rivers.
After the lapse of another long period, a third sun appears,
and the great rivers dry up. After the lapse of another long
period, a fourth sun appears, and the sources of the great
rivers in the Himalaya Mountains dry up, namely, the seven
great lakes, Sīhapapātana, Haṁsapapātana, Kaṇṇamuṇḍaka,
Rathakāradaha, Anotattadaha, Chaddantadaha, Kuṇāladaha.
After the lapse of another long period, a fifth sun appears,
and the mighty ocean gradually dries up, so that not enough
water remains to moisten the tip of one's finger. After the
lapse of another long period, a sixth sun appears, and the
whole world becomes filled with smoke, and saturated with
the greasiness of that smoke, and not only this world but a
hundred thousand times ten million worlds. After the lapse
of another long period, a seventh sun appears, and the whole
world breaks into flames; and just as this one, so also a hundred thousand times ten million worlds. All the peaks of
Mount Sineru, even those which are hundreds of leagues in
height, crumble and disappear in the sky. The flames of fire
rise up and envelop the Heaven of the Four Great Kings.
Having there burnt up all the mansions of gold, of jewels, and
of precious stones, they envelop the Heaven of the Thirty-
three. In the same manner they envelop all the heavens to
which access is given by the first trance. Having thus burnt
up three of the Brahma-heavens, they come to a stop on reaching the Heaven of the Radiant Gods. This fire does not go
out as long as anything remains; but after everything has

disappeared, it goes out, leaving no ashes, like a fire of clarified butter or sesamum oil. The upper regions of space become one with those below, and wholly dark.

Now after the lapse of another long period, a great cloud arises. And first it rains with a very fine rain, and then the rain pours down in streams which gradually increase from the thickness of a water-lily stalk to that of a staff, of a club, of the trunk of a palmyra-tree. And when this cloud has filled every burnt place throughout a hundred thousand times ten million worlds, it disappears. And then a wind arises, below and on the sides of the water, and rolls it into one mass which is round like a drop on the leaf of a lotus. But how can it press such an immense volume of water into one mass? Because the water offers openings here and there for the wind. After the water has thus been massed together by the wind, it dwindles away, and by degrees descends to a lower level. As the water descends, the Brahma-heavens reappear in their places, and also the four upper heavens of sensual pleasure. When it has descended to its original level on the surface of the earth, mighty winds arise, and they hold the water helplessly in check, as if in a covered vessel. This water is sweet, and as it wastes away, the earth which arises out of it is full of sap, and has a beautiful color, and a fine taste and smell, like the skimmings on the top of thick rice-gruel.

Then beings, who have been living in the Heaven of the Radiant Gods, leave that existence, either on account of having completed their term of life, or on account of the exhaustion of their merit, and are reborn here on earth. They shine with their own light and wander through space. Thereupon, as described in the Discourse on Primitive Ages, they taste that savory earth, are overcome with desire, and fall to eating it ravenously. Then they cease to shine with their own light, and find themselves in darkness. When they perceive this darkness, they become afraid. Thereupon, the sun's disk appears, full fifty leagues in extent, banishing their fears and producing a sense of divine presence. On seeing it, they are delighted and overjoyed, saying, "Now we have light; and whereas it has banished our fears and produced a sense

of divine presence [sura-bhāva], therefore let it be called
suriya [the sun]." Hence they named it suriya. After the
sun has given light throughout the day, it sets. Then they
are alarmed again, saying, "The light which we had has perished." Then they think: "It would be well if we had some
other light." Thereupon, as if divining their thoughts, the
disk of the moon appears, forty-nine leagues in extent. On
seeing it, they are still more delighted and overjoyed, and say,
"As if divining our wish [chanda], has it arisen: therefore is
it canda [the moon]." And therefore they named it canda.
When thus the sun and the moon have appeared, the constel-
lations and the stars arise. From that time on night and day
succeed each other, and in due course the months and half-
months, seasons and years. Moreover, on the same day with
the sun and the moon, Mount Sineru, the mountains which
encircle the world, and the Himalaya Mountains reappear.
These all appear simultaneously on the day of the full moon
of the month Phagguṇa. And how? Just as when panick-
seed porridge is cooking, suddenly bubbles appear and form
little hummocks in some places, and leave other places as depressions, while others still are flat; even so the mountains
correspond to the little hummocks, and the oceans to the
depressions, and the continents to the flat places.

Now after these beings have begun to eat the savory
earth, by degrees some become handsome and some ugly.
Then the handsome despise the ugly, and as the result of this
despising, the savoriness of the earth disappears, and the
bitter pappaṭaka plant grows up. In the same manner that
also disappears, and the padālatā plant grows up. In the
same way that also disappears, and rice grows up without any
need of cultivation, free from all husk and red granules, and
exposing the sweet-scented naked rice-grain. Then pots
appear for the rice, and they place the rice in the pots, and
place these pots on the tops of stones. And flames of fire
spring up of their own accord, and cook the rice, and it
becomes rice-porridge resembling the jasmine flower, and
needing the addition of no broth or condiments, but having
any desired flavor. Now when these beings eat this material

food, the excrements are formed within them, and in order that they may relieve themselves, openings appear in their bodies, and the virility of the man, and the femininity of the woman. Then the woman begins to meditate excessively on the man, and the man on the woman, and as a result of this excessive meditation, the fever of lust springs up, and they have carnal connection. And being tormented by the re- proofs of the wise for their low conduct, they build houses for its concealment. And having begun to dwell in houses, after a while they follow the example of some lazy one among themselves, and store up food. From that time on the red granules and the husks envelop the rice-grains, and wherever a crop has been mown down, it does not spring up again. Then these beings come together, and groan aloud, saying, "Alas! wickedness has sprung up among men; for surely we for- merly were made of mind." The full account of this is to be supplied from the Discourse on Primitive Ages.

Then they institute boundary lines, and one steals an- other's share. After reviling the offender two or three times, the third time they beat him with their fists, with clods of earth, with sticks, etc. When thus stealing, reproof, lying, and violence have sprung up among them, they come to- gether, and say, "What if now we elect some one of us, who shall get angry with him who merits anger, reprove him who merits reproof, and banish him who merits banishment. And we will give him in return a share of our rice." When, how- ever, the people of this, our world-cycle came to this decision, our Blessed One, who was at the time a Future Buddha, was of all these beings the handsomest, the most pleasing of ap- pearance, possessing the greatest influence and wisdom, and able to raise up and put down. Then they all came to him, and having gained his assent, they elected him their chief. Thus, inasmuch as he was elected by the multitude, he was called the Great Elect, and as he was lord of the fields [khetta], he was called khattiya [lord, the name for a mem- ber of the governing or warrior caste]. And as he pleased [sam-rañj-eti from root raj] his fellows by his even justice, he was called rājā [king]. Thus did he acquire these three appellations. A Future Buddha always becomes chief in that position in life which is most highly esteemed by mankind. When thus the association of warriors had been formed, with the Future Buddha at its head, by degrees the Brahmans and the other castes arose.

Now from the cycle-destroying great cloud to the termination of the conflagration constitutes one immensity, and is called the period of destruction. And from the cycle-destroying conflagration to the salutary great rains filling one hundred thousand times ten million worlds is the second immensity, and is called the continuance of destruction. From the salutary great rains to the appearing of the sun and moon is the third immensity, and is called the period of renovation. From the appearing of the sun and moon to the cycle-destroying great cloud is the fourth immensity, and is called the continuance of renovation. These four immensities form one great world-cycle.

This, then, is the order of events in a world-cycle when it perishes by fire.

But when a world-cycle perishes by water, it perishes in the manner above described, where it was said, "There arises in the beginning a cycle-destroying great cloud." But there are the following points of difference: — Instead of the second sun, there arises a cycle-destroying great cloud of salt water. At first it rains with a very fine rain which gradually increases to great torrents which fill one hundred thousand times ten million worlds, and the mountain-peaks of the earth become flooded with saltish water, and hidden from view. And the water is buoyed up on all sides by the wind, and rises upward from the earth until it engulfs the heavens to which access is given by the second trance. Having there flooded three of the Brahma-heavens, it comes to a stop at the Heaven of the Completely Lustrous Gods, and it does not settle as long as anything remains, but everything becomes impregnated with water, and then suddenly settles and disappears. And the upper regions of space become one with those below, and wholly dark. This is all as described above; only in this case the world begins to appear again at the Heaven of the Radiant Gods, and beings leave the Heaven of the Completely Lustrous Gods, and are reborn in the Heaven of the Radiant Gods, or in a lower heaven.

Now from the cycle-destroying great cloud to the termination of the cycle-destroying rain is one immensity; from the termination of the rain to the salutary great rains is the second immensity; from the salutary great rains to the appearing of the sun and moon is the third immensity; and from the appearing of the sun and moon to the cycle-destroying great cloud is the fourth immensity. These four immensities form one great world-cycle.

This is the order of events in a world-cycle when it perishes by water.

When a world-cycle is destroyed by wind, it perishes in the manner above described, where it was said, " There arises in the beginning a cycle-destroying great cloud." But there are the following points of difference : — Instead of the second sun, there arises a wind to destroy the world-cycle. And first it raises a fine dust, and then coarse dust, and then fine sand, and then coarse sand, and then grit, stones, etc., up to boulders as large as the peak of a pagoda, and mighty trees on the hill-tops. These mount from the earth to the zenith, and do not fall again, but are there blown to powder and annihilated. And then by degrees the wind arises from underneath the earth, and turns the ground upside down, and throws it into the sky, and areas of one hundred leagues in extent, two hundred, three hundred, five hundred leagues in extent, crack, and are thrown upwards by the force of the wind, and are blown to powder in the sky and annihilated. And the wind throws up also into the sky the mountains which encircle the earth, and Mount Sineru. These meet together, and are ground to powder and destroyed.

Thus are destroyed all the mansions on earth, and in the skies, also the six heavens of sensual desire, and a hundred thousand times ten million worlds. Worlds clash with worlds, Himalaya Mountains with Himalaya Mountains, and Mount Sinerus with Mount Sinerus, until they have ground each other to powder and have perished. From the earth upward does the wind prevail, until it has embraced all the heavens to which access is given by the third trance. Having there destroyed three of the Brahma-heavens, it comes to a stop at the Heaven of the Richly Rewarded Gods. When it has thus destroyed everything, it perishes. And the upper regions of space become one with those below, and wholly dark. All this is as described above. But now it is the Heaven of the Completely Lustrous Gods which first appears, and beings leave the Heaven of the Richly Rewarded Gods, and are reborn in the Heaven of the Completely Lustrous Gods, or in some lower heaven.

Now from the cycle-destroying great cloud to the termination of the cycle-destroying wind is one immensity; from the termination of the wind to the salutary great cloud is the second immensity; from the salutary great cloud to the appearing of the sun and moon is the third immensity; and from the appearing of the sun and moon to the cycle-destroying great cloud is the fourth immensity. These four immensities form one great world-cycle.

This is the order of events in a world-cycle when it perishes by wind.

Why does the world perish in these particular ways? It is on account of the special wickedness that may be at bottom. For it is in accordance with the wickedness preponderating that the world perishes. When passion preponderates, it perishes by fire; when hatred, it perishes by water. — But some say that when hatred preponderates, it perishes by fire, and that when passion preponderates it perishes by water. — When infatuation preponderates, it perishes by wind.

Now the world, in perishing, perishes seven times in succession by fire, and the eighth time by water; and then again seven times by fire, and the eighth time by water. Thus the world perishes each eighth time by water, until it has perished seven times by water, and then seven more times by fire. Thus have sixty-three world-cycles elapsed. Then the perishing by water is omitted, and wind takes its turn in demolishing the world; and when the Completely Lustrous Gods have reached their full term of existence of sixty-four world-cycles, their heaven also is destroyed.

Now it is of such world-cycles that a priest who can call
to mind former existences and former world-cycles, can call
to mind many destructions of a world-cycle, and many renovations of a world-cycle, and many destructions and renovations of a world-cycle.

And after what manner?

"*I lived in such a place,*" etc.

---

§ 70. WISDOM.

§ 70 a. — Translated from the Visuddhi-Magga (chap. xiv.).

What is Wisdom? Wisdom is manifold and various, and
an answer that attempted to be exhaustive would both fail of
its purpose and tend to still greater confusion. Therefore
we will confine ourselves to the meaning here intended, —
Wisdom is knowledge consisting in insight and conjoined
with meritorious thoughts.

§ 70 b. — Translated from the Añguttara-Nikāya (iii. 88).

And what, O priests, is the discipline in elevated wisdom?

Whenever, O priests, a priest knows the truth concerning
misery, knows the truth concerning the origin of misery,
knows the truth concerning the cessation of misery, knows
the truth concerning the path leading to the cessation of
misery, this, O priests, is called the discipline in elevated
wisdom.

§ 70 c. — Translated from the Añguttara-Nikāya (ii. 3[10]).

What advantage, O priests, is gained by training in insight? Wisdom is developed. And what advantage is gained
by the development of wisdom? Ignorance is abandoned.

§ 71. THE SUMMUM BONUM.

Translated from the Majjhima-Nikāya, and constituting Sutta 26.

Thus have I heard.

On a certain occasion The Blessed One was dwelling at Sāvatthi in Jetavana monastery in Anāthapiṇḍika's Park. Then The Blessed One, having put on his tunic in the morning, and taken his bowl and his robes, entered Sāvatthi for alms.

Then a great number of priests drew near to where the venerable Ānanda was; and having drawn near, they spoke to the venerable Ānanda as follows:

"It is a long time, brother Ānanda, since we listened to a doctrinal discourse from the mouth of The Blessed One. Come, brother Ānanda, let us obtain an opportunity to listen to a doctrinal discourse from the mouth of The Blessed One."

"Well, then, venerable sirs, draw near to the monastery of Rammaka the Brahman. Perchance you may obtain an opportunity to listen to a doctrinal discourse from the mouth of The Blessed One."

"Yes, brother," said the priests to the venerable Ānanda in assent.

Then The Blessed One, when he had gone the rounds for alms in Sāvatthi, returned from his begging, and after breakfast, addressed the venerable Ānanda:

"Let us go hence, Ānanda, and to Eastern Monastery, and to the storied mansion of Migāra's mother will we draw near for our noon-day rest."

"Yes, Reverend Sir," said the venerable Ānanda to The Blessed One in assent.

Then The Blessed One, in company with the venerable Ānanda, drew near to Eastern Monastery, and to the storied mansion of Migāra's mother, for his noon-day rest. Then The Blessed One, in the afternoon, rose from meditation, and addressed the venerable Ānanda:

"Let us go hence, Ānanda, and to Eastern Tank will we draw near to bathe our limbs."

"Yes, Reverend Sir," said the venerable Ānanda to The Blessed One in assent.

Then The Blessed One, in company with the venerable Ānanda, drew near to Eastern Tank to bathe his limbs; and having bathed his limbs in Eastern Tank and come up out of the water, he stood with but a single garment on, drying his limbs.

Then the venerable Ānanda spoke to The Blessed One as follows:

"Reverend Sir, here is the monastery of Rammaka the Brahman, but a short way off. Delightful, Reverend Sir, is the monastery of Rammaka the Brahman; enchanting, Reverend Sir, is the monastery of Rammaka the Brahman. Reverend Sir, pray let The Blessed One be so kind as to draw near to where the monastery of Rammaka the Brahman is." And The Blessed One consented by his silence.

Then The Blessed One drew near to where the monastery of Rammaka the Brahman was. Now at that time a great number of priests were seated in the monastery of Rammaka the Brahman, engaged in doctrinal discourse. Then The Blessed One stood outside in the entrance porch, and awaited the end of the discourse. Then The Blessed One, when he perceived that the discourse had come to an end, coughed, and rattled the bolt of the door. And the priests opened the door for The Blessed One. Then The Blessed One entered the monastery of Rammaka the Brahman, and sat on the seat that was spread for him. And when The Blessed One had sat down, he addressed the priests:

"What, O priests, was the subject of the present meeting? and what the discourse you were holding?"

"Reverend Sir, our doctrinal discourse was concerning The Blessed One, and then The Blessed One arrived."

"Well said, O priests! This, O priests, is worthy of you as youths of good family, who have through faith retired from the household life to the houseless one, that ye sit together in doctrinal discourse. O priests, one of two things should you do when you meet together: either hold a doctrinal discourse, or maintain a noble silence.

"There are two cravings, O priests; the noble one, and the ignoble one. And what, O priests, is the ignoble craving?

"We may have, O priests, the case of one who, himself subject to birth, craves what is subject to birth; himself subject to old age, craves what is subject to old age; himself subject to disease, . . . death, . . . sorrow, . . . corruption, craves what is subject to corruption.

"And what, O priests, should one consider as subject to birth?

"Wife and child, O priests, are subject to birth; slaves, male and female, . . . goats and sheep . . . fowls and pigs . . . elephants, cattle, horses and mares . . . gold and silver are subject to birth. All the substrata of being, O priests, are subject to birth; and enveloped, besotted, and immersed in them, this person, himself subject to birth, craves what is subject to birth.

"And what, O priests, should one consider as subject to old age . . . disease . . . death . . . sorrow . . . corruption?

"Wife and child, O priests, are subject to corruption; slaves, male and female, . . . goats and sheep . . . fowls and pigs . . . elephants, cattle, horses and mares . . . gold and silver are subject to corruption. All the substrata of being, O priests, are subject to corruption; and enveloped, besotted, and immersed in them, this person, himself subject to corruption, craves what is subject to corruption.

"This, O priests, is the ignoble craving.

"And what, O priests, is the noble craving?

"We may have, O priests, the case of one who, himself subject to birth, perceives the wretchedness of what is subject to birth, and craves the incomparable security of a Nirvana free from birth; himself subject to old age, . . . disease, . . . death, . . . sorrow, . . . corruption, perceives the wretchedness of what is subject to corruption, and craves the incomparable security of a Nirvana free from corruption.

"This, O priests, is the noble craving.

"Now I, O priests, before my Buddhaship, being not yet a Buddha, but a Future Buddha, myself subject to birth, craved what was subject to birth; myself subject to old age, . . . disease, . . . death, . . . sorrow, . . . corruption, craved what was subject to corruption. And it occurred to me, O priests, as follows:

" 'Why, myself subject to birth, do I crave what is subject to birth? myself subject to old age, . . . disease, . . . death, . . . sorrow, . . . corruption, do I crave what is subject to corruption? What if now, myself subject to birth, and perceiving the wretchedness of what is subject to birth, I were to crave the incomparable security of a Nirvana free from birth; myself subject to old age, . . . disease, . . . death, . . . sorrow, . . . corruption, I were to crave the incomparable security of a Nirvana free from corruption?'

"Subsequently, O priests, although of tender age, with the black hair of a lad, and in the hey-day of my youth, and just entering on my prime, and although my mother and my father were unwilling, and tears streamed from their eyes, I had my hair and my beard shaved off, and put on yellow garments, and retired from the household life to the houseless one. And having thus retired from the world, and craving the summum bonum, the incomparable peaceful state, I drew near to where Ālāra Kālāma was; and having drawn near, I spoke to Ālāra Kālāma as follows:

" 'Brother Kālāma, I would like to lead the religious life under your doctrine and discipline.'

"When I had thus spoken, O priests, Ālāra Kālāma spoke to me as follows:

" 'Let your venerable worship do so. Such is this doctrine that in no long time an intelligent man can learn for himself, realize, and live in the possession of all that his master has to teach.'

"Then I, O priests, in no long time, quickly acquired that doctrine. And I, O priests, and others with me, by a mere lip-profession, and a mere verbal assertion, claimed that we knew and had perceived the true knowledge and the orthodox doctrine. And it occurred to me, O priests, as follows:

" 'It is not through mere faith in this doctrine that Āḷāra Kālāma announces that he has learnt it for himself, realized it, and lives in the possession of it. Āḷāra Kālāma surely knows and perceives this doctrine.'

" Then, O priests, I drew near to where Āḷāra Kālāma was; and having drawn near, I spoke to Āḷāra Kālāma as follows :

" 'Brother Kālāma, how far does this doctrine conduct, concerning which you announce that you have learnt it for yourself, realized it, and entered upon it?'

" When I had thus spoken, O priests, Āḷāra Kālāma announced that it conducted to the realm of nothingness. And it occurred to me, O priests, as follows :

" 'Faith is not peculiar to Āḷāra Kālāma : I also have faith. Heroism . . . contemplation . . . concentration . . . wisdom is not peculiar to Āḷāra Kālāma : I also have wisdom. What if now I were to strive for the realization of that doctrine, concerning which Āḷāra Kālāma announces that he has learnt it for himself, realized it, and lives in the possession of it.' Then I, O priests, in no long time, quickly learnt that doctrine for myself, realized it, and lived in the possession of it. Then, O priests, I drew near to where Āḷāra Kālāma was; and having drawn near, I spoke to Āḷāra Kālāma as follows :

" 'Brother Kālāma, is this as far as the doctrine conducts, concerning which you announce that you have learnt it for yourself, realized it, and entered upon it?'

" 'This, brother, is as far as the doctrine conducts, concerning which I announce that I have learnt it for myself, realized it, and entered upon it.'

" 'I also, brother, have learnt this doctrine for myself, realized it, and live in the possession of it.'

" 'How fortunate, brother, are we! What supreme good fortune, brother, is ours that we should light on such a co-religionist as is your venerable worship. Thus the doctrine concerning which I announce that I have learnt it for myself, realized it, and entered upon it, that doctrine you have learnt for yourself, realized, and live in the possession of; the doctrine which you have learnt for yourself, realized, and live in the possession of, concerning that doctrine I announce that I have learnt it for myself, realized it, and entered upon it. Thus you know this doctrine, and I know this doctrine. You are the same as I am, and I am the same as you are. Come, brother, let us lead this following in common.'

"Thus, O priests, did Āḷāra Kālāma, my teacher, take me, his pupil, and make me every whit the equal of himself, and honor me with very great honor. And it occurred to me, O priests, as follows:

"'This doctrine does not lead to aversion, absence of passion, cessation, quiescence, knowledge, supreme wisdom, and Nirvana, but only as far as the realm of nothingness.'

"And I, O priests, did not honor that doctrine with my adhesion, and being averse to that doctrine, I departed on my journey.

"And craving, O priests, the summum bonum, the incomparable peaceful state, I drew near to where Uddaka, the disciple of Rāma, was; and having drawn near, I spoke to Uddaka, the disciple of Rāma, as follows:

"'Brother, I would like to lead the religious life under your doctrine and discipline.'

"When I had thus spoken, O priests, Uddaka, the disciple of Rāma, spoke to me as follows:

"'Let your venerable worship do so. Such is this doctrine that in no long time an intelligent man can learn for himself, realize, and live in the possession of all that his master has to teach.'

"Then I, O priests, in no long time, quickly acquired that doctrine. And I, O priests, and others with me, by a mere lip-profession, and a mere verbal assertion, claimed that we knew and had perceived the true knowledge and the orthodox doctrine. And it occurred to me, O priests, as follows:

"'It was not through mere faith in this doctrine that Rāma announced that he had learnt it for himself, realized it, and lived in the possession of it. Rāma surely knew and perceived this doctrine.'

"Then, O priests, I drew near to where Uddaka, the dis-

ciple of Rāma, was; and having drawn near, I spoke to
Uddaka, the disciple of Rāma, as follows:

" 'Brother, how far does this doctrine conduct, concerning
which Rāma made known that he had learnt it for himself,
realized it, and entered upon it?'

" When I had thus spoken, O priests, Uddaka, the disciple of Rāma, announced that it conducted to the realm of
neither perception nor yet non-perception. And it occurred
to me, O priests, as follows:

" 'Faith is not peculiar to Rāma: I also have faith. Heroism . . . contemplation . . . concentration . . . wisdom is
not peculiar to Rāma: I also have wisdom. What if now I
were to strive for that doctrine, concerning which Rāma announced that he had learnt it for himself, realized it, and
lived in the possession of it.' Then I, O priests, in no long
time, quickly learnt that doctrine for myself, realized it, and
lived in the possession of it. Then, O priests, I drew near to
where Uddaka, the disciple of Rāma, was; and having drawn
near, I spoke to Uddaka, the disciple of Rāma, as follows:

" 'Brother, is this as far as the doctrine conducts, concerning which Rāma announced that he had learnt it for himself,
realized it, and entered upon it?'

" 'This, brother, is as far as the doctrine conducts, concerning which Rāma announced that he had learnt it for
himself, realized, and entered upon it.'

" 'I also, brother, have learnt this doctrine for myself,
realized it, and live in the possession of it.'

" 'How fortunate, brother, are we! What supreme good
fortune, brother, is ours that we should light on such a co-
religionist as is your venerable worship. Thus the doctrine
concerning which Rāma announced that he had learnt it for
himself, realized it, and entered upon it, that doctrine you
have learnt for yourself, realized, and live in the possession
of; the doctrine which you have learnt for yourself, realized,
and live in the possession of, concerning that doctrine Rāma
announced that he had learnt it for himself, realized it, and
entered upon it. Thus you know this doctrine, and Rāma
knew this doctrine. You are the same as Rāma was, and

Rāma was the same as you are. Come, brother, lead this following.'

" Thus, O priests, did Uddaka, the disciple of Rāma, my co-religionist, make me his teacher, and honor me with very great honor. And it occurred to me, O priests, as follows:

" ' This doctrine does not lead to aversion, absence of passion, cessation, quiescence, knowledge, supreme wisdom, and Nirvana, but only as far as the realm of neither perception nor yet non-perception.'

" And I, O priests, did not honor that doctrine with my adhesion; and being averse to that doctrine, I departed on my journey.

" And craving, O priests, the summum bonum, the incomparable peaceful state, I came in the course of my journeyings among the Magadhans to Uruvelā, the General's Town. There I perceived a delightful spot with an enchanting grove of trees, and a silvery flowing river, easy of approach and delightful, and a village near by in which to beg. And it occurred to me, O priests, as follows:

" ' Truly, delightful is this spot, enchanting this grove of trees, and this silvery river flows by, easy of approach and delightful, and there is a village near by in which to beg. Truly, there is here everything necessary for a youth of good family who is desirous of struggling.'

" And there I settled down, O priests, as everything was suitable for struggling.

" And being, O priests, myself subject to birth, I perceived the wretchedness of what is subject to birth, and craving the incomparable security of a Nirvana free from birth, I attained the incomparable security of a Nirvana free from birth; myself subject to old age, . . . disease, . . . death, . . . sorrow, . . . corruption, I perceived the wretchedness of what is subject to corruption, and craving the incomparable security of a Nirvana free from corruption, I attained the incomparable security of a Nirvana free from corruption. And the knowledge and the insight sprang up within me, ' My deliverance is unshakable; this is my last existence; no more shall I be born again.' And it occurred to me, O priests, as follows:

" 'This doctrine to which I have attained is profound, recondite, and difficult of comprehension, good, excellent, and not to be reached by mere reasoning, subtile, and intelligible only to the wise. Mankind, on the other hand, is captivated, entranced, held spell-bound by its lusts; and forasmuch as mankind is captivated, entranced, and held spell-bound by its lusts, it is hard for them to understand the law of dependence on assignable reasons, the doctrine of Dependent Origination, and it is also hard for them to understand how all the constituents of being may be made to subside, all the substrata of being be relinquished, and desire be made to vanish, and absence of passion, cessation, and Nirvana be attained. If I were to teach the Doctrine, others would fail to understand me, and my vexation and trouble would be great.'

" Then, O priests, the following stanzas occurred to me, not heard of before from any one else:

" ' This Doctrine out of toil begot
I see 't is useless to proclaim :
Mankind 's by lusts and hates enthralled,
'T is hopeless they should master it.

" ' Repugnant, abstruse would it prove,
Deep, subtile, and beyond their ken ;
Th' infatuates live in clouds of lusts,
And cannot for the darkness see.'

" Thus, O priests, did I ponder, and my mind was disinclined to action, and to any proclaiming of the Doctrine.

" Then, O priests, Brahma Sahampati perceived what was in my mind, and it occurred to him as follows :

" 'Lo, the world is lost, is ruined ! For the mind of The Tathāgata, The Saint, The Supreme Buddha, is disinclined to action, and to any proclaiming of the Doctrine.'

" Then, O priests, Brahma Sahampati, as quickly as a strong man might stretch out his bent arm, or might draw in his outstretched arm, even so, having vanished from the Brahma-world, appeared in my presence.

" Then, O priests, Brahma Sahampati threw his upper

garment over his shoulder and, stretching out to me his joined palms, spoke as follows:

"'Reverend Sir, let The Blessed One teach the Doctrine, let The Happy One teach the Doctrine. There are some beings having but little moral defilement, and through not hearing the Doctrine they perish. Some will be found to understand the Doctrine.'

"Thus, O priests, spoke Brahma Sahampati, and having thus spoken, he continued as follows:

"'The Magadhans hold hitherto a doctrine
Impure, thought out by men themselves not spotless.
Ope thou the door that to the deathless leadeth:
Him let them hear who is himself unspotted.

"'As one who standeth on a rocky pinnacle,
Might thence with wide-extended view behold mankind,
Climb thou, Wise One, the top of Doctrine's palace,
And thence gaze down serene on all the peoples,
Behold how all mankind is plunged in sorrow,
And how old age and death have overwhelmed them.

"'Rise thou, O Hero, Victor in the Battle!
O Leader, Guiltless One, go 'mongst the nations!
The Doctrine let The Buddha teach,
Some will be found to master it.'

"Then I, O priests, perceiving the desire of Brahma, and having compassion on living beings, gazed over the world with the eye of a Buddha. And as I gazed over the world with the eye of a Buddha, I saw people of every variety: some having but little moral defilement, and some having great moral defilement; some of keen faculties, and some of dull faculties; some of good disposition, and some of bad disposition; some that were docile, and some that were not docile; and also some who saw the terrors of the hereafter and of blameworthy actions. Just as in a pond of blue lotuses, of water-roses, or of white lotuses, some of the blossoms which have sprung up and grown in the water, do not reach the surface of the water but grow under water; some of the blossoms which have sprung up and grown in the water, are even with the surface of the water; and some of the blossoms which have sprung up and grown in the water, shoot up above the water and are not touched by the water; in exactly the same way, O priests, as I gazed over the world with the eye of a Buddha, I saw people of every variety: some having but little moral defilement, and some having great moral defilement; some of keen faculties, and some of dull faculties; some of good disposition, and some of bad disposition; some that were docile, and some that were not docile; and also some who saw the terrors of the hereafter and of blameworthy actions. And when I had seen this, O priests, I addressed Brahma Sahampati in the following stanza:

> " ' Let those with ears to hear come give me credence,
> For lo! the door stands open to the deathless.
> O Brahma, 't was because I feared annoyance
> That I was loath to tell mankind the Doctrine.'

" Then, O priests, thought Brahma Sahampati, ' The Blessed One has granted my request that he should teach the Doctrine,' and saluting me, he turned his right side towards me, and straightway disappeared.

" Then, O priests, it occurred to me as follows:

" ' To whom had I best teach the Doctrine first? Who would quickly comprehend this Doctrine?'

" Then, O priests, it occurred to me as follows:

" ' Here is this Āḷāra Kālāma, who is learned, skilled, intelligent, and has long been a person having but little defilement. What if I teach the Doctrine to Āḷāra Kālāma first? He would quickly comprehend this Doctrine.'

" Then, O priests, a deity announced to me,

" ' Reverend Sir, Āḷāra Kālāma is dead these seven days.'

" Also in me the knowledge sprang up, ' Āḷāra Kālāma is dead these seven days.'

" Then, O priests, it occurred to me as follows:

" ' A noble man was Āḷāra Kālāma. Surely, if he could

have heard this Doctrine, he would quickly have comprehended it.'

" Then, O priests, it occurred to me as follows:

" ' To whom had I best teach the Doctrine first? Who would quickly comprehend this Doctrine?'

" Then, O priests, it occurred to me as follows:

" ' Here is this Uddaka, the disciple of Rāma, who is learned, skilled, intelligent, and has long been a person having but little defilement. What if I teach the Doctrine to Uddaka, the disciple óf Rāma, first? He would quickly comprehend this Doctrine.'

" Then, O priests, a deity announced to me,

" ' Reverend Sir, Uddaka, the disciple of Rāma, died yesterday at night-fall.'

" Also in me, O priests, the knowledge sprang up, ' Uddaka, the disciple of Rāma, died yesterday at night-fall.'

" Then, O priests, it occurred to me as follows:

" ' A noble man was Uddaka, the disciple of Rāma. Surely, if he could have heard this Doctrine, he would quickly have comprehended it.'

" Then, O priests, it occurred to me as follows:

" ' To whom had I best teach the Doctrine first? Who would quickly comprehend this Doctrine?'

" Then, O priests, it occurred to me as follows:

" ' Of great service has this band of five priests been, who waited upon me while I devoted myself to the struggle. What if I teach the Doctrine to the band of five priests first?'

" Then, O priests, it occurred to me as follows:

" ' Where does the band of five priests dwell at present?'

" And I, O priests, with my divinely clear vision surpassing that of men, saw the band of five priests dwelling at Benares, in the deer-park Isipatana.

" Then, O priests, having dwelt at Uruvelā as long as I wished, I proceeded on my wanderings in the direction of Benares. And Upaka, a naked ascetic, beheld me proceeding along the highway between the Bo-tree and Gayā. And having seen me, he spoke to me as follows:

" ' Placid, brother, are all your organs of sense; clear and bright is the color of your skin. To follow whom, brother, did you retire from the world? Who is your teacher? and whose doctrine do you approve?'

"When, O priests, Upaka, the naked ascetic, had thus spoken, I addressed him in the following stanzas:

> "'All-conquering have I now become, all-knowing;
> Untainted by the elements of being.
> I've left all things, am freed through thirst's destruction,
> All wisdom's mine: what teacher should I follow?

> "'I have no teacher anywhere;
> My equal nowhere can be found;
> In all the world with all its gods,
> No one to rival me exists.

> "'The saintship, verily, I've gained,
> I am The Teacher, unsurpassed;
> I am The Buddha, sole, supreme;
> Lust's fire is quenched, Nirvana gained.

> "'To found the Doctrine's reign I seek
> Benares, chief of Kāsi's towns;
> And for this blinded world I'll cause
> The drum of deathlessness to beat.'

"'Which is as much as to say, brother, that you profess to be a saint, an immeasurable Conqueror.'

> "'Yea, were The Conquerors like to me,
> Well rid of all depravity.
> I've conquered every evil trait;
> Thus, Upaka, a Conqueror I.'

"'You may be right, brother,' replied Upaka, the naked ascetic; and shaking his head, he took another road and departed.

"Then, O priests, I proceeded on my wanderings from place to place, and drew near to Benares, to the deer-park Isipatana, and to where the band of five priests was. And, O priests, the band of five priests saw me approaching from afar, and, when they had seen me, they made an agreement among themselves, saying:

" ' Here, brethren, is the monk Gotama approaching, that luxurious fellow who gave up the struggle and devoted himself to a life of luxury. Let us not salute him, nor rise and go to meet him, nor relieve him of his bowl and his robe. We will merely spread a seat for him: he can then sit down, if he is so inclined.'

"But, O priests, as I gradually approached, the band of five priests found themselves unable to hold to their agreement, and rising to meet me, one of them relieved me of my bowl and my robe, another spread a seat for me, and another brought water for washing my feet. But, O priests, they addressed me by my name, and by the title of 'Brother.' When, O priests, I noticed this, I spoke to the band of five priests as follows:

" ' O priests, address not The Tathāgata by his name, nor by the title of "Brother." A saint, O priests, is The Tathāgata, a Supreme Buddha. Give ear, O priests! The deathless has been gained, and I will instruct you, and teach you the Doctrine. If ye will do according to my instructions, in no long time, and in the present life, ye shall learn for yourselves, and shall realize and live in the possession of that highest good to which the holy life conducts, and for the sake of which youths of good family so nobly retire from the household life to the houseless one.'

"When I had thus spoken, O priests, the band of five priests said to me as follows:

" ' Brother Gotama, those practices of yours, that method of procedure, those stern austerities did not enable you to transcend human limitations and attain to pre-eminence in full and sublime knowledge and insight. How, then, now that you are luxurious, and have given up the struggle and devoted yourself to a life of luxury, can you have transcended human limitations and attained to pre-eminence in full and sublime knowledge and insight?'

"When they had thus spoken, O priests, I said to the band of five priests as follows:

" ' O priests, The Tathāgata is not luxurious, and has not given up the struggle and devoted himself to a life of luxury.

A saint, O priests, is The Tathāgata, a Supreme Buddha. Give ear, O priests! The deathless has been gained, and I will instruct you, and teach you the Doctrine. If ye will do according to my instructions, in no long time, and in the present life, ye shall learn for yourselves, and shall realize and live in the possession of that highest good to which the holy life conducts, and for the sake of which youths of good family so nobly retire from the household life to the houseless one.'

"And a second time, O priests, the band of five priests spoke to me as follows:

. . . .

"And a second time, O priests, I replied to the band of five priests as follows:

. . . .

"And a third time, O priests, the band of five priests spoke to me as follows:

. . . .

"When they had thus spoken, O priests, I replied to the band of five priests as follows:

"'Confess, O priests, have I ever before spoken to you as I have done this day?'

"'Nay, verily, Reverend Sir.'

"'A saint, O priests, is The Tathāgata, a Supreme Buddha. Give ear, O priests! The deathless has been gained, and I will instruct you, and teach you the Doctrine. If ye will do according to my instructions, in no long time, and in the present life, ye shall learn for yourselves, and shall realize and live in the possession of that highest good to which the holy life conducts, and for the sake of which youths of good family so nobly retire from the household life to the houseless one.'

"And I, O priests, succeeded in winning over the band of five priests.

"And I, O priests, exhorted two priests, while three priests went for alms; and the food which the three priests brought back from their begging-rounds furnished subsistence for all us six. And I, O priests, exhorted three priests,

while two priests went for alms; and the food which the
two priests brought back from their begging-rounds furnished subsistence for all us six.

"Then, O priests, the band of five priests, thus exhorted
and instructed by me, themselves subject to birth, perceived
the wretchedness of what is subject to birth, and craving the
incomparable security of a Nirvana free from birth, attained
the incomparable security of a Nirvana free from birth; themselves subject to old age, . . . disease, . . . death, . . . sorrow,
. . . corruption, . . . perceived the wretchedness of what is subject to corruption, and craving the incomparable security of a
Nirvana free from corruption, attained the incomparable security of a Nirvana free from corruption. And the knowledge
and the insight sprang up within them, 'Our deliverance is
unshakable; this is our last existence; no more shall we be
born again.'

"There are five sensual pleasures, O priests. And what
are the five? Forms perceivable by the eye, delightful, pleasant, charming, lovely, accompanied with sensual pleasure,
and exciting passion; sounds perceivable by the ear, . . .
odors perceivable by the nose, . . . tastes perceivable by the
tongue, . . . things tangible perceivable by the body, delightful, pleasant, charming, lovely, accompanied with sensual pleasure, and exciting passion. These, O priests, are the
five sensual pleasures.

"All monks and Brahmans, O priests, who partake of
these sensual pleasures, and are enveloped, besotted, immersed in them, and perceive not their wretchedness, and
know not the way of escape, of them is it to be understood
as follows: 'They have lighted on misfortune, have lighted
on destruction, and are in the power of the Wicked One.'

"Just as if, O priests, a deer of the forest were to step
into a snare, and were to be caught by it. Concerning this
deer it is to be understood as follows: 'It has lighted on
misfortune, has lighted on destruction, and is in the power of
the hunter. When the hunter shall come, it will not be able
to make its escape.' In exactly the same way, O priests, all
monks and Brahmans who partake of these sensual pleasures,

and enveloped, besotted, and immersed in them, perceive not their wretchedness, and know not the way of escape, of them is it to be understood as follows: 'They have lighted on misfortune, have lighted on destruction, and are in the power of the Wicked One.'

"On the other hand, O priests, all monks and Brahmans who partake of these sensual pleasures, and are not enveloped, besotted, and immersed in them, but perceive their wretchedness, and know the way of escape, of them is it to be understood as follows: 'They have not lighted on misfortune, have not lighted on destruction, and are not in the power of the Wicked One.'

"Just as if, O priests, a deer of the forest were to step into a snare, and were not to be caught by it. Concerning this deer it is to be understood as follows: 'It has not lighted on misfortune, has not lighted on destruction, and is not in the power of the hunter. When the hunter shall come, it will be able to make its escape.' In exactly the same way, O priests, all monks and Brahmans who do not partake of these sensual pleasures, and not enveloped, nor besotted, nor immersed in them, perceive their wretchedness, and know the way of escape, of them is it to be understood as follows: 'They have not lighted on misfortune, have not lighted on destruction, and are not in the power of the Wicked One.'

"Just as if, O priests, a deer of the forest were to roam the woods and mountain slopes; he can walk, stand, squat, and lie down in confident security. And why? Because, O priests, he is out of the reach of the hunter. In exactly the same way, O priests, a priest, having isolated himself from sensual pleasures, having isolated himself from demeritorious traits, and still exercising reasoning, still exercising reflection, enters upon the first trance which is produced by isolation, and characterized by joy and happiness. Of such a priest, O priests, is it said, 'He has blinded Māra, made useless the eye of Māra, gone out of sight of the Wicked One.'

"But again, O priests, a priest, through the subsidence of reasoning and reflection, and still retaining joy and happiness, enters upon the second trance, which is an interior tranquilization and intentness of the thoughts, and is produced by concentration. Of such a priest, O priests, is it said, 'He has blinded Māra, made useless the eye of Māra, gone out of sight of the Wicked One.'

"But again, O priests, a priest through the paling of joy, indifferent, contemplative, conscious, and in the experience of bodily happiness — that state which eminent men describe when they say, 'Indifferent, contemplative, and living happily' — enters upon the third trance. Of such a priest, O priests, is it' said, 'He has blinded Māra, made useless the eye of Māra, gone out of sight of the Wicked One.'

"But again, O priests, a priest through the abandonment of happiness, through the abandonment of misery, through the disappearance of all antecedent gladness or grief, enters upon the fourth trance, which has neither misery nor happiness, but is contemplation as refined by indifference. Of such a priest, O priests, is it said, 'He has blinded Māra, made useless the eye of Māra, gone out of sight of the Wicked One.'

"But again, O priests, a priest through having completely overpassed all perceptions of form, through the perishing of perceptions of inertia, and through ceasing to dwell on perceptions of diversity, says to himself, 'Space is infinite,' and dwells in the realm of the infinity of space. Of such a priest, O priests, is it said, 'He has blinded Māra, made useless the eye of Māra, gone out of sight of the Wicked One.'

"But again, O priests, a priest through having completely overpassed the realm of the infinity of space, says to himself, 'Consciousness is infinite,' and dwells in the realm of the infinity of consciousness. Of such a priest, O priests, is it said, 'He has blinded Māra, made useless the eye of Māra, gone out of sight of the Wicked One.'

"But again, O priests, a priest through having completely overpassed the realm of the infinity of consciousness, says to himself, 'Nothing exists,' and dwells in the realm of nothingness. Of such a priest, O priests, is it said, 'He has blinded Māra, made useless the eye of Māra, gone out of sight of the Wicked One.'

" But again, O priests, a priest through having completely
overpassed the realm of nothingness, dwells in the realm of
neither perception nor yet non-perception.   Of such a priest,
O priests, is it said, 'He has blinded Māra, made useless the
eye of Māra, gone out of sight of the Wicked One.'

" But again, O priests, a priest through having completely
overpassed the realm of neither perception nor yet non-perception, arrives at the cessation of perception and sensation, and before the clear vision of wisdom all his depravity
wastes away.   Of such a priest, O priests, is it said, 'He has
blinded Māra, made useless the eye of Māra, gone out of sight
of the Wicked One, and passed beyond all adhesion to the
world.'   He walks, stands, squats, and lies down in confident
security.   And why?   Because, O priests, he is out of the
reach of Māra."

Thus spake The Blessed One; and the delighted priests
applauded the speech of The Blessed One.

The Noble-craving Sermon.

---

§ 72. MĀRA AS PLOWMAN.

Translated from the Saṁyutta-Nikāya (iv. 2. 9).

Scene: Sāvatthi.

Now at that time The Blessed One enlightened, incited,
quickened, and gladdened the priests by a sermon on Nirvana.
And the priests, listening to the discourse with attentive ears,
became convinced, stored it up in their thoughts, and seized
upon it with their whole minds.

Then it occurred to Māra, the Wicked One, as follows :

" This monk Gotama enlightens, incites, quickens, and
gladdens the priests by a sermon on Nirvana.   And the
priests, listening to the discourse with attentive ears, become
convinced, store it up in their thoughts, and seize upon it
with their whole minds.   What if now I draw near to where
the monk Gotama is in order to perplex him."

Then Māra, the Wicked One, assumed the appearance of

a plowman. He shouldered an immense plow, took a long goad in his hand, and with dishevelled hair, a tunic of coarse hempen cloth, and mud-stained feet, he drew near to where The Blessed One was. And having drawn near, he spoke to The Blessed One as follows:

" Monk, didst thou see any oxen ? "

" What, O Wicked One, hast thou to do with oxen ? "

" Mine, O monk, is the eye ; mine are forms ; mine is the sense of sight. Where, O monk, canst thou go to escape from me ?

" Mine, O monk, is the ear ; mine are sounds ; mine is the sense of hearing. Where, O monk, canst thou go to escape from me ?

" Mine, O monk, is the nose ; mine are odors ; mine is the sense of smell. Where, O monk, canst thou go to escape from me ?

" Mine, O monk, is the tongue ; mine are tastes ; mine is the sense of taste. Where, O monk, canst thou go to escape from me ?

" Mine, O monk, is the body ; mine are things tangible ; mine is the sense of touch. Where, O monk, canst thou go to escape from me ?

" Mine, O monk, is the mind ; mine are ideas ; mine is the thinking faculty. Where, O monk, canst thou go to escape from me ? "

" Thine, O Wicked One, is the eye ; thine are forms ; thine is the sense of sight. But where, O Wicked One, there is no eye, nor any forms, nor sense of sight, there, O Wicked One, thou canst not come.

" Thine, O Wicked One, is the ear ; thine are sounds ; thine is the sense of hearing. But where, O Wicked One, there is no ear, nor any sounds, nor sense of hearing, there, O Wicked One, thou canst not come.

" Thine, O Wicked One, is the nose ; thine are odors ; thine is the sense of smell. But where, O Wicked One, there is no nose, nor any odors, nor sense of smell, there, O Wicked One, thou canst not come.

" Thine, O Wicked One, is the tongue ; thine are tastes ;

thine is the sense of taste. But where, O Wicked One, there
is no tongue, nor any tastes, nor sense of taste, there, O
Wicked One, thou canst not come.

"Thine, O Wicked One, is the body; thine are things
tangible; thine is the sense of touch. But where, O Wicked
One, there is no body, nor anything tangible, nor sense of
touch, there, O Wicked One, thou canst not come.

"Thine, O Wicked One, is the mind; thine are ideas;
thine is the thinking faculty. But where, O Wicked One,
there is no mind, nor any ideas, nor thinking faculty, there,
O Wicked One, thou canst not come."

> " Of what 't is said, ' This is of me,'
> Of what 't is said, ' These are the I,'
> If thou inclin'st thy mind to them,
> Then, monk, thou shalt not me escape."

> " Not so with me; naught is of me;
> Not so with me; they 're not the I;
> Thus, Wicked One, declare I thee,
> The path I tread thou ne'er canst find."

Then said Māra, the Wicked One :

"The Blessed One has recognized me. The Happy One
has recognized me," and sorrowful and dejected, he straightway disappeared.

The Plowman.

---

§ 73. THE FIRE-SERMON.

Translated from the Mahā-Vagga (i. 21¹)

Then The Blessed One, having dwelt in Uruvelā as long
as he wished, proceeded on his wanderings in the direction of
Gayā Head, accompanied by a great congregation of priests,
a thousand in number, who had all of them aforetime been
monks with matted hair. And there in Gayā, on Gayā Head,
The Blessed One dwelt, together with the thousand priests.

And there The Blessed One addressed the priests : —

" All things, O priests, are on fire.   And what, O priests, are all these things which are on fire ?

" The eye, O priests, is on fire; forms are on fire; eye-consciousness is on fire; impressions received by the eye are on fire; and whatever sensation, pleasant, unpleasant, or indifferent, originates in dependence on impressions received by the eye, that also is on fire.

" And with what are these on fire ?

" With the fire of passion, say I, with the fire of hatred, with the fire of infatuation; with birth, old age, death, sorrow, lamentation, misery, grief, and despair are they on fire.

" The ear is on fire; sounds are on fire; . . . the nose is on fire; odors are on fire; . . . the tongue is on fire; tastes are on fire; . . . the body is on fire; things tangible are on fire; . . . the mind is on fire; ideas are on fire; . . . mind-consciousness is on fire; impressions received by the mind are on fire; and whatever sensation, pleasant, unpleasant, or indifferent, originates in dependence on impressions received by the mind, that also is on fire.

" And with what are these on fire ?

" With the fire of passion, say I, with the fire of hatred, with the fire of infatuation; with birth, old age, death, sorrow, lamentation, misery, grief, and despair are they on fire.

" Perceiving this, O priests, the learned and noble disciple conceives an aversion for the eye, conceives an aversion for forms, conceives an aversion for eye-consciousness, conceives an aversion for the impressions received by the eye; and whatever sensation, pleasant, unpleasant, or indifferent, originates in dependence on impressions received by the eye, for that also he conceives an aversion.   Conceives an aversion for the ear, conceives an aversion for sounds, . . . conceives an aversion for the nose, conceives an aversion for odors, . . . conceives an aversion for the tongue, conceives an aversion for tastes, . . . conceives an aversion for the body, conceives an aversion for things tangible, . . . conceives an aversion for the mind, conceives an aversion for ideas, conceives an aversion for mind-consciousness, conceives an aversion for the impressions received

by the mind; and whatever sensation, pleasant, unpleasant, or
indifferent, originates in dependence on impressions received
by the mind, for this also he conceives an aversion.   And in
conceiving this aversion, he becomes divested of passion, and
by the absence of passion he becomes free, and when he is
free he becomes aware that he is free ; and he knows that rebirth is exhausted, that he has lived the holy life, that he has
done what it behooved him to do, and that he is no more for
this world."

Now while this exposition was being delivered, the minds
of the thousand priests became free from attachment and delivered from the depravities.

Here Endeth the Fire-Sermon.

§ 74.   THE FOUR INTENT CONTEMPLATIONS.

Translated from the Dīgha-Nikāya, and constituting Sutta 22.

Thus have I heard.

On a certain occasion The Blessed One was dwelling
among the Kurus where was the Kuru-town named Kam-
māsadhamma.   And there The Blessed One addressed the
priests :

" Priests ! " said he.

" Lord ! " said the priests in reply.

And The Blessed One spoke as follows : —

Priests, there is but one way open to mortals for the
attainment of purity, for the overcoming of sorrow and lamentation, for the abolition of misery and grief, for the acquisition of the correct rule of conduct, for the realization of
Nirvana, and that is the Four Intent Contemplations.[1]

---

[1] The Sumangala Vilāsinī, Cushing MS., Folio *ḍhi :* And now, just
as a skilful basket-maker, desirous of making coarse and fine mats, and
baskets, crates, hampers, and other like ware, might divide a large stalk
of bamboo into four parts, and then take some one of these sections,
split it, and make the required articles; in exactly the same way The
Blessed One, desirous of establishing for living beings a number of

And what are the four?

Whenever, O priests, a priest lives, as respects the body, observant of the body, strenuous, conscious, contemplative, and has rid himself of lust and grief; as respects sensations, observant of sensations, strenuous, conscious, contemplative, and has rid himself of lust and grief; as respects the mind, observant of the mind, strenuous, conscious, contemplative, and has rid himself of lust and grief; as respects the elements of being, observant of the elements of being, strenuous, conscious, contemplative, and has rid himself of lust and grief.

End of the Introduction.

And how, O priests, does a priest live, as respects the body, observant of the body?

Whenever, O priests, a priest, retiring to the forest, or to the foot of a tree, or to an uninhabited spot,¹ sits him down

---

avenues to proficiency, divides Right Contemplation, which is in fact but one, into four parts based on the subject-matter, saying, *There are Four Intent Contemplations. And what are the four? Whenever, O priests, a priest lives, as respects the body, observant of the body*, etc., and then takes one of these Intent Contemplations and analyzing the body begins his exposition of the subject with the words, *And how, O priests.*

¹ Folio *dhī: Retiring to the forest, or to the foot of a tree, or to an uninhabited spot* — This explains what dwelling-places should be chosen as appropriate to the exercise of intent contemplation. For in the case of this priest, his mind, having long spent itself on forms and the other objects of sense, does not readily apply itself to a subject of meditation: like a chariot harnessed to vicious oxen, it runs off the track. Therefore, even as a cowherd, desirous of breaking in a calf vicious from having been brought up on the milk of a vicious cow, will lead it away from its mother and tie it with a halter to a post planted somewhere out of her way; and even as the calf springing hither and thither and finding itself unable to escape will sit or lie down close by the post; in exactly the same way this priest, desirous of breaking in his mind, spoiled from having been brought up on the sweets of forms and of the other objects of sense, must resort to the forest, or to the foot of a tree, or to an uninhabited spot, and there with the bond of contemplation bind it to some object of intent contemplation, as it were to a post. Thus will his mind, springing hither and thither and finding none of its accustomed objects, be unable to break the bond of contemplation and escape, and will settle

cross-legged with body erect and contemplative faculty intent,
and contemplates his expirations, and contemplates his inspirations, and in making a long expiration thoroughly comprehends the long expiration he is making, and in making a long
inspiration thoroughly comprehends the long inspiration he is
making, and in making a short expiration thoroughly comprehends the short expiration he is making, and in making a
short inspiration thoroughly comprehends the short inspiration he is making, and trains himself to be conscious of all his
expirations, and trains himself to be conscious of all his inspirations, and trains himself to quiet his expirations, and trains
himself to quiet his inspirations.[1]   Just as, O priests, a skil-

---

down and lie close to the object of meditation, and attain either to neighborhood-concentration or to attainment-concentration. Therefore has it
been said by the ancients :

> " As he who wished to train a calf
> Would first him fasten to a post ;
> So should one fasten one's own mind
> Firmly by contemplation's bond."

Thus such dwelling-places are appropriate to these exercises. Therefore
have I stated : " This explains what dwelling-places should be chosen as
appropriate to the exercise of intent contemplation."

[1] Folios *ḍhī-ḍhu :* In thus training himself, he obtains the four
trances through the reflex of his respirations. And rising from his trance
he investigates either his expirations and inspirations, or else the members of his trances.

He who makes use of his respirations first investigates form, saying,
" On what are these expirations and inspirations based ? They are based
on matter, and matter is the material body, and the material body is the
four elements and form derivative from them." Secondly : " Name rests
on the same [four elements] with the addition of contact." When he
has thus grasped name, he searches for its dependence, and perceives
ignorance and the rest of Dependent Origination, and thinking, " Name
and form are merely dependence or else sprung from dependence ; there
is nothing else to form the living entity or Ego," he leaves all doubt
behind, and strengthening his insight by the application of the Three
Characteristics to dependent name and form, by degrees attains to saintship.   This is how this priest sets out on his way towards saintship.

He who makes use of his trance determines name and form in the
following manner : " On what are the members of my trance based ?
They are based on matter, and matter is the material body, and the mem-

ful turner, or turner's apprentice, in making a long turn of
the wheel thoroughly comprehends the long turn of the
wheel he is making, and in making a short turn of the wheel
thoroughly comprehends the short turn of the wheel he is
making; in exactly the same way, O priests, a priest, in
making a long expiration thoroughly comprehends the long
expiration he is making, and in making a long inspiration
thoroughly comprehends the long inspiration he is making,
and in making a short expiration thoroughly comprehends the
short expiration he is making, and in making a short inspiration thoroughly comprehends the short inspiration he is making, and trains himself to be conscious of all his expirations,
and trains himself to be conscious of all his inspirations, and
trains himself to quiet his expirations, and trains himself to
quiet his inspirations.

Thus he lives, either in his own person, as respects the
body, observant of the body, or in other persons, as respects
the body, observant of the body, or both in his own person
and in other persons, as respects the body, observant of the
body; either observant of origination in the body, or observant of destruction in the body, or observant of both origination and destruction in the body; and the recognition of the
body by his intent contemplation[1] is merely to the extent of
this knowledge, merely to the extent of this contemplation, and
he lives unattached, nor clings to anything in the world.

Thus, O priests, does a priest live, as respects the body,
observant of the body.

Section on the Contemplation of Breathing.

---

bers of my trance are form in the material body." Then he searches for
the dependence of name and form, and perceives ignorance etc., or the
formula of dependence, and thinking, "Name and form are merely
dependence or else sprung from dependence; there is nothing else to form
the living entity or Ego," he leaves all doubt behind, and strengthening
his insight by the application of the Three Characteristics to dependent
name and form, by degrees attains to saintship. This is how this priest
sets out on his way towards saintship.

[1] Folio *ḍhu: And the recognition of the body by his intent contemplation:*
— Only a body is recognized by his intent contemplation, but no living
entity, no Ego, no woman, no man, no self, nor anything pertaining to a
self, no I, no mine, no person nor anything pertaining to a person.

But again,[1] O priests, a priest, in walking thoroughly comprehends his walking, and in standing thoroughly comprehends his standing, and in sitting thoroughly comprehends his sitting, and in lying down thoroughly comprehends his

---

[1] Folios *dhu-dhū:* Having thus made of the respirations one division of the observation of the body, he now of the bodily postures makes another, and begins with the words, *But again.*

Now it is true that dogs, jackals, and other animals, when they walk, have knowledge of their walking; however, it is not with respect to knowledge of that kind that this is spoken. For such knowledge as that does not abandon the assumption of a living entity, and does not show up that belief; nor is any subject of meditation present, nor any intent contemplation. But the knowledge of this priest abandons the assumption of a living entity, shows up that belief; and a subject of meditation is present, and intent contemplation. For this was spoken with respect to complete knowledge, comprising such points as, "Who is it walks? Whose walking is it? What makes it walk?" And similarly also in regard to standing and the other bodily postures.

Now when it is asked, " *Who is it walks?* " the answer is that it is no living entity or Ego that walks. And when it is asked, " *Whose walking is it?* " the answer is that it is not the walking of any living entity or Ego. And when it is asked, " *What makes it walk?* " the answer is that walking takes place through the action of the mind, and permeation by the windy element. The following, therefore, is what he thoroughly comprehends : The thought of walking arises, and that produces the windy element, and the windy element shows itself in the action. The pulling forward of the whole body brought about by the action of the mind and permeation by the windy element is what is called walking. The explanation of standing and of the other bodily postures is similar. As follows : —

The thought of standing arises, and that produces the windy element, and the windy element shows itself in the action. The erectness of the whole body brought about by the action of the mind and permeation by the windy element is what is called standing.

The thought of sitting arises, and that produces the windy element, and the windy element shows itself in the action. The drawing in of the lower part of the body, and the erectness of the upper part brought about by the action of the mind and permeation by the windy element is what is called sitting.

The thought of lying down arises, and that produces the windy element, and the windy element shows itself in the action. The stretching out of the whole body horizontally brought about by the action of the mind and permeation by the windy element is what is called lying down.

When he has thoroughly comprehended this, he thinks as follows : —

lying down, and in whatever state his body may be thoroughly comprehends that state.

Thus he lives, either in his own person, as respects the body, observant of the body, or in other persons, as respects the body, observant of the body, or both in his own person and in other persons, as respects the body, observant of the body; either observant of origination in the body, or observant of destruction in the body, or observant of both origination and destruction in the body; and the recognition of the body by his intent contemplation is merely to the extent

"They say it is a living entity that walks, it is a living entity that stands; but is there any living entity to walk or to stand? There is not. But even as people speak of a cart's going, though there is nothing corresponding to the word cart to go or to stand, yet when the driver has yoked up four oxen and drives them, we then, by a mere convention of speech, talk of the cart's going or of the cart's standing; in exactly the same way the body on account of its lack of intelligence resembles the cart, the impulsions of the thoughts resemble the oxen, the thought resembles the driver, and when the thought of walking or of standing arises, the windy element arises and shows itself in the actions, and walking etc. are brought about by this action of the mind and permeation by the windy element.   Accordingly, to say: 'It is a living entity that walks, it is a living entity that stands; I walk, I stand,' is but a mere convention of speech.   Therefore has it been said, —

"'As ships are by the wind impelled,
As arrows by the bow-string's force,
Likewise this body is impelled,
Smit by the windy element.

"'Machines are geared to move by ropes;
So, too, this body's enginery
Is governed by a mental rope
Whene'er it stands, whene'er it sits.

"'What living entity is here
That can by its intrinsic might
Without dependence or a cause
Make shift to stand or walk about?'"

Therefore it is to be understood that it is through perceiving that walking etc. have a dependence and are produced by causes that he *in walking thoroughly comprehends his walking, and in standing . . . sitting . . . lying down thoroughly comprehends his lying down.*

of this knowledge, merely to the extent of this contemplation, and he lives unattached, nor clings to anything in the world.

Thus, O priests, does a priest live, as respects the body, observant of the body.

Section on Bodily Postures.

But again, O priests, a priest, in advancing and retiring has an accurate comprehension of what he does; in looking and gazing has an accurate comprehension of what he does; in drawing in his arm and in stretching out his arm has an accurate comprehension of what he does; in wearing his cloak, his bowl, and his robes has an accurate comprehension of what he does; in eating, drinking, chewing, and tasting has an accurate comprehension of what he does; in easing his bowels and his bladder has an accurate comprehension of what he does; in walking, standing, sitting, sleeping, waking, talking, and being silent has an accurate comprehension of what he does.

Thus he lives, either in his own person [etc., as before].

Section on the Four Accurate Comprehensions.

But again, O priests, a priest, considers this body upwards from the soles of the feet, and downwards from the crown of the head, enclosed by skin, and full of all manner of uncleanness, saying, "There is in this body hair of the head, hair of the body, nails, teeth, skin, flesh, sinew, bone, marrow of the bones, kidneys, heart, liver, pleura, spleen, lungs, intestines, mesentery, stomach, faeces, bile, phlegm, pus, blood, sweat, fat, tears, lymph, saliva, snot, synovial fluid, urine." Just as if, O priests, there were a double-mouthed vessel full of various sorts of grain, to wit, sāli-rice, common paddy, beans, pulse, sesame, and husked rice; and some intelligent man were to open it and consider its contents, saying, "This is sāli-rice, this is common paddy, these are beans, this is pulse, this is sesame, this is husked rice;" in exactly the same way, O priests, a priest considers this body upwards from the soles of the feet, and downwards from the crown of the head, enclosed by skin, and full of all manner of uncleanness, saying, "There is in this body hair of the head, hair of the body, nails, teeth, skin, flesh, sinew, bone, marrow of the bones, kidneys, heart, liver, pleura, spleen, lungs, intestines, mesentery, stomach, faeces, bile, phlegm, pus, blood, sweat, fat, tears, lymph, saliva, snot, synovial fluid, urine."

Thus he lives, either in his own person [etc., as before].

Section on Loathsomeness.

But again, O priests, a priest takes this body, whatever it may be doing, or however it may be situated, and considers it according to the elements of which it is composed, saying, " There are in this body the elements earth, water, fire, and wind." Just as, O priests, a skilful butcher, or butcher's apprentice, having slaughtered a heifer, divides her into pieces, and stations himself at a place where four roads meet; in exactly the same way, O priests, a priest takes this body,[1] whatever it may be doing, or however it may be situated, and considers it according to the elements of which it is composed, saying, " There are in this body the elements earth, water, fire, and wind."

Thus he lives, either in his own person [etc., as before].

Section on the Elements.

But again, O priests, a priest, if perchance he sees in a cemetery a decaying body one day dead, or two days dead, or

---

[1] Folio *dhe:* Just as a butcher, while rearing a cow, while leading her to the place of slaughter, and while, after bringing her there and binding her, he is placing her in position, slaughtering her, and handling her after she has been slaughtered, never ceases to think of her as a cow so long as he has not cut her up and divided her into pieces. But when he has divided her into pieces, and has seated himself ready to sell, he ceases to think of her as a cow, and thinks of her as only so much meat. He does not think, " I am selling cow; my customers come to me for cow;" but, "I am selling meat; my customers come to me for meat." In exactly the same way, while a man is an ignorant, unconverted person, whether he be a householder or a member of the Order, he never ceases to think of himself as a living entity or individual, until such time as he *takes this body, whatever it may be doing, or however it may be situated, and* analyzing it *considers it according to the elements of which it is composed.* But when he has considered it according to the elements of which it is composed, he ceases to think of it as a living entity or individual, and thinks of it as only so many elements.

three days dead, swollen, black, and full of festering putridity, he compares his own body, saying, "Verily, my body also has this nature, this destiny, and is not exempt."

Thus he lives, either in his own person [etc., as before].

Cemetery the First.

But again, O priests, a priest, if perchance he sees in a cemetery a decaying body being eaten by crows, or being eaten by eagles, or being eaten by vultures, or being eaten by dogs, or being eaten by jackals, or being eaten by various kinds of insects, he compares his own body, saying, "Verily, my body also has this nature, this destiny, and is not exempt."

Thus he lives, either in his own person [etc., as before].

Cemetery the Second.

But again, O priests, a priest, if perchance he sees in a cemetery a decaying body consisting of a skeleton with its flesh and its blood and its tendonous connections, he compares his own body, saying, "Verily, my body also has this nature, this destiny, and is not exempt."

Thus he lives, either in his own person [etc., as before].

Cemetery the Third.

But again, O priests, a priest, if perchance he sees in a cemetery a decaying body consisting of a skeleton, stripped of its flesh, but stained with blood and retaining its tendonous connections, he compares his own body, saying, "Verily, my body also has this nature, this destiny, and is not exempt."

Thus he lives, either in his own person [etc., as before].

Cemetery the Fourth.

But again, O priests, a priest, if perchance he sees in a cemetery a decaying body consisting of a skeleton without its flesh and its blood, but retaining its tendonous connections, he compares his own body, saying, "Verily, my body also has this nature, this destiny, and is not exempt."

Thus he lives, either in his own person [etc., as before].

Cemetery the Fifth.

"But again, O priests, a priest, if perchance he sees in a cemetery a decaying body with its bones unconnected and scattered in all directions— the bones of the hands in one direction, the bones of the feet in another, the bones of the shanks in another, the bones of the thighs in another, the bones of the hips in another, the bones of the spine in another, and the skull in another — he compares his own body, saying, "Verily, my body also has this nature, this destiny, and is not exempt."

Thus he lives, either in his own person [etc., as before].

Cemetery the Sixth.

But again, O priests, a priest, if perchance he sees in a cemetery a decaying body with its bones as white as a conch-shell, he compares his own body, saying, "Verily, my body also has this nature, this destiny, and is not exempt."

Thus he lives, either in his own person [etc., as before].

Cemetery the Seventh.

But again, O priests, a priest, if perchance he sees in a cemetery a decaying body with its bones scattered in piles and washed by the rains of years, he compares his own body, saying, "Verily, my body also has this nature, this destiny, and is not exempt."

Thus he lives, either in his own person [etc., as before].

Cemetery the Eighth.

But again, O priests, a priest, if perchance he sees in a cemetery a decaying body with its bones rotting and crumbling into dust, he compares his own body, saying, "Verily, my body also has this nature, this destiny, and is not exempt."

Thus he lives, either in his own person [etc., as before].

Cemetery the Ninth.

End of the Intent Contemplation of the Body.[1]

---

[1] In treating of the contemplation of the body as one of the forty subjects of meditation (see page 292), Buddhaghosa, in chapter viii. of the Visuddhi-Magga, takes up only the Section on Loathsomeness. He mentions the First Intent Contemplation as above described, but says that the Section on Breathing forms a subject of meditation by itself

And how, O priests, does a priest live, as respects sensations, observant of sensations?

Whenever, O priests, a priest, in experiencing a pleasant sensation thoroughly comprehends the pleasant sensation he is experiencing, and in experiencing an unpleasant sensation . . . an indifferent sensation . . . an interested and pleasant sensation . . . a disinterested and pleasant sensation . . . an interested and unpleasant sensation . . . a disinterested and unpleasant sensation . . . an interested and indifferent sensation . . . a disinterested and indifferent sensation thoroughly comprehends the disinterested and indifferent sensation he is experiencing.

Thus he lives, either in his own person, as respects sensations, observant of sensations, or in other persons, as respects sensations, observant of sensations, or both in his own person and in other persons, as respects sensations, observant of sensations; either observant of origination in the sensations, or observant of destruction in the sensations, or observant of both origination and destruction in the sensations; and the recognition of the sensations by his intent contemplation is merely to the extent of this knowledge, merely to the extent of this contemplation, and he lives unattached, nor clings to anything in the world.

Thus, O priests, does a priest live, as respects sensations, observant of sensations.

End of the Intent Contemplation of Sensations.

And how, O priests, does a priest live, as respects the mind, observant of the mind?

Whenever, O priests, a priest, in having a passionate mind thoroughly comprehends that passionate mind, or in having a mind free from passion . . . a mind full of hatred . . . a mind free from hatred . . . an infatuated mind . . . a

---

(the contemplation of breathing), that the Section on Bodily Postures, the Section on the Four Accurate Comprehensions, and the Section on the Elements belong under Wisdom, and the Nine Cemeteries belong in a measure under Wisdom and in a measure under the Impurities.

mind free from infatuation . . . an intent mind . . . a wandering mind . . . an exalted mind . . . an unexalted mind . . . an inferior mind . . . a superior mind . . . a concentrated mind . . . an unconcentrated mind . . . an emancipated mind . . . an unemancipated mind thoroughly comprehends that unemancipated mind.

Thus he lives, either in his own person, as respects the mind, observant of the mind, or in other persons, as respects the mind, observant of the mind, or both in his own person and in other persons, as respects the mind, observant of the mind; either observant of origination in the mind, or observant of destruction in the mind, or observant of both origination and destruction in the mind; and the recognition of the mind by his intent contemplation is merely to the extent of this knowledge, merely to the extent of this contemplation, and he lives unattached, nor clings to anything in the world.

Thus, O priests, does a priest live, as respects the mind, observant of the mind.

End of the Intent Contemplation of the Mind.

And how,[1] O priests, does a priest live, as respects the elements of being, observant of the elements of being?

Whenever, O priests, a priest lives, as respects the elements of being, observant of the elements of being in the five obstacles to the religious life.

And how, O priests, does a priest live, as respects the elements of being, observant of the elements of being in the five obstacles to the religious life?

Whenever, O priests, a priest, having existing in himself

---

[1] Folio *ḍhāu:* In the observation of the body The Blessed One treated solely of form; in the observation of the sensations and of thoughts, solely of the other groups ; but now with the words, *And how, O priests,* he begins the treatment of form and of the other groups mixed. Or, again, in the observation of the body it is only the form-group that is treated of, in the observation of the sensations it is only the sensation-group, and in the observation of thoughts it is only the consciousness-group ; but now with the words, *And how, O priests,* he begins the treatment of the perception-group, and of the predisposition-group.

a sensual disposition thoroughly comprehends the sensual disposition as existing in himself, or not having existing in himself a sensual disposition thoroughly comprehends the sensual disposition as not existing in himself, and thoroughly comprehends how a sensual disposition not yet arisen may arise, and thoroughly comprehends how a sensual disposition already arisen may be abandoned, and thoroughly comprehends how a sensual disposition that has been abandoned may be kept from arising again in the future; or having existing in himself a malevolent disposition . . . a slothful and torpid disposition . . . a proud and unmannerly disposition . . . a doubting disposition thoroughly comprehends the doubting disposition as existing in himself, or not having existing in himself a doubting disposition thoroughly comprehends the doubting disposition as not existing in himself, and thoroughly comprehends how a doubting disposition not yet arisen may arise, and thoroughly comprehends how a doubting disposition already arisen may be abandoned, and thoroughly comprehends how a doubting disposition that has been abandoned may be kept from arising again in the future.

Thus he lives, either in his own person, as respects the elements of being, observant of the elements of being, or in other persons, as respects the elements of being, observant of the elements of being, or both in his own person and in other persons, as respects the elements of being, observant of the elements of being; either observant of origination in the elements of being, or observant of destruction in the elements of being, or observant of both origination and destruction in the elements of being; and the recognition of the elements of being by his intent contemplation is merely to the extent of this knowledge, merely to the extent of this contemplation, and he lives unattached, nor clings to anything in the world.

Thus, O priests, does a priest live, as respects the elements of being, observant of the elements of being.

Exposition of the Obstacles.

But again, O priests, a priest lives, as respects the elements of being, observant of the elements of being in the five attachment-groups.

And how, O priests, does a priest live, as respects the elements of being, observant of the elements of being in the five attachment-groups ?

Whenever, O priests, a priest grasps the nature of form, and how form arises, and how form perishes ; the nature of sensation, and how sensation arises, and how sensation perishes ; the nature of perception, and how perception arises, and how perception perishes ; the nature of the predispositions, and how the predispositions arise, and how the predispositions perish ; the nature of consciousness, and how consciousness arises, and how consciousness perishes.

Thus he lives, either in his own person [etc., as before].

Exposition of the Groups.

But again, O priests, a priest lives, as respects the elements of being, observant of the elements of being in the six organs of sense and the six objects of sense.

And how, O priests, does a priest live, as respects the elements of being, observant of the elements of being in the six organs of sense and the six objects of sense ?

Whenever, O priests, a priest thoroughly comprehends the eye, thoroughly comprehends forms, thoroughly comprehends the bondage that arises in dependence on the two, and thoroughly comprehends how this bondage not yet arisen may arise, and thoroughly comprehends how this bondage may be abandoned, and thoroughly comprehends how this bondage that has been abandoned may be kept from arising again in the future ; thoroughly comprehends the ear, thoroughly comprehends sounds, . . . thoroughly comprehends the nose, thoroughly comprehends odors, . . . thoroughly comprehends the tongue, thoroughly comprehends tastes, . . . thoroughly comprehends the body, thoroughly comprehends things tangible, . . . thoroughly comprehends the mind, thoroughly comprehends ideas, thoroughly comprehends the bondage that arises in dependence on the two, and thoroughly comprehends how this bondage not yet arisen may arise, and thoroughly comprehends how this bondage may be abandoned, and thoroughly comprehends how this bondage that has been abandoned may be kept from arising again in the future.

Thus he lives, either in his own person, as respects the elements of being [etc., as before].

Exposition of the Organs of Sense and of the Objects of Sense.

But again, O priests, a priest lives, as respects the elements of being, observant of the elements of being in the seven constituents of enlightenment.

And how, O priests, does a priest live, as respects the elements of being, observant of the elements of being in the seven constituents of enlightenment?

Whenever, O priests, a priest, having existing in himself the constituent of enlightenment contemplation thoroughly comprehends the constituent of enlightenment contemplation as existing in himself, or not having existing in himself the constituent of enlightenment contemplation thoroughly comprehends the constituent of enlightenment contemplation as not existing in himself, and thoroughly comprehends how the constituent of enlightenment contemplation not yet arisen may arise, and thoroughly comprehends how the constituent of enlightenment contemplation already arisen may be brought to full development; or having existing in himself the constituent of enlightenment investigation of doctrine . . . the constituent of enlightenment heroism . . . the constituent of enlightenment joy . . . the constituent of enlightenment tranquillity . . . the constituent of enlightenment concentration . . . the constituent of enlightenment indifference thoroughly comprehends the constituent of enlightenment indifference as existing in himself, or not having existing in himself the constituent of enlightenment indifference thoroughly comprehends the constituent of enlightenment indifference as not existing in himself, and thoroughly comprehends how the constituent of enlightenment indifference not yet arisen may arise, and thoroughly comprehends how the constituent of enlightenment indifference already arisen may be brought to full development.

Thus he lives, either in his own person [etc., as before].

Exposition of the Constituents of Enlightenment.

Here Endeth the First Lesson.

But again, O priests, a priest lives, as respects the elements of being, observant of the elements of being in the four noble truths.

And how, O priests, does a priest live, as respects the elements of being, observant of the elements of being in the four noble truths ?

Whenever, O priest, a priest knows the truth concerning misery, knows the truth concerning the origin of misery, knows the truth concerning the cessation of misery, knows the truth concerning the path leading to the cessation of misery.

And what, O priests, is the noble truth of misery ?

Birth is misery; old age is misery; disease is misery; death is misery; sorrow, lamentation, misery, grief, and despair are misery; to wish for what one cannot have is misery; in short, all the five attachment-groups are misery.

And what, O priests, is birth ?

When of such and such a being, into such and such a class of beings, takes place the birth, the being born, the descent into the womb, the rebirth, the appearance of the groups, the obtaining of the organs of sense, this, O priests, is called birth.

And what, O priests, is old age ?

When to such and such a being, in such and such a class of beings, there comes old age, decrepitude, toothlessness, hoariness, wrinkledness of the skin, subsidence of the vital powers, decay of the faculties, this, O priests, is called old age.

And what, O priests, is death ?

When of such and such a being, from such and such a class of beings, takes place the passing, the passing away, the breaking up, the disappearance, the dying, the death, the meeting its end, the breaking up of the groups, the laying away of the corpse, this, O priests, is called death.

And what, O priests, is sorrow ?

Whenever, O priests, in any one who has experienced some great loss, or is afflicted by some misfortune, there arises sorrow, sorrowing, sorrowfulness, heart-sorrow, heart-sorrowfulness, this, O priests, is called sorrow.

And what, O priests, is lamentation ?

Whenever, O priests, any one who has experienced some

great loss, or is afflicted by some misfortune, gives way to lamenting, lamentation, laments, lamenting cries, lamentable cries, cries of lamentation, this, O priests, is called lamentation.

And what, O priests, is misery?

Bodily misery, O priests, bodily discomfort, misery and sensations of discomfort experienced in the impressions received by the body, this, O priests, is called misery.

And what, O priests, is grief?

Mental misery, O priests, mental discomfort, misery and sensations of discomfort experienced in the impressions received by the mind, this, O priests, is called grief.

And what, O priests, is despair?

Whenever, O priests, in any one who has experienced some great loss, or is afflicted by some misfortune, there arises desperation, despair, a state of desperation, a state of despair, this, O priests, is called despair.

And what, O priests, is meant by saying, " To wish for what one cannot have is misery?"

In beings, O priests, subject to birth there arises the wish, " O that we were not subject to birth! O that birth might never come to us!" Nevertheless this cannot be obtained by wishing. This is what is meant by saying, " To wish for what one cannot have is misery."

To beings, O priests, subject to old age . . . disease . . . death . . . sorrow . . . lamentation . . . misery . . . grief . . . despair there arises the wish, " O that we were not subject to despair! O that despair might never come to us!" Nevertheless this cannot be obtained by wishing. This is what is meant by saying, " To wish for what one cannot have is misery."

And what, O priests, are meant by saying, " In short, all the five attachment-groups are misery?" The form-attachment-group, the sensation-attachment-group, the perception-attachment-group, the predisposition-attachment-group, the consciousness-attachment-group, — these, O priests, are what are meant by saying, "In short, all the five attachment-groups are misery."

This, O priests, is called the noble truth of misery.

End of the Exposition of Misery.

And what, O priests, is the noble truth of the origin of misery ?

It is desire leading to rebirth, joining itself to pleasure and passion, and finding delight in every existence, — desire, namely, for sensual pleasure, desire for permanent existence, desire for transitory existence.

But where, O priests, does this desire spring up and grow ? where does it settle and take root?

Where anything is delightful and agreeable to men, there desire springs up and grows, there it settles and takes root.

And what is delightful and agreeable to men, where desire springs up and grows, where it settles and takes root ?

The eye is delightful and agreeable to men ; there desire springs up and grows, there it settles and takes root.

The ear . . . the nose . . . the tongue . . . the body . . . the mind is delightful and agreeable to men; there desire springs up and grows, there it settles and takes root.

The Six Organs of Sense.

Forms . . . sounds . . . odors . . . tastes . . . things tangible . . . ideas are delightful and agreeable to men ; there desire springs up and grows, there it settles and takes root.

The Six Objects of Sense.

Eye-consciousness . . . ear-consciousness . . . nose-con-sciousness . . . tongue-consciousness . . . body-consciousness . . . mind-consciousness is delightful and agreeable to men; there desire springs up and grows, there it settles and takes root.

The Six Consciousnesses.

Contact of the eye . . . ear . . . nose . . . tongue . . . body . . . mind is delightful and agreeable to men; there desire springs up and grows, there it settles and takes root.

The Six Contacts.

Sensation produced by contact of the eye . . . ear . . . nose . . . tongue . . . body . . . mind is delightful and agreeable to men; there desire springs up and grows, there it settles and takes root.

The Six Sensations.

Perception of forms . . . sounds . . . odors . . . tastes . . . things tangible . . . ideas is delightful and agreeable to men; there desire springs up and grows, there it settles and takes root.

The Six Perceptions.

Thinking on forms . . . sounds . . . odors . . . tastes . . . things tangible . . . ideas is delightful and agreeable to men; there desire springs up and grows, there it settles and takes root.

The Six Thinkings.

Desire for forms . . . sounds . . . odors . . . tastes . . things tangible . . . ideas is delightful and agreeable to men; there desire springs up and grows, there it settles and takes root.

The Six Desires.

Reasoning on forms . . . sounds . . . odors . . . tastes . . . things tangible . . . ideas is delightful and agreeable to men; there desire springs up and grows, there it settles and takes root.

The Six Reasonings.

Reflection on forms . . . sounds . . . odors . . . tastes . . . things tangible . . . ideas is delightful and agreeable to men; there desire springs up and grows, there it settles and takes root.

The Six Reflections.

This, O priests, is called the noble truth of the origin of misery.

End of the Exposition of the Origin of Misery.

And what, O priests, is the noble truth of the cessation of misery?

It is the complete fading out and cessation[1] of this desire, a giving up, a loosing hold, a relinquishment, and a non-adhesion.

But where, O priests, does this desire wane and disappear? where is it broken up and destroyed?

Where anything is delightful and agreeable to men; there desire wanes and disappears, there it is broken up and destroyed.

And what is delightful and agreeable to men, where desire wanes and disappears, where it is broken up and destroyed?

The eye is delightful and agreeable to men; there desire wanes and disappears, there it is broken up and destroyed.

[Similarly respecting the other organs of sense, the six objects of sense, the six sense-consciousnesses, the six contacts, the six sensations, the six perceptions, the six thinkings, the six desires, the six reasonings, and the six reflections.]

This, O priests, is called the noble truth of the cessation of misery.

End of the Exposition of the Cessation of Misery.

And what, O priests, is the noble truth of the path leading to the cessation of misery?

---

[1] Folio *ṇāi: Complete fading out and cessation*, etc. are all simply synonyms for Nirvana. For in Nirvana there is a complete fading out and cessation of desire; therefore is it called the complete fading out and cessation of that desire. In Nirvana, also, desire decays, is relinquished, does not adhere; therefore is Nirvana called a letting go, a loosing hold, a relinquishment, and a non-adhesion. For Nirvana is but one, but its names based on its oppositions are many. To wit, complete fading out, complete cessation, a letting go, a loosing hold, a relinquishment, a non-adhesion, the perishing of passion, the perishing of hatred, the perishing of infatuation, the perishing of desire, non-origination, the non-existent, the unconditioned, the desireless, the non-production of karma, deliverance from conception, deliverance from rebirth, deliverance from renewed existence, the unborn, the undecaying, deliverance from disease, the deathless, the sorrowless, deliverance from lamentation, deliverance from despair, the incorrupt, etc.

It is this noble eightfold path, to wit, right belief, right resolve, right speech, right behavior, right occupation, right effort, right contemplation, right concentration.

And what, O priests, is right belief?

The knowledge of misery, O priests, the knowledge of the origin of misery, the knowledge of the cessation of misery, and the knowledge of the path leading to the cessation of misery, this, O priests, is called "right belief."

And what, O priests, is right resolve?

The resolve to renounce sensual pleasures, the resolve to have malice towards none, and the resolve to harm no living creature, this, O priests, is called "right resolve."

And what, O priests, is right speech?

To abstain from falsehood, to abstain from backbiting, to abstain from harsh language, and to abstain from frivolous talk, this, O priests, is called "right speech."

And what, O priests, is right behavior?

To abstain from destroying life, to abstain from taking that which is not given one, and to abstain from immorality, this, O priests, is called "right behavior."

And what, O priests, is right occupation?

Whenever, O priests, a noble disciple, quitting a wrong occupation, gets his livelihood by a right occupation, this, O priests, is called "right occupation."

And what, O priests, is right effort?

Whenever, O priests, a priest purposes, makes an effort, heroically endeavors, applies his mind, and exerts himself that evil and demeritorious qualities not yet arisen may not arise; purposes, makes an effort, heroically endeavors, applies his mind, and exerts himself that evil and demeritorious qualities already arisen may be abandoned; purposes, makes an effort, heroically endeavors, applies his mind, and exerts himself that meritorious qualities not yet arisen may arise; purposes, makes an effort, heroically endeavors, applies his mind, and exerts himself for the preservation, retention, growth, increase, development, and perfection of meritorious qualities already arisen, this, O priest, is called "right effort."

And what, O priests, is right contemplation?

Whenever, O priests, a priest lives, as respects the body, observant of the body, strenuous, conscious, contemplative, and has rid himself of lust and grief; as respects sensations, observant of sensations, strenuous, conscious, contemplative, and has rid himself of lust and grief; as respects the mind, observant of the mind, strenuous, conscious, contemplative, and has rid himself of lust and grief; as respects the elements of being, observant of the elements of being, strenuous, conscious, contemplative, and has rid himself of lust and grief, this, O priests, is called "right contemplation."

And what, O priests, is right concentration?

Whenever, O priests, a priest, having isolated himself from sensual pleasures, having isolated himself from demeritorious traits, and still exercising reasoning, still exercising reflection, enters upon the first trance which is produced by isolation and characterized by joy and happiness; when, through the subsidence of reasoning and reflection, and still retaining joy and happiness, he enters upon the second trance, which is an interior tranquilization and intentness of the thoughts, and is produced by concentration; when, through the paling of joy, indifferent, contemplative, conscious, and in the experience of bodily happiness — that state which eminent men describe when they say, "Indifferent, contemplative, and living happily" — he enters upon the third trance; when, through the abandonment of happiness, through the abandonment of misery, through the disappearance of all antecedent gladness and grief, he enters upon the fourth trance, which has neither misery nor happiness, but is contemplation as refined by indifference, this, O priests, is called "right concentration."

This, O priests, is called the noble truth of the path leading to the cessation of misery.

End of the Exposition of the Path Leading to the Cessation of Misery.

Thus he lives, either in his own person, as respects the elements of being, observant of the elements of being, or in other persons, as respects the elements of being, observant of the elements of being, or both in his own person and in other persons, as respects the elements of being, observant of the elements of being; either observant of origination in the elements of being, or observant of destruction in the elements of being, or observant of both origination and destruction in the elements of being; and the recognition of the elements of being by his intent contemplation is merely to the extent of this knowledge, merely to the extent of this contemplation, and he lives unattached, nor clings to anything in the world.

Thus, O priests, does a priest live, as respects the elements of being, observant of the elements of being.

End of the Intent Contemplation of the Elements of Being.

———

Any one, O priests, who for seven years shall thus practise these Four Intent Contemplations, may expect one or the other of two rewards — either he will attain to perfect knowledge in his present life, or, if at death the groups still remain, to never returning.

But setting aside, O priests, all question of seven years, any one, O priests, who for six years shall thus practise the above Four Intent Contemplations, may expect one or the other of two rewards — either he will attain to perfect knowledge in his present life, or, if at death the groups still remain, to never returning.

But setting aside, O priests, all question of six years, . . . five years, . . . four years, . . . three years, . . . two years, . . . one year, . . . seven months, . . . six months, . . . five months, . . . four months, . . . three months, . . . two months, . . . one month, . . . a half month, any one, O priests, who for seven days shall thus practise the above Four Intent Contemplations, may expect one or the other of two rewards — either he will attain to perfect knowledge in his present life, or, if at death the groups still remain, to never returning.

This, therefore, is the meaning of my opening words: "Priests, there is but one way open to mortals for the attain-

ment of purity, for the overcoming of sorrow and lamentation, for the abolition of misery and grief, for the acquisition
of the correct rule of conduct, for the realization of Nirvana,
and that is the Four Intent Contemplations."

Thus spake The Blessed One, and the delighted priests
applauded the speech of The Blessed One.

End of the Sermon on the Four Intent Contemplations.

---

§ 75.   THE ATTAINMENT OF THE PATHS.

Translated from the Visuddhi-Magga (chap. xxi.).

> " Behold how empty is the world,
> Mogharāja !   In thoughtfulness
> Let one remove belief in self
> And pass beyond the realm of death.
> The king of death can never find
> The man who thus the world beholds."

When in the course of his application of the Three Characteristics the ascetic has thus considered the constituents of
being in the light of their emptiness, he abandons all fear
and joy in regard to them, and becomes indifferent and neutral, and does not deem them as " I " or " mine," like a man
who has given up his wife.

Just as a man might have a wife beloved, delightful, and
charming, from whom he could not bear to be separated for
a moment, and on whom he excessively doted.   If he then
were to see that woman standing or sitting in company with
another man, and talking and joking with him, he would be
angry and displeased, and experience bitter grief.   But if
subsequently he were to discover that she had been guilty of
a fault, he would lose all desire for her and let her go, and
no longer look on her as " mine."   From that time on, whenever he might see her engaged with any one else, he would
not be angry or grieved, but simply indifferent and neutral.
In exactly the same way the ascetic by grasping the constit-

uents of being with the reflective insight becomes desirous of
being released from them, and perceiving none of them worthy of being deemed "I" or "mine," he abandons all fear
and joy in regard to them, and becomes indifferent and
neutral. When he has learnt and perceived this, his mind
draws in, contracts, and shrinks away from the three modes
of existence, the four species of being, the five destinies in
rebirth, the seven stages of consciousness, the nine grades of
being, and does not spread out, and only indifference or disgust abides.

Just as drops of water on a gently inclined lotus-leaf draw
in, contract, and shrink away, and do not spread out; in exactly the same way his mind draws in, contracts, and shrinks
away from the three modes of existence, the four species of
being, the five destinies in rebirth, the seven stages of consciousness, the nine grades of being, and does not spread out,
and only indifference or disgust abides. Just as a cock's
feather, . . . if thrown into the fire, draws in, contracts, and
shrinks away, and does not spread out; in exactly the same
way his mind draws in, contracts, and shrinks away from the
three modes of existence, the four species of being, the five
destinies in rebirth, the seven stages of consciousness, the
nine grades of being, and does not spread out, but only indifference or disgust abides. Thus has he attained to the
knowledge consisting in indifference to the constituents of
being.

If this knowledge be such that it sees Nirvana, the abode
of peace, to be the good, then it gives up everything made of
the constituents of being, and leaps towards it; but if it be
not such that it sees Nirvana to be the good, it will again
and again take the constituents of being as its object, resembling in this the crow of the sailors.

They say that sea-faring traders take what is called a
land-sighting crow when they go aboard ship. And when
the ship is tossed about by the winds, and out of its course,
and land no longer to be seen, then they let go that land-
sighting crow. Such a bird springs into the air from the
mast-head, and going to all the quarters and intermediate

quarters flies to the shore if he sees it; but if he does not see it, he returns again and again and alights on the mast.   In exactly the same way, if the knowledge consisting in indifference to the constituents of being be such that it sees Nirvana, the abode of peace, to be the good, then it gives up everything made of the constituents of being, and leaps towards it; but if it be not such that it sees Nirvana to be the good, it will again and again take the constituents of being as its object.   It grasps the constituents of being in many different ways, as if they were so much meal being sorted in the kitchen, or so much cotton unrolled and being shredded, and having abandoned all fear and joy in regard to them and become neutral by its sifting of the constituents of being, it abides as the threefold insight.   And abiding thus, it becomes the threefold starting-point of deliverance, and the dependence for the distinction of the seven noble individuals.

Now this knowledge, existing as the threefold insight, becomes by the predominance of three qualities the threefold starting-point of deliverance.   For the three insights are called the three starting-points of deliverance.   As it is said :

" Moreover, deliverance has three starting-points for escape from the world: the consideration of the beginnings and endings of the constituents of being for the thoughts to spring to the unconditioned; the agitating of the mind concerning the constituents of being for the thoughts to spring to the desireless; the consideration of all the elements of being as not an Ego for the thoughts to spring to the empty. These are the three starting-points of deliverance for escape from the world."

Here *the beginnings and endings* — the beginnings and endings in the springing up and disappearance of things. For the insight into transitoriness, by coming to the conclusion, " The constituents of being did not exist before they sprang up," determines beginnings ; and by observing their destiny, and coming to the conclusion, " They continue no more after they have disappeared, but vanish right then," determines endings.

The *agitating of the mind* — the agitating of the thoughts. For by insight into the misery of the constituents of being the thoughts are agitated.

The *consideration of all the elements of being as not an Ego* — considering them as not an "I" or "mine."

Accordingly these three propositions are to be understood as spoken concerning the insight into transitoriness etc. Therefore was it thereafter said in answer to a question,

" To one who considers them in the light of their transitoriness the constituents of being seem perishable. To one who considers them in the light of their misery they seem frightful. To one who considers them in the light of their want of an Ego they seem empty.

But how many are the deliverances of which these insights are the starting-points? There are three: the unconditioned, the desireless, and the empty. For it has been said as follows:

" He who considers them [the constituents of being] in the light of their transitoriness abounds in faith and obtains the unconditioned deliverance; he who considers them in the light of their misery abounds in tranquillity and obtains the desireless deliverance; he who considers them in the light of their want of an Ego abounds in knowledge and obtains the empty deliverance."

Here *the unconditioned deliverance* is the Noble Path realized by meditation on Nirvana in its unconditioned aspect. For the Noble Path is unconditioned from having sprung out of the unconditioned, and it is a deliverance from being free from the corruptions. In the same way the Noble Path when realized by meditation on Nirvana in its desireless aspect is to be understood as *desireless;* when realized by meditation on Nirvana in its empty aspect as *empty.*

§ 76. NIRVANA TO BE ATTAINED AT DEATH.

Translated from the Visuddhi-Magga (chap. xxii.).

Just as, however, a man displeased with the flowers, fruit, etc. of a tree, will pierce it on each of its four sides with the poisonous thorn called the maṇḍu-thorn, and then that tree, when its earth-extracted juices and its sap have become exhausted by the application of that poison, will arrive at a state of inability to bear fruit and not be able to reproduce itself; in exactly the same way a youth of good family, displeased with the existence of the groups, will, like the man who applied poison to the tree on each of its four sides, begin to apply the meditation of the Four Paths to the series of his groups. And then the series of his groups, when the rebirth-causing corruptions have become exhausted by the application of the poison of the Four Paths, resolves itself into such bodily and other kinds of karma as constitute barren action;[1] and arriving at a state of not being liable to be reborn in the future, and unable to reproduce itself in the next existence, by the cessation of the last consciousness becomes like a fire without fuel, and passes into Nirvana without attachment.

§ 77. THE ATTAINMENT OF NIRVANA BY GODHIKA.

Translated from the Dhammapada, and from Buddhaghosa's Commentary to stanza 57.

54.   The flower's fragrance goes not to the windward,
　　　　Nor sandal-wood, the tagara, or jasmine;
　　　　But of the good the fragrance goes to windward —
　　　　The holy man suffuses every quarter.

55.   Or sandal-wood, or tagara,
　　　　Or lotus-flower, or jessamine —
　　　　Of all these various kinds of scents,
　　　　The virtuous give the scent most rare.

----

[1] See page 216.

56. A feeble fragrance is it comes
    From tagara and sandal-wood ;
    But fragrance that the virtuous give,
    Sublimely floats the gods among.

57. Of such as these, in virtues rich,
    Of vigilant and sober lives,
    With minds by perfect knowledge freed,
    No track or path the Slayer finds.

"*Of such as these, in virtues rich.*"   This doctrinal instruction was given by The Teacher while dwelling at Bamboo
Grove in the vicinity of Rājagaha; and it was concerning the
attainment of Nirvana by Godhika the elder.

This venerable man, while dwelling at Black Rock on
the slopes of Isigili, being vigilant, austere, and strenuous,
attained release for his mind in ecstatic meditation, and then
through the power of a disease which beset him, the trance
was broken up.   A second time, a third time, up to the sixth
time was his trance broken up.

At the seventh time, he thought,

" Six times has my trance been broken up, and doubtful is
the fate of those who fail in trance.   This time I will resort
to the knife."

And taking a razor for shaving the hair, he lay down on
a couch in order to cut his windpipe.

Māra, the Slayer, perceived his intention, and thought,

" This priest is about to use the knife; but they who do
so are indifferent to life, and such attain to insight and saintship.   If I should attempt to dissuade him, he would not
heed me.   I will get The Teacher to dissuade him."

Then he disguised himself, and drawing near to The
Teacher, he spoke as follows:

" Thou Hero Great, profoundly wise,
Whose magic power full brightly shines,
Who hast o'ercome all sin and fear,
Thy feet I worship, Seeing One.

> " Thy follower, O thou Hero Great,
> Although o'er death victorious,
> Doth long for death, and plotteth it;
> Dissuade him, O thou Radiant One.

> " Pray, shall thy follower, Blessed One,
> Whose keen delight is in thy law
> With goal unreached, not perfect trained,
> So soon expire, O Chief of Men?"

At this instant the elder used the knife.

The Teacher recognized the Slayer, and pronounced the following stanza:

> " Thus, verily, the valiant act,
> Nor think to hanker after life!
> Lo! Godhika uproots desire,
> And, dying, has Nirvana gained."

Then The Blessed One, with a great number of priests, went to the place where the elder had lain down and used the knife.

At that moment the Slayer, the Wicked One, had become a pillar of smoke, as it were, or a bunch of darkness; and wondering to himself, "Where can it have fixed itself?" was searching in all directions for the elder's rebirth-consciousness.

The Blessed One pointed out to the priests the smoke and darkness, and said,

"That, O priests, is the Slayer, the Wicked One. He is searching for the consciousness of the noble Godhika, to find out where it has fixed itself. But the noble Godhika, O priests, has attained Nirvana, and his consciousness has not fixed itself."

The Slayer, being unable to find out where the elder's consciousness was, assumed the appearance of a youth with a lute of the white wood of the bel-tree, and drawing near to The Teacher, he said,

"Where has Godhika gone? Though I search upwards

and downwards, and to all the points and intermediate points
of the compass, I do not meet him."

Then said The Teacher to him,

> "Always in meditation found
> That brave, strong man his best delight;
> Each day and night he practised it,
> And recked not, cared not, for his life.

> "Thus vanquished he Namuci's host;
> No more to rebirth he returns.
> Lo! Godhika uproots desire,
> And, dying, has Nirvana gained."

> The Demon sorely mortified,
> Down from his side let fall the lute;
> And in a sore, dejected mood,
> He straightway disappeared from sight.

And The Teacher said:

"O Wicked One, what have you to do with the place of
rebirth of the noble Godhika?   A hundred or a thousand
such as you could never detect his place of rebirth."   So
saying, he pronounced the stanza,

> "Of such as these, in virtues rich,
> Of vigilant and sober lives,
> With minds by perfect knowledge freed,
> No track or path the Slayer finds."

The Story of the Attainment of Nirvana by Godhika the Elder.

---

§ 78. THE TRANCE OF CESSATION.

§ 78 a. — Translated from the Saṁyutta-Nikāya (xli. 6⁵).

Inspirations and expirations, O householder, are bodily
functions, therefore inspirations and expirations constitute
bodily karma; first occur reasoning and reflection and afterwards articulate utterance, therefore reasoning and reflection
constitute vocal karma; perception and sensation are mental

functions and occur in association with the mind, therefore perception and sensation constitute mental karma.

And moreover, O priest, I have taught the gradual cessation of karma. Of one who has entered the first trance the voice has ceased; of one who has entered the second trance reasoning and reflection have ceased; of one who has entered the third trance joy has ceased; of one who has entered the fourth trance the inspirations and the expirations have ceased; of one who has entered the realm of the infinity of space the perception of form has ceased; of one who has entered the realm of the infinity of consciousness the perception of the realm of the infinity of space has ceased; of one who has entered the realm of nothingness the perception of the realm of the infinity of consciousness has ceased; of one who has entered the realm of neither perception nor yet non-perception, the perception of the realm of nothingness has ceased; of one who has entered the cessation of perception and sensation, perception and sensation have ceased. Of the priest who has lost all depravity, passion has ceased, hatred has ceased, infatuation has ceased.

What is the trance of cessation?

It is the stoppage of all mentality by a gradual cessation. . . . A priest who is desirous of entering on cessation will take his breakfast, wash carefully his hands and his feet, and seat him cross-legged on a well-strewn seat in some retired spot, with body erect, and contemplative faculty active. He then enters the first trance, and rising from it obtains insight into the transitoriness, misery, and lack of an Ego of the constituents of being.

This insight, however, is threefold: the insight into the constituents of being, the insight belonging to the attainment of the Fruits, and the insight belonging to the trance of cessation.

Whether the insight into the constituents of being be dull or keen, it is in either case a preparation for the Paths.

The insight belonging to the attainment of the Fruits can only be keen, like the realization of the Paths.

The insight, however, belonging to the trance of cessation should not be too dull nor yet too keen. Therefore he will contemplate the constituents of being with an insight that is neither very dull nor very keen.

Thereupon he enters the second trance, and rising from it obtains insight into the constituents of being in the same manner as before. Thereupon he enters the third trance, . . . the fourth trance, . . . the realm of the infinity of space, . . . the realm of the infinity of consciousness, and rising from it obtains insight into the constituents of being in the same manner as before. Then he enters the realm of nothingness, and rising from it performs the four preliminary duties; the protection of less intimate belongings, respect for the Order, a summons from The Teacher, limitation of time.

The protection of less intimate belongings : — That which is not intimately joined to the person of the priest, but is more loosely connected, such as his bowl and his robes, his couch and his bench, his dwelling, or any other of the requisites, should be protected from fire, water, wind, robbers, rats, etc., by means of a firm resolve. The manner of making this firm resolve is as follows:

He makes a firm resolve, saying, "For the space of seven days let not this and that article be burnt by fire, borne away by a flood, blown to pieces by the wind, carried off by robbers, or eaten by rats and the like." Then for the space of seven days no harm will touch them, any more than it did in the case of the elder, Nāga the Great; but if he does not make this firm resolve, they are liable to perish by fire etc.

In regard to this elder, tradition has it that he went for alms to the village where lived his mother, a lay devotee. The lay devotee gave him some rice-gruel and asked him to sit down in a reception-hall. The elder sat down and entered on cessation. While he was sitting there, the reception-hall

took fire, and all the other priests took up the several mats
on which they had been sitting, and fled away.   The inhabitants of the village came together, and seeing the elder, cried
out, "The lazy monk! the lazy monk!"   The fire blazed up
in the grass, bamboo, sticks of wood, etc., completely surrounding the elder.   The people brought water in pitchers
and put it out, removed the ashes and made the ground neat
again, and scattering flowers stood worshiping him.   The
elder rose from his trance, when the fixed term had elapsed,
and seeing the people gazing at him, sprang up into the air,
and went to the island Piyaṅgu.   This is the protection of
less intimate belongings.

Articles, however, which are intimately joined to the person of the priest, such as his tunic, his upper garment, or the
seat on which he may be sitting, do not need any special resolve.   The trance is sufficient to protect them, as in the case
of the venerable Sañjīva.   For it has been said as follows:

"The concentration of the venerable Sañjīva possesses
magical power; the concentration of the venerable Sāriputta
possesses magical power."

Respect for the Order — respect, regard for the Order.
The sense is the Order cannot hold a function without his
presence.   Here it is not respect for the Order but reflection
on the respect due it which is his preliminary duty.   Therefore let him reflect as follows:

"If, during the seven days I am sitting in a trance of cessation, the Order should wish to pass a resolution, or perform
some other ecclesiastical function, I will arise before a priest
comes and summons me."

If he does this before entering his trance, he will rise
from it at the time set; but if he does not do it, and the Order
comes together and misses him, and inquires, "Where is such
and such a priest?" and hearing that he has entered a
trance of cessation sends some priest, saying, "Go, summon
him by authority of the Order!" then he will have to rise
from his trance when that priest has come within hearing and
has called him, saying, "Brother, the Order sends you its
respects."   For such is the imperativeness of a command

from the Order. Therefore he must reflect on this, and so enter his trance as to rise from it of his own accord.

A summons from The Teacher : — Here, also, it is reflection on a summons of The Teacher that is his duty. Therefore let it be reflected upon as follows:

"If, during the seven days I am sitting in a trance of cessation, The Teacher should take occasion to lay down some precept, or, apropos of some particular event, should teach the Doctrine, I will rise from my trance before any one summons me."

If he does this before sitting down, he will rise from it at the time set; but if he does not do it, and The Teacher misses him when the Order assembles, and inquires, "Where is such and such a priest?" and hearing that he has entered a trance of cessation sends some priest, saying, "Go, summon him by my authority!" then he will have to rise from his trance when that priest has come within hearing and has called him, saying, "The Teacher sends for your venerable worship." For such is the imperativeness of a summons from The Teacher. Therefore he must reflect on this, and so enter his trance as to rise from it of his own accord.

Limitation of time — limitation of the time of life. For this priest should be skilful respecting the limitation of time. He should not enter this trance without first reflecting whether his span of life is to last seven days longer or not. For if he were to enter this trance without perceiving that his vital powers were to break up within the seven-day limit, his trance of cessation would not be able to ward off death, and as death cannot take place during cessation, he would have to rise from the midst of his trance. Therefore he must enter it only after having made the above reflection. For it has been said that it is permissible to neglect the other reflections, but not this one.

When he has thus entered the realm of nothingness, and risen from it and performed these preliminary duties, he enters the realm of neither perception nor yet non-perception; and having passed beyond one or two thoughts, he stops thinking and reaches cessation. But why do I say that beyond

two thoughts the thoughts cease? Because of the priest's
progress in cessation. For the priest's progress in gradual
cessation consists in an ascent through the eight attainments
by the simultaneous use of both the quiescence and insight
methods, and does not result from the trance of the realm of
neither perception nor yet non-perception alone. Thus it is
because of the priest's progress in cessation that beyond two
thoughts the thoughts cease.

Now the priest who should rise from the realm of nothingness, and enter the realm of neither perception nor yet
non-perception without having performed his preliminary
duties would not be able to lose all thought, but would fall
back into the realm of nothingness. In this connection I
will add a simile of a man traveling on a road over which he
has never passed before.

A certain man traveling on a road over which he has
never passed before, comes on his way to a deep ravine containing water, or to a slough in which is a stepping-stone
that has been over-heated by the sun; and essaying to descend into the ravine, without having first adjusted his tunic
and his upper garment, he is obliged to retreat again to the
top of the bank, through fear of wetting his requisites; or
stepping upon the stone he scorches his feet so badly that he
jumps back to the hither bank. In the above simile, just as
the man, through not having adjusted his tunic and his upper
garment, retreated to where he had started from, as soon as he
had descended into the ravine, or had stepped on the heated
stone; in exactly the same way the ascetic, if he have not
performed the preliminary duties, as soon as he reaches the
realm of neither perception nor yet non-perception, retreats
again into the realm of nothingness.

As, however, another man who has traveled on that road
before, when he reaches that spot, will gird his tunic tightly
and cross the ravine with the other garment in his hand,
or will touch the stone as little as possible in passing to
the further bank; in exactly the same way a priest who
has performed his preliminary duties, and entered the realm
of neither perception nor yet non-perception, will pass beyond and lose all thought, and dwell in cessation.

How long will he stay in it? He who has entered it in the above-described manner will remain in it during the limit of time which he has set for it, provided that the termination of his life, or respect for the Order, or a summons from The Teacher does not interfere.

How does he rise from it? In a twofold manner. The priest who is in the path of never returning, with the attainment of the fruit of never returning, the saint with the attainment of the fruit of saintship.

When he has risen from it, to what is his mind inclined? It is inclined to Nirvana. For it has been said as follows:

"Brother Visākha, the mind of a priest who has risen from the trance of the cessation of perception and sensation is inclined to isolation, has a tendency to isolation, is impelled to isolation."

What is the difference between a dead man and one who has entered this trance? This matter also is treated of in this discourse. As it is said:

"Brother, of the man who has died and become a corpse, bodily karma has ceased and become quieted, vocal karma has ceased and become quieted, mental karma has ceased and become quieted, vitality has become exhausted, natural heat has subsided, and the senses have broken up. Of the priest who has entered on the cessation of perception and sensation, bodily karma has ceased and become quieted, vocal karma has ceased and become quieted, mental karma has ceased and become quieted, but vitality has not become exhausted, natural heat has not subsided, and the senses have not broken up."

In regard to the questions "Is the trance of cessation conditioned or unconditioned?" etc., it cannot be said either that it is conditioned or that it is unconditioned, either that it is worldly or that it is transcendent. And why not? On account of the non-existence of any positive reality. Inasmuch, however, as it can be entered upon, therefore it is correct to say that it is brought about, not that it is not brought about.

Whereas the wise who cultivate
The wisdom which doth make a saint
Are they who reach this holy trance —
This trance by saints at all times prized,
And ever by them held to be
Nirvana in the present life —
Therefore the faculty to reach
This state of trance which is conferred
By wisdom in the holy paths
A blessing' of those paths is called.

§ 79. THE ATTAINMENT OF NIRVANA.

Translated from the Visuddhi-Magga (chap. xxiii.).

Acquisition of honor etc.: — The blessings to be derived from the realization of this transcendent wisdom include not only the ability to enter the trance of cessation, but also the acquisition of honor etc. For the individual who has developed his wisdom by the development of the fourfold wisdom of the paths is worthy of the worship, the veneration, the votive offerings, and the reverence of all the world of gods and men, and is an unsurpassed source of merit for the world.

To particularize : —

He who, being of weak faculties, develops the wisdom of the first path with a dull insight is reborn seven times at most; after seven rebirths in states of bliss he will make an end of misery: he who develops it with medium faculties and insight is a roamer; after two or three rebirths he will make an end of misery: he who develops it with keen faculties and insight takes root but once, only one human birth will he pass through and make an end of misery.

He who develops the wisdom of the second path returns once; once more will he return to this world and then make an end of misery.

He who develops the wisdom of the third path never returns. His destiny is fivefold, as follows: In the descending order of the worth of his faculties he passes into Nirvana in the midst, at the end, without instigation, with instigation, or passes up current to the Sublime Gods.

Here the one who passes into Nirvana *in the midst* is reborn in some one of the Pure Abodes and passes into Nirvana before attaining half the normal length of life of that heaven; he who passes into Nirvana *at the end* passes into Nirvana after attaining half the normal length of life; he who passes into Nirvana *without instigation* achieves the fourth path without instigation or urging; he who passes into Nirvana *with instigation* achieves the higher path with instigation or urging; and he who *passes up current to the Sublime Gods* starts from the particular heaven into which he may be reborn, and ascends as far as to the Sublime Gods and there passes into Nirvana.

Of those who develop the wisdom of the fourth path, one is freed by faith, another is freed by wisdom, another is doubly freed, another possesses the threefold knowledge, another the Six High Powers, but the greatest of all is he who has mastered the four analytical sciences and has lost all depravity. Concerning this last it has been said: —

" At the time he is in the paths he is disentangling the snarl, at the time he is in the fruits he has disentangled the snarl, and there is in all the world of gods and men none more worthy of votive gifts."

> Since, then, such blessings manifold
> From noble wisdom take their rise,
> Therefore the understanding man
> Should place therein his heart's delight.

The above constitutes the explanation of the development of wisdom and of its blessings in the Way of Purity as taught in the stanza,

> " What man his conduct guardeth, and hath wisdom,
> And thoughts and wisdom traineth well,
> The strenuous and the able priest,
> He disentangles all this snarl."

CHAPTER V.

THE ORDER.

INTRODUCTORY DISCOURSE.

UNLIKE Christ, The Buddha instituted an Order, or Church, during his own lifetime; and in the course of his long ministry of forty-five years, and as occasion arose, he made a great many regulations for its guidance. To give these rules and ordinances at length would be a large undertaking, and make this book too technical. The desultory selections of this chapter are therefore mainly illustrative in character, and designed to show what the Buddhists understand by the monastic life, and the duties and position of the laity. It is curious that the aversion which The Buddha showed to having women as members of the Order appears to have been shared by the Buddhist Church in the ages subsequent to his death. The nuns seem never to have played an influential rôle in the history of Buddhism, and there are now no nuns in Ceylon.

§ 80.   CONDUCT.

Translated from the Aṅguttara-Nikāya (iii. 88).

And what, O priests, is the discipline in elevated conduct?

Whenever, O priests, a priest is correct in his conduct, and lives restrained by the restraints of the Pātimokkha, is exemplary in his habits and associations, and afraid of even the smallest fault, and adopts and disciplines himself in the precepts, this, O priests, is called the discipline in elevated conduct.

---

§ 81.   THE ADMISSION AND ORDINATION CEREMONIES.

Reprinted from a paper by J. F. Dickson, B. A., in the Journal of the Royal Asiatic Society for 1874.

In May, 1872, I was invited by my learned friend and pandit Kewiṭiyāgala Unnānsē, of the Malwattē Monastery in Kandy, to be present at an ordination service, held, according to custom, on the full-moon day of Wesak, (May, June), being the anniversary of the day on which Gautama Buddha attained Nirvāna, B. C. 543. I gladly availed myself of this opportunity of witnessing the celebration of a rite of which Englishmen have but little knowledge, and which has rarely, if ever, been witnessed by any European in Ceylon.

Nothing could be more impressive than the order and solemnity of the proceedings. It was impossible not to feel that the ceremony was being conducted precisely as it was more than two thousand years ago.

The chapter house (Sinhalese, Poya-ge) is an oblong hall, with rows of pillars forming an inner space and leaving broad aisles at the sides. At the top of this inner space sat the aged Abbot (Sinhalese, Maha Nāyaka), as president of the chapter; on either side of him sat the elder priests, and down the sides sat the other priests in number between thirty and

forty. The chapter or assembly thus formed three sides of
an oblong. The president sat on cushions and a carpet; the
other priests sat on mats covered with white calico. They
all sat cross-legged. On the fourth side, at the foot, stood
the candidates, behind the pillars on the right stood the deacons, the left was given up to the visitors, and behind the
candidates at the bottom was a crowd of Buddhist laymen.

To form a chapter for this purpose not less than ten duly
ordained priests are required, and the president must be not
less than ten years' standing from his Upasampadā ordination. The priests attending the chapter are required to give
their undivided, unremitting, and devout attention throughout the service. Every priest is instructed to join heart and
mind in the exhortations, responses, formulas, etc., and to
correct every error, lest the oversight of a single mistake
should vitiate the efficacy of the rite. Previously to the
ordination the candidates are subjected to a strict and searching examination as to their knowledge of the discourses of
Buddha, the duties of a priest, etc. An examination and
ordination is held on the full-moon day in Wesak, and on
the three succeeding Poya days, or days of quarters of the
moon.

After witnessing the celebration of this rite, I read the
Upasampadā-Kammavācā or book setting forth the form
and manner of ordering of priests and deacons, and I was
subsequently induced to translate it. This manual was
translated into Italian in 1776, by Padre Maria Percoto
(missionary in Ava and Pegu), under the title of "Kam-
muva, ossia trattato della ordinazione dei Talapoini del
secondo ordine detti Pinzi," and a portion of it was edited
in 1841, in Pāli and Latin, by Professor Spiegel. Clough
translated it in 1834, and Hardy has given an interesting
summary of it in his Eastern Monachism; but neither the
text nor any complete translation is readily accessible, and I
have therefore thought that this edition might possibly be
acceptable to those who desire information respecting the
practice of Buddhism in Ceylon, where, as is well pointed
out by Mr. Childers, in his Pāli Dictionary, (s.v. Nibbā-

naṁ, p. 272, note), "Buddhism retains almost its pristine purity."

With regard to the transliteration, I have used the system adopted (after Fausböll) by Mr. Childers in his Dictionary. In the translation I have placed in italics the rubrical directions in the text, and all explanations and amplifications of the text I have placed in square brackets. I have thus endeavoured to give a translation of the text as it stands, and, at the same time, to set out the ordination service fully and completely, precisely in the form in use in Ceylon at the present time, as I have myself witnessed it. No one who compares this form with that given in Article XV. of Hodgson's "Literature and Religion of the Buddhists in Nepaul," can fail to be struck with the purity and simplicity of the Ceylon rite as contrasted with that in use among the Northern Buddhists.

KANDY, 9th January, 1873.   J. F. D.

THE ORDINATION SERVICE.

Praise be to the Blessed One, the Holy One, to him who has arrived at the knowledge of all Truth.

[*The candidate, accompanied by his Tutor, in the dress of a layman, but having the yellow robes of a priest in his arms, makes the usual obeisance and offering to the President of the chapter, and standing says,*]

Grant me leave to speak. Lord, graciously grant me admission to deacon's orders. *Kneels down.* Lord, I pray for admission as a deacon. Again, lord, I pray for admission as a deacon. A third time, lord, I pray for admission as a deacon. In compassion for me, lord, take these yellow robes, and let me be ordained, in order to the destruction of all sorrow, and in order to the attainment of Nirvāṇa. *To be repeated three times.* [The President takes the bundle of robes.] In compassion for me, lord, give me those yellow robes, and let me be ordained, in order to the destruction of all sorrow, and in order to the attainment of Nirvāṇa. *To be repeated three times.* [And the President then gives the bundle of robes, the yellow band of which he ties round the neck of the candidate, reciting the while the tacapañcakaṁ, or formula of meditation on the perishable nature of the human body, as follows: kesā lomā nakhā dantā taco — taco dantā nakhā lomā kesā. Hair of the head, hair of the body, nails, teeth, skin — skin, teeth, nails, hair of the body, hair of the head. The candidate then rises up, and retires to throw off the dress of a layman, and to put on his yellow robes. While changing his dress he recites the following: In wisdom I put on the robes, as a protection against cold, as a protection against heat, as a protection against gadflies and musquitoes, wind and sun, and the touch of serpents, and to cover nakedness, *i. e.* I wear them in all humility, for use only, and not for ornament or show. Having put on the yellow robes, he returns to the side of his tutor, and says,] Grant me leave to speak. I make obeisance to my lord. Lord, forgive me all my faults. Let the merit that I have gained be shared by my lord. It is fitting to give me to share in the merit gained by my lord. It is good, it is good. I share in it. Grant me leave to speak. Graciously give me, lord, the three refuges and the precepts. [He kneels down.] Lord, I pray for the refuges and the precepts.

[The tutor gives the three refuges and the ten precepts as follows, the candidate still kneeling, and repeating them after him sentence by sentence.

I.

THE THREE REFUGES.

I put my trust in Buddha.
I put my trust in the Law.
I put my trust in the Priesthood.
Again I put my trust in Buddha.
Again I put my trust in the Law.
Again I put my trust in the Priesthood.
Once more I put my trust in Buddha.
Once more I put my trust in the Law.
Once more I put my trust in the Priesthood.

II.

THE TEN PRECEPTS OR LAWS OF THE PRIESTHOOD.

Abstinence from destroying life;

Abstinence from theft;

Abstinence from fornication and all uncleanness;

Abstinence from lying;

Abstinence from fermented liquor, spirits and strong drink which are a hindrance to merit;

Abstinence from eating at forbidden times;

Abstinence from dancing, singing, and shows;

Abstinence from adorning and beautifying the person by the use of garlands, perfumes and unguents;

Abstinence from using a high or a large couch or seat;

Abstinence from receiving gold and silver;

are the ten means (of leading a moral life).

[The candidate says,]

I have received these ten precepts. Permit me. [He rises up, and makes obeisance to his Tutor.] Lord, I make obeisance. Forgive me all my faults. May the merit I have gained be shared by my lord. Give me to share in the merit of my lord. It is good, it is good. I share in it.

[This completes the ordination of a deacon, and the candidate retires.]

The foregoing ceremony is gone through previous to the ordination of a priest in all cases, even where the candidate has already been admitted as a deacon. If the candidate is duly qualified for the priestly office, he can proceed at once from deacon's to priest's orders; otherwise he must pass a term of instruction as a deacon: but a candidate who has received deacon's orders must solicit them again, and go through the above ceremony when presented for priest's orders.

The candidate being duly qualified, returns with his tutor, and goes up to the President of the chapter, presenting an offering, and makes obeisance, saying,]

Permit me to speak. Lord, graciously grant me your sanction and support. *He kneels down.* Lord, I pray for

your sanction and support; a second time, lord, I pray
for your sanction and support; a third time, lord, I pray for
your sanction and support. Lord, be my superior. *This is
repeated three times.* [The President says,] It is well. [And
the candidate replies,] I am content. *This is repeated three
times.* From this day forth my lord is my charge. I am
charge to my lord. [This vow of mutual assistance] *is
repeated three times.*

[The candidate rises up, makes obeisance, and retires
alone to the foot of the assembly, where his alms-bowl is
strapped on his back. His tutor then goes down, takes him
by the hand, and brings him back, placing him in front of
the President. One of the assembled priests stands up, and
places himself on the other side of the candidate, who thus
stands between two tutors. The tutors say to the assembly,]
With your permission, [and then proceed to examine the candidate as to his fitness to be admitted to priest's orders].
Your name is Nāga? It is so, lord. Your superior is the
venerable Tissa? It is so, lord. [The two tutors together
say,] Praise be to the Blessed One, the Holy One, to him
who has arrived at the knowledge of all Truth. [They then
recite the following commands of Buddha.] First it is right
to appoint a superior. When the superior has been appointed, it is right to inquire whether the candidate has
alms-bowl and robes [which they do as follows]. Is this
your alms-bowl? It is so, lord. Is this the stole? It is so,
lord. Is this the upper robe? It is so, lord. Is this the
under robe? It is so, lord. Go and stand there. [The candidate here retires, going backwards in a reverential posture,
and stands at the lower corner of the assembly. The tutors
remain in front of the President, and one of them says,]
Priests, hear me. The candidate desires ordination under
the venerable Tissa. Now is the time of the assembly of
priests. I will instruct the candidate. [The tutors make
obeisance to the President, and go down to the foot of the
assembly, and join the candidate, whom they instruct and
examine as follows.] Listen, Nāga. This is the time for
you to speak the truth, to state what has occurred. When

asked concerning anything in the midst of the assembly, if it be true, it is meet to say so; if it be not true, it is meet to say that it is not. Do not hesitate. Conceal nothing. *They inquire of the candidate as follows.* Have you any such diseases as these? Leprosy? No, lord. Boils? No, lord. Itch? No, lord. Asthma? No, lord. Epilepsy? No, lord. Are you a human being? Yes, lord. Are you a male? Yes, lord. Are you a free man? Yes, lord. Are you free from debt? Yes, lord. Are you exempt from military service? Yes, lord. Have you come with the permission of your parents? Yes, lord. Are you of the full age of twenty years? Yes, lord. Are your alms-bowl and robes complete? Yes, lord. What is your name? Lord, I am called Nāga. What is the name of your superior? Lord, my superior is called the venerable Tissa. [The two tutors here go to the top of the assembly, and make obeisance to the President, and one of them says,] Priests, hear me. The candidate desires ordination under the venerable Tissa. He has been duly instructed by me. Now is the time of the assembly of priests. If the candidate is here, it is right to tell him to approach. [One of the tutors says.] Come hither. [The candidate comes up, and stands between the tutors, makes obeisance to the assembly, and kneels down.] Priests, I ask the assembly for ordination. Priests, have compassion on me, and lift me up. A second time, lords, I ask the assembly for ordination; lords, have compassion on me, and lift me up. A third time, lords, I ask the assembly for ordination. Lords, have compassion on me, and lift me up. [The candidate rises up, and makes obeisance. The tutors say,] Priests, hear me. This candidate desires ordination under the venerable Tissa. Now is the time of the assembly of priests. I will examine the candidate respecting the disqualifications for the priestly office. Listen, Nāga, This is the time for you to speak the truth, to state what has occurred. I will inquire of you concerning facts. If a thing is, it is right to say it is; if a thing is not, it is right to say it is not. Have you any such diseases as these? Leprosy? No, lord. Boils? No, lord. Itch? No, lord. Asthma?

No, lord. Epilepsy? No, lord. Are you a human being? Yes, lord. Are you a male? Yes, lord. Are you free from debt? Yes, lord. Are you exempt from military service? Yes, lord. Have you come with the permission of your parents? Yes, lord. Are you of the full age of twenty years? Yes, lord. Are your alms-bowl and robes complete? Yes, lord. What is your name? Lord, I am called Nāga. What is the name of your superior? My superior, lord, is called the venerable Tissa. [Here ends the examination in the midst of the assembly, and one of the tutors reports the result as follows.] This candidate desires ordination under the venerable Tissa. He is free from disqualifications. He has his alms-bowl and robes complete. The candidate asks the assembly for ordination under his superior the venerable Tissa. The assembly gives the candidate ordination under his superior the venerable Tissa. If any of the venerable assembly approves the ordination of the candidate under the venerable Tissa, let him be silent; if any objects, let him speak. A second time I state this matter. Priests, hear me. This candidate desires ordination under the venerable Tissa. He is free from disqualifications for the priestly office. His alms-bowl and robes are complete. The candidate asks the priesthood for ordination under his superior the venerable Tissa. The assembly gives the candidate ordination under his superior the venerable Tissa. If any of the venerable assembly approve the ordination of the candidate under his superior the venerable Tissa, let him be silent; if any objects, let him speak. A third time I state this matter. Priests, listen. This candidate desires ordination under the venerable Tissa. He is free from disqualifications for the priestly office. His alms-bowl and robes are complete. The candidate asks the priesthood for ordination under his superior the venerable Tissa. The assembly gives the candidate ordination under his superior the venerable Tissa. If any of the venerable assembly approves the ordination of the candidate under his superior the venerable Tissa, let him be silent; if any objects, let him speak. [The two tutors here again make obeisance to the

President, and say,] The candidate has received ordination from the priesthood under his superior the venerable Tissa. The assembly approves the resolution: therefore it keeps silence. So I understand your wish.

---

§ 82. THE SERPENT WHO WANTED TO BE A PRIEST.

Translated from the Mahā-Vagga (i. 63¹).

Now at that time a certain serpent was distressed at, ashamed of, and loathed his state as a serpent. Then it occurred to the serpent as follows:

" By what means can I gain release from my state as a serpent, and quickly become a human being ? "

Then it occurred to the serpent as follows:

" Here, these Sakyaputta monks are virtuous, tranquil, religious, truthful, moral, and noble. If I were to retire from the world under these Sakyaputta monks, thus might I gain release from my state as a serpent, and quickly become a human being."

Then the serpent, in the guise of a youth, drew near to the priests, and asked leave to retire from the world into the Order. And the priests received him into the Order, and ordained him.

Now at that time the serpent dwelt with a certain priest in a cell on the outskirts of the monastery. And the priest arose at the waning of the night, and paced up and down under the open sky. Then the serpent, when the priest had gone out, felt safe and went to sleep; and the whole cell became filled with the snake, and his coils hung out at the windows. And the priest, wishing to enter the dwelling, pushed open the door, and saw the whole house filled with the snake, and his coils hanging out at the windows. And when he had seen this, he was frightened and shrieked aloud. And the other priests came running up, and spoke to the priest as follows:

" Brother, wherefore did you shriek ? "

" Brethren, this whole house is filled with a snake, and his coils hang out at the windows."

Thereupon the serpent awoke at the noise, and sat in his seat. And the priests spoke to him as follows:

" Who are you, brother ? "

" Reverend sirs, I am a serpent."

" But wherefore, brother, have you behaved in this manner ? "

Then the serpent announced the matter to the priests, and the priests announced the matter to The Blessed One.

Then The Blessed One, on this occasion and in this connection, having called together the congregation of the priests, spoke to the serpent as follows:

" You, verily, are a serpent, and not capable of growth in this Doctrine and Discipline; go you, remain in your state as a serpent, and keep fast-day on the fourteenth, fifteenth, and eighth day of the half-month; thus shall you gain release from your state as a serpent, and quickly become a human being."

" He says I am not capable of growth in this Doctrine and Discipline," said the serpent, and with tears and shrieks he sorrowfully and dejectedly departed.

---

§ 83.   THE BUDDHIST CONFESSION OF PRIESTS.

§ 83 *a*. — Translated from the Mahā-Vagga (ii. 1¹).

Now at that time The Buddha, The Blessed One, was dwelling at Rājagaha on Vulture Peak. And at that time the heretical sect of wandering ascetics met together on the fourteenth, fifteenth, and eighth day of the half-month, and recited their doctrine. And the people drew near to listen to their doctrine, and conceived a liking for the heretical sect of wandering ascetics, and put faith in their teachings ; and the heretical sect of wandering ascetics gained adherents.

Now it happened to Seniya Bimbisāra, king of Magadha, being in seclusion and plunged in meditation, that a consideration presented itself to his mind, as follows:

"Here the heretical sect of wandering ascetics meet together on the fourteenth, fifteenth, and eighth day of the half-month, and recite their doctrine. And the people draw near to listen to their doctrine, and conceive a liking for the heretical sect of wandering ascetics, and put faith in them; and the heretical sect of wandering ascetics gain adherents. What if now the reverend ones also were to meet together on the fourteenth, fifteenth, and eighth day of the half-month."

Then drew near Seniya Bimbisāra, king of Magadha, to where The Blessed One was; and having drawn near and greeted The Blessed One, he sat down respectfully at one side. And seated respectfully at one side, Seniya Bimbisāra, king of Magadha, spoke to The Blessed One as follows:

"Reverend Sir, it happened to me, as I was just now seated in seclusion and plunged in meditation, that a consideration presented itself to my mind, as follows: 'Here the heretical sect of wandering ascetics meet together on the fourteenth, fifteenth, and eighth day of the half-month, and recite their doctrine. And the people draw near to listen to their doctrine, and conceive a liking for the heretical sect of wandering ascetics, and put faith in them; and the heretical sect of wandering ascetics gain adherents. What if now the reverend ones also were to meet together on the fourteenth, fifteenth, and eighth day of the half-month?'"

Then The Blessed One enlightened, incited, quickened, and gladdened Seniya Bimbisāra, king of Magadha, with a doctrinal discourse. And Seniya Bimbisāra, king of Magadha, enlightened, incited, quickened, and gladdened by The Blessed One with a doctrinal discourse, rose from his seat and saluted The Blessed One; and keeping his right side toward him, he departed.

Then The Blessed One, on this occasion and in this connection, after he had delivered a doctrinal discourse, addressed the priests:

"I prescribe, O priests, that ye meet together on the fourteenth, fifteenth, and eighth day of the half-month."

Now at that time the priests, having understood that The Blessed One had prescribed that they should meet together on the fourteenth, fifteenth, and eighth day of the half-month, met together on the fourteenth, fifteenth, and eighth day of the half-month, and sat in silence. And the people drew near to listen to the Doctrine, and were angered, annoyed, and spoke indignantly:

"How is it, pray, that the Sakyaputta monks, when they meet together on the fourteenth, fifteenth, and eighth day of the half-month, sit in silence like dumb hogs? Why should they meet together, if not to recite the Doctrine?"

And the priests heard that the people were angered, annoyed, and spoke indignantly. And the priests announced the matter to The Blessed One.

Then The Blessed One, on this occasion and in this connection, after he had delivered a doctrinal discourse, addressed the priests:

"I prescribe, O priests, that when ye have met together on the fourteenth, fifteenth, and eighth day of the half-month, ye recite the Doctrine."

Now it happened to The Blessed One, being in seclusion and plunged in meditation, that a consideration presented itself to his mind, as follows:

"What if now I prescribe that the priests recite a confession [pātimokkha] of all those precepts which have been laid down by me; and this shall be for them a fast-day duty?"

Then The Blessed One, in the evening of the day, rose from his meditation, and on this occasion and in this connection, after he had delivered a doctrinal discourse, addressed the priests:

"O priests, it happened to me, as I was just now seated in seclusion and plunged in meditation, that a consideration presented itself to my mind, as follows: 'What if now I prescribe that the priests recite a confession of all those precepts which have been laid down by me; and this shall be for them a fast-day duty?' I prescribe, O priests, that

ye recite a confession. And after this manner, O priests, is it
to be recited :

" Let a learned and competent priest make announcement
to the congregation, saying, ' Let the reverend congregation
hear me. To-day is the fast-day of the fifteenth day of the
half-month. If the congregation be ready, let the congregation keep fast-day, and recite the confession. What is the
first business before the congregation? Venerable sirs, the
proclaiming of your innocency. I will recite the confession,
and let as many of us as are here present listen carefully and
pay strict attention. If any one have sinned, let him reveal
the fact; if he have not sinned, let him remain silent; by
your silence I shall know that your reverences are innocent.
But now, in assemblages like this, proclamation is made up to
the third time, and each one must make confession as if
individually asked. But if, when proclamation up to the
third time has been made, any priest shall remember a sin and
not reveal it, it will be a conscious falsehood. But a conscious falsehood, reverend sirs, has been declared by The
Blessed One to be a deadly sin. Therefore, if a priest remember having committed a sin, and desire again to be pure,
let him reveal the sin he committed, and when it has been
revealed, it shall be well for him.' "

§ 83 *b.* — Reprinted from a paper, by J. F. Dickson, M. A., in the Journal
of the Royal Asiatic Society for 1875.

On the 2nd of January, 1874, being the full-moon day of
the month Phussa, I was permitted, by the kindness of my
friend Kæwiṭiyāgala Unnānsē, to be present at a chapter of
priests assembled for the recitation of the Pātimokkha or
office of the confession of priests. The chapter was held
in the Sīmā or consecrated space in the ancient Lohapāsāda,
or Brazen Palace, in the city of Anurādhapura, and under
the shadow of the sacred Bo-tree, grown from a branch of the
tree at Buddha Gayā, under which, as tradition relates, the
prince Siddhārtha attained to supreme Buddhahood. The
branch was sent to Devānampiyatissa, King of Ceylon, by
the Emperor Açoka, in the year 288 B. C., now upwards of

two thousand years ago. It was in this remarkable spot, under the shadow of the oldest historical tree, and in probably the oldest chapter-house in the world, that it was my good fortune to be present at this service. The building has none of its original magnificence. The colossal stone pillars alone remain as a memorial of the devotion of the kings and people of Ceylon to the religion which was taught them by Mahendra, the great apostle of Buddhism. In place of the nine storeys which these pillars once supported, a few in the centre are now made to carry a poor thatched roof no larger than that of a cotter's hut, and hardly sufficient to protect the chapter from the inclemencies of the weather. Still there was a simple and imposing grandeur in the scene. At the back of some dozen or more of these gigantic pillars were stretched pieces of white calico, to form the sides of the room: the ceiling in like manner was formed by stretching white calico above the pillars to conceal the shabby roof, the bare ground was covered with clean mats, two lamps gave a dim light, the huge columns, grey with age, stood out against the white calico. At the top of the long room thus formed was hung a curtain of bright colors, and through a space left for the entrance were visible, row after row, the pillars of the ancient palace, their broad shadows contrasting with the silvery brightness of the tropical moon.

Accompanied by a friend, I went to the chapter-house about seven o'clock in the evening; we were met at the door by the priests, who showed us to the places prepared for us — two cushions on the floor at the bottom of the room, at a distance of about two fathoms from the place reserved for the priests. The ordinances of Buddha require that all persons who are not ordained priests, free at the time from all liability to ecclesiastical censure, shall keep at a distance of two and a half cubits from the assembled chapter. It was on my pointing out that this was the only direction of Buddha on the subject, that the priests consented to make an exception in my favor, and to break their rule of meeting in secret conclave.

After we were seated the priests retired two and two together, each pair knelt down face to face and made confession of their faults, one to another, in whispers. Their confessions being ended, they took their seats on mats covered with white calico, in two rows facing each other. The senior priest, the seniority being reckoned from the date of ordination, sat at the head of one row, the next in order at the head of the opposite row, the third next to the senior priest, and so on right and left down the room. The senior priest remained sitting, the others knelt and made obeisance to him, saying —

Permit me. Lord, give me absolution from all my faults committed in deed, or word, or thought.

The senior then says —

I absolve you, brother. It is good to grant me absolution.

All reply —

Permit me. Lord, I absolve you.

The second in order of seniority now resumes his seat, and all his juniors kneel and receive and give absolution, saying, Permit me, etc., as above; he then takes his seat, and the others kneel to him, and so on, till no one has a junior present, that is to say, if there are thirty priests present, the senior will receive obeisance from the twenty-nine others together, the second from the twenty-eight, and so on down to the twenty-ninth, who will receive obeisance from one. After all are seated, they fall together on their knees and say —

Praise be to the blessed one, the holy one, the author of all truth. (This is said three times.)

We believe in the Blessed one, the holy one, the author of all truth, who has fully accomplished the eight kinds of supernatural knowledge and the fifteen holy practices, who came the good journey which led to the Buddhahood, who knows the universe, the unrivalled, who has made subject to him all mortal beings, whether in heaven or in earth, the Teacher of Gods and men, the blessed Buddha. Through life till I reach Nirvāṇa I will put my trust in Buddha.

> I worship continually
> The Buddhas of the ages that are past,
> And the Buddhas of the ages that are yet to come,
> And the Buddhas of this present age.

> I have no other Refuge,
> Buddha is the best Refuge ;
> By the truth of these words
> May I conquer and win the victory.
>
> I bow my head to the ground, and worship
> The sacred dust of his holy feet.
> If in aught I have sinned against Buddha,
> May Buddha forgive me my sin.

The Law was graciously preached by Buddha, its effects are immediate, it is unlimited by time, it is conducive to salvation, it invites all comers, it is a fitting object of contemplation, the wise ponder it in their hearts. Through life till I reach Nirvāṇa I will put my trust in the Law.

> The Law as it has been in the ages that are past,
> The Law that will be in the ages that are yet to come,
> The Law as it is in this present age,
> I worship continually.
>
> I have no other Refuge,
> The Law is my best Refuge ;
> By the truth of these words
> May I conquer and win the victory.
>
> I bow my head to the ground and worship
> The Law, the noble doctrine of the Three Baskets.
> If in aught I have sinned against the Law,
> May the Law forgive me my sin.

Buddha's holy Church, the congregation of righteous men that lead a godly life, that walk in the straight way, in the way of wisdom, that walk faithfully in the four paths of holiness, the eight orders of the elect, worthy of offerings from afar, worthy of fresh offerings, worthy of offerings of the daily necessaries of life, entitled to receive the respectful salutation of joined hands raised in homage to the forehead, this holy Church produces merit which, like unto a rich field, yields its increase for the benefit of this world of men.

Through life till I reach Nirvāṇa I will put my trust in the Church.

> The Church as it has been in the ages that are past,
> The Church as it will be in the ages that are yet to come,
> The Church as it is in this present age,
> I worship continually.

> I have no other Refuge,
> The Church is my noble Refuge
> By the truth of these words
> May I worship and win the victory.

> I bow my head to the ground and worship
> The Church, threefold and best.
> If in aught I have sinned against the Church,
> May the Church forgive me my sin.

> Buddha and the Law, the Pacceka-buddhas,
> And the Church are my lords.
> I am their slave.
> May their virtues ever rest on my head.

> The three refuges, the three symbols and equanimity,
> And lastly, Nirvāṇa,
> Will I worship with bowed head, unceasingly.
> Thus shall I receive the benefit of that threefold power.

> May the three refuges rest on my head,
> On my head may there rest the three symbols.
> May peace rest on my head,
> May Nirvāṇa rest on my head.

> I worship the Buddhas, the all-pitiful,
> The Law, the Pacceka-buddhas;
> The Church and the three sages
> I worship with bowed head.

> I worship every saying
> And every word of the Great Teacher.
> I worship every shrine,
> My spiritual superior and my tutor.
> By virtue of these feelings of reverence
> May my thoughts be freed from sin.

The priests here rise from their knees and resume their seats. The senior, or some other deputed in his stead to officiate, then takes a seat at the top between the two rows. The interrogatories are then proceeded with as will be found explained in the following translation of the Pātimokkha. The interrogatories being ended, the Pātimokkha is intoned after the manner followed to this day by the Roman Church.

. . . .

The office for priestesses . . . has been omitted in the present edition, because the order of priestesses is not now recognized by the orthodox Buddhists.

The text of this edition is derived from MSS. in use at the Malwattē Monastery in Kandy, and it will be found divided into ten chapters, as follows:—

    I. Interrogatories relating to the requisites for forming a chapter.

    II. The Introduction.

    III. The four deadly sins.

    IV. The thirteen faults involving temporary separation from the priesthood.

    V. The two undetermined offences.

    VI. The thirty faults requiring confession and absolution, and involving forfeiture of the article in reference to which the offence has been committed.

    VII. The ninety-two faults requiring confession and absolution.

    VIII. Four offences requiring confession.

    IX. The seventy-five rules of conduct.

    X. The seven rules for settling cases.

The whole is sometimes known as the two hundred and twenty-seven precepts.

J. F. D.

Harmondsworth, Slough, March 19th, 1875.

§ 84. THE ORDER RECEIVE LEAVE TO DWELL IN HOUSES.

Translated from the Culla-Vagga (vi. 1¹).

At that time The Buddha, The Blessed One, was dwelling at Rājagaha in Bamboo Grove, which is in Kalandakanivāpa. Now at that time The Blessed One had not given permission to the priests to use dwelling-houses. And the priests of his following dwelt wherever they could, — in the forests, at the foot of trees, on the hills, in the valleys, in mountain caves, in cemeteries, in groves of trees, in open spaces, or in heaps of straw. And they would return early in the morning from their various resting-places, — from the forests, from the foot of trees, from the hills, from the valleys, from the mountain caves, from the cemeteries, from the groves of trees, from the open spaces, or from the heaps of straw, winning the minds of men with their advancing and their retiring, with their looking and their gazing, with their drawing in their arms and their stretching out their arms, and having their eyes cast down, and perfect in their deportment.

Now at that time a Rājagaha treasurer went early in the morning to the park. And the Rājagaha treasurer saw those priests as they returned early in the morning from their various resting-places, — from the forests, from the foot of trees, from the hills, from the valleys, from the mountain caves, from the cemeteries, from the groves of trees, from the open spaces, or from the heaps of straw, winning the minds of men with their advancing and their retiring, with their looking and their gazing, with their drawing in their arms and their stretching out their arms, and having their eyes cast down, and perfect in their deportment, — and when he had seen them, his mind was won. Then the Rājagaha treasurer drew near to where those priests were, and having drawn near, he spoke to those priests as follows :

" Reverend sirs, if I were to build some monastery cells, would ye dwell in those my monastery cells ? "

"O householder, The Blessed One has not given permission to use monastery cells."

"In that case, reverend sirs, ask The Blessed One about the matter, and announce to me his answer."

"Very well, O householder," said those priests to the Rājagaha treasurer in assent, and drew near to where The Blessed One was; and having drawn near and greeted The Blessed One, they sat down respectfully at one side. And seated respectfully at one side, they spoke to The Blessed One as follows:

"Reverend Sir, a Rājagaha treasurer is desirous of building some monastery cells. Reverend Sir, how shall we act in the matter?"

Then The Blessed One, on that occasion, after he had delivered a doctrinal discourse, addressed the priests:

"O priests, I permit places of retreat of five different kinds; monastery cells, Bengal houses, storied mansions, mansions with attics, and huts."

Then those priests drew near to where the Rājagaha treasurer was; and having drawn near, they spoke to the Rājagaha treasurer as follows:

"O householder, The Blessed One has given permission to use monastery cells. Pray, suit your own convenience."

Then the Rājagaha treasurer in one day established sixty monastery cells. And the Rājagaha treasurer, having completed those sixty monastery cells, drew near to where The Blessed One was; and having drawn near and greeted The Blessed One, he sat down respectfully at one side. And seated respectfully at one side, the Rājagaha treasurer spoke to The Blessed One as follows:

"Reverend Sir, let The Blessed One consent to take breakfast at my house to-morrow, together with the congregation of the priests."

And The Blessed One consented by his silence.

Then the Rājagaha treasurer, perceiving that The Blessed One had given his consent, rose from his seat, and saluted The Blessed One; and keeping his right side toward him, he departed.

Then the Rājagaha treasurer, when night was over, prepared excellent food, both hard and soft, and sent word to The Blessed One :

" Reverend Sir, breakfast is ready."

Then The Blessed One, having put on his tunic in the morning, took his bowl and his robes, and drew near to where the house of the Rājagaha treasurer was ; and having drawn near, together with the congregation of the priests, he sat down in the seat that was spread for him. Then the Rājagaha treasurer served The Buddha and the congregation of the priests that followed him with excellent food, both hard and soft, with his own hands, until they were satisfied, and would take no more. And when The Blessed One had finished eating, and had washed his bowl and his hands, the Rājagaha treasurer sat down respectfully at one side. And seated respectfully at one side, he spoke to The Blessed One as follows :

" Reverend Sir, I have built these sixty monastery cells in the hope of merit, and in the hope of heaven. Reverend Sir, how shall I act in the matter of these monastery cells ? "

" In that case, O householder, dedicate these sixty monastery cells to the Order, both present, and to come, and throughout the world."

" Very well, Reverend Sir," said the Rājagaha treasurer to The Blessed One in assent, and dedicated those sixty monastery cells to the Order, both present, and to come, and throughout the world.

Then The Blessed One gave thanks to the Rājagaha treasurer in the following stanzas : —

> " The cold, the heat, it beateth back,
>   And ravenous beasts of every sort,
>   The snakes that creep, the gnats that bite,
>   The winter's cold, the heavy rains ;
>   And when the dreaded, torrid winds
>   Spring up, they, too, are beaten back.
>
> " A place for refuge, and for ease,
>   To meditate, and insight gain,
>   Are monasteries, best of gifts,
>   And of The Buddha highly praised.

" Therefore, if any man is wise,
And cherisheth his weal at heart,
Then monasteries let him build,
And lodge therein the erudite.

" Let food to eat, and also drink,
And clothes, and bedding in full store,
Be given to the holy men,
By him with a believing heart.

" To him the Doctrine they shall teach,
And all his miseries put to flight;
And he, when once he sees the truth,
Depraved no more, Nirvana gains."

Then The Blessed One, having given thanks to the Rājagaha treasurer in the foregoing stanzas, rose from his seat and departed.

---

§ 85. RESIDENCE DURING THE RAINY SEASON.

§ 85 *a*. — Translated from the Mahā-Vagga (iii. 1[1]).

At that time The Buddha, The Blessed One, was dwelling at Rājagaha in Bamboo Grove, which is in Kalanda-kanivāpa. Now at that time residence during the rainy season had not been prescribed for the priests by The Blessed One. And the priests went about on their wanderings, both in the cold season, and in the hot season, and in the rainy season. And the people were angered, annoyed, and spoke indignantly:

" Pray, why should the Sakyaputta monks go about on their wanderings both in the cold season, and in the hot season, and in the rainy season, and crush the green grass, and injure beings having but one of the organs of sense, and bring to destruction many small animals? Verily, the followers of heretical sects, possessing but a poorly expounded doctrine, must lie by and compose themselves for residence during the rainy season. Verily, the birds must make their nests in the tops of the trees, and lie by and compose themselves for residence during the rainy season. But these Sakyaputta monks go about on their wanderings, both in the cold season, and in the hot season, and in the rainy season, and crush the green grass, and injure beings having but one of the organs of sense, and bring to destruction many small animals."

And the priests heard that the people were angered, annoyed, and were speaking indignantly; and the priests brought the matter to the notice of The Blessed One.

Then The Blessed One, on this occasion and in this connection, after he had delivered a doctrinal discourse, addressed the priests as follows :

" I prescribe, O priests, that ye enter upon residence."

Then it occurred to the priests as follows :

" At what time, pray, ought residence to begin ? " And they brought the matter to the notice of The Blessed One.

" I prescribe, O priests, that ye enter upon residence at the time of the annual rains."

Then it occurred to the priests as follows :

" How many, pray, are the days for beginning residence ? " And they brought the matter to the notice of The Blessed One.

" There are two days, O priests, on which to begin residence, an earlier and a later. The earlier one is the day after the full moon in the month Āsāḷhī, and the later is one month after the full moon in the month Āsāḷhī. These, O priests, are the two days for beginning residence."

And at that time the band of six priests entered upon residence, and in the midst of their residence they went about on their wanderings. And the people were angered, annoyed, and spoke indignantly :

" Pray, why should the Sakyaputta monks go about on their wanderings, both in the cold season, and in the hot season, and in the rainy season, and crush the green grass, and injure beings having but one of the organs of sense, and bring to destruction many small animals ? Verily, the followers of heretical sects, possessing but a poorly expounded doctrine, must lie by and compose themselves for residence during the rainy season. Verily, the birds must make their nests in the tops of the trees, and lie by and compose themselves for residence during the rainy season. But these Sakyaputta monks go about on their wanderings in the cold season, and in the hot season, and in the rainy season, and crush the green grass, and injure beings having but one of the organs of sense, and bring to destruction many small animals."

And the priests heard that the people were angered, annoyed, and spoke indignantly; and those that were moderate were angered, annoyed, and spoke indignantly:

"Pray, why should the band of six priests, having once entered upon residence, go about on their wanderings in the midst of the season for residence?" And they brought the matter to the notice of The Blessed One.

Then The Blessed One, on this occasion and in this connection, after he had delivered a doctrinal discourse, addressed the priests:

"O priests, it is not allowed that ye go about on your wanderings after having once entered upon residence, and not having finished either the former or the latter period of three months. If any one go about on his wanderings, he shall be guilty of a misdemeanor."

§ 85 *b*. — Translated from the Mahā-Vagga (iv. 1¹³).

"I prescribe, O priests, that at the end of residence, the priests shall invite criticism in respect to three points ; what has been seen, or heard, or suspected. Thus shall ye live in accord with one another, and be released from your offences, and keep the rules of discipline before your eyes. And after this manner, O priests, shall ye invite criticism : By a learned and competent priest shall the motion be brought before the congregation :

"'Reverend sirs, let the congregation hear me! This is the day of inviting criticism. If the congregation is ready, let the congregation invite criticism.'

"Then the senior priest, throwing his cloak over one shoulder, squatting on the ground, and holding forth his joined hands, shall say to the congregation of the priests:

" ' Brethren, I invite the criticism of the congregation with respect to what has been seen, or heard, or suspected. Let the venerable brethren have compassion and speak, and when I have seen my offence, I will atone for it. Brethren, a second time . . . a third time I invite the criticism of the congregation with respect to what has been seen, or heard, or suspected. Let the venerable brethren have compassion and speak, and when I have seen my offence, I will atone for it.'

" Then each junior priest, throwing his cloak over one shoulder, squatting on the ground, and holding forth his joined hands, shall say to the congregation of the priests :

" ' Reverend sirs, I invite the criticism of the congregation with respect to what has been seen, or heard, or suspected. . . . Reverend sirs, a second time . . . a third time I invite the criticism of the congregation with respect to what has been seen, or heard, or suspected. Let the venerable brethren have compassion and speak, and when I have seen my offence, I will atone for it.' "

---

§ 86. THE MENDICANT IDEAL.

Translated from the Saṁyutta-Nikāya (xvi. 3[1]).

Thus have I heard.

On a certain occasion The Blessed One was dwelling at Sāvatthi in Jetavana monastery in Anāthapiṇḍika's Park. And there The Blessed One addressed the priests :

" Priests," said he.

" Lord," said the priests to The Blessed One in reply.

And The Blessed One spoke as follows :

" Take pattern by the moon, O priests, when ye go a-begging. Hold aloof, O priests, both in body and in mind, never weary your welcome, nor be impudent to your benefactors.

" Just as a man, O priests, would regard a dilapidated well, or a rugged mountain, or a river difficult to ford, and hold aloof both in body and in mind, in exactly the same

way, O priests, take pattern by the moon when ye go a-begging, hold aloof both in body and in mind, never weary your
welcome, nor be impudent to your benefactors.

"Kassapa, O priests, takes pattern by the moon when he
goes a-begging. He holds aloof both in body and in mind,
never wearies his welcome, nor is impudent to his benefactors.

"What do you say to this, O priests? What sort of a
priest is worthy to go a-begging?"

"Reverend Sir, our beliefs derive from The Blessed One,
have The Blessed One for their guide and their authority.
Pray, Reverend Sir, let the answer to this find expression in
the mouth of The Blessed One. Anything the priests hear
from The Blessed One will be kept in mind."

Then The Blessed One waved his hand in the air: "Just
as my hand, O priests, is not caught, nor seized, nor held fast
by the air, in exactly the same way, O priests, when the mind
of a priest who goes a-begging is not caught, nor seized, nor
held fast, and when, willing that they should gain who wish
for gain, and that they should acquire merit who wish to acquire merit, he is as delighted and pleased with the gains of
others as with his own, such a priest, O priests, is worthy to
go a-begging.

"The mind of Kassapa, O priests, when he goes a-begging
is not caught, nor seized, nor held fast, and willing that they
should gain who wish for gain, and that they should acquire
merit who wish to acquire merit, he is as delighted and pleased
with the gains of others as with his own.

"What do you say to this, O priests? What sort of a
priest is an unworthy teacher of the Doctrine? And what
sort of a priest is a worthy teacher of the Doctrine?"

"Reverend Sir, our beliefs derive from The Blessed One,
have The Blessed One for their guide and their authority.
Pray, Reverend Sir, let the meaning of this saying find expression in the mouth of The Blessed One. Anything the
priests hear from The Blessed One will be kept in mind."

"Then listen, O priests, and pay strict attention, and I
will speak."

" Yes, Reverend Sir," said the priests to The Blessed One in assent.

And The Blessed One spoke as follows :

" Any priest, O priests, who in teaching the Doctrine to others thinks as follows : ' O that they may hear from me the Doctrine ! and be won over by what they hear, and manifest delight towards me,' such a priest, O priests, is an unworthy teacher of the Doctrine.

" Any priest, O priests, who in teaching the Doctrine to others thinks as follows : ' The Doctrine has been well taught by The Blessed One, avails even in the present life, is immediate in its results, is inviting and conducive to salvation, and may be mastered by any intelligent man for himself. O that they may hear from me the Doctrine, and be enlightened by what they hear, and as a result of their enlightenment begin to act accordingly ! ' and thus teaches the Doctrine to others because of that Doctrine's intrinsic goodness, and because of compassion, mercy, and kindness, such a priest, O priests, is a worthy teacher of the Doctrine.

" Kassapa, O priests, in teaching the Doctrine to others, thinks as follows : ' The Doctrine has been well taught by The Blessed One, is of advantage even in the present life, is immediate in its results, is inviting and conducive to salvation, and may be mastered by any intelligent man for himself. O that they may hear from me the Doctrine, and be enlightened by what they hear, and as a result of their enlightenment begin to act accordingly ! ' and thus teaches the Doctrine to others because of that Doctrine's intrinsic goodness, and because of compassion, mercy, and kindness.

" I will admonish you, O priests, by the example of Kassapa, or by that of any one who may resemble Kassapa, and when you have been admonished, begin to act accordingly."

§ 87. THE VALUE OF TRAINING IN RELIGION.

Translated from the Milindapañha (264²⁹).

" Bhante Nāgasena, you priests say, ' If a layman reach saintship, there are two courses open to him, and none other: on the self-same day he either retires from the world or passes into Nirvana; he cannot wait until the morrow.' Now if, bhante Nāgasena, he should not succeed in obtaining either professor or preceptor, or bowl and robes on that day, would that man who had reached saintship retire from the world without any assistance? or would he wait until another day? or would some other saint come by magical power and receive him into the Order? or would he pass into Nirvana?"

" Your majesty, this layman who had attained to saintship, would not retire from the world without assistance, or if he did so, he would be guilty of theft, nor could he wait for another day; and whether any one who had attained to saintship came or not, he would pass into Nirvana that self-same day."

" In that case, bhante Nāgasena, saintship has forfeited all claim to be a quiet haven, if it slaughters its possessor."

" Your majesty, inferiority is characteristic of a layman; and it is through this characteristic inferiority and weakness that a householder, when he has attained to saintship, on the self-same day either retires from the world or passes into Nirvana; and this weakness, your majesty, is not a fault of saintship, it is a fault belonging to the lay state. Just as food, your majesty, sustains the vital force, and preserves the life of all beings, but kills, through its indigestibility, any one who has a poor stomach and a slow and weak digestion, yet this weakness of digestion is not the fault of the food, but the fault of the stomach; in exactly the same way, your majesty, it is through his characteristic weakness and inferiority that a householder, when he has attained to saintship, on the self-same day either retires from the world or passes into Nirvana; and this characteristic weakness, your majesty, is not a fault of saintship, it is a fault belonging to the lay state. Or, again, your majesty, as a small stalk of grass will break and double over if a heavy stone be placed upon it; in exactly the same way, your majesty, a layman who has attained to saintship, cannot, so long as he remains a layman, sustain saintship, but on the self-same day he either retires from the world or passes into Nirvana. Or, again, your majesty, just as a man who is weak, feeble, of low extraction, and of few meritorious works, if he succeeds to a large kingdom, falls at once, perishes, and breaks down, and proves unable to sustain princely power; in exactly the same way, your majesty, a layman who has attained to saintship, cannot, so long as he stays a layman, sustain saintship. For this reason, then, on the self-same day he either retires from the world or passes into Nirvana."

"Well done, bhante Nāgasena! Thus it is, and you have my assent."

---

§ 88. THE COLORLESS LIFE.

Translated from the Milindapañha (76^{23}).

Said the king, "Bhante Nāgasena, what is the difference between one who has passion and one who is free from passion?"

"Your majesty, the one clings, the other does not cling."

"Bhante, what do you mean by 'clings' and 'does not cling'?"

"Your majesty, the one covets, the other does not covet."

"Bhante, this is the way I look at the matter: both he who has passion and he who is free from passion have the same wish, that his food, whether hard or soft, should be good; neither wishes for what is bad."

"Your majesty, he that is not free from passion experiences both the taste of that food, and also passion due to that taste; while he who is free from passion experiences the taste of that food, but no passion due to that taste."

"You are an able man, bhante Nāgasena."

§ 89.　CAN THE SAINT SUFFER?

Translated from the Saṁyutta-Nikāya (xxii. 1¹⁸).

"And how, O householder, is one wretched of body but not wretched of mind?

"We may have, O householder, a learned and noble disciple, who is a follower of noble disciples, conversant with the Noble Doctrine, disciplined in the Noble Doctrine, a follower of good people, conversant with the Doctrine held by good people, disciplined in the Doctrine held by good people. He does not consider form in the light of an Ego — neither the Ego as possessing form, nor form as comprised in the Ego, nor the Ego as comprised in form — and is thus not possessed with the idea, 'I am form; form belongs to the I.' And not being possessed with the idea, 'I am form; form belongs to the I,' when form alters and changes, the alteration and change of form do not cause sorrow, lamentation, grief, and despair to arise in him.

"He does not consider sensation . . . perception . . . the predispositions . . . consciousness in the light of an Ego — neither the Ego as possessing consciousness, nor consciousness as comprised in the Ego, nor the Ego as comprised in consciousness — and is thus not possessed with the idea, 'I am consciousness; consciousness belongs to the I.' And not being possessed with the idea, 'I am consciousness; consciousness belongs to the I,' when consciousness alters and changes, the alteration and change of consciousness do not cause sorrow, lamentation, grief, and despair to arise in him.

"Thus, O householder, is one wretched of body but not wretched of mind."

Thus spake the venerable Sāriputta, and the delighted householder Nakulapitā applauded the speech of the venerable Sāriputta.

§ 90. THE BODY IS AN OPEN SORE.

Translated from the Milindapañha (73²⁴).

Said the king, "Bhante Nāgasena, are they who have retired from the world fond of their bodies?"

"No, your majesty, they who have retired from the world are not fond of their bodies."

"Then why, bhante, do you indulge your body, and lavish attention on it?"

"Pray, your majesty, have you ever at any time been hit in battle by an arrow?"

"Yes, bhante; I have."

"And was the wound, your majesty, anointed with ointment, smeared with oil, and bandaged with a strip of fine cloth?"

"Yes, bhante. It was anointed with ointment, smeared with oil, and bandaged with a strip of fine cloth."

"Pray, your majesty, were you fond of that wound, that you anointed it with ointment, smeared it with oil, and bandaged it with a strip of fine cloth?"

"No, bhante. I was not fond of my wound; but it was in order that my flesh might heal that I anointed it with ointment, smeared it with oil, and bandaged it with a strip of fine cloth."

"In exactly the same way, your majesty, they who have retired from the world are not fond of their bodies; but, without being attached to them, they take care of their bodies in order to advance in the religious life. The body, your majesty, has been likened to a wound by The Blessed One; and, therefore, they who have retired from the world take care of their bodies as though they were wounds, without thereby becoming attached to them. And The Blessed One, your majesty, has spoken as follows:

> "'This monstrous wound hath outlets nine,
> A damp, wet skin doth clothe it o'er;
> At every point this unclean thing
> Exudeth nasty, stinking smells.'"

"You are an able man, bhante Nāgasena."

§ 91. HEAVEN NOT THE HIGHEST GOOD.

Translated from the Aṅguttara-Nikāya (iii. 18).

"If wandering ascetics, O priests, members of another sect, were to say to you, 'Sirs, is it in order to be reborn in the world of the gods that the monk Gotama leads a holy life?' would ye not, O priests, if that question were put to you, be distressed at, ashamed of, and loathe the idea?"

"Yes, Reverend Sir."

"So it appears, O priests, that ye are distressed at, ashamed of, and loathe the idea of life in heaven, heavenly beauty, heavenly happiness, heavenly glory; that ye are distressed at, ashamed of, and loathe the idea of heavenly power. But much more, O priests, should ye be distressed at, ashamed of, and loathe doing evil with the body; be distressed at, ashamed of, and loathe doing evil with the voice; be distressed at, ashamed of, and loathe doing evil with the mind."

---

§ 92. THE SAINTS SUPERIOR TO THE GODS.

Translated from the Aṅguttara-Nikāya (iii. 37).

In former times, O priests, Sakka, the leader of the gods, was admonishing the Gods of the Suite of the Thirty-three, and on that occasion pronounced the following stanza:

> "Come, tell me, where's the man like me,
> The fourteenth day, the fifteenth day,
> And eke the eighth of each half-month,
> To celebrate as days of fast,
> And keep the vows, in number eight,
> Through all the months of residence!"

Now this stanza, O priests, which was sung by Sakka, the leader of the gods, was inapposite, not apposite, ill-spoken, not well-spoken. And why do I say so? Because Sakka, the leader of the gods, O priests, was not free from passion, was not free from hatred, was not free from infatuation. But that priest, O priests, who is a saint, who has lost all depravity, who has led the holy life, who has done what it behooved him to do, who has laid aside the burden, who has achieved the supreme good, who has destroyed every fetter that binds him to existence, who is released by perfect knowledge, such a priest, O priests, can truly say,

> "Come, tell me where's the man like me,
> The fourteenth day, the fifteenth day,
> And eke the eighth of each half-month,
> To celebrate as days of fast,
> And keep the vows, in number eight,
> Through all the months of residence!"

And why do I say so? Because that priest, O priests, is free from passion, is free from hatred, is free from infatuation.

In former times, O priests, Sakka, the leader of the gods, was admonishing the Gods of the Suite of the Thirty-three, and on that occasion pronounced the following stanza:

> "Come, tell me where's the man like me,
> The fourteenth day, the fifteenth day,
> And eke the eighth of each half-month,
> To celebrate as days of fast,
> And keep the vows, in number eight,
> Through all the months of residence!"

Now this stanza, O priests, which was sung by Sakka, the leader of the gods, was inapposite, not apposite, ill-spoken, not well-spoken. And why do I say so? Because Sakka, the leader of the gods, O priests, is not released from birth, old age, death, sorrow, lamentation, misery, grief, and despair; in short, he is not released from misery. But that priest, O priests, who is a saint, who has lost all depravity, who has led the holy life, who has done what it behooved him to do, who has laid aside the burden, who has achieved the supreme good, who has destroyed every fetter that binds him to existence, who is released by perfect knowledge, such a priest, O priests, can truly say,

> " Come, tell me where 's the man like me,
> The fourteenth day, the fifteenth day,
> And eke the eighth of each half-month,
> To celebrate as days of fast,
> And keep the vows, in number eight,
> Through all the months of residence ! "

And why do I say so? Because that priest, O priests, is released from birth, old age, death, sorrow, lamentation, misery, grief, and despair; in short, he is released from misery.

---

§ 93. THE ANGER–EATING DEMON.

Translated from the Saṁyutta-Nikāya (xi. 3.2[1]).

Thus have I heard.

On a certain occasion The Blessed One was dwelling at Sāvatthi in Jetavana monastery in Anāthapiṇḍika's Park. And there The Blessed One addressed the priests:

" Priests ! " said he.

" Lord ! " said the priests in reply.

And The Blessed One spoke as follows:

Once upon a time, O priests, a certain sickly-looking and decrepit demon took his seat on the throne of Sakka, the leader of the gods. And the Gods, O priests, of the Suite of the Thirty-three, were angered, annoyed, and spoke indignantly: " O wonderful is it ! O marvellous is it ! Here this sickly-looking and decrepit demon has taken his seat on the throne of Sakka, the leader of the gods ! " Now, O priests, in proportion as the Gods of the Suite of the Thirty-three were angered, annoyed, and spoke indignantly, in the same proportion did the demon grow handsomer, better-looking, and more pleasing.

Then, O priests, the Gods of the Suite of the Thirty-three drew near to where Sakka, the leader of the gods, was; and having drawn near, they spoke to Sakka, the leader of the gods, as follows:

"Sir, a certain sickly-looking and decrepit demon has come here and taken his seat on your throne. And the Gods, sir, of the Suite of the Thirty-three, are angered, annoyed, and speak indignantly: 'O wonderful is it! O marvellous is it! Here this sickly-looking and decrepit demon has taken his seat on the throne of Sakka, the leader of the gods.' And, sir, in proportion as the Gods of the Suite of the Thirty-three are angered, annoyed, and speak indignantly, in the same proportion does the demon grow handsomer, better-looking, and more pleasing. Sir, surely now, it must be an anger-eating demon."

Then, O priests, Sakka, the leader of the gods, drew near to where the anger-eating demon was; and having drawn near, he threw his upper garment over his shoulder, and planting his right knee-pan on the ground, he stretched out his joined palms to the demon, and thrice announced himself:

"Sir, your obedient servant, Sakka, the leader of the gods! Sir, your obedient servant, Sakka, the leader of the gods! Sir, your obedient servant, Sakka, the leader of the gods!"

And the more, O priests, Sakka, the leader of the gods, proclaimed his own name, the more sickly-looking and decrepit became the demon; and straightway he disappeared.

Then, O priests, Sakka, the leader of the gods, resumed his seat on his throne, and took occasion to induce in the gods a more fitting frame of mind, by means of the following stanzas:

> "My mind's not easily cast down,
> Nor lightly swerveth from its course;
> Long angry can I never be,
> For anger finds in me no place.
>
> "I ne'er in anger say harsh words,
> And ne'er proclaim my virtue's fame;
> Myself I seek to keep subdued
> In interest of my future weal."

§ 94. CONTENTMENT IS RICHES.

Translated from the Visuddhi-Magga (chap. iii.).

By *dwelling-place* is meant either a chamber, or a hut, or a whole monastery. Now a dwelling-place is not a hindrance to everybody. But any one who spends much thought on building operations or the like, or accumulates many goods, or for any reason devotes much attention to his house and becomes engrossed by it, to him it is a hindrance, but not to any other. The following story will illustrate.

They say there were two young men of good family, who issued forth from Anurādhapura, and retired from the world in a monastery surrounding a relic-shrine. One of these learnt two tables of contents by heart, and when five years had elapsed from his ordination, he went, after the solemnity of inviting criticism, to Pācīnakhaṇḍarāji. The other one remained where he was. The one who had gone to Pācīnakhaṇḍarāji dwelt there a long time, and having become an elder, he reflected, "This place is very suitable for retirement. Come now, I will tell it to my comrade." And he issued forth, and in due course of travel arrived at the monastery surrounding the relic-shrine. His friend saw him coming, and, notwithstanding he was also an elder, and had been a member of the Order for the same length of time, went to meet him, and taking his bowl and his robe, he performed for him the duties of respect. When the visiting elder had entered his sleeping-quarters, he thought, "Now my friend will send me either some clarified butter, or some treacle, or something to drink; for he has dwelt in this city a long time." But when he received nothing at night, in the morning he thought, "Now he will send me some rice-gruel, or some hard food, given by some of his charitable friends." But when he saw nothing, he thought, "There are none to send. Methinks they will give when he goes to the village," and went with him early in the morning to the village. After walking through one street and securing only

a ladleful of rice-gruel, they sat down in a hall where there
was a seat, and drank it up.   Then the stranger elder
thought, "Methinks it cannot be rice-gruel all the time;
surely at dinner-time the people will give some good rice-
porridge."   So at dinner-time he went his rounds for alms,
and getting nothing to eat but such as had already been
given him, he said to his friend:

"Reverend sir, do you always live in this way?"

"Yes, brother."

"Reverend sir, it is very pleasant at Pācīnakhaṇḍarāji.
Let us go thither."

The elder issued from the city by the southern gate, and
started off by way of the potter's village.

"Reverend sir," said his friend, "why do you take this
road?"

"Brother, did you not celebrate the praises of Pācīnakhaṇḍarāji?"

"But, reverend sir, in all this time that you have inhabited this place, have you acquired no spare requisites?"

"Yes, brother; the bed and the bench that belong to the
congregation.   But I have put them back where they belong,
and have nothing else."

"But I, reverend sir, am leaving behind a walking-stick,
a measure of sesamum oil, sandals, and a scrip."

"Brother, have you accumulated all those in one day's
time?"

"Yes, reverend sir," said the other; and pleased in mind,
he did obeisance, and said, "Reverend sir, for such as you it
is everywhere as though you dwelt in the wood, and as
though every place contained a relic-shrine, and held the
remains of the four Buddhas, and as though you could hear
profitable sermons in the Brazen Palace, and had sight of
great temples, and of holy elders.   For you it is as if The
Buddha were alive.   Stay you here!"

And on the next day, with his bowl and his robe, he
departed alone.

For such a one, a *dwelling-place* is no hindrance.

§ 95. THE STORY OF A PRIEST.

Translated from the Dhammapada, and from Buddhaghosa's comment.

> 222. "What man his rising anger curbs,
> Like chariot circling o'er the plain,
> He, truly, is the charioteer —
> Holders of reins all other folk."

"*What man his rising anger.*" This doctrinal instruction was given by The Teacher while dwelling in the Aggālava shrine; and it was concerning a certain priest.

For when The Teacher had given permission to the congregation of the priests to use houses, and houses were being built for them by the Rājagaha treasurer and others, a certain priest who dwelt in the forest, in making for himself a house, saw a particular tree, and began to cut it down. But the goddess who had been born therein and had a young son, took the child on her hip, and stood and begged, saying,

"My lord, do not cut down my mansion. I cannot, with my little son, wander about with no place of abode."

"It would not be possible for me to find another tree like this," thought the priest, and heeded not her request.

"At least, consideration for the child will cause him to stop," thought the goddess, and placed her son on a bough of the tree; but the priest was unable to check his uplifted axe, and cut off the child's arm.

The goddess, in a violent rage, had lifted up both her hands to smite the priest dead, when she thought,

"This priest observes the precepts: if I kill him, I shall go to hell. And the other goddesses, also, when they see their trees cut down by priests, will follow my example, and kill the priests, thinking, 'It was thus that such and such a goddess killed a priest.' But this priest has a master: I will tell it to his master."

Then she lowered her uplifted hands, and went weeping to The Teacher. And having done him obeisance, she stood respectfully at one side.

Then said The Teacher, " What is it, goddess ? "

" Reverend Sir," said she, "your disciple did so and so to me. I, however, when desirous of killing him, made such and such a reflection, and have come hither without killing him." And she related the whole story in full.

" Well done, well done, goddess ! " said The Teacher, when he had heard her story. " You did well in keeping your mounting anger under control, as one would a chariot circling hither and thither." And he pronounced this stanza :

> " What man his rising anger curbs,
> Like chariot circling o'er the plain,
> He, truly, is the charioteer —
> Holders of reins all other folk."

Other folk : — By " other folk " are meant the charioteers of the king, of the deputy king, and so on. These are called *holders of reins,* but not charioteers in the highest sense.

At the end of this instruction, the goddess became established in the fruit of conversion ; and the instruction was of profit also to the assembled throng.

But the goddess, though converted, continued to weep.

Then said The Teacher, " What is it, goddess ? "

" Reverend Sir," said she, "my mansion is destroyed. What am I now to do ? "

" Nay, goddess, be not anxious. I will give you a mansion." And indicating a tree the goddess of which had passed into another existence on the previous day, and which was situated in the neighborhood of the perfumed chamber of Jetavana monastery, he said to her, " In such and such a spot is a deserted tree ; go thither."

And she went thither ; and from that time on, even powerful goddesses did not dare to come and attempt to expel her from a tree that had been given her by The Buddha.

The Teacher, when he had performed this benefaction, laid down for the priests the precept concerning vegetation.

The Story of a Priest.

§ 96. THE YOUNG STONE–THROWER.

Translated from the Dhammapada, and from Buddhaghosa's
commentary on stanza 362.

360. " The guarding of the eye is good :
And good the guarding of the ear.
The guarding of the nose is good :
And good the guarding of the tongue.

361. " The guarding of the body 's good :
And good the guarding of the voice.
The guarding of the mind is good :
And good is guarding everywhere.
The priest that guarded is in all,
From every misery frees himself.

362. " Restrained of hand, restrained of foot,
Restrained of voice, restrained in all,
Reflective, calm, content alone,
'T is he that is a priest in truth.

363. " That priest who keeps his tongue controlled,
Who Scripture quotes, is not puffed up,
Who all things good and right explains, —
How sweet to listen to his voice ! "

" *Restrained of hand.*" This doctrinal instruction was
given by The Teacher while dwelling at Jetavana monastery ;
and it was concerning a priest who killed a goose. The
account runs as follows :

Two friends, inhabitants of Sāvatthi, entered the Order,
and having received ordination as priests, generally went
about together. One day they had been bathing in the
Aciravatī River, and as they were afterwards basking in the
sun, they fell into friendly conversation. At that instant
two wild geese came flying through the sky. Thereupon the
younger of the two priests said,

" I can take a potsherd and hit this gosling in the eye."

" No, you can't," said the other.

" I can do even better; I can hit the eye on the other side."

" That you surely cannot do."

" Just wait and see!" And so saying, he took a triangular piece of pottery, and threw it at the goose's hinder parts.

The goose, when it heard the whiz of the potsherd, turned its head to look. Then the priest, snatching up a round fragment, hit the eye belonging to the further side, so that the potsherd came out at the eye belonging to this side. The goose screamed, and rolling over fell down at their feet.

Then came up other priests, who happened to be at hand, and had seen what had happened.

" Brother," said they, " you, who have retired from the world under the dispensation of a Buddha, have done something very unseemly in taking life." And they took the priest with them, and showed him to The Tathāgata.

" Is it true," asked The Teacher, " what they say, that you have taken life?"

" Reverend Sir, it is true."

" Priest, . . . it was a very serious sin for you to take life after you had retired from the world under the dispensation of such a Buddha as I. A priest should always keep his hands, his feet, and his voice under restraint." So saying, he pronounced this stanza:

> " Restrained of hand, restrained of foot,
> Restrained of voice, restrained in all,
> Reflective, calm, content alone,
> 'T is he that is a priest in truth."

The Story of the Goose-killing Priest.

§ 97. "AND HATE NOT HIS FATHER AND MOTHER."

Translated from the Visuddhi-Magga (chap. iii.).

For some persons even _mother and father_ are no hindrances, as in the case of the young priest, the nephew on his mother's side of an elder who dwelt in Koraṇḍaka monastery.

It is related that the young priest had gone to Rohaṇa to hear the precepts read, and the elder's sister, who was a lay devotee, used constantly to ask the elder for news of her son. One day the elder determined to go and fetch the lad, and set out in the direction of Rohaṇa. The youth also had left his quarters, and had issued forth from Rohaṇa. For he said to himself, "It is a long time that I have lived here. I will go now and see my preceptor, and having learnt how the lay woman is doing, I will return again." And they both met on the banks of the Ganges. Then the young priest performed his respectful duties to the elder at the foot of a certain tree, and when the latter asked him, "Whither are you going?" he told him. Said the elder, "You do well; the lay woman is always asking after you, and it is for this very reason that I am come. By all means go, and I will stay and keep residence here." And thus he dismissed him.

The young priest arrived home at the monastery on the day for beginning residence, and they assigned to him a cell which had been built by his father. On the next day his father came, and inquired of one of the priests, "Reverend sir, to whom has my cell been assigned?" And when he heard it had been assigned to a young stranger, he drew near, and having done obeisance, he said,

"Reverend sir, any one who enters upon residence in my cell has a garment given him."

"What mean you, O layman?"

"For the next three months you must beg your food at our house, and when, after the solemnity of inviting criticism, you wish to depart, come and take leave of us."

The other assented by his silence.

Then the layman went home, and said to his wife, " A certain reverend stranger is in the dwelling I put up, and we must wait on him attentively."

" Very well," said the lay woman in assent, and prepared excellent food, both hard and soft.

At breakfast-time the lad came to the house of his mother and father, but no one recognized him. And he remained three months, and always ate his alms at their house. And when residence was over, he announced to them that he was about to depart.

Then said his mother and father, " Reverend sir, you can go on the morrow." And the next day they fed him in their house, and then filled up a measure of sesamum oil and gave it to him, and also a lump of sugar, and nine cubits' length of cloth, and said, " You can go now, reverend sir." And he returned thanks, and set out in the direction of Rohaṇa.

And his preceptor, after the solemnity of inviting criticism, was coming in the opposite direction, and met him in the place where they had met before. The lad performed his respectful duties to the elder at the foot of a certain tree. Then said the elder,

" Well, my friend, did you see the lay woman ? "

" Yes, reverend sir," said he in reply, and told him all the news. And having anointed the feet of the elder with the sesamum oil, and made him a drink with the lump of sugar, and given him the cloth, he did obeisance before him and saying, " Reverend sir, Rohaṇa is the place for me," he departed on his way.

The elder came to the monastery, and on the next day entered the village of Koraṇḍaka. And the lay woman, who was always looking up the road, and saying, " Now, now my brother is coming with my son," saw him approaching alone, and fell at his feet, and wept, and lamented, saying, " My son, methinks, must be dead, inasmuch as the elder comes alone."

Then thought the elder, " Surely, the lad, through the moderateness of his passions, must have gone away without announcing himself." And he comforted her, and told her the whole story, and drawing forth the cloth from the scrip in which he carried his bowl, he showed it to her.

The lay woman was pleased, and lying prostrate, with her face in the direction in which her son had gone, she worshiped, saying,

"Methinks The Blessed One must have had in mind a body of priests like my son when he preached the relay course of conduct, the Nālaka course of conduct, the tuvaṭṭaka course of conduct, and the course of conduct customary with the great saints, showing how to take delight in the cultivation of content with the four reliances. This man ate for three months in the house of the mother who bore him, and never said, 'I am thy son, and thou art my mother.' O the wonderful man!"

For such a one *mother and father* are no hindrances, much less any other lay devotees.

---

§ 98. NO BUDDHIST SHOULD COMMIT SUICIDE.

Translated from the Milindapañha (195[1]).

"Bhante Nāgasena! The Blessed One has said as follows: 'Priests, let no one destroy himself, and whosoever would destroy himself, let him be dealt with according to law.' But on the other hand you priests say, 'Whenever The Blessed One taught the Doctrine to his disciples, he would in many different ways teach the extirpation of birth, old age, disease, and death. And, verily, if any one overcame birth, old age, disease, and death, him he would praise in the highest terms.'

"If, bhante Nāgasena, The Blessed One has said as follows: 'Priests, let no one destroy himself, and whosoever would destroy himself, let him be dealt with according to law,' then, surely, it was a mistake to say that he would teach the extirpation of birth, old age, disease, and death. If he would teach the extirpation of birth, old age, disease, and death, then surely, it was a mistake to say, 'Priests, let no one destroy himself, and whosoever would destroy himself, let him be dealt with according to law.'

"This is another dilemma come to you to solve."

"The Blessed One, your majesty, has said as follows: 'Priests, let no one destroy himself, and whosoever would destroy himself, let him be dealt with according to law.' And whenever The Blessed One taught the Doctrine to his disciples, he would in many different ways teach the extirpation of birth, old age, disease, and death. But there was a reason for the interdiction, and also for the exhortation of The Blessed One."

"But what was the reason, bhante Nāgasena, for the interdiction, and what also for the exhortation of The Blessed One?"

"The virtuous and well-conducted man, your majesty, is like a medicine in destroying the poison of human corruption; is like a healing herb in quieting the disease of human corruption; is like water in removing the dirt and defilement of human corruption; is like the magic jewel in giving all good fortune to men; is like a ship in crossing to the further shore of the four torrents of human viciousness; is like a caravan-leader in conducting men through the wilderness of birth; is like the wind in extinguishing the heat of man's threefold fever; is like a great cloud in satisfying man's longings; is like a teacher in training men in the acquirement of merit; and is like a skilful preceptor in pointing out to men the way of peace.

"It was, your majesty, in order that the virtuous man, whose good qualities are so many, so numerous, so infinitely multiplied, who is such an embodiment and aggregation of good qualities, such a cause of welfare to men, might not perish, that The Blessed One, your majesty, out of compassion for men, laid down this precept: 'Priests, let no one destroy himself, and whosoever would destroy himself, let him be dealt with according to law.'

"This, your majesty, was the reason for the interdiction of The Blessed One.

"Moreover, your majesty, the following was said by the brilliant preacher, the elder Kumāra-Kassapa, in an exposition of the next world which he made to prince Pāyāsi: 'The longer, O prince, virtuous and noble monks and Brahmans live, the more they avail for the welfare of the multitude, for the happiness of the multitude, for compassionating the world, for the advantage, the welfare, and the happiness of gods and men.'

"But what was the reason for the exhortation of The Blessed One?

"Your majesty, birth is misery; old age is misery; disease is misery; death is misery; sorrow is misery; lamentation is misery; misery is misery; grief is misery; despair is misery; association with those we do not love is misery; separation from those we love is misery; to have a mother die is misery; to have a father die is misery; to have a brother die is misery; to have a sister die is misery; to have a son die is misery; to have a wife die is misery; to have a relative die is misery; to have misfortunes happen to a relative is misery; the loss of health is misery; the loss of wealth is misery; the loss of character is misery; the loss of orthodoxy is misery; to be in danger from the king is misery; to be in danger from bandits is misery; to be in danger from enemies is misery; to be in danger of famine is misery; to be in danger from fire is misery; to be in danger from water is misery; to be in danger from the waves is misery; to be in danger from whirlpools is misery; to be in danger from crocodiles is misery; to be in danger from sea-monsters is misery; self-reproach is misery; the reproach of others is misery; to be fined is misery; poverty is misery; stage-fright is misery; to be in danger from the naked ascetics is misery; to be in danger of death is misery; to be beaten with rattans is misery; to be beaten with whips is misery; to be beaten with short sticks is misery; to have one's hands cut off is misery; to have one's feet cut off is misery; to have one's hands and feet cut off is misery; to have one's ears cut off is misery; to have one's nose cut off is misery; to have one's ears and nose cut off is misery; the 'kettle of gruel' is misery; the 'sea-shell tonsure' is misery; the 'Rāhu-mouth' is misery; the 'wreath of flame' is misery; the 'hands of flame' is misery; the 'blades of grass' is misery; the 'bark-dress' is misery; the 'black antelope is misery; the 'hook-meat' is misery; the 'penny-bit' is misery; 'carving by caustics' is misery; the 'pivot' is misery; the 'straw-bolster' [1] is misery; to be sprinkled with boiling oil is

---

[1] Extract from the Native Commentary to the Aṅguttara-Nikāya, ii. 1, 1:

Kettle of gruel: — In the pot-of-gruel torture they cut open the skull, and with a pair of tongs take up a heated iron ball, and throw it in; whereby the brains boil, and run over.

Sea-shell tonsure: — In the sea-shell-tonsure torture they first make an incision through the skin, beginning on either side of the upper lip, and continuing by the roots of the ears, and around by the neck. And drawing together all the hair into one knot, they twist it by means of a stick until they have raised the scalp. Then they rub the dome of the skull with coarse gravel, and wash it until it presents the appearance of a polished sea-shell.

Rāhu-mouth: — In the Rāhu-mouth torture they keep the mouth open by means of a peg, and burn a candle inside. Or, beginning from the roots of the ears, they dig out the teeth, so that the blood gushes forth, and fills the mouth.

Wreath of flame: — They envelop the entire body in cloth that has been steeped in oil, and then set fire.

Hands of flame: — Having enveloped the hands in cloth that has been steeped in oil, they cause them to flame up like torches.

Blades of grass: — In the blades-of-grass torture they begin at the neck, and cut the skin downwards in blade-like strips as far as to the ankles, and then let them fall. Then they put a halter on the man, and drag him forward, so that he stumbles and falls over the blade-like strips of his own skin.

Bark-dress: — In the bark-dress torture they cut strips the same as before, leaving off at the hips; and from the hips they cut other strips, leaving off at the ankles. Then the strips of the upper part of the body form, as it were, a bark tunic for the lower part.

Black antelope: — In the black-antelope torture they drive the points of four iron stakes through the two elbows and the two knees, so that the man remains pinioned to the ground by means of these four iron stakes. Then they build a fire all around him; and in order to make the fire-surrounded black antelope, mentioned in the text, they remove the

misery; to be devoured by dogs is misery; to be impaled alive is misery; to be beheaded with a sword is misery. Such, such, your majesty, are the various and manifold miseries which one encounters in the course of rebirth.

"As the water, your majesty, of the Ganges River, after having rained down in the Himalaya Mountains, encounters on its way stones, grit, . . . whirlpools, eddies, . . . obstructions, hindrances, roots, and branches; in exactly the same way, your majesty, men have to encounter various and manifold miseries in the course of rebirth.

"The existent, your majesty, is misery; the non-existent is happiness; and it was, your majesty, while The Blessed One was explaining how good is the non-existent, and how terrible the existent, that he gave the exhortation to realize the non-existent by overcoming birth, old age, disease, and death.

"This, your majesty, is the reason for the exhortation of The Blessed One."

"Well done, bhante Nāgasena! The difficulty has been well straightened out; the reason ably presented. You have my assent that thus it is."

---

stakes from time to time, and set the man on his protruding bones. There is no torture equal to this one.

Hook-meat: — They strike him with double hooks, and thus tear away skin, flesh, and tendons.

Penny-bit: — Beginning at the top, they cut off bits of the size of a penny from the whole body by means of sharp razors, and let them fall to the ground.

Carving by caustics: — They cut the man's body here and there with weapons, and then, by means of combs, they rub in caustic, so that skin, flesh, and gristle trickle away, and only the bony skeleton remains.

Pivot: — Having made him lie down on one side, they drive an iron stake through his ear, and make him fast to the ground. Then they take him by the feet and whirl him around.

Straw-bolster: — A skilful executioner, without cutting through the skin, will break his bones by means of small hand-millstones, so that when lifted up by the hair, he hangs a limp mass of flesh. Then they wind him round and round with his hair, and dispose him in a coil like a straw-pad.

§ 99. THE ADMISSION OF WOMEN TO THE ORDER.

Translated from the Culla-Vagga (x. 1¹).

At that time The Buddha, The Blessed One, was dwelling among the Sakkas at Kapilavatthu in Banyan Park.   Then drew near Mahā-Pajāpatī the Gotamid to where The Blessed One was; and having drawn near and greeted The Blessed One, she stood respectfully at one side.   And standing respectfully at one side, Mahā-Pajāpatī the Gotamid spoke to The Blessed One as follows :

"Pray, Reverend Sir, let women retire from household life to the houseless one, under the Doctrine and Discipline announced by The Tathāgata."

"Enough, O Gotamid, do not ask that women retire from household life to the houseless one, under the Doctrine and Discipline announced by The Tathāgata."

And a second time Mahā-Pajāpatī the Gotamid spoke to The Blessed One as follows :

"Pray, Reverend Sir, let women retire from household life to the houseless one, under the Doctrine and Discipline announced by The Tathāgata."

"Enough, O Gotamid, do not ask that women retire from household life to the houseless one, under the Doctrine and Discipline announced by The Tathāgata."

And a third time Mahā-Pajāpatī the Gotamid spoke to The Blessed One as follows :

"Pray, Reverend Sir, let women retire from household life to the houseless one, under the Doctrine and Discipline announced by The Tathāgata."

"Enough, O Gotamid, do not ask that women retire from household life to the houseless one, under the Doctrine and Discipline announced by The Tathāgata."

Then thought Mahā-Pajāpatī the Gotamid, "The Blessed One permitteth not that women retire from household life to the houseless one, under the Doctrine and Discipline announced by The Tathāgata ; " and she was sorrowful, sad, and tearful, and wept.   And saluting The Blessed One, and keeping her right side toward him, she departed.

Then The Blessed One, after dwelling at Kapilavatthu as long as he wished, departed on his wanderings toward Vesālī; and wandering from place to place, he came to where Vesālī was.   And there The Blessed One dwelt at Vesālī, in Great Wood, in Pagoda Hall.

Then Mahā-Pajāpatī the Gotamid had her hair cut off, put on yellow garments, and with a number of Sakka women departed towards Vesālī; and going from place to place, she drew near to where Vesālī was, and Great Wood, and Pagoda Hall.   And Mahā-Pajāpatī the Gotamid with swollen feet, and covered with dust, sorrowful, sad, and tearful, stood weeping outside in the entrance porch.

Now the venerable Ānanda saw Mahā-Pajāpatī the Gotamid with swollen feet, and covered with dust, sorrowful, sad, and tearful, stand weeping outside in the entrance porch. And he spoke to Mahā-Pajāpatī the Gotamid as follows:

"Wherefore dost thou, O Gotamid, with swollen feet, and covered with dust, sorrowful, sad, and tearful, stand weeping outside in the entrance porch?"

"Because, alas! O Ānanda, reverend sir, The Blessed One permitteth not that women retire from household life to the houseless one, under the Doctrine and Discipline announced by The Tathāgata."

"In that case, O Gotamid, stay thou here a moment, and I will beseech The Blessed One that women retire from household life to the houseless one, under the Doctrine and Discipline announced by The Tathāgata."

Then the venerable Ānanda drew near to where The Blessed One was; and having drawn near and greeted The Blessed One, he sat down respectfully at one side.   And seated respectfully at one side, the venerable Ānanda spoke to The Blessed One as follows:

"Reverend Sir, here this Mahā-Pajāpatī the Gotamid with swollen feet, and covered with dust, sorrowful, sad, and tearful, stands weeping outside in the entrance porch, and says that The Blessed One permitteth not that women retire from household life to the houseless one, under the Doctrine and Discipline announced by The Tathāgata. Pray, Reverend Sir, let women retire from household life to the houseless one, under the Doctrine and Discipline announced by The Tathāgata."

" Enough, Ānanda, do not ask that women retire from household life to the houseless one, under the Doctrine and Discipline announced by The Tathāgata."

And a second time the venerable Ānanda spoke to The Blessed One as follows :

" Pray, Reverend Sir, let women retire from household life to the houseless one, under the Doctrine and Discipline announced by The Tathāgata."

" Enough, Ānanda, do not ask that women retire from household life to the houseless one, under the Doctrine and Discipline announced by The Tathāgata."

And a third time the venerable Ānanda spoke to The Blessed One as follows :

" Pray, Reverend Sir, let women retire from household life to the houseless one, under the Doctrine and Discipline announced by The Tathāgata."

" Enough, Ānanda, do not ask that women retire from household life to the houseless one, under the Doctrine and Discipline announced by The Tathāgata."

Then thought the venerable Ānanda, " The Blessed One permitteth not that women retire from household life to the houseless one, under the Doctrine and Discipline announced by The Tathāgata; what if now, by another route, I beseech The Blessed One that women retire from household life to the houseless one, under the Doctrine and Discipline announced by The Tathāgata ? "

Then the venerable Ānanda spoke to The Blessed One as follows :

" Are women competent, Reverend Sir, if they retire from household life to the houseless one, under the Doctrine and Discipline announced by The Tathāgata, to attain to the fruit of conversion, to attain to the fruit of once returning, to attain to the fruit of never returning, to attain to saintship ? "

" Women are competent, Ānanda, if they retire from household life to the houseless one, under the Doctrine and Discipline announced by The Tathāgata, to attain to the fruit of conversion, to attain to the fruit of once returning, to attain to the fruit of never returning, to attain to saintship."

" Since, then, Reverend Sir, women are competent, if they retire from household life to the houseless one, under the Doctrine and Discipline announced by The Tathāgata, to attain to the fruit of conversion, to attain to the fruit of once returning, to attain 'to the fruit of never returning, to attain to saintship, consider, Reverend Sir, how great a benefactress Mahā-Pajāpatī the Gotamid has been. She is the sister of the mother of The Blessed One, and as foster-mother, nurse, and giver of milk, she suckled The Blessed One on the death of his mother. Pray, Reverend Sir, let women retire from household life to the houseless one, under the Doctrine and Discipline announced by The Tathāgata."

" If, Ānanda, Mahā-Pajāpatī the Gotamid will accept eight weighty regulations, let it be reckoned to her as her ordination : —

" A priestess of even a hundred years' standing shall salute, rise to meet, entreat humbly, and perform all respectful offices for a priest, even if he be but that day ordained. This regulation shall be honored, esteemed, revered, and worshiped, and is not to be transgressed as long as life shall last.

" A priestess shall not keep residence in a district where there are no priests. This regulation shall be honored, esteemed, revered, and worshiped, and is not to be transgressed as long as life shall last.

" On each half-month a priestess shall await from the congregation of the priests the appointing of fast-day, and some one to come and administer the admonition. This regulation shall be honored, esteemed, revered, and worshiped, and is not to be transgressed as long as life shall last.

" At the end of residence a priestess shall invite criticism in both congregations in regard to what has been seen, or heard, or suspected. This regulation shall be honored, esteemed, revered, and worshiped, and is not to be transgressed as long as life shall last.

"If a priestess be guilty of serious sin, she shall undergo penance of half a month toward both the congregations. This regulation shall be honored, esteemed, revered, and worshiped, and is not to be transgressed as long as life shall last.

"When a female novice has spent her two years in the practice of the six rules, she shall seek ordination from both the congregations. This regulation shall be honored, esteemed, revered, and worshiped, and is not to be transgressed as long as life shall last.

"A priestess shall not revile or abuse a priest in any manner. This regulation shall be honored, esteemed, revered, and worshiped, and is not to be transgressed as long as life shall last.

"From this day on the priestesses shall not be allowed to reprove the priests officially, but the priests shall be allowed to reprove the priestesses officially. This regulation shall be honored, esteemed, revered, and worshiped, and is not to be transgressed as long as life shall last.

"If, Ānanda, Mahā-Pajāpatī the Gotamid will accept these eight weighty regulations, let it be reckoned to her as her ordination."

Then the venerable Ānanda, when he had received from The Blessed One these eight weighty regulations, drew near to Mahā-Pajāpatī the Gotamid; and having drawn near, he spoke to Mahā-Pajāpatī the Gotamid as follows:

"If now, O Gotamid, you will accept eight weighty regulations, it shall be reckoned to you as your ordination : —

"A priestess of even a hundred years' standing shall salute, rise to meet, entreat humbly, and perform all respectful offices for a priest, even if he be but that day ordained. This regulation shall be honored, esteemed, revered, and worshiped, and is not to be transgressed as long as life shall last.

"A priestess shall not keep residence in a district where there are no priests. This regulation shall be honored, esteemed, revered, and worshiped, and is not to be transgressed as long as life shall last.

" On each half-month a priestess shall await from the congregation of the priests the appointing of fast-day, and some one to come and administer the admonition. This regulation shall be honored, esteemed, revered, and worshiped, and is not to be transgressed as long as life shall last.

" At the end of residence a priestess shall invite criticism in both congregations in regard to what has been seen, or heard, or suspected. This regulation shall be honored, esteemed, revered, and worshiped, and is not to be transgressed as long as life shall last.

" If a priestess be guilty of serious sin, she shall undergo penance of half a month toward both the congregations. This regulation shall be honored, esteemed, revered, and worshiped, and is not to be transgressed as long as life shall last.

" When a female novice has spent her two years in the practice of the six rules, she shall seek ordination from both the congregations. This regulation shall be honored, esteemed, revered, and worshiped, and is not to be transgressed as long as life shall last.

" A priestess shall not revile or abuse a priest in any manner. This regulation shall be honored, esteemed, revered, and worshiped, and is not to be transgressed as long as life shall last.

" From this day on the priestesses shall not be allowed to reprove the priests officially, but the priests shall be allowed to reprove the priestesses officially. This regulation shall be honored, esteemed, revered, and worshiped, and is not to be transgressed as long as life shall last.

" If now, O Gotamid, you will accept these eight weighty regulations, it shall be reckoned to you as your ordination."

" Just as, O Ānanda, reverend sir, a woman or a man, youthful, young, and fond of ornament, having bathed his head, and obtained a wreath of blue lotuses, or a wreath of jasmine flowers, or a wreath of atimuttaka flowers, would take it up with both hands, and place it on the head, the noblest part of the body; in exactly the same way do I, O Ānanda, reverend sir, take up these eight weighty regulations, not to be transgressed as long as life shall last."

Then the venerable Ānanda drew near to where The Blessed One was; and having drawn near and greeted The Blessed One, he sat down respectfully at one side. And seated respectfully at one side, the venerable Ānanda spoke to The Blessed One as follows:

"Mahā-Pajāpatī the Gotamid, Reverend Sir, has accepted the eight weighty regulations; the sister of the mother of The Blessed One has become ordained."

"If, Ānanda, women had not retired from household life to the houseless one, under the Doctrine and Discipline announced by The Tathāgata, religion, Ānanda, would long endure; a thousand years would the Good Doctrine abide. But since, Ānanda, women have now retired from household life to the houseless one, under the Doctrine and Discipline announced by The Tathāgata, not long, Ānanda, will religion endure; but five hundred years, Ānanda, will the Good Doctrine abide. Just as, Ānanda, those families which consist of many women and few men are easily overcome by burglars, in exactly the same way, Ānanda, when women retire from household life to the houseless one, under a doctrine and discipline, that religion does not long endure. Just as, Ananda, when the disease called mildew falls upon a flourishing field of rice, that field of rice does not long endure, in exactly the same way, Ānanda, when women retire from household life to the houseless one, under a doctrine and discipline, that religion does not long endure. Even as, Ānanda, when the disease called rust falls upon a flourishing field of sugar-cane, that field of sugar-cane does not long endure, in exactly the same way, Ānanda, when women retire from household life to the houseless one, under a doctrine and discipline, that religion does not long endure. And just as, Ānanda, to a large pond a man would prudently build a dike, in order that the water might not transgress its bounds, in exactly the same way, Ānanda, have I prudently laid down eight weighty regulations, not to be transgressed as long as life shall last."

§ 100. A FAMILY OF MAGICIANS.

Translated from the Mahā-Vagga (vi. 34¹).

Now at that time there dwelt in the city of Bhaddiya a householder named Meṇḍaka. And his magical power was such that if he bathed his head, had his granary swept out, and sat outside by the door, a shower of grain would fall from the sky and fill the granary. Of his wife the magical power was such that if she sat down by a pint-pot of boiled rice and a dish of sauce and curry, she could serve a meal to the slaves and serving-men; and as long as she did not get up, the food was not exhausted. Of the son the magical power was such that with only a purse of a thousand pieces of money he could pay six months' wages to the slaves and serving-men; and as long as the purse was in his hand, the money was not exhausted. Of the daughter-in-law the magical power was such that if she sat down by a four-bushel basket, she could give six months' rations of rice to the slaves and serving-men; and as long as she did not get up, the rice was not exhausted. Of the slave the magical power was such that with one plow he could plow seven furrows at once.

And it came to the ears of Seniya Bimbisāra, king of Magadha:

"They say that in the city of Bhaddiya, which is in our territory, there dwells a householder named Meṇḍaka. And his magical power is such that if he bathes his head, has his granary swept out, and sits outside by the door, a shower of grain will fall from the sky and fill the granary. Of his wife the magical power is such that if she sits down by a pint-pot of boiled rice, and a dish of sauce and curry, she can serve a meal to the slaves and serving-men; and as long as she does not get up, the food is not exhausted. Of the son the magical power is such that with only a purse of a thousand pieces of money he can pay six months' wages to the slaves and serving-men; and as long as the purse is in his hand, the money is not exhausted. Of the daughter-in-law the magical power is such that if she sits down by a four-bushel basket, she can give six months' rations of rice to the slaves and serving-men; and as long as she does not get up, the rice is not exhausted. Of the slave the magical power is such that with one plow he can plow seven furrows at once."

Then Seniya Bimbisāra, king of Magadha, said to a certain minister who had charge of general affairs:

"Look you now! They say that in the city of Bhaddiya, which is in our territory, there dwells a householder named Meṇḍaka. And his magical power is such that if he bathes his head, has his granary swept out, and sits outside by the door, a shower of grain will fall from the sky and fill the granary. Of his wife the magical power is such that if she sits down by a pint-pot of boiled rice and a dish of sauce and curry, she can serve a meal to the slaves and serving-men; and as long as she does not get up, the food is not exhausted. Of the son the magical power is such that with only a purse of a thousand pieces of money he can pay six months' wages to the slaves and serving-men; and as long as the purse is in his hand, the money is not exhausted. Of the daughter-in-law the magical power is such that if she sits down by a four-bushel basket, she can give six months' rations of rice to the slaves and serving-men; and as long as she does not get up, the rice is not exhausted. Of the slave the magical power is such that with one plow he can plow seven furrows at once. Look you now! Go and find out about this. When you have seen this magical power, it will be as if I myself had seen it."

"Yes, sire," said the minister to Seniya Bimbisāra, king of Magadha, in assent, and set out with a fourfold army in the direction of Bhaddiya. And going from place to place, he drew near to Bhaddiya, and to where Meṇḍaka the householder was; and having drawn near, he spoke to Meṇḍaka the householder as follows:

"I, O householder, have been commanded by the king, as follows: 'Look you now! They say that in the city of Bhaddiya, which is in our territory, there dwells a householder named Meṇḍaka. And his magical power is such that if he bathes his head, has his granary swept out, and sits outside by the door, a shower of grain will fall from the sky and fill the granary. Of his wife the magical power is such that if she sits down by a pint-pot of boiled rice and a dish of sauce and curry, she can serve a meal to the slaves and serving-men; and as long as she does not get up, the food is not exhausted. Of the son the magical power is such that with only a purse of a thousand pieces of money he can pay six months' wages to the slaves and serving-men; and as long as the purse is in his hand, the money is not exhausted. Of the daughter-in-law the magical power is such that if she sits down by a four-bushel basket, she can give six months' rations of rice to the slaves and serving-men; and as long as she does not get up, the rice is not exhausted. Of the slave the magical power is such that with one plow he can plow seven furrows at once. Look you now! Go and find out about this. When you have seen this magical power, it will be as if I myself had seen it.' Let us see, O householder, your magical power."

Then Meṇḍaka the householder bathed his head, had his granary swept out, and sat outside by the door, and a shower of grain fell from the sky and filled the granary.

"We have seen, O householder, your magical power. We will see that of your wife."

Then Meṇḍaka the householder commanded his wife:

"Serve, then, the fourfold army with food."

Then the wife of Meṇḍaka the householder sat down by a pint-pot of boiled rice and a dish of sauce and curry, and served a meal to the fourfold army; and as long as she did not get up, the food was not exhausted.

"We have seen, O householder, the magical power of your wife. We will see that of your son."

Then Meṇḍaka the householder commanded his son:

"Pay, then, my child, six months' wages to the army."

Then the son of Meṇḍaka, with only a purse of a thousand pieces of money, paid six months' wages to the fourfold army; and as long as the purse was in his hand, the money was not exhausted.

"We have seen, O householder, the magical power of your son. We will see that of your daughter-in-law."

Then Meṇḍaka the householder commanded his daughter-in-law:

"Give, then, six months' rations of rice to the fourfold army."

Then the daughter-in-law of Meṇḍaka the householder sat down by a four-bushel basket, and gave six months' rations of rice to the fourfold army; and as long as she did not get up, the rice was not exhausted.

"We have seen, O householder, the magical power of your daughter-in-law. We will see that of your slave."

"Sir, the magical power of my slave is to be seen in the field."

"Enough, O householder; we have seen the magical power of your slave."

Then the minister returned to Rājagaha with the fourfold army, and drew near to where Seniya Bimbisāra, king of Magadha, was; and having drawn near, he told the matter to Seniya Bimbisāra, king of Magadha.

---

§ 101. THE STORY OF VISĀKHĀ.

Translated from the Dhammapada, and from Buddhaghosa's comment.

> 53.   "As flowers in rich profusion piled
> Will many a garland furnish forth;
> So all the years of mortal man
> Should fruitful be in all good works."

"*As flowers in rich profusion piled.*" This doctrinal instruction was given by The Teacher while dwelling near Sāvatthi in Eastern Monastery; and it was concerning Visākhā, a female lay disciple. She was born, we are told, in the city of Bhaddiya, in the kingdom of Bengal. Her father Dhanañjaya, son of Meṇḍaka[1] the treasurer, ranked

---

[1] Identical with the Meṇḍaka of the last selection.

also as treasurer, and her mother was the lady Sumanā, his principal wife.

When Visākhā was seven years old, The Teacher, perceiving that the Brahman Sela, and others of her city, were competent to attain to salvation, went thither on his wanderings, accompanied by a great congregation of priests.

Now at that time Meṇḍaka, who was filling the office of treasurer in that city, was head of a household of five persons of great merit. The five persons of great merit were: Meṇḍaka the treasurer; Padumā, his principal wife; Dhanañjaya, his eldest son; the latter's wife, Sumanā; and Meṇḍaka's slave, Puṇṇa. Now Meṇḍaka the treasurer was not the only person of illimitable wealth in Bimbisāra's territory. There were five of them: Jotiya, Jaṭila, Meṇḍaka, Puṇṇaka, Kākavaḷiya.

When Meṇḍaka the treasurer heard of the arrival of The One Possessing the Ten Forces, he sent for the little maid Visākhā, the daughter of his son Dhanañjaya the treasurer, and said to her,

"Dear girl, this is an auspicious day for you and for me! With your five hundred girl-attendants mount five hundred chariots, and with these five hundred female slaves as your retinue go to welcome The One Possessing the Ten Forces."

"Very well," said she, and did so. But as she well knew what etiquette required, when she had gone as far in her carriage as was proper for carriages to go, she alighted, and on foot drew near to The Teacher. Then she did him obeisance, and stood respectfully at one side. Pleased with her behavior, The Teacher taught her the Doctrine, and at the end of the discourse, she attained to the fruit of conversion, together with her five hundred maidens.

Also Meṇḍaka the treasurer drew near to The Teacher, and listening to a sermon, attained to the fruit of conversion, and invited him for the morrow to breakfast. On the next day at his own house he served The Buddha and the congregation of the priests with excellent food, both hard and soft; and thus for half a month he gave liberally. And when The Teacher had stopped in the city of Bhaddiya as long as he wished, he departed.

Now at that time Bimbisāra and Pasenadi the Kosalan were connected by marriage, being each of them the husband of the other's sister. And one day it occurred to the Kosalan king: "In Bimbisāra's territory dwell five men of illimitable wealth, while there is not one in mine. Suppose, now, I go to Bimbisāra, and ask him for one of these persons of great merit."

And going to king Bimbisāra, he was received cordially by the latter, who then asked,

"What was your purpose in coming?"

"In your territory dwell five men of illimitable wealth, persons of great merit. I have come with the intention of taking one of them back with me. Let me have one."

"It would be impossible for me to move one of those great families."

"I will not go without," was the reply.

The king took counsel with his ministers, and then said to him:

"To move such powerful personages as Joti and the others, would be like moving the world. But Meṇḍaka the great treasurer has a son called Dhanañjaya the treasurer: I will consult with him, and then give you my reply."

Then Bimbisāra sent for Dhanañjaya the treasurer, and said to him,

"Dear friend, the king of the Kosalans says he will not return home unless you go with him. Therefore, go with him, pray."

"Sire, I will go, if you send me."

"Then make your preparations, dear friend, and go."

So he got himself ready, and the king was full of kind attentions to him, and at parting formally intrusted him to Pasenadi the king. And Pasenadi the king set out for Sāvatthi, intending to spend one night on the way. And coming to a pleasant spot, they bivouacked there.

Then said Dhanañjaya the treasurer,

"Whose territory are we on now?"

"Mine, O treasurer."

"How far is it from here to Sāvatthi?"

" Seven leagues."

" It is very crowded in a city, and my suite is a large one. Sire, if it so please you, I will dwell here."

" Very good," said the king in assent; and mapping out for him a city, he gave it to him, and went away. And from the circumstance that the settlement in that place was made in the evening [sā-yaṁ], the city received the name of Sāketa.

Now there was dwelling at Sāvatthi a young man named Puṇṇavaḍḍhana, who was the son of a treasurer named Migāra, and had just come of age. And his mother and father said to him,

" Son, choose yourself a wife from what family you please."

" Oh! I have no use for anything of that sort."

" Son, act not so! No family can last without children."

" Well, then," said he, when they continually insisted, " if I can have a girl endowed with the five beauties, I will do as you say."

" But, son, what are these five beauties?"

" Beauty of hair; beauty of flesh; beauty of bone; beauty of skin; and beauty of youth."

(The hair of a woman who is experiencing the reward of great merit is like a peacock's tail, and, when it is loosened and allowed to fall, reaches to the bottom of the tunic, where the ends turn and point upwards. This is " Beauty of hair." The lips are of a fine color, resembling a bright red gourd, and are smooth and pleasant to the touch. This is " Beauty of flesh." The teeth are white, with even interstices, resembling a row of diamonds set upright, or evenly cut mother-of-pearl. This is " Beauty of bone." The skin, even without the application of sandal-wood perfume, or any rouge, or other cosmetic, is glossy like a blue-lotus wreath, and white like a wreath of kaṇikāra flowers. This is " Beauty of skin." She possesses a youthfulness as fresh when she has brought forth ten times, as if she had brought forth but once. This is " Beauty of youth.")

Then his mother and father invited and entertained one hundred and eight Brahmans, and inquired of them,

" Are there any women endowed with the five beauties ? "

" Assuredly there are."

" Then let eight of you go in search of a girl of this description."

And giving them a liberal present, they continued : " When you return, we will remember you again. Go, search for a girl of this description, and as soon as you find her, put on her this decoration." And with that they placed in their hands a gold wreath worth a hundred thousand pieces of money, and dismissed them.

So the eight Brahmans went searching through all the large cities, but discovered no girl endowed with the five beauties. Then they turned back, and as they were returning, they chanced to arrive at Sāketa on Public Day. " Now," thought they, " our mission will be effected."

It seems that every year in that city there was held a festival called " Public Day." Then all those ladies who are not in the habit of going out of doors issue forth from their homes with their attendants, and show themselves in public, going on foot to the banks of the river. And on the same day they do this, all the rich men's sons of the warrior and other castes station themselves alongside the paths in order to put garlands on the heads of any pretty girl they may see of equal rank with themselves.

And these Brahmans came also, and stationed themselves in a hall on the banks of the river. At that moment Visākhā, then some fifteen or sixteen years of age, came to that place on her way to bathe in the river, being decked in all her ornaments, and attended by five hundred maidens. And suddenly a cloud arose, and it began to rain. The five hundred maidens took to running, and sought refuge in the hall. The Brahmans scanned them carefully, but saw not one among them endowed with the five beauties. Then Visākhā came up at her natural gait, and entered the hall, and her garments and ornaments were wet.

The Brahmans perceived that she had four of the beauties, and being desirous of seeing her teeth, they began conversing among themselves, saying,

"Our daughter is of a lazy disposition; her husband, we must needs suppose, will have to content himself with sour gruel."

Then said Visākhā, "What is that you are saying?"

"Dear girl, we say thus and so."

(They say the sound of her voice was sweet, sounding forth like the tones of a gong of bell-metal.)

Then with a sweet voice, she asked them again,

"Why do you say that?"

"Your attendant women came running to this hall, and did not get their garments or their ornaments wet. But though it is but a little way, you did not run at all, and got your garments and ornaments wet. This is why we speak as we do."

"Good sirs, say not so. I am better able to run than they; but I had my reasons for not running."

"What were they, dear girl?"

"Good sirs, there are four things which do not appear to advantage when running. And there is another reason."

"Dear girl, what are the four things?"

"Good sirs, an anointed and richly dressed king does not appear to advantage when he binds up his loin-cloth, and runs in the royal court. Every one finds fault, saying, 'How is it this great king rushes around like any householder?' He appears to advantage when walking at a slow gait. The king's caparisoned state elephant does not appear to advantage when running. He appears to advantage when marching at an elephant's natural dignified pace. A man who has retired from the world does not appear to advantage when running. Every one finds fault, saying, 'How is it this monk rushes about like any layman?' He appears to advantage when adopting a tranquil gait. No woman appears to advantage when running. People justly find fault with her, saying, 'How is it this woman rushes about like a man?' These four do not appear to advantage when running."

"But what, dear girl, was your other reason?"

"Good sirs, a daughter is brought up by her mother and father, who put a value on every limb in her body. For we are goods for sale. They bring us up in order to marry us into another family. If we should run and stumble, either over our skirts or over some obstacle on the ground, and in falling should break either a hand or a foot, we should remain as burdens on our families. But articles of ornament, if they get wet, can dry. This, good sirs, was my reason for not running."

All the while she was talking, the Brahmans were beholding the splendor of her teeth, such splendor as they felt they had never seen before. And having applauded her speech, they took the gold wreath, and placed it on her head, and said:

"You, dear girl, are the one whom this befits."

Then she asked them: "Good sirs, from what city are you come?"

"From Sāvatthi, dear girl."

"The treasurer, the head of the family, what is his name?"

"His name, dear girl, is Migāra the treasurer."

"And my young master, what is his name?"

"He is the young Puṇṇavaḍḍhana, dear girl."

Having thus ascertained that the family was of equal caste to her own, she sent a message to her father to send the chariot. For although she had come on foot, it is not allowed to maidens to return in that manner when once they have been decorated with the wreath. The daughters of influential families return in chariots and the like; others, either mount ordinary carriages, or walk under a palm-leaf parasol, or, if that is lacking, they raise the skirts of their cloaks and throw them over their shoulders. In the present instance, her father sent her five hundred chariots, and she and her attendants mounted and returned home, while the Brahmans accompanied them.

Then said the treasurer to the Brahmans,

"Whence are ye come?"

"From Sāvatthi, great treasurer."

"The treasurer, what is his name?"

"Migāra the treasurer."

" What is the son's name ? "

" Young Puṇṇavaḍḍhana."

" The riches, how great are the riches ? "

" Four hundred millions, great treasurer."

" His riches, by the side of ours, are but as a farthing. However, from the time one obtains a protector for a maiden, why look for anything else ? " Thus he gave his consent.

After a day or two of hospitable entertainment, he dismissed them. And they returned to Sāvatthi, and announced to Migāra the treasurer:

" We have found the girl."

" Whose daughter is she ? "

" Dhanañjaya the treasurer's."

" That is a powerful personage whose daughter you have secured for us. We must go quickly to fetch her." Then he went and announced to the king the circumstances of the case, and that he must needs absent himself for a while.

And the king thought to himself : " This is the great personage whom I removed from before Bimbisāra and settled in Sāketa. I ought to pay him some attention." And he said to Migāra the treasurer,

" I, too, will go."

" Very good, sire," replied the other, and sent the following message to Dhanañjaya the treasurer: " When I come, the king will come also, and the king's army is large. Shall you be able to take care of so many people, or not ? "

The return message came : " Let ten kings come, if they wish."

Then Migāra the treasurer took all the inhabitants of that large city, leaving barely enough to guard the houses, and when he had come within half a league of Sāketa, he halted, and sent a message announcing his arrival.

Then Dhanañjaya the treasurer, after sending out to them a large present, consulted with his daughter :

" My dear," said he, " I hear that your father-in-law has come with the king of the Kosalans. Which house shall we get ready for him, which for the king, and which ones for the deputy kings ? "

Now clever was the treasurer's daughter, with a fully matured and keen intellect, the result of longing expressed and aspiration cherished through a hundred thousand world-cycles. And she gave orders: "Let such and such a house be got ready for my father-in-law, such another for the king, and such others for the deputy kings." After making these arrangements, she next summoned the slaves and servants, and said to them: "Let so many of you wait on the king, and so many on the deputy kings; and do you who are hostlers and the like take care of the elephants, horses, and other beasts; for our guests must have a merry time while they are here." Such were her orders. And why? So that none might say: "We came to Visākhā's merrymaking and got nothing for our pains, but spent our time looking after our beasts."

That same day, Visākhā's father sent for five hundred goldsmiths, and giving them a thousand nikkhas of red gold, besides silver, gems, pearls, coral, diamonds, etc., enough to go with it, he said: "Make for my daughter what is called the great creeper parure."

After remaining a few days, the king sent a message to Dhanañjaya the treasurer, saying,

"It is too great a load for a simple treasurer to feed and take care of us. Be pleased to appoint a time for the maiden's departure."

But Dhanañjaya the treasurer returned word to the king:

"The rainy season is now come, and you can well afford to remain four months. Let everything pertaining to your army be my care. It will be time enough for your majesty to go when I dismiss you."

From that time on it was like a continual festival for the city of Sāketa. From the king down, every one was provided with garlands, perfumes, garments, and other gifts, so that each one felt himself the especial object of the treasurer's hospitality.

Thus three months went by, but the parure was not yet finished.

Then came the masters of ceremonies, and announced to the treasurer:

" There is no lack of anything else, but the army has not
sufficient wood to cook its meals."

" Go, my dear sirs, take all the tumble-down elephant
stables, and other buildings of the kind in the city, and all
the dilapidated houses, and use them for cooking-fuel."

This wood did the cooking for half a month, and thereupon they again announced to the treasurer:

" There is no wood."

" At this time in the year one cannot go for wood. But
open the store-houses where stuffs are kept, and make wicks
of the coarse cloths, dip them in vessels of oil, and so cook
your meals."

They did so for half a month, and thus four months had
gone by, and the parure was finished. There was no thread
in this parure; silver was used instead. When this parure
was on, it extended from head to foot. At the latter place
were bunches of gold medals, and silver dies. On the crown
of the head was a medal, at the top of the ears two, at the
throat one, at the knees two, at the elbows two, and at the
sides of the waist two.

Now a part of this parure consisted of a peacock, and
there were five hundred feathers of red gold in the wing on
the right side, and five hundred in the one on the left side.
The beak was of coral, the eyes were of jewels, and likewise
the neck and the tail-feathers. The midribs of the feathers
were of silver, and likewise the shanks of the legs. When
placed in position on Visākhā's head, it appeared like a peacock dancing on the summit of a mountain, and the sound
which came from the thousand midribs rolled forth like the
tones of celestial choruses and orchestras. And it was only
when people had come quite close that they knew it was not
a real peacock.

This parure was worth ninety millions, and a hundred
thousand was spent on the workmanship. But what was the
deed in a previous existence which caused her to obtain this
parure? They say that in the time of Kassapa Buddha she
gave cloth for robes to twenty thousand priests, also thread
and needles and dyeing material, all her own property; and

the parure was the result of this liberality. For the giving of robes by a woman attains its fruition in the great creeper parure; by a man, in the supernatural bowl and robes.

When the great treasurer had thus spent four months in getting ready his daughter's trousseau, he began giving her the dowry. He gave five hundred carts full of money, five hundred carts full of gold dishes, five hundred full of silver dishes, five hundred full of copper dishes, five hundred full of silk garments, five hundred full of clarified butter, five hundred full of husked rice, and five hundred full of plow-shares and other implements. They say the reason why he thus gave her all manner of implements was for fear that his daughter in her new home might need something, and be obliged to send to a neighbor's for it. And he gave fifteen hundred waiting-maids whose duties were to bathe, feed, and dress her, — all of them handsome slaves, and richly dressed, and riding in five hundred chariots, three to each several chariot.

Then he determined to give his daughter some cattle, and gave orders to his men:

"Look you now! Go and open the door of my lesser cattle-fold, and post yourselves for a distance of three quarters of a league, and at every quarter-league have a drum. And let the space across from side to side be a hundred and forty cubits, and let not the cows transgress those limits. And as soon as you get them in position, sound your drums."

They did so. When the cows passed out of the fold, and had gone a quarter-league, the men gave a signal with the drum, and again at the end of the second quarter-league, and again at the third quarter-league. And they hemmed them in at the sides. Thus, for a space of three-quarters of a league in length, and a hundred and forty cubits across, the cows stood so close that they chafed one another.

Then said the great treasurer, "That is enough cows for my daughter. Shut the door." So they shut the door of the fold; but, notwithstanding the door was shut, such was the effect of Visākhā's merit that the vigorous bulls and the milch cows leaped up and got out. And·in spite of all the men could do to prevent them, sixty thousand vigorous bulls and sixty thousand milch cows got out, and behind the milch cows followed vigorous bull calves.

What was the deed in a previous existence by reason of which the cattle thus got out? Because once she kept on giving, in spite of the efforts people made to stop her. As tradition has it, in the time of The Supreme Buddha Kassapa, she was the youngest of the seven daughters of king Kiki, and her name was Servant-of-the-Congregation. And as she was once giving the five products of the cow in alms to twenty thousand priests, the young priests and the novices cried, " Enough, enough! " and closed their hands up tight. But, notwithstanding their efforts to prevent her, she kept on giving, saying, " Here is a sweet bit; here is a dainty morsel." This was the reason the cattle kept on coming out, notwithstanding the efforts made to prevent them.

When the treasurer had got thus far in his giving, his wife said to him,

" You have assigned goods to my daughter, but no male and female vassals to do her bidding. Why is this ? "

" Because I want to find out who are fond of her, and who are not. Of course, I shall send vassals with her to do her bidding. When she comes to mount her chariot to depart, I shall make proclamation : ' Let all who wish to go with my daughter, do so; and let all others stay at home.' "

Now the day before she was to depart, the treasurer sat in his room and had his daughter sit by him, and he admonished her, telling her what rules of conduct she should adopt when she came to dwell in her husband's family. And it happened that Migāra the treasurer was seated in the next room, and overheard the admonition of Dhanañjaya the treasurer, which was as follows :

" My child, as long as you dwell in your father-in-law's family, the in-door fire is not to be taken out of doors ; outdoor fire is not to be brought within doors ; give only to him who gives ; give not to him who does not give ; give both to him who gives, and to him who does not give ; sit happily; eat happily; sleep happily; wait upon the fire; and reverence the household divinities." This was the tenfold admonition.

On the next day he assembled the different guilds of artisans, and in the presence of the royal army he appointed eight householders to be sponsors for his daughter, saying, "You are to try any charge of sin that may be brought against my daughter in her new home." Next he had his daughter put on her great creeper parure that was worth ninety millions, and gave her besides five hundred and forty millions with which to buy aromatic powders for her bath. And causing her to mount a chariot, he took her about in the neighborhood of Sāketa as far as to Anurādhapura, through fourteen villages that were subject to him; and as he went through one after another, he caused proclamation to be made: "Let all who wish to go with my daughter, go." On hearing the proclamation, all the inhabitants of the fourteen villages, without exception, issued forth, saying, "When our mistress is on the point of leaving, why stay we here?" Then Dhanañjaya the treasurer, full of polite attentions to the king and Migāra the treasurer, accompanied them a short distance on their way; and having intrusted his daughter into their hands, he there took leave of them.

And Migāra the treasurer rode in a conveyance behind the others, and beholding a great crowd of people following, he asked,

"Pray, who are these?"

"They are male and female vassals to do the bidding of your daughter-in-law."

"Who could ever feed so many? Beat and drive them away, and keep only those who do not run."

"Hold!" cried Visākhā; "do not drive them away! The one army can feed the other."

But the treasurer persisted, saying, "My dear girl, we have no use for them. Who is there to feed them?" And he caused his men to fling clods of earth at them, and to beat them with sticks, and all those who did not run he took with him, saying, "These are a plenty."

When Visākhā approached the gate of the city of Sāvatthi, she began to reflect, "Shall I enter seated in a
covered conveyance, or standing erect in a chariot?" Then
she thought, "If I am in a covered conveyance when I enter,
no one will see the elegance of my great creeper parure."
So she entered the city standing in her chariot, and showing
herself to the whole town. And when the inhabitants of
Sāvatthi beheld the magnificence of Visākhā, they said,
"This, then, is Visākhā. Truly, her magnificence becomes
her well!" And thus it was in great pomp she entered the
treasurer's house.

Then all the inhabitants of the city sent gifts to her,
according to their power, and according to their ability;
for they thought, "Dhanañjaya the treasurer was exceedingly hospitable to us when we went to his city." But
Visākhā took all the gifts that were sent her, and distrib-
uted them to the different families everywhere throughout
the city. And in sending, she accompanied each gift with an
affectionate message: "This is for my mother, this for my
father, this for my brother, and this for my sister;" thus
treating each one according to age, and making, as it were,
all the inhabitants of the city her relatives.

Now towards the end of the night, her thoroughbred
mare gave birth to a foal. And Visākhā, accompanied by
her female slaves bearing torches, went to the stable, and
superintended while they washed the mare with warm water,
and anointed her with oil. Then she returned to her own
quarters.

Now Migāra the treasurer had for a long time been favorably disposed to the sect of naked ascetics. And urged by
this feeling, though The Buddha was dwelling in a neighbor-
ing monastery, he neglected him in the festivities of his son's
wedding, but determined to do the naked ascetics an honor.
So, on a certain day, he had some rice porridge cooked in
several hundred new dishes, and extended an invitation to
five hundred of the unclothed. And when he had got them
all into his house, he sent a message to Visākhā, saying,
"Let my daughter-in-law come and do reverence to the
saints."

When Visākhā heard the word "saints" she was greatly delighted, for she had been converted, and was a noble disciple. But when she came to the place where they were eating, and beheld them, she was angry with the treasurer, and returned to her own quarters, saying reproachfully, "These persons so devoid of shame and fear of sinning cannot be saints. Why did my father-in-law have me summoned?"

When the unclothed caught sight of her, they all with one mouth reproached the treasurer:

"Why, O householder, did you not find some one else for a daughter-in-law? You have introduced into your house an arrant misfortune-breeder, a disciple of the monk Gotama. Make haste and have her expelled from the house."

"It is out of the question," thought the treasurer, "for me to expel her just because these men tell me to do so. She is from too powerful a family." And he dismissed them, saying,

"Your reverences, young people sometimes act without knowing what they are about. Hold your peace!"

Then he sat down on a costly seat, and began to eat the sweet rice porridge from a golden bowl. At that moment a [Buddhist] elder on his begging rounds entered the house. Visākhā was standing fanning her father-in-law, and saw him. And thinking, "It would not be fitting for me to announce him to my father-in-law," she moved off in such a way as to call his attention to the elder. But the foolish, unconverted man, although he saw the elder, made as if he did not see him, and with head bent down, he kept on eating.

"Pass on, reverend sir," said Visākhā, when she perceived that her father-in-law made no sign, notwithstanding he had seen the elder; "my father-in-law is eating stale fare."

The treasurer, although he had borne with the talk of the naked ascetics, the moment she said, "He is eating stale fare," removed his hand from his bowl, and exclaimed,

"Take away this rice porridge, and turn the girl out of the house! To think that she should accuse *me*, and in a time of festivity, too, of eating anything unclean!"

But all the slaves and servants in the house belonged to Visākhā. Who was there to seize her by hand or foot? There was not one who dared so much as open his mouth.

"Father," said Visākhā, after listening to him; "I'll not leave so easily as you seem to think. I am not a common prostitute, picked up at some river bathing-place; and daughters whose parents are still living are not turned off so easily. Now my father has provided for this very case. When I was starting to come hither, he summoned eight householders, and put me in their charge, saying, 'If any charge of sin be made against my daughter, investigate it.' Have these men summoned, and establish my guilt or innocence."

"She speaks well," said the treasurer, and had the eight householders summoned.

Said he: "This young girl, when I was seated, in a time of festivity, eating rice porridge from a golden bowl, said I was eating what was unclean. Find her guilty and turn her out."

"Dear girl, is it so, as he says?"

"That is not as *I* say: — but when a certain elder on his begging-rounds came and stood in the door-way, my father-in-law, who was eating sweet rice porridge, paid no attention to him. Then I thought: 'My father-in-law is not acquiring any merit in this existence, but is consuming old, stale merit.' So I said: 'Pass on, reverend sir; my father-in-law is eating stale fare.' Now, what fault is there here of mine?"

"There is none. Our daughter speaks justly. Why are you angry with her?"

"Sirs, granted that this is no fault: but one night in the middle watch, she went out behind the house, accompanied by her male and female slaves."

"Dear girl, is it so, as he says?"

"Good sirs, I went for no other reason but that I thought when a thoroughbred mare was bringing forth in this very house, it would not do to sit still and make no sign. So I had my slave-girls take torches, and went and caused the mare to receive the attentions suitable for a time of foaling."

"Sir, our daughter does in your house work that is unfit even for slave-girls. What fault can you discover here?"

" Sirs, granted that here also there is no fault. Her father, however, was admonishing her at the time she was starting to come hither, and gave her ten admonitions of a deeply hidden meaning; and I do not understand them. Let her tell me their meaning. For instance, her father said, ' The in-door fire is not to be taken out of doors.' Is it possible, pray, for us to get on with our neighbors, without ever sending fire to their households ? ''

" Is it so, as he says, dear girl ? "

" Good sirs, my father did not mean that by what he said; but this is what he meant : ' Dear girl, if you notice any fault in your mother-in-law, or your father-in-law, or your husband, do not tell of it outside in some one else's house. There is no worse fire than this.' "

" Sirs, so be it : but her father said : ' Out-door fire is not to be brought within doors.' Would it be possible, if our in-door fire were to go out, for us not to fetch fire from out-side ? "

" Is it so, as he says, dear girl ? "

" Good sirs, my father did not mean that by what he said; but this is what he meant : ' If any of your neighbors, whether male or female, speak ill of your father-in-law, or of your husband, do not bring their talk home, and repeat it saying, " So and so has this or that to say of you." For there is no fire comparable to this fire.' "

Thus, in this point also she was guiltless. And as in this case, so also in the others; and the following is their purport : —

When her father said to her : " Give only to him who gives," he meant, " Give only to those who give borrowed articles back again."

And " Give not to him who does not give," meant, " Give not to those who do not give back again what they borrow."

" Give both to him who gives, and to him who does not give," meant, " When your needy relatives and friends come to you, you should give to them, whether they are able to repay you or not."

" Sit happily," meant, " When you see your mother-in-law,

or your father-in-law, or your husband, you should rise, and not keep your seat."

"Eat happily," meant, "You should not eat before your mother-in-law, or your father-in-law, or your husband. You must eat after you have waited on them, and they have been helped to everything they wish."

"Sleep happily," meant, "Do not ascend your couch to lie down to sleep before your mother-in-law, or your father-in-law, or your husband; but when you have done for them all the different services which should be done, you can afterwards yourself lie down to sleep."

"Wait upon the fire," meant, "You should look upon your mother-in-law, your father-in-law, and your husband, as if they were a flame of fire, or a royal serpent."

"Reverence the household divinities," meant, "You should look upon your mother-in-law, your father-in-law, and your husband, as your divinities."

When thus the treasurer had heard the meaning of the ten admonitions, he was unable to find any reply, and sat with downcast eyes. The householders then said to him,

"Treasurer, is there any other sin in our daughter?"

"Sirs, there is none."

"Then, if she is guiltless, why did you attempt without cause to turn her out of doors?"

"Good sirs," said Visākhā, at this point in the discussion, "although at first it was not fitting that I should leave at the command of my father-in-law, yet now that you whom my father appointed to try charges which might be brought against me, have found me guiltless, it is a good time to go."

So saying, she gave orders to her male and female slaves to get ready the carriages and make the other necessary preparations.

"Dear girl, I spoke in ignorance; pardon me," said then the treasurer, speaking half to the householders.

"Good sir, I do pardon you all there is to pardon. I am, however, daughter in a family that has studied and has faith in the religion of The Buddha, and to see something of the congregation of the priests is necessary to us. If I can be allowed to wait on the congregation of the priests at my pleasure, I will stay."

" Dear girl, wait on your monks as much as you please," was the reply.

Visākhā, accordingly, sent an invitation to The One Possessing the Ten Forces, and on the next day received him at her house. And the naked monks, when they heard that The Teacher had gone to the house of Migāra the treasurer, went also, and sat down outside the house encompassing it. Visākhā, having given the water of donation, sent a message to her father-in-law :

" All the arrangements for the entertainment are ready. Let my father-in-law come and wait on The One Possessing the Ten Forces."

But as he was about to go, the naked ascetics restrained him, saying,

" O householder, go not near the monk Gotama."

So he sent back word: " Let my daughter-in-law wait on him herself."

When she had waited on The Buddha and on the congregation of the priests that followed him, and the meal was now at an end, she again sent a message :

" Let my father-in-law come and hear the sermon."

" If I were not to go now, it would not do at all," said then the treasurer; for he was very desirous of hearing the Doctrine.

" Well, then," said the naked monks, when they saw he was bent on going, " you may listen to the Doctrine of the monk Gotama, if you will sit outside of a curtain." Then they went ahead of him, and drew a curtain around, and he went and sat down outside of the curtain.

But The Teacher thought, " Sit outside of a curtain, if you will, or beyond a wall, or beyond a mountain, or at the end of the world. I am The Buddha, and can make you hear my voice." And marching as it were with a mighty Jambu trunk held aloft, and showering down as it were showers of ambrosia, he began to teach the Doctrine in consecutive discourse.

Now when a Supreme Buddha teaches the Doctrine, those in front, and those behind, and those beyond a hundred or a thousand worlds, and those, even, who inhabit the abode of the Sublime Gods, exclaim: "The Teacher is looking at me; The Teacher is teaching the Doctrine to me." To each one it seems as if The Teacher were beholding and addressing him alone. The Buddhas, they say, resemble the moon: as the moon in the midst of the heavens appears to every living being as if over his head, so The Buddhas appear to every one as if standing in front of him. This gift is said to be their reward for liberality in previous existences, when, for the benefit of others, they cut off their own garlanded heads, gouged out their own eyes, tore out their own hearts, and gave away to be slaves sons such as Jāli, daughters such as Kanhājinā, and wives such as Maddī.

And Migāra the treasurer, as he sat outside the curtain, and turned over and over in his mind the teaching of The Tathāgata, became established in the thousandfold ornamented fruit of conversion, and acquired an immovable and unquestioning faith in the three refuges. Then, raising the curtain, he approached his daughter-in-law, and taking her breast in his hand, he said: "From this day forth you are my mother," thus giving her the position of mother. And henceforth she was known as "Migāra's mother;" and when, later on, she had a son, she named him Migāra.

The great treasurer then let go his daughter-in-law's breast, and went and fell at the feet of The Blessed One, and stroking them with his hands, and kissing them with his lips, he three times proclaimed his own name, "Reverend Sir, I am Migāra."

"Reverend Sir," continued he, "all this time have I been without knowing that on you should one bestow alms to obtain great reward. But now I have learnt it, thanks to my daughter-in-law, and am released from all danger of being reborn in a lower state of existence. Truly, it was for my advantage and for my welfare that my daughter-in-law came to my house." So saying, he pronounced the following stanza:

> " Now have I learnt where rich reward
> Will surely follow every gift !
> Truly a happy day for me,
> When first my daughter sought my home ! "

Visākhā invited The Teacher again for the next day on her own account, and on the day after her mother-in-law also attained to the fruit of conversion. And henceforth that house kept open doors for the religion of The Buddha.

Then thought the treasurer, " My daughter-in-law is a great benefactress to me; I must make her a present. And, truly, her present parure is too heavy for every-day wear. I will have a very light one made, which she can wear both by day and by night in all the four postures."

And he had made what is called a highly polished parure, worth a thousand pieces of money: and when it was finished, he invited The Buddha and the congregation of the priests, and assiduously waited on them at breakfast. And causing Visākhā to bathe herself with sixteen pitcherfuls of perfumed water, he placed her in front of The Teacher, and putting her parure upon her, he had her do obeisance. Then The Teacher, after giving thanks for the repast, returned to the monastery.

And Visākhā continued to give alms, and do other deeds of merit, and she received the eight boons from The Teacher. And as the crescent of the moon waxes great in the sky, so did she increase in sons and daughters. They say she had ten sons and ten daughters, and of these each had ten sons and ten daughters, and of these also each had ten sons and ten daughters. Thus the children and children's children which had sprung from her numbered eight thousand and four hundred and twenty persons.

She lived to be a hundred and twenty years old, but there was not a single gray hair on her head, — always she appeared as if about sixteen. When people saw her on her way to the monastery, surrounded by her children and children's children, there were always those who inquired: " Which of these is Visākhā ? " Those who saw her as she walked would think: " I hope she will walk a little further;

our lady looks well when she walks." And those who saw her stand, or sit, or lie, would think: " I hope she will lie a little longer now; our lady looks well when she is lying down." Thus in respect of the four postures, it could not be charged against her that there was any one posture in which she did not look well.

Moreover, she was as strong as five elephants. And the king, hearing that Visākhā was currently reported to be as strong as five elephants, was desirous of testing her strength; and one day, as she was on her way back from the monastery where she had been to hear a sermon, he let loose an elephant against her. The elephant, lifting his trunk, came on to meet Visākhā. Of her five hundred attendant women, some fled away, while others threw their arms about her. And when she asked what the matter was, they replied: " They say the king is desirous of testing your iron strength, and has let loose an elephant against you." When Visākhā saw the elephant, she thought, " What is the need of my running away ? It is only a question how I shall take hold of him." And, being afraid that if she seized him roughly it might kill him, she took hold of his trunk with two fingers, and pressed him back. The elephant was unable either to resist or to keep his feet, and fell back on his haunches in the royal court. Thereupon the crowd shouted " Bravo ! " and she and her attendants reached home in safety.

Now at that time Visākhā, Migāra's mother, lived at Sāvatthi, and had many children and many children's children, and the children were free from disease, and the children's children were free from disease, and she was considered to bring good luck. Among her thousands of children and children's children not one had died. And when the inhabitants of Sāvatthi had their festivals and holidays, Visākhā was always the first to be invited, and the first to be feasted.

Now on a certain day of merry-making, the populace were going in their fine clothes and ornaments to the monastery to listen to the Doctrine. And Visākhā, having come from a place of entertainment, and wearing the great creeper parure, was likewise proceeding with the populace to the monastery. There she took off her ornaments, and gave them to her slave-girl. Concerning which it is said,

"Now at that time there was a merry-making at Sāvatthi; and the people in gorgeous array went to the park. Visākhā, also, Migāra's mother, in gorgeous array went to the monastery. Then Visākhā, Migāra's mother, took off her ornaments, and tying them up in a bundle in her cloak, gave them to her slave-girl, saying, 'Here, take this bundle.'"

It would appear that she thought it not seemly to enter the monastery wearing such an extremely costly and showy parure, — a decoration which, when put on, adorned her from head to foot. Thus it was that, as she was proceeding to the monastery, she took it off, and made of it a bundle, and gave it to a slave-girl, who had been born with the strength of five elephants as the result of former good deeds, and hence was able to carry it. Thus her mistress could say to her, "Dear girl, take this parure. I will put it on when I return from The Teacher."

Having put on her highly polished parure, she drew near The Teacher, and listened to the Doctrine. And at the close of the sermon she rose, did obeisance to The Blessed One, and went forth from his presence. The slave-girl, however, forgot the parure. Now it was the custom of Ānanda the elder, when the assembly had listened to the Doctrine, and had departed, to put away anything that had been forgotten. And so this day he noticed the great creeper parure, and announced to The Teacher,

"Reverend Sir, Visākhā has gone forgetting her parure."

"Lay it aside, Ānanda."

The elder lifted it up, and hung it on the side of the staircase.

And Visākhā, in company with her friend Suppiyā, wandered about the monastery to see what could be done for the in-coming, for the out-going, for the sick, and others. Now it was the custom of the young priests and novices, when they saw the devout ladies bringing clarified butter, honey, oil, and other medicaments, to draw near with basins of various kinds. And on that day also they did so.

Thereupon Suppiyā saw a certain sick priest, and asked him,

"Sir, of what do you stand in need?"

"Meat broth," was the reply.

"Very well, sir; I will send you some."

But as she failed on the next day to obtain any suitable meat, she made the preparation with flesh from her own thigh; and afterwards by the favor of The Teacher her body was made whole.

When Visākhā had attended to the sick and to the young priests, she issued forth from the monastery. But before she had gone far, she stopped and said,

"Dear girl, bring me the parure; I will put it on."

Instantly the slave-girl remembered that she had forgotten it, and had left it behind. And she said,

"Mistress, I forgot it."

"Go, then, and get it, and bring it hither. But if my master, Ānanda the elder, has taken it up and laid it away anywhere, then do not fetch it. It is a present to my master." It appears she knew that the elder was in the habit of putting away valuables which highborn personages had forgotten; and this was why she spoke as she did.

When the elder saw the slave-girl, he said to her,

"Why have you returned?"

"I went away forgetting my mistress's parure," said she.

"I have put it by the staircase," said the elder; "go and get it."

"My lord," said the slave-girl, "an article which has been touched by your hand is not to be reclaimed by my mistress." And so she returned empty-handed.

"How was it, dear girl?" said Visākhā. And she told her.

"Dear girl, never will I wear an article which my master has touched. I make him a present of it. Nevertheless, it would be troublesome for my masters to take care of it. I will sell it, and give them things which are more suitable. Go fetch it."

And the slave-girl went and fetched it.

Visākhā did not put it on, but sent for some goldsmiths and had it appraised.

" It is worth ninety millions," said they ; " and the workmanship is worth a hundred thousand."

" Then put the parure in a wagon," said Visākhā, " and sell it."

" There is no one who is able to take it at such a price, and a woman worthy to wear such a parure is difficult to find. For in all the circuit of the earth only three women have the great creeper parure : Visākhā, the great female lay disciple ; the wife of Bandhula, the general of the Mallas ; and Mallikā, daughter of a treasurer of Benares."

So Visākhā paid the price herself ; and, putting ninety millions and a hundred thousand into a cart, she took the amount to the monastery.

" Reverend Sir," said she, when she had made her obeisance to The Teacher, " my master, Ānanda the elder, has touched with his hand my parure, and from the time he has touched it, it is impossible for me to wear it again. I have endeavored to sell it, thinking that with the amount I should get for it, I would give things suitable for priests. But when I saw there was no one else able to buy it, I made up the price myself, and have now brought the money with me. Reverend Sir, which one of the four reliances shall I give ? "

" Visākhā, a dwelling-place at the east gate for the congregation of the priests would be fitting."

" The very thing, Reverend Sir ! "

And Visākhā, with a joyous mind, bought a site for ninety millions, and with another ninety millions she began constructing a monastery.

Now one day, as The Teacher at dawn was gazing over the world, he perceived that a son, Bhaddiya, had been born from heaven into the family of a treasurer of the city of Bhaddiya, and was competent to attain to salvation. And after taking breakfast at the house of Anāthapiṇḍika, he directed his steps towards the north gate of the city. Now it was the custom of The Teacher, if he took alms at the house of Visākhā, to issue forth from the city by the south gate and

lodge at Jetavana monastery. If he took alms at the house
of Anāthapiṇḍika, he would issue forth by the east gate, and
lodge in Eastern Park; but if The Blessed One was perceived at sunrise making his way to the north gate, then
people knew that he was setting out on his travels.

So when Visākhā heard on that day that he had gone in
the direction of the north gate, she hastened to him, and
making an obeisance, said,

" Reverend Sir, are you desirous of going traveling? "

" Yes, Visākhā."

" Reverend Sir, at this vast expense am I having a monastery built for you. Reverend Sir, turn back."

" Visākhā, this journey admits not of my turning back."

" Assuredly," thought Visākhā, " The Blessed One has
some special reason in all this." Then she said, " Reverend
Sir, in that case, before you go, command some priest to stay
behind who will know how the work should be done."

" Visākhā, take the bowl of any one you wish."

Then Visākhā, though fond of Ānanda, thought of the
magical power of the elder, Moggallāna the Great, and how
swiftly the work would progress with him to assist, and took
his bowl.

The elder then looked at The Teacher.

" Moggallāna," said The Teacher, " take five hundred
priests in your train and turn back."

And he did so: and by his supernatural power they would
go a distance of fifty or sixty leagues for logs and stones; and
having secured logs and stones of tremendous size, they would
bring them home on the same day. And they who placed the
logs and stones on the carts were not exhausted, nor did the
axles break. And in no long time they had erected a two-
story building on high foundations and approached by steps.
The building contained a thousand apartments, — five hundred
apartments being in the lower story, and the same number
in the upper.

After traveling about for nine months, The Teacher came
again to Sāvatthi; and in these nine months Visākhā had put
up her building, and was now at work on the peak, which was

intended to hold the water-pots, and was finished in solid, beaten, red gold.

And Visākhā, hearing that The Teacher was proceeding towards Jetavana monastery, went to meet him; and, conducting him to her monastery, she exacted of him a promise:

"Reverend Sir, dwell here for four months with the congregation of the priests, and I will have the building completed."

The Teacher consented; and thenceforth she gave alms to The Buddha, and to the congregation of the priests in the monastery.

And it came to pass that a certain female friend of Visākhā came to her with a piece of stuff that was worth a thousand pieces of money.

"Dear friend," said she, "I want to replace some of the floor-covering in your pavilion, and spread this instead. Tell me a place in which to spread it."

"Dear friend, if I were to tell you there was no place left, you would think, 'She does not want to let me have a place.' But look through the two floors of the pavilion and the thousand apartments yourself, and find a place in which to spread it."

Then the other took the piece of stuff worth a thousand pieces of money, and went through the building; but finding no stuff there of less value than hers, she was overcome with grief; for she thought: "I shall have no share in the merit of this building." And stopping still, she wept.

And Ānanda the elder happened to see her, and said, "Why do you weep?" And she told him the matter.

"Let not that trouble you," said the elder; "I will tell you a place in which to spread it. Make a door-mat of it, and spread it between the place for washing the feet and the staircase. The priests, after washing their feet, will wipe them upon the mat before they enter the building: thus will your reward be great." This spot, it appears, had been overlooked by Visākhā.

For four months did Visākhā give alms in her monastery to The Buddha and to the congregation which followed him; and at the end of that time she presented the congregation of

the priests with stuff for robes, and even that received by the
novices was worth a thousand pieces of money. And of medi-
cines, she gave the fill of every man's bowl. Ninety millions
were spent in this donation. Thus ninety millions went for
the site of the monastery, ninety for the construction of the
monastery, and ninety for the festival at the opening of the
monastery, making two hundred and seventy millions in all
that were expended by her on the religion of The Buddha.
No other woman in the world was as liberal as this one who
lived in the house of a heretic.

On the day the monastery was completed, when the shadows
of eventide were lengthening, she walked with her children
and her children's children round and round the building,
delighted with the thought that her prayer of a former existence had now attained its complete fruition. And with a
sweet voice, in five stanzas, she breathed forth this solemn
utterance : —

> " ' O when shall I a mansion give,
> Plastered with mud and stuccoed o'er,
> A pleasing monastery-gift ? ' —
> O this my prayer is now fulfilled !

> " ' O when shall I give household goods,
> Benches and stools to sit upon,
> And bolsters, pillows for the couch ? ' —
> O this my prayer is now fulfilled !

> " ' O when shall I provisions give,
> The ticket-food so pure and good,
> Smothered in broths of various meats ? ' —
> O this my prayer is now fulfilled !

> " ' O when shall I give priestly robes,
> Garments of fine Benares cloth,
> And linen, cotton goods as well ? ' —
> O this my prayer is now fulfilled !

> " ' O when shall I give medicines,
> Fresh butter, butter clarified,
> And honey, treacle, purest oil ? ' —
> O this my prayer in now fulfilled ! "

When the priests heard her, they brought word to The Teacher:

" Reverend Sir, in all this time we have never known Visākhā to sing; but now, surrounded by her children and her children's children, she walks singing round and round the building. Pray, is her bile out of order? or has she become mad?"

"Priests," said The Teacher, "my daughter is not singing; but the desire of her heart having come to pass, in her delight she breathes forth a solemn utterance."

" But when was it, Reverend Sir, she made the prayer?"

" Priests, will you listen?"

" Reverend Sir, we will."

Whereupon he related a tale of ancient times: —

" Priests, a hundred thousand cycles ago, a Buddha was born into the world by the name of Padumuttara. His term of life was a hundred thousand years; his retinue of those in whom depravity had become extinct was a hundred thousand; his city was Haṁsavatī; his father, king Sunanda; and his mother, queen Sujātā. The chief benefactress of this Teacher, a lay devotee, had obtained the eight boons and held the position of mother, and used to provide him with the four reliances. Every evening and morning she used to wait on him at the monastery, and a certain female friend constantly accompanied her.

" When this friend saw on what intimate terms she conversed with The Teacher, and how much she was beloved, she began to consider: 'What do people do to be beloved by The Buddhas?' And she said to The Teacher:

" ' Reverend Sir, what is this woman to you?'

" ' She is the chief of my benefactresses.'

" ' Reverend Sir, by what means does one thus become chief benefactress?'

" ' By praying for a hundred thousand world-cycles to become one.'

" ' Reverend Sir, could I become one, if I now made my prayer?'

" ' Assuredly, you could.'

" ' In that case, Reverend Sir, come with your hundred thousand priests and take alms of me for seven days.'

" The Teacher consented; and for seven days she gave alms of food, and on the last day stuff for robes. Then she did obeisance to The Teacher, and, falling at his feet, made her prayer:

" ' Reverend Sir, I do not pray for rule among the gods, or any other such reward as the fruit of this alms-giving; but that from some Buddha like yourself I may obtain the eight boons, and have the position of mother, and be chief of those able to provide the four reliances.'

" The Teacher looked into the future for a hundred thousand cycles to see if her prayer would be fulfilled, and said:

" ' At the end of a hundred thousand cycles a Buddha named Gotama shall arise, and you shall be a female lay disciple of his, and have the name Visākhā. From him you shall obtain the eight boons, and obtain the position of mother, and become chief of the benefactresses who shall provide the four reliances.'

" . . . and after a life of meritorious deeds, she was reborn in the world of the gods. And continuing to be reborn in the world of the gods and the world of men, she was born in the time of The Supreme Buddha Kassapa as the youngest of the seven daughters of Kiki, king of Benares. In this existence she was called Servant-of-the-Congregation; and having married, and with her sisters for a long time given alms and done other meritorious deeds, she fell at the feet of The Supreme Buddha Kassapa, and prayed: ' At a future time may I hold the position of mother to a Buddha such as you, and become chief of the female givers of the four reliances.' Now, after further rebirths in the world of the gods and the world of men, she has been born in this existence as the daughter of Dhanañjaya the treasurer, the son of Meṇḍaka the treasurer, and has done many meritorious deeds for my religion. Thus it is, O priests, that I say my daughter is not singing, but that, at the realization of her prayer, she breathes forth a solemn utterance."

And The Teacher continued his instruction, and said,

"Priests, just as a skilful garland-maker, if he obtain a large heap of various kinds of flowers, will go on and on and making all manner of garlands, even so does the mind of Visākhā incline to do all manner of noble deeds." So saying, he pronounced this stanza:

> 53.   " As flowers in rich profusion piled
>   Will many a garland furnish forth;
>   So all the years of mortal man
>   Should fruitful be in all good works."

---

§ 102. THE BUDDHIST APOCALYPSE.

[The following is the account given by Prof. J. Minayeff, of St. Petersburg, of the second of the Manuscripts used by him in editing the Anāgata-Vaṁsa (History of Future Events), but with the Pāli passages translated into English. See *Journal of the Pāli Text Society* for 1886, page 33.]

II. B.   A MS. on paper, 24 pages, marked by the letters (k–b). It is a copy from the MS. in the Library of Mg. Hpo Hmyin at Rangoon. This recension is a mixed one, in prose and in verse. It begins—

Hail to that Blessed One, that Saint, and Supreme Buddha!

Thus have I heard.

On a certain occasion The Blessed One was dwelling at Kapilavatthu in Banyan Grove on the banks of the Rohaṇī River.

Then the venerable Sāriputta questioned The Blessed One concerning the future Conqueror:

> " The Hero that shall follow you
> As Buddha, of what sort is he?
> Th' account in full I fain would learn.
> Declare to me, thou Seeing One."

> When he had heard the elder's speech,
> The Blessed One vouchsafed reply:
> " I'll tell it thee, Sāriputta,
> Pray lend your ears, for I will speak.

" Our cycle is a happy one,
Three Leaders have already lived,
Kakusandha, Koṇāgamana,
And eke the leader Kassapa.

" The Buddha now Supreme am I,
But after me Metteyya comes,
While still this happy cycle lasts,
Before its tale of years shall lapse.

" This Buddha, then, Metteyya called,
Supreme, and of all men the chief —"

Then follows a history of the previous existence of Metteyyo, with the three Buddhas, *Sumitto*, *Metteyyo*, and *Muhutto*,
during twenty-seven Buddhas, and finally at the time of the
Buddha gotama, when he was born as son of Ajātaçattu,
prince of Ajita (pp. ka — ca). On page *ca* begins the future
history of Metteyya with a quotation of the recension com-
piled in verse. Then follows the description of the gradual
declension of the holy religion:

" How will it occur? After my decease, first will occur
the five disappearances. And what are the five disappearances? The disappearance of the attainments, the disappearance of the method, the disappearance of learning,
the disappearance of the symbols, the disappearance of the
relics. These are the five disappearances that are to occur.

" First: —

" *The attainments:* — Only for a thousand years from the
time The Blessed One passes into Nirvana will the priests
be able to acquire the analytical sciences. Then as time goes
on my disciples will attain only to never returning, to once
returning, to conversion. As long as such exist the disappearance of the attainments will not yet have occurred. But
with the death of the last disciple that has attained to conversion the attainments will have disappeared.

" This, O Sāriputta, is the disappearance of the attainments.

" *Disappearance of the method:* — My disciples being un-

able to realize the trances, the insights, the Paths, and the
Fruits, will keep only the four purities of conduct. Then as
time goes on they will keep only the commandments forbidding the four deadly sins. As long as there are a hundred
or a thousand priests who keep the commandments forbidding
the four deadly sins, the disappearance of the method will not
have occurred. But when the last priest shall break the precepts, or shall die, the method will have disappeared.

"This, O Sāriputta, is the disappearance of the method.

"*Disappearance of learning :* — As long as the text of the
Three Baskets, which is the word of The Buddha, and as long
as their commentaries are extant, the disappearance of learning will not have occurred. But as time goes on there will
be irreligious kings of base extraction, and the courtiers and
others in authority will be irreligious, and then the country
people throughout the kingdom will be irreligious. On account of their irreligion the god will not rain in due season,
and the crops will not flourish properly. And when the crops
do not flourish, those who are wont to give the reliances to the
congregation of the priests will be unable to do so any more.
And the priests, not receiving the reliances, will not teach the
novices, and as time goes on learning will disappear. When
it disappears, it is the Great Work [i. e. Paṭṭhāna. See page
xviii] that first disappears ; when that has disappeared, then
the Yamaka, the Kathā-Vatthu, the Puggala-Paññatti, the
Dhātu-Kathā, the Vibhaṅga, and the Dhamma-Saṅgaṇi do so.
When the Abhidhamma-Piṭaka has disappeared, the Suttanta-
Piṭaka will also disappear. When the Suttanta disappears, it
is first the Aṅguttara-Nikāya that disappears, and when the
Aṅguttara-Nikāya disappears, then the Saṁyutta-Nikāya, the
Majjhima-Nikāya, the Dīgha-Nikāya, the Khuddaka-Nikāya
will disappear. My disciples will only remember the Jātaka
together with the Vinaya-Piṭaka. It is, however, only the
well-conducted priests that will remember the Vinaya-Piṭaka.
But as time goes on they will be unable to remember the
Jātaka, and first the Vessantara Birth-Story will disappear,
and when the Vessantara Birth-Story has disappeared . . .
the Apaṇṇaka Birth-Story will disappear. When the Jātaka

has disappeared, they will only remember the Vinaya-Piṭaka.
As time goes on the Vinaya-Piṭaka will disappear, but as long
as a four-line stanza remains among men, so long the disappearance of learning will not have occurred. But when a
pious king shall cause a purse containing a thousand pieces of
money to be placed in a golden casket on the back of an elephant, and shall cause proclamation up to the second and third
time to be made throughout the city to the sound of the drum,
as follows : ' Any one who knows a single stanza spoken by
The Buddhas, let him take these thousand coins together with
this elephant,' and yet shall fail to find any one who knows a
four-line stanza, and shall receive again the purse containing
the thousand pieces into the royal palace, then the disappearance of learning will have occurred.

"This, O Sāriputta, is the disappearance of learning.

"Now as time goes on the last of the priests will carry
their robes, their bowls, and their tooth-sticks after the manner
of the naked ascetics. They will take a bottle-gourd, make
of it a begging-bowl, and carry it in their arms, or in their
hands, or in the balance of a carrying-pole. And as time goes
on a priest will say, ' What is the good of this yellow robe?'
and cut a small piece of yellow cloth, and tie it around his
neck, or his ears, or his hair, and devote himself to hus-
bandry or trade and the like, and to taking care of wife and
children. Then he will give gifts to the southern congregation. And the fruit of this gift, say I, will be a myriadfold.
As time goes on the priests will say, ' What do we want with
this?' and they will throw away the piece of yellow cloth and
persecute the wild animals and birds of the forest, and thus
the disappearance of the symbols will have occurred.

"This, O Sāriputta, is *the disappearance of the symbols.*

"Thereupon, the dispensation of The Supreme Buddha
being now five thousand years old, the relics will begin to fail
of honor and worship, and will go wherever they can receive
honor and worship. But as time goes on they will not receive
honor and worship in any place. Then, when the dispensation
has disappeared, the relics will come from every place; from
the serpent world, from the world of the gods, and from the

Brahma-world; and having congregated together at the throne under the Great Bo-tree, they will make an effigy of The Buddha and perform a miracle resembling the double-miracle, and will teach the Doctrine. Not a single human being will be found at that place; but all the gods from ten thousand worlds will come together and listen to the Doctrine, and many thousands of them will attain to the Doctrine. And these will cry aloud, saying, 'Divine sirs, on the seventh day from now our One Possessing the Ten Forces will pass into Nirvana.' Then they will weep, saying, 'From henceforth we shall be in darkness.' Then the relics will put forth flames of fire and burn up that effigy without remainder.

"This, O Sāriputta, is *the disappearance of the relics.*"

Immediately after this, there follows an account of the destruction of the *Kappa* [World-Cycle]. The verse recension does not run on continuously in the compilation. The verses are interrupted by prose insertion, *e. g.*, on page *ṅa* there is inserted the ancient history of Mahāpaṇāda; on page *ṭha* there is a description of the capital of King Saṅkha. Further on page *ḍa* there is described the attainment of *pāramita* [the Perfections], the conception and birth of *Metteyya*, his palaces, his life there, his departure from home, and his death. On page *na* is depicted the sacred tree and the body of the future teacher. This recension ends thus:

f. [i. e., Folio] *ba.* "But who shall not behold Metteyya, The Blessed One? and who shall behold him?

"One who creates a schism in a church, as it is said, 'Devadatta remains in hell for the entire world-cycle,' as well as all others born in the Avīci hell, from performing the five crimes that constitute 'proximate karma,' those cherishing wholly heretical views, and those who slander the noble disciples, shall not see him. The naked ascetics who create a schism by denying the congregation allowable privileges shall not see him. All other beings who give gifts, keep the precepts, keep fast-days, fulfil their religious duties, found shrines, plant sacred fig-trees, parks and groves, make bridges, clear the highways, take their stand in the precepts, and dig wells, shall see him. Those who, in their longing for a Blessed One, shall make a gift even if only of a handful of flowers, or of a single lamp, or of a mouthful of food, shall see him. Those who feel pleasure at meritorious deeds shall see him. Those who further the religion of The Buddha, prepare the pavilion and the seats for the preachers of the Doctrine, bring forward the fan, make offerings of cloth, canopies, garlands, incense, or lamps, or are stanch sustainers of the ministrations of the Doctrine, shall see him. Those who listen to the Vessantara Birth-Story shall see him, likewise those who give to the congregation offerings of food etc. shall see him. Those who wait on their mothers and their fathers, and perform respectful duties for their elders among their kinsfolk shall see him. Those who give ticket-food, fortnightly food, and food on fast-days, those who practise the ten means of acquiring merit shall see him. And when they have listened to the Doctrine of The Blessed Metteyya, they shall attain to saintship."

Then our Blessed One, in order to show who of those about him were to become Buddhas, said:

> "Metteyya excellent, Rāma,
> Pasenadi Kosala, 'Bhibhū,
> Dīghasoni and Saṃkacca,
> Subha, the Brahman Todeyya,

> "Nāḷāgiri, Palāleyya,
> These ten are Future Buddhas now,
> And in due course, in time to come,
> Wisdom Supreme shall they attain."

End of the Metteyya Discourse and History of Future Events.

APPENDIX.

§ 103. THE FIVE GROUPS.

ALTHOUGH it has not been my plan to go deeply into technical matters, I have been obliged to give such prominence to the groups that constitute the human being, that it seems necessary to give a statement of how these groups are made up, in order that the reader may understand what they are like. Of the translations which follow, the final one entitled "Karma and the Consciousnesses" is made from the seventeenth chapter of the Visuddhi-Magga; the other translations and the materials for the lists are from the fourteenth chapter of that work.

1. THE FORM-GROUP.

A. Elementary forms.
    1. Earthy element.
    2. Watery element.
    3. Fiery element.
    4. Windy element.
B. Derivative forms.
    1. Eye.
    2. Ear.
    3. Nose.
    4. Tongue.
    5. Body.
    6. Form.
    7. Sound.
    8. Odor.
    9. Taste.
10. Femininity.
11. Masculinity.
12. Vitality.
13. Organ of the heart.
14. Bodily intimation.
15. Vocal intimation.
16. Space.
17. Buoyancy of form.
18. Softness of form.
19. Suppleness of form.
20. Growth of form.
21. Continuation of form.
22. Growing old of form.
23. Transitoriness of form.
24. Material food.

2. THE SENSATION-GROUP.

Sensation conjoined with a meritorious consciousness is a meritorious sensation; conjoined with a demeritorious consciousness, it is a demeritorious sensation; conjoined with an indeterminate consciousness, it is an indeterminate sensation. It has a fivefold division peculiar to itself; namely, happiness, misery, gladness, grief, and indifference.

3. THE PERCEPTION-GROUP.

Perception conjoined with a meritorious consciousness is a meritorious perception; conjoined with a demeritorious consciousness, it is a demeritorious perception; conjoined with an indeterminate consciousness, it is an indeterminate perception. For there is no consciousness that is not conjoined with perception. Accordingly perception has the same number of divisions as consciousness.

4. THE PREDISPOSITION-GROUP.

1. Contact.
2. Thinking.
3. Reasoning.
4. Reflection.
5. Joy.
6. Courage.
7. Life.
8. Concentration.
9. Faith.
10. Contemplation.
11. Shame.
12. Fear of sinning.
13. Freedom from covetousness.
14. Freedom from hatred.
15. Freedom from infatuation.
16. Bodily tranquillity.
17. Mental tranquillity.
18. Buoyancy of body.
19. Buoyancy of mind.
20. Softness of body.
21. Softness of mind.
22. Suppleness of body.
23. Suppleness of mind.
24. Skilfulness of body.
25. Skilfulness of mind.
26. Erectness of body.
27. Erectness of mind.
28. Will.
29. Determination.
30. Attention.
31. Neutrality.
32. Compassion.
33. Rejoicing.
34. Abstinence from doing evil with the body.
35. Abstinence from doing evil with the voice.
36. Abstinence from wrong occupations.
37. Shamelessness.
38. Freedom from fear of sinning.
39. Covetousness.
40. Infatuation.
41. Heresy.
42. Haughtiness.
43, 44. Idleness and sloth.
45. Pride.
46. Hatred.
47. Envy.
48. Miserliness.
49. Ill-behavior.
50. Steadiness of mind.
51. Doubt.

5. THE CONSCIOUSNESS–GROUP.

MERITORIOUS CONSCIOUSNESSES.
[Good Karma.]

Belonging to the realm of sensual pleasure.

1. Coupled with gladness, conjoined with knowledge, and uninstigated.
2. Coupled with gladness, conjoined with knowledge, and instigated.
3. Coupled with gladness, not conjoined with knowledge, and uninstigated.
4. Coupled with gladness, not conjoined with knowledge, and instigated.
5. Coupled with indifference, conjoined with knowledge, and uninstigated.
6. Coupled with indifference, conjoined with knowledge, and instigated.
7. Coupled with indifference, not conjoined with knowledge, and uninstigated.
8. Coupled with indifference, not conjoined with knowledge, and instigated.

Belonging to the realm of form.

9. Conjoined with reasoning, reflection, joy, happiness, and concentration.
10. Conjoined with reflection, joy, happiness, and concentration.
11. Conjoined with joy, happiness, and concentration.
12. Conjoined with happiness and concentration.
13. Conjoined with indifference and concentration.

Belonging to the realm of formlessness.

14. Conjoined with the trance of the realm of the infinity of space.
15. Conjoined with the trance of the realm of the infinity of consciousness.
16. Conjoined with the trance of the realm of nothingness.
17. Conjoined with the trance of the realm of neither perception nor yet non-perception.

Transcendent.

18. Conjoined with the first path.
19. Conjoined with the second path.
20. Conjoined with the third path.
21. Conjoined with the fourth path.

DEMERITORIOUS CONSCIOUSNESSES.
[Bad Karma.]

Belonging to the realm of sensual pleasure.

Rooted in covetousness.

22. Coupled with gladness, conjoined with heresy, and uninstigated.
23. Coupled with gladness, conjoined with heresy, and instigated.
24. Coupled with gladness, not conjoined with heresy, and uninstigated.
25. Coupled with gladness, not conjoined with heresy, and instigated.
26. Coupled with indifference, conjoined with heresy, and uninstigated.
27. Coupled with indifference, conjoined with heresy, and instigated.
28. Coupled with indifference, not conjoined with heresy, and uninstigated.
29. Coupled with indifference, not conjoined with heresy, and instigated.

Rooted in hatred.

30. Coupled with grief, conjoined with anger, and uninstigated.
31. Coupled with grief, conjoined with anger, and instigated.

Rooted in infatuation.

32. Coupled with indifference and conjoined with doubt.
33. Coupled with indifference and conjoined with haughtiness.

E CONSCIOUSNESSES.

INDETERMINATE CONSCIOUSNESSES.

FRUITION.
[Fruition of Karma.]

34. Eye-consciousness.
35–8. Ear-, nose-, tongue-, body-consciousness.
39. Mind in its noticing capacity.
40. Mind-consciousness in its cognitive and so forth capacity and joined with gladness.
   a. Cognizing.
   b. Identical object.
41. Mind-consciousness in its cognitive and so forth capacity and joined with indifference.
   a. Cognizing.
   b. Identical object.
   c. Conception.
   d. Existence-substratum.
   e. Passing-away.
42. Coupled with gladness, conjoined with knowledge, and uninstigated.
43. Coupled with gladness, conjoined with knowledge, and instigated.
44. Coupled with gladness, not conjoined with knowledge, and uninstigated.
45. Coupled with gladness, not conjoined with knowledge, and instigated.
46. Coupled with indifference, conjoined with knowledge, and uninstigated.
47. Coupled with indifference, conjoined with knowledge, and instigated.
48. Coupled with indifference, not conjoined with knowledge, and uninstigated.
49. Coupled with indifference, not conjoined with knowledge, and instigated.
50. Eye-consciousness.
51–4. Ear-, nose-, tongue-, body-consciousness.
55. Mind in its noticing capacity.
56. Mind-consciousness in its cognizing capacity in five divisions.
57. Conjoined with reasoning, reflection, joy, happiness, and concentration.
58. Conjoined with reflection, joy, happiness, and concentration.
59. Conjoined with joy, happiness, and concentration.
60. Conjoined with happiness and concentration.
61. Conjoined with indifference and concentration.
62. Conjoined with the trance of the realm of the infinity of space.
63. Conjoined with the trance of the realm of the infinity of consciousness.
64. Conjoined with the trance of the realm of nothingness.
65. Conjoined with the trance of the realm of neither perception nor yet non-perception.
66. Conjoined with the first path.
67. Conjoined with the second path.
68. Conjoined with the third path.
69. Conjoined with the fourth path.

ACTION.
[Barren Karma.]

Without a cause.

70. Mind.
71. Mind-consciousness, general, and coupled with indifference.
72. Mind-consciousness, specific, and coupled with gladness.

Belonging to the realm of sensual pleasure. Having a cause.

73. Coupled with gladness, conjoined with knowledge, and uninstigated.
74. Coupled with gladness, conjoined with knowledge, and instigated.
75. Coupled with gladness, not conjoined with knowledge, and uninstigated.
76. Coupled with gladness, not conjoined with knowledge, and instigated.
77. Coupled with indifference, conjoined with knowledge, and uninstigated.
78. Coupled with indifference, conjoined with knowledge, and instigated.
79. Coupled with indifference, not conjoined with knowledge, and uninstigated.
80. Coupled with indifference, not conjoined with knowledge, and instigated.

Belonging to the realm of form.

81. Conjoined with reasoning, reflection, joy, happiness, and concentration.
82. Conjoined with reflection, joy, happiness, and concentration.
83. Conjoined with joy, happiness, and concentration.
84. Conjoined with happiness and concentration.
85. Conjoined with indifference and concentration.

Belonging to the realm of formlessness.

86. Conjoined with the trance of the realm of the infinity of space.
87. Conjoined with the trance of the realm of the infinity of consciousness.
88. Conjoined with the trance of the realm of nothingness.
89. Conjoined with the trance of the realm of neither perception nor yet non-perception.

The Functions of the Consciousnesses.

The consciousnesses are in all eighty-nine in number and occur on fourteen different occasions; in conception, existence-substratum, attention, seeing, hearing, smelling, tasting, touching, noticing, cognizing, defining, the swiftnesses, identical object, and passing away. And how?

When, through the power of the eight meritorious consciousnesses belonging to the realm of sensual pleasure, living beings are born in the world of gods and men, then, at the moment of conception, occur nine fruition-consciousnesses; namely, eight fruition-consciousnesses belonging to the realm of sensual pleasure and possessing a cause, having as their object any karma, karma-reflex, or destiny-reflex, that might have been present at the time of death, and also, in the case of those who in the world of men become eunuchs and the like, a meritorious fruition-mind-consciousness, coupled with indifference, which, as having its two causes weak, is called without a cause. When, through the power of the meritorious consciousnesses belonging to the realms of form and formlessness, these beings are born in the realms of form and formlessness, then, at the moment of conception occur nine fruition-consciousnesses of the realms of form and formlessness, having as their object any karma-reflex that might have been present at the time of death. When, however, through the power of the demeritorious consciousnesses, they are born in hell, then, at the moment of conception, there occurs only a demeritorious fruition-mind-consciousness without a cause, having as its object any karma, karma-reflex, or destiny-reflex, that might have been present at the time of death. Accordingly, therefore, it is to be understood that nineteen fruition-consciousnesses occur in *conception.*

But when conception-consciousness ceases, then, close on its heels, occurs the precisely similar existence-subtratum-consciousness, being the fruition of the same karma and having the same object. This repeats itself, as does the stream of a river, as long as no other thought arises to interrupt the series, and this process continues indefinitely during dreamless sleep and like occasions. Accordingly, therefore, it is to be understood that the same nineteen consciousnesses occur in *existence-substratum.*

But when in the course of the existence-substratum series the sense-apertures of a living being have grown to be competent to grasp their objects, then, when form comes within the visual field, the irritability of the eye for form is stimulated, and through the force of this stimulus existence-substratum is interrupted. When existence-substratum ceases, action-mind arises to take its place, with that form as its object, and accomplishing the function of attention. Similarly in respect of the ear-aperture etc. In the case of the mind-aperture, however, when the six objects of sense come within range and existence-substratum has been interrupted, then arises action-mind-consciousness to take its place, being without a cause and coupled with indifference and accomplishing the function of attention. Accordingly it is to be understood that two action-consciousnesses occur in *attention.*

But after attention there occurs the eye-consciousness, having for its instrument the irritability of the eye and accomplishing the function of sight in the eye-aperture, and there occur the ear-consciousness, nose-consciousness, tongue-consciousness, and body-consciousness, accomplishing the functions of hearing etc. in the ear-aperture etc. These are meritorious fruitions when their objects are desirable or desirable-neutral, and demeritorious fruitions when their objects are undesirable or undesirable-neutral. Accordingly it is to be understood that ten fruition-consciousnesses occur during *seeing, hearing, smelling, tasting,* and *touching.*

But when it is said that after eye-consciousness has sprung up and ceased there arises the thought, mentality, mind due to it, this is fruition-mind which springs up after the sense-consciousnesses, and notices their objects. When it succeeds a meritorious sense-consciousness, it is a meritorious fruition; when it succeeds a demeritorious sense-consciousness, it is a demeritorious fruition. Accordingly it is to be understood that two fruition-consciousnesses occur in *noticing.*

But when it is said that after mind has sprung up and ceased there arises the thought, mentality, mind-consciousness due to it, this is fruition-mind-consciousness without a cause springing up and cognizing what has been noticed by the mind. When it succeeds the demeritorious fruition-mind in an undesirable-neutral object, it is a demeritorious fruition. When it succeeds the meritorious fruition-mind, it is a meritorious fruition, being coupled with gladness in the case of a desirable object, and coupled with indifference in the case of a desirable-neutral one. Accordingly it is to be understood that three fruition-consciousnesses occur in the case of *cognizing*.

After cognizing there arises action-mind-consciousness without a cause and coupled with indifference. This defines the object. Accordingly it is to be understood that one solitary action-consciousness occurs in *defining*.

After defining, in case the object, form or the like, is large, then in respect of the defined object there hasten six or seven swiftnesses. These are made up either from the eight meritorious consciousnesses belonging to the realm of sensual pleasure, or from the twelve demeritorious ones, or from the nine action-consciousnesses belonging to the realm of sensual pleasure. This is how the case stands in respect to the five apertures; but in the case of the mind-aperture, only after attention in the mind-aperture. Beyond *gotrabhū* there occur five meritorious consciousnesses and five action-consciousnesses belonging to the realm of form, four meritorious consciousnesses and four action-consciousnesses belonging to the realm of formlessness, and four path-thoughts and four fruition-thoughts transcending the world, — all according as they may have obtained a dependence. Accordingly it is to be understood that the meritorious consciousnesses, demeritorious consciousnesses, action-consciousnesses, and fruition-consciousnesses amount to fifty-five in number in the *swiftnesses*.

But at the end of the swiftnesses, in case the object in the five apertures is excessively large, or that in the mind-aperture is vivid, then any dependence possessed by beings in the realm of sensual pleasure at the termination of the swiftnesses belonging to that realm, such dependence, namely, as desirable objects etc., and previous karma, swiftnesses, thoughts, etc., will have as its result some one of the eight fruition-consciousnesses belonging to the realm of sensual pleasure and possessing a cause, or else some one of the three fruition-minds without a cause. And, as water pursues, though only at an interval, the stern of a vessel that is proceeding up stream, so this fruition-consciousness, once or twice repeated, pursues the swiftness that has spent itself on some object other than an object of existence-substratum. As this fruition-consciousness, at the same time with being able at the end of the swiftnesses to exist in an existence-substratum-object, exists also in an object of a swiftness, it is called identical object. Accordingly it is to be understood that eleven fruition-consciousnesses occur in *identical object*.

But at the end of identical object, existence-substratum occurs again, and when existence-substratum is interrupted, then attention and the rest occur again. A series of thoughts which has thus obtained a dependence always recurs in the regular round of attention following existence-substratum, and of seeing etc. following attention, until in any given existence existence-substratum perishes. The passing away in the last existence of existence-substratum-thought is called passing away [death]. Accordingly the passing-away-consciousness, like existence-substratum, has nineteen sub-divisions. Accordingly it is to be understood that nineteen fruition-consciousnesses occur in *passing-away*.

But after passing-away comes conception, and after conception existence-substratum again. Accordingly the series of thoughts of beings in their rounds of rebirth through modes of existence, destinies, halting-places, and abodes, is without interruption. But in the case of one who has attained saintship it ceases as soon as passing-away-consciousness ceases.

Karma and the Consciousnesses.

Karma is so called because it makes whatever is made. Moreover, there are two kinds of karma; karma depending on ignorance, and other karmas.

There are six karmas depending on ignorance; namely, the triplet consisting of meritorious karma, demeritorious karma, and karma leading to immovability; and the triplet consisting of bodily karma, vocal karma, and mental karma. All these are nothing but worldly meritorious and demeritorious thoughts.[1]

The other karmas are four in number; namely, static karma, constituent karma, active karma, and strenuous karma.

In such phrases as "All the constituents of being are transitory," *static karma* is meant; namely, all the elements of being possessing a dependence.

In the commentaries, all the elements of being, both those with form and those without, which have sprung from karma,[1] and are comprised in the three modes of being, are called *constituent karma*.[2] They are included in the phrase, "All the constituents of

---

[1] That is, consciousnesses 1–17 and 22–33 in the list above.

[2] That is, the four lower groups in so far as they are sprung from karma, and the fruition-consciousnesses of the consciousness-group.

being are transitory;" but there is no passage quotable for them separately.

Meritorious and demeritorious thoughts belonging to the three modes of being are, moreover, *active karma.* For them is quotable the passage, "This ignorant individual, O priest, performs meritorious karma etc." [1]

Bodily and mental heroism is called *strenuous karma.* This is quotable in the passage, "It went as far as there was room for karma, and then it stopped, as if struck in the axle." [2]

But there are not merely these, there are also others. In such quotations as, "Brother Visākha, when any priest enters upon the trance of the cessation of perception and sensation, first vocal karma ceases, then bodily karma, and then mental karma," several karmas are mentioned, but there is no one of these that is not included under *static karma.*

---

[1] Compare page 182, line 8.

[2] This quotation probably refers to the wheel of empire (see 64 and 101), and symbolically expresses the victorious progress of a Universal Monarch in subduing the world. (Compare Wheel of Doctrine, *s. v.* Doctrine, in Index.)

HENRY CLARKE WARREN (1854-1899) was born in Cambridge, Massachusetts and was educated at Harvard, Johns Hopkins, and Oxford. He was a student of James B. Greenough, Charles R. Lanman, and Maurice Bloomfield in Sanskrit; and of Rhys Davids, the founder of the Pali Text Society. Despite severe and life-long physical handicaps, Warren became a leading figure in Indian studies and the first American scholar to attain distinction in the field of Pali. He did not live to complete his *magnum opus,* a translation of Buddhagosa's *Way of Purity.* His generosity made possible the publication of the Harvard Oriental Series.